SHEPHERDING
GOD'S FLOCK

SHEPHERDING GOD'S FLOCK

Biblical Leadership
in the New Testament and Beyond

BENJAMIN L. MERKLE *and*
THOMAS R. SCHREINER, *editors*

Kregel
Ministry

Shepherding God's Flock: Biblical Leadership in the New Testament and Beyond
© 2014 by Benjamin L. Merkle and Thomas R. Schreiner

Published by Kregel Publications, a division of Kregel, Inc., 2450 Oak Industrial Dr. NE, Grand Rapids, MI 49505-6020.

The Greek font GraecaU and the Hebrew font NewJerusalemU are available from www.linguistsoftware.com/lgku.htm, +1-425-775-1130.

ISBN 978-0-8254-4256-8

Printed in the United States of America
14 15 16 17 18 / 5 4 3 2 1

CONTENTS

INTRODUCTION

Shepherding God's flock is an important task and a high calling. When Jesus restored the apostle Peter, he was told by the risen Lord to "feed my sheep" (John 21:17). Jesus' words of restoration and acceptance included the mandate to take care of God's people. Shepherding God's flock is important because the sheep belong to God. There are his flock, his people, his church because they were "purchased with His own blood" (Acts 20:28 NASB). Shepherding is important because there are many dangers that God's people face and shepherds help protect the flock from such dangers. Just as Paul warned the Ephesian elders to "Pay careful attention to yourselves and all the flock," today shepherds must likewise be diligent because it is still the case that "savage wolves" can "come in . . . and will not spare the flock" (Acts 20:28–29 NIV).

Furthermore, shepherds are given a high calling because they serve as "examples to the flock" (1 Peter 5:3). Although ultimately sheep are led by the "chief Shepherd" (1 Peter 5:4), under-shepherds are given to the church to provide godly examples of what it means to be a follower of the "Shepherd and Overseer" of their souls (1 Peter 2:25). Consequently, who leads the church, the type of authority they are given, how they relate to one another, to whom they are accountable, and how they are selected are of utmost importance to the life and health of God's people. We believe that the Scriptures provide us with a solid foundation as to who is to lead the church and how it is to be done.

This book, however, is not intended to provide pithy answers to practical questions on leadership, for there are scores of books and seminars in which such answers are given. This book is designed to take a step back and to consider what the Scriptures teach about leadership. Before answering practical questions, it is imperative to determine the message of the Scriptures on leadership. As evangelicals, we believe the Scriptures are sufficient and normative for every dimension of life, and thus they have supreme authority. Jim Hamilton seeks to answer the question concerning the relationship of the Old Testament elders and synagogue leaders to leaders in New Testament churches. The following three chapters seek to provide the biblical foundation for church leaders found in the Gospels (Andreas Köstenberger), Acts and Paul's letters to churches (Benjamin Merkle), Paul's letters to individuals and the General Epistles (Thomas Schreiner).

We also recognize, however, that we are not the first ones to think about this matter. Christians throughout history have reflected on the pattern of leadership in individual churches and among all the churches. If we want to dig our roots deep, we must consider those who have gone before us, those who have labored in the Lord's vineyard during previous eras. Thus, we consider the papacy in two chapters (Michael Haykin and Gregg Allison), for the Roman Catholic understanding has exerted an enormous influence throughout church history—an influence which continues to this day. Obviously, many other patterns of leadership could be investigated, but space precludes covering them all, and so we have restricted our study to Presbyterians (Nathan Finn), Anglicans (Jason Duesing), and Baptists (Shawn Wright). By sampling different polity structures, we are introduced to some of the configurations and structures that have played a significant role during the history of the church. The understanding of church leadership among these groups is not only described but also evaluated.

The book before you is not written from a detached and neutral standpoint. All the contributors are Baptists, and we are convinced that the Baptist understanding of church government comports with the Scriptures. Saying that we don't write neutrally should not lead anyone to think that this book is propaganda. It is our contention that a careful consideration of the Scriptures supports a baptistic understanding, and hence the scriptural chapters presented here attempt to make the case for our view biblically. We understand if some disagree, but we do hope that the case made here gets a fair hearing. The intensive study of Scripture and history is the platform for Bruce Ware's essay where he puts together the case we are making biblically and theologically. We hope readers see the beauty and coherency of the view of church leadership defended here. Finally, we believe what we argue here has practical ramifications, for theory must ultimately lead to practice. Andy Davis helps us think about what the study means for us today as we serve and lead God's people.

Our prayer is that God will raise up pastors and leaders who will lead our churches with humility and with vision.

ABBREVIATIONS

AB   Anchor Bible
ANF   *Ante-Nicene Fathers*, ed. A. Roberts and J. Donaldson. 10
            vols. 1885. Peabody, MA: Hendrickson, reprint, 2004.
AUSS   *Andrews University Seminary Studies*
BBR   *Bulletin for Biblical Research*
BDAG   W. Bauer, F. W. Danker, W. F. Arndt, and F. W. Gingrich.
            *Greek-English Lexicon of the New Testament and Other
            Early Christian Literature.* 3rd ed. Chicago: University of
            Chicago Press, 2000.
BECNT   Baker Exegetical Commentary on the New Testament
BTNT   Biblical Theology of the New Testament
DNTB   *Dictionary of New Testament Background.* Edited by
            Craig A. Evans and Stanley E. Porter. Downers Grove, IL:
            InterVarsity, 2000.
HCSB   Holman Christian Standard Bible
HNTC   Harper's New Testament Commentaries
ICC   International Critical Commentary
ISBE   *International Standard Bible Encyclopedia.* Edited by G. W.
            Bromiley. 4 vols. Grand Rapids, 1979–1988.
IVPNTCS   IVP New Testament Commentary Series
JSNT   *Journal for the Study of the New Testament*
JTS   *Journal of Theological Studies*
KJV   King James Version
LTJ   *Lutheran Theological Journal*
NAC   New American Commentary
NIBC   New International Biblical Commentary
NICNT   New International Commentary on the New Testament
NIDNTT   *New International Dictionary of New Testament Theology.*
            Edited by Colin Brown. 4 vols. Grand Rapids: Zondervan,
            1975–85.

NIDOTTE	*New International Dictionary of Old Testament Theology and Exegesis. Edited by Willem A. VanGemeren. 5 vols. Grand Rapids, 1997.*
NIGTC	New International Greek Testament Commentary
NIV	New International Version
NIV[84]	New International Version (1984)
NIVAC	NIV Application Commentary
NKJV	New King James Version
NLT	New Living Translation
NovT	*Novum Testamentum*
NPNF[2]	*Nicene and Post-Nicene Fathers*, Series 2
NSBT	New Studies in Biblical Theology
NTS	*New Testament Studies*
ODNB	*Oxford Dictionary of National Biography*
PNTC	Pillar New Testament Commentary
SBJT	*The Southern Baptist Journal of Theology*
SBT	Studies in Biblical Theology
SE	*Studia evangelica*
SP	Sacra pagina
TDNT	*Theological Dictionary of the New Testament.* Edited by G. Kittel and G. Friedrich. Translated by G. W. Bromiley. 10 vols. Grand Rapids, 1964–1976.
TEV	Today's English Version
TNTC	Tyndale New Testament Commentaries
TrinJ	*Trinity Journal*
TU	Texte und Untersuchungen
TynBul	*Tyndale Bulletin*
WBC	Word Biblical Commentary
ZECNT	Zondervan Exegetical Commentary on the New Testament

CHAPTER 1

Did the Church Borrow Leadership Structures from the Old Testament or Synagogue?

James M. Hamilton Jr.[1]

The pastors of the early churches were referred to as elders and overseers. These terms are used interchangeably at several points in the New Testament (see esp. Acts 20:17, 28 and 1 Peter 5:1–2; cf. also Titus 1:5, 7; 1 Tim. 3:1–7; Phil. 1:1; James 5:14). Why were these men referred to as elders?[2] Were they called elders because there were elders in Old Testament Israel and in the synagogues of the second temple period? Is there a relationship between the leadership structure of the nation of Israel, the synagogue, and the church?

The short answer is yes and no, but less yes than no. The yes part is in the way the church took up a term that the Greek translation of the Old Testament had used to designate a group of leaders that we read about across the Old Testament.[3] There are elders in the Old Testament, and the authors of the New Testament indicate that the early church referred to their leaders as elders, pastors, and overseers. There is less yes than no, though, because the similarities basically end with the fact

---

1. James M. Hamilton Jr. (PhD, The Southern Baptist Theological Seminary) is Professor of Biblical Theology at The Southern Baptist Theological Seminary in Louisville, Kentucky.

2. And they would have been men, as passages like 1 Timothy 2:12 and 5:17 make clear (cf. also Acts 20:30). See further Thomas R. Schreiner and Andreas J. Köstenberger, *Women in the Church: An Analysis and Application of 1 Timothy 2:9–15*, 2nd ed. (Grand Rapids: Baker, 2005); and James M. Hamilton, "What Women Can Do in Ministry: Full Participation Within Biblical Boundaries," in *Women, Ministry and the Gospel: Exploring New Paradigms* (Downers Grove, IL: InterVarsity Press, 2007), 32–52.

3. In the overwhelming majority of instances, the Greek translators rendered the Hebrew term זָקֵן with πρεσβύτερος. For the statistics, see Benjamin L. Merkle, *The Elder and Overseer: One Office in the Early Church* (New York: Peter Lang, 2003), 30.

of leadership and the use of the term. The differences between Old and New Testament elders are too significant to permit the conclusion that the elders of the church were a natural development of the elders of Israel. Against G. K. Beale, who writes, "I contend that the office of elder in the church, the new Israel, is to some degree the continuation of the position of elder in Israel,"[4] L. Coenen is correct: "the examples do not permit any direct connection to be drawn between the OT and the later office of episkopos, or bishop."[5]

More extensive treatments of the elders in the Old Testament can be found elsewhere,[6] and Merkle has provided the decisive treatment of the question being considered here, summarizing other positions and outlining positives and negatives.[7]

The existence of this body of work makes it unnecessary for this essay either to present an exhaustive round-up or summarize the various perspectives. Here we need only summarize what we know about elders in the OT and in the synagogue to show that Merkle and others are correct to conclude that the office of elder is "an almost entirely new position."[8] The final section of this essay, however, will consider the Old Testament's major contribution to the New Testament concept of leadership, that of the suffering righteous shepherd.

ELDERS IN THE OLD TESTAMENT

Although elders in the Old Testament are frequently mentioned, they are also easily ignored. There is never an outright definition of who they were, never a set of qualifications or requirements for them, never an overt statement of where they stand in relationship to other leading figures, and only once are individual elders named (Num.

---

4. G. K. Beale, *A New Testament Biblical Theology: The Unfolding of the Old Testament in the New* (Grand Rapids: Baker, 2011), 929.
5. L. Coenen, "Bishop," *NIDNTT*, 1:190.
6. See Hanoch Reviv, *The Elders in Ancient Israel: A Study of a Biblical Institution* (Jerusalem: Magnes Press, 1989); and Timothy M. Willis, *The Elders of the City: A Study of the Elders-Laws in Deuteronomy* (Atlanta: Society of Biblical Literature, 2001); cf. also John L. McKenzie, "The Elders in the Old Testament," *Biblica* 40 (1959): 522–40. See also M. R. Jacobs, "Leadership, Elders," *Dictionary of the Old Testament Pentateuch*, ed. T. Desmond Alexander and David W. Baker (Downers Grove: InterVarsity Press, 2003), 515–18.
7. Merkle, *The Elder and Overseer*, 23–56.
8. Ibid., 65.

11:26). There is nothing like a sustained focus on what particular elders did, when they became elders, or how they functioned as elders.[9] The evidence in the Old Testament indicates that ancient Israel and its neighbors recognized the authority and standing of older males. That is to say, Israel was not the only society that had elders. We read of elders of the house of Pharaoh and of the land of Egypt (Gen. 50:7; cf. Ps. 105:22), of Midian and Moab (Num. 22:4, 7), of Gibeon (Josh. 9:11) and of Gebal (Ezek. 27:9).

Because the elders are never defined and no qualifications are ever given, in order to get any traction on who they were we are left to the meaning of the terms used to describe them and the roles they are called to play. As to the terms used to describe elders, Merkle observes, "The noun [*zaqen*] is derived from the Hebrew term 'beard' [*zaqan*], a relationship that is attested in most Semitic languages."[10] For this reason, F. C. Fensham writes that an "elder" is "An elderly person; also, an authority, or a person with judicial office. It is commonly accepted that the origin of this latter meaning is to be sought in the ancient patriarchal family institution of the Hebrews."[11] Similarly, Kenneth Aitken explains, "The office of elder has its roots in the tribal structure of early Israelite society. Elders were the heads of the families and the leaders and representatives of the tribes. They exercised a patriarchal authority based on kinship and the wisdom of experience."[12]

To see exactly how the elders are presented in the Old Testament, what follows is a summary of the references to the elders in the Old Testament. This review of the evidence lays the foundation for the affir-

---

9. Cf. C. J. H. Wright: "the heads of houses acted judicially in the local civic assembly—'the gate.' This was probably their major public function as 'elders' in the everyday life of the community. The OT never spells out exactly the identity of the elders nor their qualifications for eldership, so there has been room for debate among scholars on the matter. But the most likely view is that they were composed of the senior males from each household . . ., who were qualified by their substance—their family and land. . . ." ("Family," *Anchor Bible Dictionary*, ed. D. N. Freedman [Doubleday: New York, 1992], 2:764). Similarly L. Coenen writes, "Although their role was in origin neither religious nor cultic but socio-political, the existence of elders *as an institution* was of considerable significance in the life of Israel and the Jewish synagogue community, as it was among other peoples of the ancient world (cf. the elders of Egypt in Gen. 50:7). The institution was already established when Israel became a people. It is assumed in every strand of OT tradition" ("Bishop," *NIDNTT*, 1:194).
10. Merkle, *The Elder and Overseer*, 23.
11. F. C. Fensham, "Elder in the OT," *ISBE*, 2:53.
12. Kenneth T. Aitken, "זקן," in *NIDOTTE*, 1:1137–39.

mation of the conclusion that there is more discontinuity than continuity between the old and new covenant elders.

In accordance with the patriarchal authority the elders held, when the Lord sends Moses back to Egypt, he sends him to gather the elders of Israel (Ex. 3:16). Wegner observes, "It appears that as far back as the Egyptian captivity, the Israelites were led by elders (Ex. 3:16), and it is commonly accepted that this concept originated in the Hebrew patriarchal family institution."[13] We repeatedly read of the elders of Israel or of the people (Ex. 3:16, 18; 4:29; 12:21; 17:5; 18:12; 19:7, etc.).[14] The elders are listed with heads of tribes (e.g., Deut. 5:23; Josh. 24:1) and with officers (Deut. 29:10; 31:28) and judges (Josh. 8:33; 23:2). Moses gave the Torah to the priests, Levites, and elders (Deut. 31:9).

The elders feature prominently in the narrative when seventy of them ascend the mount with Moses, Aaron, Nadab, and Abihu (Num. 24:1, 9, 14). Exodus 24:10 says, "They saw the God of Israel," and 24:11 calls them "the chief men of the people of Israel." The only time individual elders are named in the narratives is when Eldad and Medad remained in the camp when the seventy were given some of the Spirit that was upon Moses (Num. 11:16–30, see 11:17, 26). The seventy were thus equipped to bear the burden of the people with Moses (11:17).

As for what the Law required elders to do, if the whole congregation of Israel sinned unintentionally, Leviticus 4:15 called for the elders of the congregation to lay their hands on the head of the bull to be sacrificed. In Deuteronomy 19:23, "the elders of his city" were responsible for punishing a murderer, in 21:2–6, the "elders of the city" handled atonement for unsolved murder, while the man fleeing to a city of refuge had to "explain his case to the elders of the city" (Josh. 20:4). In Deuteronomy 21:19–20, the "elders of his city" take on the punishing of a rebellious son, in 22:15–18, the "elders of the city" examine the evidence of virginity, and in 25:7–9, the "elders of his city" see to the shaming the man who will not do his Levirate duty. In keeping with these instructions, Boaz brought ten of the elders of the city to witness the Levirate interaction between himself and the nearer kinsman regarding Ruth (Ruth 4:2–11). On the basis of

---

13. Paul D. Wegner, "זָקֵן," in *NIDOTTE*, 1:1135.
14. See Merkle, *The Elder and Overseer*, 24 n. 4 for a full summary of all the phrases that qualify the term "elders," whether "of Israel" or "of the city" etc.

this evidence, Wegner observes, "Once the Israelites settled in the Promised Land, it appears that each city also had its own elders who sat at the city gate to attend to certain internal matters (Deut. 21:19; 22:15). . . . It does not appear that the elders created laws or established precedents, but were there to administer and maintain societal standards."[15]

The elders of Israel mourned with Joshua after the defeat at Ai (Josh. 7:6), and then after the judgment of Achan, Joshua and the elders led the people back to Ai for victory (8:10). The elders of Joshua's generation apparently helped preserve piety among the people after Joshua's death (24:31). We read of elders at several points in Judges (Judg. 8:14, 16; 11:5–11; 21:16), then in Samuel the elders act foolishly by taking the ark into battle (1 Sam. 4:3) and demanding a king (8:4). The elders are relevant enough to warrant Saul's concern for their opinion (15:30) and for David to send them spoil (30:26).

Abner confers with the elders of Israel to make David king (2 Sam. 3:17), and David covenants with the elders of Israel (5:3) who then anoint him king (1 Chron. 11:3). David and the elders brought the ark into Jerusalem (1 Chron. 15:25), and the elders of David's house try to raise him up from mourning (1 Sam. 12:17).

When Absalom rebelled against David, Ahithophel's advice pleased Absalom and the elders of Israel (2 Sam. 17:4). Hushai overturned Ahithophel's counsel before the same (17:15). The elders of Judah were called to restore David after the rebellion (19:11), and 1 Chronicles 21:16 describes David and the elders clothed in sackcloth when the angel was destroying Jerusalem.

At the dedication of the temple "Solomon assembled the elders of Israel and all the heads of the tribes, the leaders of the fathers' houses of the people of Israel" (1 Kings 8:1, cf. 8:3; 2 Chron. 5:2, cf. 5:4). Ahab and Jezebel interacted with the elders (1 Kings 20:7–8; 21:8), and the elders sat both with Elisha (2 Kings 6:32) and in exile before Ezekiel (Ezek. 8:1; 14:1; 20:1). Jehu wrote to the rulers, elders, and guardians of Ahab's sons (1 Kings 10:1, 5). Josiah gathered the elders as he initiated reforms (23:1; 2 Chron. 34:29).

When Israel returned to the land after the exile to rebuild temple and city, Ezra 5:5 tells us, "the eye of their God was on the elders of the

---

15. Wegner, "זָקֵן," 1135.

Jews" (cf. Ezra 5:9; 6:7, 8), and 6:14 states "the elders of the Jews built and prospered."[16] When Ezra led the people to confront the mixed marriage crisis, the people were summoned to appear "by order of the officials and the elders" (10:8), and then "the elders and the judges of every city" (10:14) were involved in the process of dealing with the problem.

Psalm 107:32 refers to "the assembly of the elders," and this assembly is probably also in view in Proverbs 31:23, where the husband of the virtuous woman is known among the elders at the gate. Certain elders speak in Jeremiah's defense and appeal to the precedent of Micah of Moresheth (Jer. 26:17–19). Jeremiah addresses the surviving elders in the letter he sends to Babylon (Jer. 29:1).

Various prophetic texts indicate that when the Lord judged his people he held the elders responsible for the failures of the people (Isa. 3:14; Jer. 19:1; cf. Lam. 1:19; 2:10; 4:16; 5:12; Ezek. 7:26; 8:11–12; 9:6; Joel 1:2, 16; 2:16). This reality indicates that the elders were both representative of and responsible for the people.

Perhaps the most unique text on elders in the Old Testament is Isaiah 24:23, which envisions Yahweh reigning on Mount Zion, "and his glory will be before his elders." This description of the Lord's eschatological triumph probably informs the 24 elders on thrones around the throne in Revelation 4:4. Because in Revelation the elders are classed with heavenly beings rather than with humans, it seems that the earthly elders have a heavenly counterpart in the divine council in heaven.

Elders in the Synagogue

Our knowledge of the synagogue is limited.[17] Chilton and Yamauchi comment briefly on the relationship between synagogue and temple: "Before the synagogue was felt to replace the temple, it had complemented it. The official function of receiving taxes for its upkeep is one

---

16. These references to elders in Ezra 5–6 are in the Aramaic portion of Ezra (Ezra 4:8–6:18 and 7:12–26 are in Aramaic, with the rest of the book in Hebrew), so the Aramaic equivalent to the Hebrew term for "elders" is used.
17. Merkle, *The Elder and Overseer*, 55 n. 127. On the synagogue, see Rainer Riesner, "Synagogues in Jerusalem," in *The Book of Acts in Its Palestinian Setting*, ed. Richard Bauckham (Grand Rapids: Eerdmans, 1995), 179–211.

example. Another is its function as a gathering of elders for the purpose of administering justice."[18]

As a result of the paucity of evidence, assumptions must be made about its leadership, as can be seen from Schnabel's words: "In regard to the villages of Palestine, we can assume that each one had a spokesperson. Larger villages and smaller towns may have had councils or elders, identical with or closely connected to the leaders of the local synagogues."[19] Similarly, Chilton and Yamauchi tell us what was "probably" the case: "A group of elders would direct the activities of the synagogue. The *archisynagogos* was probably chosen from among them. An almoner would collect and distribute alms. The *hazzan*, or 'attendant,' was the one who took care of the Scripture scrolls."[20] Schnabel nicely summarizes the synagogue functionaries:

> The sources attest the following offices: leaders or presidents of the synagogues (*archisynagogoi*), leaders, officials (*archontes*), council of elders (*gerousia*) and elders (*presbyteroi*), scribes (*grammateis*), readers (*anagnostai*), servants (*diakonoi*), priests (*hiereis*), singers of psalms (*psalmologoi*), finance officials (*phrontistai*) and defenders or benefactors (*prostatai*).[21]

Emil Schürer writes, "the 'elders' were not looked upon as officials in the technical sense of the word. They were the representatives and advisers of their community, but not officials with specific functions entrusted to them."[22] Sanders states, "According to Philo, Sabbath instruction was led by a priest or elder . . . ."[23] Schnabel comments at more length on the difficulty of knowing whether what we can know about one synagogue would have prevailed more generally:

---

18. B. Chilton and E. Yamauchi, "Synagogues," in *DNTB*, 1149.
19. Eckhard Schnabel, *Early Christian Mission* (Downers Grove, IL: InterVarsity Press, 2004), 191.
20. Chilton and Yamauchi, "Synagogues," 1146.
21. Schnabel, *Early Christian Mission*, 646.
22. Emil Schürer, *A History of the Jewish People in the Time of Jesus Christ*, trans. John MacPherson, Sophia Taylor, and Peter Christie (Peabody, MA: Hendrickson, 1994), 2.2:249.
23. E. P. Sanders, *Judaism: Practice and Belief, 63 BCE–66 CE* (Philadelphia: Trinity Press International, 1992), 177.

In regard to the leadership of the synagogues, Donald Binder distinguishes between the archon (*prostates, archiprostates*), who was responsible for the legislative and legal concerns of the village and town community, and the *archisynagogos*, who led the religious services; both *archon* and *archisynagogos* were members of a council of elders (*presbyteroi, gerontes, dynatoi*) who functioned as advisers and representatives of the synagogue members. This differentiation can be demonstrated only for a few synagogues, however, and it is too 'neat' to be a valid description for all local situations. . . . The function of the 'elders' (*presbyteroi*) cannot be determined with certainty: the priest Samuel ben Yedaya is the archon of the synagogue in Dura-Europos, but at the same time (in a Greek inscription) he is *presbyteros*. The function of the 'elders' presumably was different, depending on local circumstances: they probably carried out administrative and financial, and perhaps also religious-liturgical, tasks. Small communities probably managed without a council of elders.[24]

The Gospels and Acts in the New Testament provide us with a number of references to synagogues and leadership in Israel, and for the purposes of this investigation, this NT evidence is most relevant. We are asking whether the early church borrowed leadership structures from the Old Testament or synagogue, so the references to the synagogue and to Jewish elders in writings from the early church are most pertinent for our purposes.[25]

What we see of pre-Christian elders in the New Testament is very similar to what we have seen in the Old Testament, with some developments. The centurion sends elders of the Jews to Jesus in Luke 7:3. In Mark (7:3, 5) there are references to the traditions of the elders related to hand-washing (cf. Matt. 15:2). These traditions of the elders indicate

---

24. Schnabel, *Early Christian Mission*, 193.
25. For a broader survey than will be given here, see Merkle, *The Elder and Overseer*, who discusses elders in the apocryphal writings (32–35), in writings from Qumran (35–37), in Josephus (38), in the Mishna (38–39), in papyri and inscriptions (39–42), and in Plutarch (42–43).

that the elders have led the way in prescribing how the Mosaic Law was to be lived out.

Jesus repeatedly indicates that he will suffer and be rejected by "the elders and the chief priests and the scribes" (Mark 8:31; cf. 11:27; 14:43; Matt. 16:21; Luke 9:22; 20:1; 22:66). Chief priests and elders challenge the authority of Jesus in Matthew 21:23, then they plot to arrest and kill Jesus in 26:3–4 (cf. Matt. 27:1, 3). They put their plan into action (Luke 22:52). The chief priests and elders accuse Jesus before Pilate in Matthew 27:12 and persuade the crowd against him in 27:20. They bribe the soldiers from Jesus' tomb in Matthew 28:12.

What we see the pre-Christian elders doing in the Gospels matches the role they have played in the Old Testament, particularly the instructions of Deuteronomy, where they are given responsibility to uphold the Torah. Along these lines, Chilton and Yamauchi note, "Offenders could be judged before the elders in the synagogues and flogged forty stripes save one by the *hazzan* (Mark 13:9; 2 Cor. 11:24). Apostates could be excommunicated (John 9:22; 12:42; 16:2)."[26] In their actions against Jesus, the elders think (wrongly) that they are upholding Torah.

The elders play a similar role in the book of Acts. When Peter and John are arrested for "proclaiming in Jesus the resurrection from the dead" (Acts 4:2), the "rulers and elders and scribes gathered" to hear the case against them in Acts 4:5, and Peter addresses them in 4:8. Peter and John report back to the church what "the chief priests and elders had said to them" (4:23). Elders and scribes seized Stephen (6:12; cf. 7:58; 8:1; 22:5). The elders play a similar role later in the book with respect to Paul: the forty plus who conspire to kill Paul report their plan "to the chief priests and elders" (23:14). The high priest Ananias accuses Paul "with some elders" (24:1; cf. 25:15).

ELDERS IN THE CHURCH

Did the church borrow the leadership structure of eldership from Old Testament Israel or the synagogue of early Judaism? As in the introduction, yes and no, but more no than yes. We have seen that eldership was widely established in the ancient world. Israel, as well as Egypt, Midian,

---

26. Chilton and Yamauchi, "Synagogues," 1147.

and other nations, all had elders. The evidence in the Old Testament indicates that eldership arose from the standing that derives from age and
the wisdom and stature that tends to accompany life experience. Being
a patriarchal society, in Israel the men of standing who would have
been recognized as elders would naturally have been clan and tribal
fathers, so the elders would have had an intrinsically familial standing.

The most superficial examination shows that the early church adopted a term widely employed in their social environment, a term
with a long history of designating male leadership. The question here
is whether the church used that term to designate an office that cor-
responded to or grew out of the elders we read about in the Old Testament and in the descriptions of early pre-Christian Judaism. In order
to gain traction on the issue, we must summarize differences between
the old and new covenant peoples of God, and we must consider what
the New Testament shows and tells about the elders in the early church.

The first and most significant difference between old and new covenant elders is the simple fact that whereas membership in the old covenant was based on familial descent, in the new covenant this is not
so. The old covenant people of God was a nation, a collection of twelve
tribes, with those tribes made up of clans, all descending from Abraham through Isaac and Jacob. Thus, the people of God were one ethnic
group. They were genealogically connected, and in a very real sense
they were a collection of families descending from father Abraham. In
such a situation, the heads of fathers' houses would naturally take on
leadership. In Old Testament Israel, fathers led families. It takes very
little imagination to see how this would result in a situation where the
elders in a particular city would be the responsible, engaged, wise, and
willing fathers of that city.

The reason no qualifications are explicitly stated probably comes
down to the fact that no qualifications were felt to be needed. The requirements of the covenant were already there. The book of Proverbs
gives dramatized exposition of what it looks like to keep the command-
ments. Texts like Psalms 127 and 128 describe the blessed life of the
man who walks according to Torah in the context of his family.[27] The

27. For discussion of family relationships in the Old Testament, see James M. Hamilton, "That
the Coming Generation Might Praise the Lord," *Journal of Family Ministry* 1 (2010): 10–17;

man who was faithful to his wife, diligent with his children, disciplined in his farming and shepherding, and faithful to his neighbors would be visibly successful as he enjoyed the blessings of the covenant by faith. The virtues and prosperity of such a man would be on display in all areas of his life, as Proverbs 14:24 states, "The crown of the wise is their wealth, but the folly of fools brings folly."[28] Such a man would be easy to get along with, as Proverbs 16:7 says, "When a man's ways please the Lord, he makes even his enemies to be at peace with him."

If we could ask someone like Ezra why no qualifications for the Old Testament's "elders" were ever stated in the books of the Old Testament, Ezra would probably give us a puzzled look and respond that such qualifications are obvious and practically stated on every page of the Scriptures.

The situation changes when the Lord blasts out the ethnic boundaries around his people and Jesus sends his followers out to make disciples of all nations. No longer are the people of God gathered in one land. No longer are they a political entity of clans and tribes forming a patriarchal nation. No longer are the people of God defined by a line of descent. When Jesus sends his followers to make disciples of all nations, the people of God cease to be defined by the fact that they descend from Abraham. Where one was born, who one was born to, these issues no longer determine whether one belongs to God's people. These changed realities affect what we see in the Old Testament and in the synagogue about elders.

If genealogical descent and ethnic identity no longer determine membership in the people of God, what does? The key statement in the Old Testament comes in Jeremiah 31:34, "they shall all know me, from the least of them to the greatest, declares the Lord." This means that everyone in the promised new covenant will know God (Jer. 31:31–34). In the New Testament it becomes clear that people are enabled to know God by means of the new birth, and to experience the new birth is to

---

idem, "A Biblical Theology of Motherhood," *Journal of Discipleship and Family Ministry* 2 (2012): 6–13.

28. For discussion of the theology of the Old Testament showing that the Old Testament is not teaching prosperity theology but everywhere assumes that the old covenant was only to operate by faith, see James M. Hamilton, *God's Glory in Salvation through Judgment: A Biblical Theology* (Wheaton, IL: Crossway, 2010), 67–353, esp. 107–14, 344.

be made alive or regenerated. The Old Testament refers to this new birth with various circumcision metaphors, whether of the heart or ears (e.g., Deut. 30:6; Jer. 6:10, etc.).[29]

The first difference, then, between the old and new covenant elders is that whereas an Israelite man with much common grace who did not know God might be an elder in old covenant Israel (and if the elders of Jesus' day had known the Father they would have known Jesus, John 14:7), the new covenant church consists of those who have been born again by the Holy Spirit and thereby know God.

Old covenant Israel had stipulations for the wicked being cut off from God's people, but theoretically a man with an uncircumcised heart could stay within the boundaries of the Torah as far as the human eye could see and remain an elder. What I have in mind here are the indications in the New Testament Gospel accounts that there were respected elders among the people of Israel who rejected Jesus and his teachings. These were men who had the outward appearance of keeping the law, but if their hearts had been changed they would have responded to Jesus the way that Simeon did (Luke 2:25–32). The teaching of Jesus in the Sermon on the Mount (Matt. 5–7) seems pointed at just these kinds of people, people who seem to be keeping the law on the outside, but their hearts were foul. Jesus described them as whitewashed tombs full of dead bones (Matt. 23:27). In keeping with the teaching of Jesus in the sermon on the mount, the new covenant church received instructions for the process of disciplining an unrepentant elder (1 Tim. 5:19–25). These instructions go with other instructions given in the New Testament that pertain to the removal of the unrepentant from the congregation (Matt. 18:15–18; 1 Cor. 5:1–13).

This change in what makes people members of the people of God changes the pool of candidates from which the elders will be drawn. Just as the nation is no longer the people of God, the elders are no longer the men of visible standing in the communities within the nation. The making of converts into disciples introduces people into the congregations who have little or no background in the Torah,

---

29. For discussion of the regeneration and indwelling of the Holy Spirit, see James M. Hamilton, *God's Indwelling Presence: The Holy Spirit in the Old and New Testaments,* NAC Studies in Bible and Theology (Nashville: B&H, 2006).

resulting in the need for qualifications to be spelled out more explicitly. This results in the lists of qualifications found in 1 Timothy 3:1–7 and Titus 1:5–9.

We find another difference between old and new covenant elders in these lists of qualifications, most prominently in the requirement that new covenant elders of churches be "able to teach" (1 Tim. 3:2) and "able to give instruction in sound doctrine and also to rebuke those who contradict it" (Titus 1:9). The change here arises from the fact that while the Torah was entrusted to the priests, Levites, and elders (Deut. 31:9), the priests and Levites seem to have been particularly charged with the responsibility to teach (e.g., Lev. 10:11; 1 Kings 17:27; Ezra 7:10). This is not to say that elders never taught in Israel: all fathers were to teach the Torah to their children (Deut. 6:7), but they don't seem to have a more formal teaching role. In the new covenant church, however, the teaching of the scriptures to the people of God is specifically entrusted to the elders in a way that we do not see in the Old Testament. There are no more Levites. Jesus is the high priest, and all believers constitute God's royal priesthood (1 Peter 2:9). Moreover, the elders are specifically called to refute those who contradict (Titus 1:9), to shepherd the flock (Acts 20:28), and to do this under Christ the chief-shepherd (1 Peter 5:4), building on the foundation of the church laid down by the apostles (Eph. 2:20; 1 Cor. 3:10–17).

THE OLD TESTAMENT'S MAJOR CONTRIBUTION

If the new covenant office of elder does not grow directly out of the elders we read about in the Old Testament and in the synagogue, what did the Old Testament contribute to New Testament conceptions of leadership? Focusing on the word "elder" to the exclusion of more thematic issues could keep us from seeing the massive continuity between the Old and New Testaments regarding the righteous sufferer who shepherds God's people.

Far more significant than the contribution of a term to New Testament vocabulary is the typological pattern that the Old Testament provides for New Testament conceptions of leadership. The pattern of leadership the Old Testament contributes to the New can be summarized in the phrase: the suffering righteous shepherd.

The biblical authors themselves noticed and highlighted this pattern, beginning with Moses.[30] Moses noticed certain correspondences between himself and other suffering shepherds who were faithful to Yahweh whom he learned about in the traditions that came down to him. Under the inspiration of the Holy Spirit, Moses then chose to include and frame these details he had noticed in his own narrative in the Pentateuch. The way that Moses selected, arranged, and presented this material made it possible for his audience to notice these correspondences. The audience of Moses included later Old Testament authors, who picked up on the patterns Moses wove through his narrative. These later biblical authors also saw correspondences between those prior suffering righteous shepherds and either themselves or those about whom they wrote. As the patterns piled up on one another, they gained significance and the expectations mounted for an ultimate fulfillment of this pattern.

Thus, all across the Old Testament we find contributions to the pattern of the suffering righteous shepherd. The first instance of this is Abel, "keeper of sheep" (Gen. 4:2), whose offering "the Lord had regard for" (4:4), but for whose life Cain had no regard, killing him (4:8). The next prominent shepherd we meet is Abraham (see Gen. 12:16; 13:5–7). Abraham's life anticipates the exodus from Egypt: he went down to Egypt in response to a famine (Gen. 12:10), the same reason Jacob and his sons will later sojourn there. In Egypt, just as the nation was enslaved, Abraham's wife was taken captive by Pharaoh (12:15), in response to which the Lord plagues Pharaoh (12:17), Abraham plunders Egypt (12:16), then the Lord brings Abraham into the land of promise (13:3–4). Moses invites his audience to connect these correspondences through the similar statements in Genesis 15:7 and Exodus 20:1. In addition to trouble from Pharaoh and Egypt, Abraham has trouble with the Philistines in the land (Gen. 20:1–18; 21:32), again foreshadowing Israel's future. The trouble Isaac has is very similar to what his father Abraham experienced (26:6–11). The similarities in the sister-fib narrative invite readers to note the correspondences between Abraham

---

30. This way of approaching the issue reflects my view that biblical theology seeks to understand and embrace the interpretive perspective of the biblical authors, which keeps biblical theology connected to authorial intent—the intent not only of the divine author but of the individual human authors as well.

and Isaac. Just as Abraham and Isaac have the same trouble, they have the same promise: the Lord confirming for Isaac the oath he made to Abraham (26:1–4).[31]

That same oath is passed to Jacob (Gen. 28:4), the next shepherd we meet (30:43), who faces enmity from the seed of the serpent (27:41).[32] Cain murdered Abel; Pharaoh and the Philistines troubled Abraham; Ishmael mocked Isaac; Esau wants to kill Jacob; and then Joseph, who was keeping the flock of his father (37:2), is nearly murdered by his brothers (37:20).[33]

The theme of the suffering righteous shepherd receives yet more treatment in the life of Moses, who was shepherding the flock of his father in law (Ex. 3:1) when Yahweh sent him back to Egypt to face Pharaoh, only to have the Israelites reject him just as Cain had rejected Abel and the older brothers rejected Joseph. Moses learned the pattern of the suffering righteous shepherd from the traditions that he received, which he incorporated in the book of Genesis, and then he interpreted his own experience in light of the pattern, setting the trajectory that would continue through David and find ultimate fulfillment in Jesus.

Timothy Laniak observes, "Moses and David are prototypical leaders. More importantly, YHWH reveals himself as the true Shepherd Ruler of Israel."[34] Laniak elaborates on this statement when he writes, "Prototypes are exemplars for phenomenological categories, ideal members that possess the primary attributes by which we define a class." He goes on to say that there are "two prototypical shepherd rulers in biblical literature, Moses and David. To use theological language, these figures 'typologically' anticipate the role of Christ as the ultimate shepherd."[35] Like Joseph, David was shepherding his father's flock, and his father sent him to see about his older brothers (1 Sam. 17:12–15).

---

31. On the blessing of Abraham, see James M. Hamilton, "The Seed of the Woman and the Blessing of Abraham," *TynBul* 58 (2007): 253–73.

32. See further James M. Hamilton, "The Skull Crushing Seed of the Woman: Inner-Biblical Interpretation of Genesis 3:15," *SBJT* 10, no. 2 (2006): 30–54.

33. For more on Joseph typology, see James M. Hamilton, "Was Joseph a Type of the Messiah? Tracing the Typological Identification Between Joseph, David, and Jesus," *SBJT* 12 (2008): 52–77.

34. Timothy S. Laniak, *Shepherds after My Own Heart: Pastoral Traditions and Leadership in the Bible*, NSBT 20 (Downers Grove, IL: InterVarsity Press, 2006), 25.

35. Ibid., 34.

Just as Joseph's older brothers did not respond favorably to him, David's brothers were not happy about his arrival (17:28). Just as Abraham and Isaac had trouble with Philistines in the land, David had trouble with them, and the superscription of Psalm 34 identifies Achish king of Gath with Abimelech, forging a connection between the Philistines who troubled Abraham and Isaac and those who troubled David.

The Psalms of the righteous sufferer are heavily Davidic. In fact, this theme of the righteous sufferer receives its major contribution from the Psalms: The one who has been faithful to Yahweh is continually afflicted by those who have set themselves against the Lord and his Messiah (Ps. 2:2). Through persecution and affliction, Yahweh vindicates his anointed one.

Deuteronomy 18:15–18 describes a prophet like Moses whom the Lord would raise up for Israel. The prophets who follow Moses are like him in the sense that they spoke the true word of God, and like Moses they were rejected by Israel, persecuted, afflicted, and ultimately vindicated. Amos depicts himself as a rejected prophet like Moses, and he uses Davidic terms to do so. In Amos 7:10–13, Amos recounts how the false priest of the man-made calf-worshiping cult at Bethel told him not to prophesy—an Israelite rejecting God's true prophet. In his reply to Amaziah, Amos uses Davidic imagery when he says, "The Lord took me from following the flock" (Amos 7:15). This statement is almost an exact quotation of 2 Samuel 7:8, where the Lord tells David, "I took you from the pasture, from following the flock" (my translation). Amos prophesied "in the days of Uzziah" (Amos 1:1, 792–740 BC). The book of Samuel was likely available by then, but even if not, the very significant oracle that Nathan spoke to David in 2 Samuel 7 was probably well known even before the book of Samuel was written. Thus, Amos consciously[36] combines themes of the rejected prophet like Moses, in

---

36. I am convinced that the interpretations of the OT found in the NT are largely in keeping with the intentions of the human authors of the OT. Thus, John presents the people recognizing Jesus as the prophet like Moses (John 6:14) after the feeding of the 5,000 (6:4–13), and in response to this John presents Jesus "perceiving then that they were about to come and take him by force to make him king" (6:15). John here presents the recognition of Jesus as the prophet like Moses leading to the impulse to make him king, as though the Old Testament has swirled these two lines of expectation—prophetic and royal—into one. Passages like Amos 7:10–15 provide Old Testament warrant for the combination of these expectations, and I am convinced that Amos presenting himself

partial fulfillment of Deuteronomy 18:15–18, and Amos brings in over-
tones of the Davidic suffering righteous shepherd.

Similar interpretive moves can be seen in the prophesy of Isaiah,
where he predicts a shoot from the stump of Jesse (Isa. 11:1). Why
would Jesse's line be a stump? Because the nation, depicted as a tree,
will be chopped down at the exile (6:9–13; 10:5–15). Isaiah 11 depicts
the reigning king from David's line that will grow up after exile, but
Isaiah 53:2 describes a root out of dry ground. The tree imagery in
Isaiah 11 and 53 is one of the key indicators that the suffering servant
of Isaiah 53 is a royal figure from David's line. His work of bearing
the sins of God's people (53:4–6) fulfills the theme of the righteous
sufferer. The fact that the term used in the phrase "the stripes of the
sons of men" in 2 Samuel 7:14 appears in Isaiah 53:4 and 8 establishes
the suffering servant as a king from David's line. We can also note
that God said to Nathan, "thus you shall say to my servant David"
(2 Sam. 7:8), which gives the passages about the servant in Isaiah a
Davidic overtone as well.

Daniel develops the idea that the fulfillment of the theme of the
righteous sufferer will be found in the death of the Messiah when he
speaks of the Messiah being cut off in Daniel 9:26, and Zechariah likewise depicts the fulfillment of these themes in passages such as Zechariah 12:10–11 and 13:7. Along these lines, Zechariah presents himself
as a type of a shepherd who is rejected and sold out for 30 pieces of
silver (Zech. 11:1–17), and the man struck in 13:7 is the Lord's own
shepherd. Matthew claims these passages were fulfilled in what happened when Jesus was betrayed and crucified (Matt. 26:15, 31; 27:9).

Both Matthew and Luke present Jesus himself highlighting the
theme of the righteous sufferer, summarizing it as one that goes from
the beginning to the end of the Old Testament. Matthew presents Jesus pointing to a future that will be just like the whole history of Israel
when he says,

---

as a rejected prophet like Moses with Davidic language reflects his consciously having
made the interpretive move to combine the two lines of interpretation. In other words,
I think that Amos intended to communicate to his audience that the expected prophet
like Moses was to be understood in Davidic terms and that the coming king and the
coming prophet would be the same person (and Amos would have known that David
was a prophet).

> Therefore I send you prophets and wise men and scribes, some of whom you will kill and crucify, and some you will flog in your synagogues and persecute from town to town, so that on you may come all the righteous blood shed on earth, from the blood of righteous Abel to the blood of Zechariah the son of Barachiah, whom you murdered between the sanctuary and the altar. (Matt. 23:34–35; cf. Luke 11:49–51)[37]

Here Jesus not only summarizes the theme of the righteous sufferer from Abel to Zechariah, he says that this theme will continue to be enacted by those whom he himself will send.

Jesus himself is the ultimate fulfillment of the typological pattern of the suffering righteous shepherd. The apostles whom Jesus sent also partook in their share of Christ's sufferings. In fact, they seem to understand themselves to be fulfilling the appointed messianic woes, an amount of suffering that must be completed before the return of Christ.[38] As the Apostle Paul appoints elders in every church in the book of Acts, he tells them that the path into the kingdom goes through many tribulations (Acts 14:22–23). Similarly, Peter calls Christians to follow in the footsteps of Jesus by suffering for doing what is right (1 Peter 2:18–25). In addition, the section on church leaders in 1 Peter 4–5 includes the exhortation to "rejoice insofar as you share Christ's sufferings" (1 Peter 4:13).[39]

There are many similarities between the accounts of the crucifixion of Jesus and the martyrdom of Stephen.[40] Luke hereby narrates what John presents Jesus saying in John 15:20, "If they persecuted me, they will also persecute you." G. K. Beale has argued that the churches needed elders precisely because of the tribulation, affliction, and persecution that they would face.[41] Thus, the elders of the churches will

---

37. Cf. Hamilton, "Was Joseph a Type of the Messiah?," 53.
38. On the messianic woes, see table 6.2 on p. 493 in Hamilton, *God's Glory in Salvation through Judgment* along with the surrounding discussion.
39. See the exposition in Thomas R. Schreiner, *1, 2 Peter, Jude*, NAC 37 (Nashville: B&H, 2003).
40. On these, see Mitchell L. Chase, "Luke-Acts Parallels Between Jesus and Stephen" (ThM thesis, Southwestern Seminary, 2008).
41. Beale, "The Inaugurated End-Time Tribulation and Its Bearing on the Church Office of Elder and on Christian Living in General," 19.

shepherd the flock of God through the messianic woes,[42] continuing the pattern of the suffering righteous shepherd.

Conclusion

Did the early church get their *concept of leadership* from the Old Testament? Absolutely. The pages of the Old Testament are full of righteous sufferers, many of whom were either literal shepherds or figuratively shepherded God's people. This theme finds its fulfillment in Jesus, and those who belong to Jesus follow in his steps, enduring persecution, affliction, and tribulation on the way to the kingdom of God.

Did the early church get the *office of elder* from the Old Testament and/or the synagogue? The word was certainly in common use to refer to leaders who were fatherly males, but the theological and sociological differences between the nation of Israel and the new covenant church are too great to allow the conclusion that the elders of the church were a natural outgrowth of either the elders of the synagogue or the elders of Israel. Moreover, what the elders do in the Old Testament has a good deal to do with the regulation of society at large—judging cases and enforcing the law. By contrast, the elders in the New Testament have authority only within the church, as the church is no longer a civic body in the way that the nation of Israel was. The church transcends all ethnic and political distinctions and has no geographic boundaries. Her elders would do well to heed the call of the Apostle Paul:

> Pay careful attention to yourselves and to all the flock, in which the Holy Spirit has made you overseers, to shepherd the church of God, which he obtained with his own blood. (Acts 20:28)

---

42. Cf. Hamilton, *God's Glory in Salvation through Judgment*, 527.

CHAPTER 2

Shepherds and Shepherding in the Gospels

Andreas J. Köstenberger[1]

Shepherds and their flocks are a pervasive motif throughout the biblical literature. This chapter focuses on the shepherding motif in the four Gospels with particular attention to its application to pastoral theology and leadership. Because of the salvation-historical constraints of Jesus' ministry, the church and its leaders are not explicitly mentioned in the Gospels. Nevertheless, there is much to learn from Jesus' teaching and practice as to how pastors should go about shepherding God's people as Christ's undershepherds. The chapter begins with a brief introduction to the shepherding motif in the Old Testament. The bulk of the chapter is taken up with a discussion of all the relevant passages in the Gospels. I conclude with some reflections on how the portrait of shepherding drawn from the Gospels can inform our understanding of the role and duties of a shepherd of God's flock in the twenty-first century.

BACKGROUND AND PROCEDURE

In the Old Testament, God is presented as the "Shepherd" of Israel and the people of Israel as the "sheep of his pasture."[2] Throughout Israel's

---

1. Andreas J. Köstenberger (PhD, Trinity Evangelical Divinity School) is Senior Research Professor of New Testament and Biblical Theology at Southeastern Baptist Theological Seminary in Wake Forest, North Carolina.
2. For God as the shepherd, see Genesis 48:15; 49:24; Psalm 23:1; 28:9; 77:20; 78:52; 80:1; Isaiah 40:11; Jeremiah 31:10; and Ezekiel 34:11–31. For Israel as the sheep of God's pasture, see Psalm 74:1; 78:52; 79:13; 95:7; 100:3; Ezekiel 34:31; and Micah 2:12. See also chapter 1 in this volume.

history, God's shepherding activity extended to the human rulers of the Israelites who are also described as shepherds (Num. 27:17; 2 Sam. 7:7; 1 Kings 22:17; 1 Chron. 17:6; Jer. 3:15). David, the shepherd-king, served as the prototype of God-honoring shepherd leadership (2 Sam. 5:2; Ps. 78:70–72; Jer. 23:3–6; Ezek. 34:23–24),[3] while other leaders, who fed and served only themselves, are described as bad shepherds (Isa. 56:11; Jer. 10:21; 23:1–2; 50:6–7; Ezek. 34:1–31; Zech. 10:2–3; 11:15–17).[4] Old Testament prophetic expectations concerning God's future rescue of his people from poor human shepherds (Jer. 23:3–6; Ezek. 34:23–24; cf. Jer. 3:15) lay the foundation for our study of shepherding in the Gospels. In the future, "An anticipated shepherd ruler (Mosaic and/or Davidic) would lead his renewed community in a second exodus, provide for God's flock in their exilic wilderness, and renew his covenant with them there."[5] The Gospel writers develop these ideas associated with shepherding in the Old Testament and present Jesus as the eschatological shepherd ruler, the Jewish leaders who rejected Jesus as bad shepherds of the flock, and the apostles as Christ's undershepherds, leading the flock and feeding the sheep. Jesus' teaching and shepherding set the example his undershepherds are to follow—particularly with regard to exercising compassion toward the sheep, feeding them and sacrificing their lives for them, and going after any lost sheep.

A fitting way to begin any study of a particular motif or concept in the Bible is to conduct a thorough study of all the relevant and re-

---

3. See, e.g., Ezekiel 34:23–24: "And I will set up over them one shepherd, my servant David, and he shall feed them: he shall feed them and be their shepherd. And I, the LORD, will be their God, and my servant David shall be prince among them. I am the LORD; I have spoken." See also Moses as a secondary prototypical "good shepherd" in passages such as Psalm 77:20 and Isaiah 63:11.

4. "Son of man, prophecy against the shepherds of Israel; prophesy, and say to them, even to the shepherds, Thus says the Lord GOD: Ah, shepherds of Israel who have been feeding yourselves! Should not shepherds feed the sheep? You eat the fat, you clothe yourselves with the wool, you slaughter the fat ones, but you do not feed the sheep. The week you have not strengthened, the sick you have not healed, the injured you have not bound up, the strayed you have not brought back, the lost you have not sought, and with force and harshness you have ruled them. So they were scattered, because there was no shepherd, and they became food for all the wild beasts. My sheep were scattered; they wandered over all the mountains and on every high hill. My sheep were scattered over all the face of the earth, with none to search or seek for them" (Ezek. 34:2–6).

5. Timothy S. Laniak, *Shepherds after My Own Heart: Pastoral Traditions and Leadership in the Bible*, NSBT 20 (Downers Grove: InterVarsity Press, 2006), 171.

lated terminology.[6] To be sure, this approach must guard against lexical reductionism, the assumption that one can fully study a concept by means of scrutinizing the vocabulary alone. For example, an exploration of "love" in the New Testament must go beyond an investigation of the relevant vocabulary (*agapaō*, *phileō*, etc.) and include in its purview acts or expressions of love found in narrative texts as well as other words often associated with love such as mercy, forgiveness, or grace. With this caution in mind, however, studies of biblical terminology are still an excellent place to start any in-depth exploration of a motif or concept because such studies help us to identify the passages most relevant to the discussion. The Greek words related to the shepherding motif include *poimnē* (flock), *poimnion* (flock), *poimainō* (to shepherd [verb]), *probaton* (sheep), *poimēn* (shepherd [noun]), *boskō* (feed, herd), *amnos*, *arēn*, and *arnia* (all meaning "lamb").[7] A study of each occurrence of these words in the Gospels surfaces the passages that need to be studied in the following sections in order to conduct a thorough analysis of the shepherding motif in Matthew, Mark, Luke, and John.

SHEPHERDING IN THE GOSPELS

References to shepherds and shepherding are not spread equally across the four Gospels. Matthew and John develop the theme in the most detail, while Mark and Luke feature a smaller amount of relevant passages, and those that are relevant often duplicate material found in the other Gospels. Matthew, in particular, features a considerable number of significant references to shepherding, while John exhibits a pronounced "shepherding motif" in two of his major discourses. The following sur-

---

6. For a much more detailed discussion of the relationship between words and concepts and a rigorous application of a semantic field approach to interpreting the concept of "mission" in the Gospel of John, see Andreas J. Köstenberger, *The Missions of Jesus and the Disciples according to the Fourth Gospel: With Implications for the Fourth Gospel's Purpose and the Mission of the Contemporary Church* (Grand Rapids: Eerdmans, 1998), 17–44.

7. Some passages that contain this vocabulary are not relevant to the current study because they are simply recounting elements of the narrative. Examples include the shepherds at the birth of Jesus (Luke 2:8–20) and the separation of the sheep from the goats at the final judgment (Matt. 25:31–33). Other shorter examples include Matthew 12:11–12; Luke 17:7; John 2:14–15. See Laniak, *Shepherds after My Own Heart*, 187–92, 196–200, for a discussion of Matthew 12:11–12; 25:31–33; and Luke 2:8–10.

vey will show that the motif of Jesus as God's shepherd and of his followers as his flock or sheep, building on the Old Testament characterization of Israel as God's flock, pervades all four canonical Gospels. In this, the Gospels provide an important bridge from the Old Testament to the teaching on shepherding in the New Testament Epistles and the Book of Revelation.

Matthew

The Birth of a Ruler Who Will Shepherd God's People (Matt. 2:6)
The first relevant passage for our study is found in the Matthean birth narrative of Jesus. In Matthew 2:6 we read, "'And you, O Bethlehem, in the land of Judah, are by no means least among the rulers of Judah; for from you shall come a ruler who will shepherd [*poimainō*] my people Israel.'" This quotation from Micah 5:2 and 2 Samuel 5:2, provided to King Herod by the chief priests and teachers of the law, illuminates Jewish messianic expectation concerning both the location of the Messiah's birth and his functions: to rule and to shepherd. The placement of this quotation near the beginning of Matthew's Gospel sets the stage for the development of the shepherding theme throughout the Gospel: Jesus is the promised eschatological Messiah-shepherd who will rule and shepherd—guide, protect, and care for—his people Israel.[8] What past Israelite kings, including its present leadership, "often failed to carry out, the Messiah will now perform properly."[9]

False Prophets Who Come in Sheep's Clothing (Matt. 7:15)
In Jesus' Sermon on the Mount, the first major discourse of Jesus presented in Matthew's Gospel, Jesus warns his followers as follows: "Be-

---

8. Hagner connects this prophecy that the Messiah would shepherd his people with the "statement in 1:21 that 'he will save his people'" (Donald A. Hagner, *Matthew 1–13*, WBC 33A [Dallas: Word, 1993], 30). Good shepherding involves saving.
9. Craig L. Blomberg, *Matthew*, NAC 22 (Nashville: Broadman, 1992), 64. Witherington rightly draws attention to how this passage critiques "obdurate Jerusalem leadership" by contrasting Herod's response to the birth of Jesus (attempted murder) with the response of pagan astrologers (worship) (Ben Witherington, *Matthew*, Smyth & Helwys Bible Commentary [Macon, GA: Smyth & Helwys, 2006], 61). On the "contrast between Jesus as the genuine Davidic shepherd of Israel and Herod," see David L. Turner, *Matthew*, BECNT (Grand Rapids: Baker Academic, 2008), 84.

ware of false prophets, who come to you in sheep's [*probaton*] clothing but inwardly are ravenous wolves" (Matt. 7:15). Jesus' warning against false prophets draws attention to the deception employed by them to blend in with the genuine flock in order to harm, attack, and devour it. This is likely an allusion to Israel as the flock of God which was in danger of being deceived by religious leaders, although the precise identity of the false prophets is left open.[10] The flock is vulnerable, and part of Jesus' shepherding activity is fulfilled in warning his sheep and teaching them how to discover wolves disguised as sheep—by their fruit.

People Are Like Sheep without a Shepherd (Matt. 9:36)

In the context of Jesus' commissioning of the Twelve, Jesus' second major discourse in Matthew's Gospel, we find a cluster of references related to sheep and shepherding. Just prior to Jesus' sending out of the Twelve, Matthew characterizes the state of the people as follows: "When he saw the crowds, he [Jesus] had compassion for them, because they were harassed and helpless, like sheep [*probaton*] without a shepherd [*poimēn*]" (Matt. 9:36; cf. Mark 6:34). The passage squarely alludes to Moses' request, "Let the LORD . . . appoint a man over the congregation who shall go out before them and come in before them, who shall lead them out and bring them in, that the congregation of the LORD may not be as sheep that have no shepherd" (Num. 27:16–17). God answered Moses' prayer by providing Joshua to succeed Moses as Israel's leader.

The trajectory of shepherding in the Old Testament, thus, is grounded in Moses and continues through Joshua all the way to David. Matthew 9:36, along with the surrounding context, highlights Jesus' activity as Israel's messianic shepherd. The passage also indirectly indicts the Jewish leaders as worthless shepherds who failed to adequately shepherd God's flock and shows how Jesus' compassion for the sheep found expression in his commissioning and sending out of the twelve apostles.[11] Jesus is primarily characterized here by compassion—a compassion that enables him to perceive the true needs of the people and to act to meet those needs.[12] Jesus' compassion is often tied

---

10. John Nolland, *The Gospel of Matthew*, NIGTC (Grand Rapids: Eerdmans, 2005), 336–37.
11. Ibid., 407.
12. Hagner notes that "[w]hat causes Jesus' deep compassion at this point is not the abundance of sickness he has seen but rather the great spiritual need of the people, whose lives have

to concrete actions throughout the Gospel (Matt. 14:14; 15:32; 20:34). What is more, Matthew 9:37–38 links the metaphor of sheep without a shepherd with that of a harvest and explicitly involves the disciples in meeting the need for harvesters.[13]

Jesus' Followers Are Sent Out to the Lost Sheep of Israel, as Sheep in the Midst of Wolves (Matt. 10:5–6, 16)

On the heels of Jesus' statement concerning the crowds being sheep without a shepherd comes Jesus' commissioning of the Twelve. As Matthew writes, "These twelve Jesus sent out, instructing them, 'Go nowhere among the Gentiles and enter no town of the Samaritans, but go rather to the lost sheep [*probaton*] of the house of Israel. . . . Behold, I am sending you out as sheep [*probaton*] in the midst of wolves, so be wise as serpents and innocent as doves'" (Matt. 10:5–6, 16). Jesus' instructions to his disciples in Matthew 10:5–6 show the ministry of the Twelve to be part of the fulfillment of the prayer for harvesters (Matt. 9:37–38) and an expression of his compassion for the shepherdless sheep (Matt. 9:35).[14] The flock of Israel is desperately in need of shepherding—involving spiritual guidance, protection, instruction, and help (Matt. 10:7–8).

The salvation-historical constraints of Jesus' instructions to his disciples are apparent again in Matthew 15:24 where Jesus responds to a Canaanite woman's cry for help by noting that he was only sent to the "lost sheep of the house of Israel."[15] Yet even during his earthly ministry Jesus anticipates the Gentile mission (Matt. 8:11; 10:18; 21:43; 22:9; 24:14), and following his resurrection he explicitly commands his disciples to go and make disciples of all the nations (Matt. 28:19).[16] As Turner notes, "This stress in Jesus's ministry underlines the priority of Israel in redemptive history."[17]

---

no center, whose existence seems aimless, whose experience is one of futility. The whole Gospel is a response to just this universal human need" (*Matthew 1–13*, 260).

13. Turner states, "If the shepherdless-flock imagery expresses the desperation of Israel's situation, the harvest imagery expresses the urgency of this desperation" (*Matthew*, 263).

14. Turner describes the disciples as "shepherd-harvesters" (ibid.).

15. Witherington writes, "It should not be surprising then that the mission of the Twelve is described in the same terms as the mission of Jesus, as it is simply an extension of Jesus' ministry (cf. 9:35–37 to 10:1–4)" (*Matthew*, 216).

16. Turner, *Matthew*, 268–69.

17. Ibid.

Even as Jesus sends out his disciples as undershepherds to meet the needs of the flock, he reminds them that they are sheep themselves in the midst of dangerous wolves and that they therefore must be wise and continually on their guard (Matt. 10:16).[18] Nevertheless, their vulnerability as sheep should not lead them to fearfulness but rather dependence on God who would be with them and speak through them (Matt. 10:19–20).[19] Intriguingly, serpents are here used positively as an example of wisdom or shrewdness in dealing with potential dangers, while doves serve as an emblem of moral innocence.

Jesus' and the Disciples' Mission of Going after Lost Sheep (Matt. 18:10–14)

In a chapter that features Jesus' fourth major discourse in Matthew's Gospel, including several parables, Jesus tells the following parable:

> See that you do not despise one of these little ones. For I tell you that in heaven their angels always see the face of my Father who is in heaven. What do you think? If a man has a hundred sheep [*probaton*], and one of them has gone astray, does he not leave the ninety-nine on the mountains and go in search of the one that went astray? And if he finds it, truly, I say to you, he rejoices over it more than over the ninety-nine that never went astray. So it is not the will of my Father who is in heaven that one of these little ones should perish. (Matt. 18:10–14)

The broader context of this passage suggests that references to the "little ones" in Matthew 18:1–14 are to child-like disciples rather than children.[20] This indicates that the parable of the lost sheep is emphasizing the importance and value of every individual disciple (sheep) to the Father, particularly those who have wandered away and have been lost

---

18. Daniel J. Harrington, *The Gospel of Matthew*, SP 1 (Collegeville, MN: Liturgical Press, 1991), 144.
19. This point is also made in a similar context in Luke's Gospel (the sending of the seventy-two): "Behold, I am sending you out as lambs in the midst of wolves" (Luke 10:3).
20. So Donald A. Hagner, *Matthew 14–28*, WBC 33B (Dallas: Word, 1995), 521–22; Nolland, *Gospel of Matthew*, 735; Blomberg, *Matthew*, 276–77.

(Matt. 18:10, 14). This observation, in turn, lays the foundation for the broader instructions concerning proper conduct among Christians: they are not to despise each other (Matt. 18:10) and they are to do all they can to bring straying sheep back to the flock (implied by Matt. 18:14).[21]

In Ezekiel 34, the shepherds of Israel are criticized for failing to do what Jesus describes the shepherd as doing in the parable ("the strayed you have not brought back, the lost you have not sought"; Ezek. 34:4), while God promises to do what Jesus describes in the parable ("I will seek the lost, and I will bring back the strayed"; Ezek. 34:16).[22] These connections with Ezekiel invite reflection on Matthew's presentation of Jesus as the one who will shepherd his people Israel (Matt. 2:6), who has compassion on the flock (Matt. 9:36), and who will seek and save the sheep that is lost (Matt. 18:12). As Hagner notes, "Very probably Matthew and his original readers think of Jesus as the shepherd who goes in search of the straying (see 26:31; cf. 9:36; 15:24; elsewhere in the NT, John 10:11–30)."[23]

The Shepherd Will Be Stricken, and the Sheep Scattered (Matt. 26:31; cf. Mark 14:27)

In Matthew's Gospel, Jesus has now denounced the religious leaders, instructed his followers about the end times, and told several more parables (chaps. 23–25). He celebrated the Last Supper with his disciples and identified Judas as the one who would shortly betray him (Matt. 26:1–30). Predicting Peter's imminent denial of his Master, Jesus told his followers, "You will all fall away because of me this night. For it is written, 'I will strike the shepherd [*poimēn*], and the sheep [*probaton*] of the flock [*poimnē*] will be scattered'" (Matt. 26:31; cf. Mark 14:28), plainly alluding to Zechariah 13:7.[24]

The setting and function of this saying is similar enough in both Matthew and Mark that both passages can be discussed together. As

---

21. Nolland argues that "[t]hose who act as the parable challenges them to act are modeling themselves on the priorities that God himself has. In light of Mt. 9:36; 15:24, Matthew likely sees Jesus in a shepherd role as occupying a middle position between God as shepherd and Christians as shepherds to each other" (*Gospel of Matthew*, 743).
22. Cf. Harrington, *Gospel of Matthew*, 265.
23. Hagner, *Matthew 14–28*, 527.
24. For a masterful treatment of Jesus and his use of messianic passages in Zechariah, see R. T. France, *Jesus and the Old Testament* (London: Tyndale, 1971), 208–9 *et passim*.

mentioned, Jesus makes this statement following the Last Supper (Matt. 26:20–30; Mark 14:12–26). His words clearly indicate that Jesus viewed himself as the shepherd and his disciples as sheep in fulfillment of Zechariah's prophecy concerning God's eschatological shepherd.[25] Jesus quickly follows up this dire prediction with the consolation that he and the disciples would soon be reunited (Matt. 26:32; Mark 14:28). As recorded in both Matthew and Mark, Jesus adapts the quotation to emphasize divine causality and necessity—that God himself would do the striking.[26] Salvation-historical divine necessity dictated that the striking—the crucifixion—had to occur in order that prophecy could be fulfilled and the purification and regathering of the remnant could ensue (Zech. 13:9; Matt. 26:32; Mark 14:28).

Mark

The Crowds Are Like Sheep without a Shepherd (Mark 6:34)
As mentioned, references to shepherding and sheep are not as common in Mark's Gospel as they are in Matthew. The first relevant passage in Mark's Gospel is found in the context of Jesus' feeding of the 5,000. After relating the setting of the miracle, Mark provides the following commentary: "When he went ashore he saw a great crowd, and he had compas-

---

25. Space precludes a discussion of the context of the quotation in Zechariah. See Edwards who argues that in "its original context, Zechariah 13:7 referred to the martyrdom of the eschatological good shepherd" (James R. Edwards, *The Gospel according to Mark*, PNTC [Grand Rapids: Eerdmans, 2002], 428). The identity of the shepherd in Zechariah is complicated by the presence of an eschatological bad shepherd (Zech. 11:15–17). The striking of the shepherd in Zechariah 13:7 results in a process of judgment, purification, and salvation (Zech. 13:8–9).

26. Harrington comments, "The OT quotation is taken from Zech 13:7 and carries on the Matthean fulfillment theme. Both the Hebrew and Greek texts read 'Strike the shepherd ...' The Markan/Matthean 'I will strike' suggest that God does the striking, continuing the idea of the divine plan" (*Gospel of Matthew*, 368). But see Stein who notes that "[i]t is uncertain whether Zech. 13:7 is the source of Jesus's prediction (Scripture says this will happen, so Jesus knew that his disciples would fall away) or served as supporting evidence to what he already knew (my disciples will fall away, and this is in accordance with what Scripture in Zech. 13:7 says). However, the divinely ordained nature of Jesus's passion and death is shown in the quotation by 'It is written' (... cf. 1:2; 7:6; 9:12; 11:17; 14:21) and the words 'I will strike the shepherd.' It is God himself who is ultimately the cause of his Son's suffering and death" (Robert H. Stein, *Mark*, BECNT [Grand Rapids: Baker Academic, 2008], 654). See also R. T. France, *The Gospel of Mark: A Commentary on the Greek Text*, NIGTC (Grand Rapids: Eerdmans, 2002), 575–76.

sion on them, because they were like sheep [*probaton*] without a shepherd [*poimēn*]. And he began to teach them many things" (Mark 6:34).

This description of Jesus' attitude and actions shares some similarities with Matthew 9:36 (discussed above), but the contexts are markedly different. In Mark, Jesus had already sent out the Twelve (Mark 6:7–13), the disciples had just returned (Mark 6:30), and they were seeking solitude and rest which were precluded by the persistent crowds of people (Mark 6:31–33). Instead of responding in impatience and anger to the people who would not allow them to rest, Jesus views them as sheep without a shepherd. He has compassion on them and meets their spiritual needs by teaching them (Mark 6:34) and their physical needs by feeding them (Mark 6:35–44).[27] As R. T. France perceptively notes,

> The description of the crowd . . . is an obvious metaphor for lack of care and leadership, and one used in the OT for Israel in the wilderness after Moses (Nu. 27:17, where the problem is solved by the appointment of Joshua), for Ahab's army after his death in battle (1 Ki. 22:17), for the people of God when their appointed leaders have failed in their trust (Ezk. 34:5–6), and for their helplessness when their (messianic) leader is taken away (Zc. 13:7). While the metaphor in itself would suit a military context . . ., it clearly has also a wider application (cf. its use in a different context in Mt. 9:36, where it forms the basis for the disciples' mission of teaching and healing). Here it denotes the "untended" state of the ordinary people of Galilee (perhaps a reflection on the inadequacy of their current leadership; cf. 7:1–23; 12:38–40), which arouses Jesus'

---

27. Edwards helpfully notes the primary focus of the shepherding metaphor: "Although this image elicits pictures of Jesus helping weak and helpless sheep (Matt 9:36), a pastoral connotation is not its primary connotation in Jewish tradition. As a metaphor, the shepherd of sheep was a common figure of speech in Israel for a leader of Israel like Moses (Isa 63:11), or more often of a Joshua-like military hero who would muster Israel's forces for war (Num 27:17; 1 Kgs 22:17//2 Chr 18:16; Jer 10:21; Ezek 34:5; 37:24; Nah 3:18; Zech 13:7; Jdt 11:19). It is, in other words, a metaphor of hegemony, including military leadership and victory. In his compassion, Jesus sees a whole people without direction, without purpose, without a leader. Jesus utilizes the opportunity to teach the people, but as is usual in Mark, it is not the content of the teaching but the one who teaches who is the focus of interest" (*Gospel according to Mark*, 191).

compassion and to which he responds as in 4:1–2 by an extended period of teaching.[28]

The phrase "sheep without a shepherd," as stated above, likely recalls Moses' prayer preceding Yahweh's appointment of Joshua: "Let the LORD . . . appoint a man over the congregation . . . who shall lead them . . ., that the congregation of the LORD may not be as sheep that have no shepherd" (Num. 27:16–17). In Numbers 27:18, the prayer is answered by the appointment of Joshua to succeed Moses, but Mark 6:34 points toward its greater fulfillment in Jesus. As Stein observes, "Now a greater Joshua ('Jesus' in Greek), who possesses even more of the Spirit of God (cf. Num. 27:18 and Mark 1:10), has come to lead Israel (cf. Heb. 4:8). The promised shepherd of Ezek. 34:23 would 'feed' Israel, and Jesus now feeds his people."[29] Jesus came in order to permanently fill the shepherd-vacuum that existed among God's people in a way that prior shepherds—Moses, Joshua, David—were unable to fill because of sin and death.

Luke

The Disciples Are Jesus' "Little Flock" (Luke 12:32)

As stated above, references to shepherding are not as frequent in Luke as they are in Matthew. In the context of Jesus' teaching on his kingdom, we find this statement: "Fear not, little flock [*poimnion*], for it is your Father's good pleasure to give you the kingdom" (Luke 12:32). This passing reference to Jesus' disciples as a little flock indicates Jesus' perception of himself as a shepherd and his followers as sheep. The immediate context contains general instruction from Jesus concerning anxiety (Luke 12:22–31) and generosity (Luke 12:33). Jesus assures his followers that they are to give generously, without fear or worry because the Father will give the kingdom to Jesus' flock, those who were following him faithfully.

The Parable of the Lost Sheep (Luke 15:4–7)

As part of his "Travel Narrative" tracing Jesus' journey to Jerusalem (Luke 9:51–19:27), Luke features several of Jesus' parables dealing with "lost

---

28. France, *Gospel of Mark*, 265.
29. Stein, *Mark*, 313.

things." The second of these is the Parable of the Lost Sheep: "What man of you, having a hundred sheep [*probaton*], if he has lost one of them, does not leave the ninety-nine in the open country, and go after the one that is lost, until he finds it? And when he has found it, he lays it on his shoulders, rejoicing. And when he comes home, he calls together his friends and his neighbors, saying to them, 'Rejoice with me, for I have found my sheep [*probaton*] that was lost.' Just so, I tell you, there will be more joy in heaven over one sinner who repents than over ninety-nine righteous persons who need no repentance" (Luke 15:4–7).

Differences in vocabulary, context, and content distinguish this parable of the lost sheep from the one in Matthew 18:10–14. This is probably due to the fact that Jesus, as an itinerant rabbi, would have naturally shared similar stories in different places and times to make various points. At the same time, it is also possible that the respective Gospel writers themselves set different emphases—Matthew stressing the need to value and seek after strayed disciples in the context of Jesus' instructions concerning the community of believers and Luke focusing on God's love for sinful humanity and sinners' need to repent in the context of a defense of Jesus' outreach to sinners.

Despite the differences, in Luke as in Matthew, "the parable takes up the theme of God's care for his flock (Ezk. 34:12, 23f) which is now fulfilled in the Messiah."[30] God's care for his flock, both for strayed disciples and for lost sinners, is embodied in the ministry and activity of Jesus: "The implication is that in some sense Jesus takes the place of God; he performs the acts of God."[31] This is evident because it is "the behavior of Jesus that is being defended. Clearly there is some sense in which Jesus is performing the acts of God here."[32] The identification of the shepherd with Jesus is strengthened by Jesus' statement following his successful outreach to Zacchaeus, the tax-collector: "For the Son of Man came to seek and to save the lost" (Luke 19:10).

All three of the parables in Luke 15—the lost sheep, lost coin, and lost son—are told by Jesus in response to the Pharisees and teachers of the law grumbling, saying, "This man receives sinners and eats with

---

30. I. Howard Marshall, *The Gospel of Luke*, NIGTC (Grand Rapids: Eerdmans, 1978), 601.
31. John Nolland, *Luke 9:21–18:34*, WBC 35B (Dallas: Word, 1993), 771.
32. Ibid., 773.

them" (Luke 15:2).[33] The set of parables explains and defends Jesus'
practice of seeking out tax-collectors and "sinners," with the Pharisees representing the older brother in the parable of the lost son (Luke
15:25–32). The three parables are united by the shared themes of something lost; someone searching (or, in the case of the father, seeing and
running from a long way off); and the joy over finding that which was
lost (sheep, coin, son, or sinners). As Nolland observes, "The motif of
shared joy runs as a thread through the parables of chap. 15; it functions to encourage in the church a reiteration of the pattern of Jesus'
preoccupations: an outward-looking concern for the winning of sinners and participation in the joy of those who are successfully involved
in such outreach."[34] Jesus' outreach to tax-collectors and "sinners" is
cast in the parables as a quest that is deeply rooted in the nature of
all human experience—the persistent looking for things that are lost,
whether a sheep, a coin, and or even a son, and the rejoicing over finding what had been lost.

John

Jesus Is the "Lamb of God" (John 1:29, 36)

Together with the Gospel of Matthew, John's Gospel provides the most
sustained expression of the shepherding motif in the Gospels. In the first
chapter of John's Gospel, John affirms that Jesus' ministry is firmly rooted in the witness of his predecessor, John the Baptist. Subsequent to the
Baptist's interchange with a group of priests and Levites from Jerusalem
regarding his identity as a "voice of one crying out in the wilderness,
'Make straight the way of the Lord,'" we read the following statement by
John the evangelist: "The next day he [the Baptist] saw Jesus coming toward him, and said, 'Behold the Lamb [*amnos*] of God, who takes away
the sin of the world!' . . . and he looked at Jesus as he walked by and said,
'Behold, the Lamb [*amnos*] of God!'" (John 1:29, 36).

---

33. Bock notes that the parables of the lost sheep and lost coin "represent Jesus' explanation of
why he relates to tax collectors and sinners (15:1–2). God will go to great effort and rejoice
with great joy to find and restore a sinner to himself. Jesus wishes to emphasize that God
is not a God of the few, a God of the wise, or a God only of those who think they pursue
God. He is a God who searches, finds, and cares for the sinner" (Darrell L. Bock, *Luke
9:51–24:53*, BECNT [Grand Rapids: Baker Academic, 1996], 1295).
34. Nolland, *Luke 9:21–18:34*, 773–74.

These initial two utterances by John the Baptist highlight the universal significance of Jesus' sacrificial, substitutionary death as the Lamb of God.[35] Jesus is not here presented as God's eschatological shepherd but rather as an eschatological lamb—the final, complete, and sufficient sacrifice that dealt with the sin of the world. As we will see further below, Jesus describes himself as the Good Shepherd who "lays down his life for the sheep" (John 10:11). Both as lamb and as shepherd, Jesus is described as laying down his life to rescue God's people and flock.

Jesus Is the Good Shepherd, and His Followers Are His Sheep (John 10)
Following the healing of the man born blind, which was fiercely opposed by the Pharisees (John 9, esp. vv. 39–40), Jesus delivers his "Good Shepherd Discourse": "Truly, truly, I say to you, he who does not enter the sheepfold by the door but climbs in by another way, that man is a thief and a robber. But he who enters by the door is the shepherd of the sheep. To him the gatekeeper opens. The sheep hear his voice, and he calls his own sheep by name and leads them out. When he has brought out all his own, he goes before them, and the sheep follow him, for they know his voice. A stranger they will not follow, but they will flee from him, for they do not know the voice of strangers" (John 10:1–5).

He continues, "Truly, truly, I say to you, I am the door of the sheep. All who came before me are thieves and robbers, but the sheep did not listen to them. I am the door. If anyone enters by me, he will be saved and will go in and out and find pasture. The thief comes only to steal and kill and destroy. I came that they may have life and have it abundantly. I am the good shepherd. The good shepherd lays down his life for the sheep" (John 10:7–11). And again, "I am the good shepherd. I know my own and my own know me, just as the Father knows me and

---

35. See Andreas J. Köstenberger, *John*, BECNT (Grand Rapids: Baker Academic, 2004), 66–68; Leon Morris, *The Gospel according to John*, rev. ed., NICNT (Grand Rapids: Eerdmans, 1995), 130. The expression invites textual associations with the slaughtered lamb of Isaiah 53:7; the Passover lamb of Exodus 12 (Gary M. Burge, *The Gospel of John*, NIVAC [Grand Rapids: Zondervan, 2000], 73–74; C. K. Barrett, *The Gospel according to St. John*, 2nd ed. [Philadelphia: Westminster, 1978], 176); the lamb provided by God for Abraham (Gen. 22:8, 13); the apocalyptic warrior lamb (*1 Enoch* 90:9–12; *T. Jos.* 19:8; *T. Ben.* 3:8; George R. Beasley-Murray, *John*, WBC 36 [Waco, TX: Word, 1987], 24–25); the gentle lamb of Jeremiah 11:19; the scapegoat of Leviticus 16; and the guilt offering of Leviticus 14 and Numbers 6 (though involving bulls and goats).

I know the Father, and I lay down my life for the sheep. And I have other sheep that are not of this fold. I must bring them also, and they will listen to my voice. So there will be one flock, one shepherd. For this reason the Father loves me, because I lay down my life that I may take it up again" (John 10:13–17).

Later on, at the occasion of the Feast of Dedication, Jesus returns to the topic once more: "The works that I do in my Father's name bear witness about me, but you do not believe because you are not among my sheep. My sheep hear my voice, and I know them, and they follow me. I give them eternal life, and they will never perish, and no one will snatch them out of my hand. My Father, who has given them to me, is greater than all, and no one is able to snatch them out of the Father's hand. I and the Father are one" (John 10:25–30).[36]

Notably, there is no real transition from the account of Jesus' healing of the blind man in John 9 to his presentation of himself as the Door and the Good Shepherd in John 10. This lack of transition indicates that the audience is likely the same and that the thieves and robbers of John 10 are meant to describe the Pharisees who had just expelled the healed blind man from the synagogue (John 9:34).[37] John 10 thus includes a strong polemic as the passage contrasts Jesus the Good Shepherd of God's flock with the current Jewish leadership which is shown to be part of the trajectory of bad shepherds throughout Old Testament history who served and nurtured only themselves and, shockingly, fed on the sheep rather than caring for them (John 10:1, 5, 8, 10, 12; cf. Isa. 56:11; Jer. 10:21; 23:1–2; 50:6–7; Ezek. 34:1–31; Zech. 10:2–3; 11:15–17).[38]

Although shepherds in ancient Israel were widely considered to be members of the lower class, this cultural background is surmounted

---

36. Shepherding language pervades these verses: *probaton* in John 10:1, 2, 3, 4, 7, 8, 11, 12, 13, 15, 16, 26, 27; *poimēn* in John 10:2, 11, 12, 14, 16; and *poimnē* in John 10:16.

37. Continuity is also suggested by the fact that the double *amēn* construction never begins a discourse in the Gospel of John. Cf. Morris, *Gospel according to John*, 446.

38. I elsewhere note that the "spectrum of 'thieves and robbers' may also encompass pseudo-prophets such as the ones mentioned by Luke and Josephus . . . , the Zealots, and even the high-priestly circles that controlled Judaism in Jesus' day. Sadducees in particular were known to use temple religion for their own profit, and elsewhere both the Pharisees (Luke 16:14) and the scribes (Mark 12:40) are denounced for their greed. Perhaps the closest connection in the present context is with the Pharisees, whose attitude toward the man born blind exemplifies a blatant usurpation of religious authority and a perversion of godly leadership (cf. John 9)" (Köstenberger, *John*, 303).

by the Gospel writers throughout the Gospels in favor of the positive Old Testament depiction of God and his Messiah as the shepherds of Israel.[39] There is a great deal that could be said regarding John 10:1–30, but several points in particular are relevant to the present study:[40] the Good Shepherd knows his sheep individually by name (John 10:3, 14, 27); the sheep know the voice of the shepherd and can distinguish his voice from that of others (John 10:3–5, 14, 16, 27); the Good Shepherd sacrificially lays down his own life on behalf of the sheep (John 10:11, 15, 17–18); and salvation and life for the sheep are found with the shepherd (John 10:9–10, 28–29).

The image of the shepherd calling his sheep by name indicates a deep level of care and intimacy as well as highlighting the value of the individual (John 10:3, 14, 27). There is evidence for the practice of Palestinian shepherds giving nicknames to some of their sheep, but the more relevant background is to be found in God's calling of his closest servants and Israel as a whole "by name" (Ex. 33:12, 17; Isa. 43:1).[41] God's people—sheep—are never just numbers to the Good Shepherd.

Not only does the Good Shepherd call his sheep by name, but his sheep know his voice and can distinguish it from that of a stranger. Even though sheep are helpless, vulnerable, and in need of guidance, they can discern the voice of their shepherd. In the Old Testament, God's people listened to his voice by living in obedience to the instructions of the law and the prophets, but now Jesus is presenting his own voice as that which will be followed by God's sheep. Jesus does not elevate his voice over the law and the prophets but contrasts it with the "strangers" whom God's sheep will not follow (John 10:5; cf. the thieves and robbers of John 10:1, 8, 10). Those who do not listen to Jesus' voice (i.e., believe; John 10:25) demonstrate that they are not God's sheep, which strikingly includes the Jewish leaders themselves (John 10:26).

As noted by John the Baptist at the beginning of the Gospel, Jesus as the Lamb of God will take away the sin of the world (John 1:29, 36). This sacrificial idea is expanded here by the different metaphor of a shepherd laying down his life on behalf of his sheep (John 10:11,

---

39. See the discussion above.
40. For a more detailed treatment of this discourse, see Köstenberger, *John*, 297–320.
41. For the background of Palestinian shepherds "naming" their sheep, see Craig S. Keener, *The Gospel of John*, 2 vols. (Peabody, MA: Hendrickson, 2003), 805.

15, 17–18).[42] The repeated references to Jesus' selfless sacrifice for the sheep in John 10:11–18 indicate that this is the defining characteristic of the Good Shepherd—it is the reason why he is called "good." The description of Jesus as the Good Shepherd confirms his role as God's eschatological shepherd in the trajectory of Moses and David (2 Sam. 5:2; Ps. 77:20; 78:70–72; Isa. 63:11; Ezek. 37:24; Mic. 5:4), and in contrast to the bad shepherds that had preyed on God's flock throughout its history (Jer. 23:1–4; Ezek. 34; Zech. 11:4–17). These verses also indicate that God's eschatological Good Shepherd extends the benefits of his sacrificial death to the Gentiles who are united with God's sheep so as for there to be "one flock and one shepherd" (John 10:16; cf. Isa. 56:6–8; Ezek. 37:15–28; Mic. 2:12).[43] Although the Gentile mission was carried out by Jesus' followers, it was still Jesus who was calling, brining, and shepherding them from his exalted position with the Father (John 10:16; cf. John 10:12).[44]

Finally, this text makes clear that the sheep will only find salvation and life by entering through the gate and by following the shepherd (John 10:9–10, 28–29). The metaphor of Jesus being a gate (cf. Ps. 118:20) may seem far removed from the metaphor of him being a shepherd, but both metaphors are unified by their relationship to sheep: they are both essential for the life and safety of the flock.[45] The imagery of the gate stresses that salvation and fullness of life—going in and out and finding pasture—for the sheep is only found through Jesus (John 10:9–10).[46] It is evident from the Gospel as a whole that the reference

---

42. See D. A. Carson, *The Gospel according to John*, PNTC (Grand Rapids: Eerdmans, 1991), 386; Barrett, *Gospel according to St. John*, 375; Gerald L. Borchert, *John 1–11*, NAC 25A (Nashville: B&H, 1996), 334; Burge, *Gospel of John*, 291.

43. Cf. H. Ridderbos, *The Gospel According to John*, trans. J. Vriend (Grand Rapids: Eerdmans, 1997), 362–63.

44. On John 10:16, see especially Andreas J. Köstenberger, "Jesus the Good Shepherd Who Will Also Bring Other Sheep (John 10:16): The Old Testament Background of a Familiar Metaphor," *BBR* 12 (2002): 67–96.

45. Laniak notes that as "the door he is the exclusive means of entrance into the protected fold. As the shepherd he is the one who leads the flock to pastures (abundant life). By both metaphors Jesus contrasts himself with others—those who do not use the door and those who care for themselves rather than the flock" (*Shepherds after My Own Heart*, 214).

46. This is made clear by the emphatic placement of *di' emou* ("through me"). Cf. Morris, *Gospel according to John*, 452. It was common in the ancient world among Greeks, Romans, and Jews to visualize entering heaven through a gate (Gen. 28:17; Ps. 78:23; Matt. 7:7, 13–14; 18:8–9; 25:10; *1 Enoch* 72–75; *3 Bar.* 6:13).

to having abundant life (John 10:10) refers both to eternal life (John 10:28–29) and to abundant life in the here and now (cf. the present tense "give" in John 10:28). The certainty of eternal life for the flock is stressed by the fact that no one will be able to snatch the sheep out of the shepherd's (John 10:28) or God's hand (John 10:29)—and the shepherd and God are one (John 10:30)![47]

To sum up, the shepherd discourse of John 10 contrasts Jesus, the eschatological Good Shepherd who protects, provides for, and brings salvation to his sheep, with the thieves, robbers, and hired hands who harmed the flock through neglect and predatory activities. In contrast to those who harm the flock out of self-interest, the Good Shepherd sacrifices his own life to save and preserve those who are his. Salvation is available only to those who listen and believe in and follow the Good Shepherd.

Jesus Commissions Peter as His Undershepherd (John 21)

The concluding scene of John's Gospel follows up on Jesus' "Good Shepherd Discourse." John writes, "When they had finished breakfast, Jesus said to Simon Peter, 'Simon, son of John, do you love me more than these?' He said to him, 'Yes, Lord; you know that I love you.' He said to him, 'Feed [boskō] my lambs [arnia].' He said to him a second time, 'Simon, son of John, do you love me?' He said to him, 'Yes, Lord; you know that I love you.' He said to him, 'Tend [poimainō] my sheep [probaton].' He said to him the third time, 'Simon, son of John, do you love me?' Peter was grieved because he said to him the third time, 'Do you love me?' and he said to him, 'Lord, you know everything; you know that I love you.' Jesus said to him, 'Feed [boskō] my sheep [probaton].' . . . 'Follow me'" (John 21:15–17, 19c).

With its reference to a charcoal fire and three questions concerning Peter's stance toward Jesus, this passage is clearly meant to mirror Peter's threefold denial of Jesus prior to the crucifixion.[48] In response

---

47. "To be sure, the emphasis here is on the unity of their works . . ., yet an ontological (not just functional) unity between Jesus and the Father seems presupposed" (Köstenberger, *John*, 312). Cf. Carson, *Gospel according to John*, 394–95.

48. For Peter's three denials, see John 18:15–18, 25–27; his three affirmations of his love for Jesus are in John 21:15, 16, and 17. John 18:18 and 21:9 contain the only two instances of *anthrakia* (charcoal fire) in the Gospel (and, in fact, in the entire New Testament). See Gerald L. Borchert, *John 12–21*, NAC 25B (Nashville: B&H, 2002), 335.

to Peter's repeated affirmations of his love for him, Jesus gives him the thrice-repeated command to shepherd his sheep. The different words used, "feed/tend" *(boskō/poimainō)* and "lambs/sheep" *(arnia/probaton)*, likely indicate mere stylistic variety and through synonymous parallelism emphasize the overarching command to feed, take care of, and tend—that is, shepherd—the sheep.[49] Jesus' final command to Peter to follow him (John 21:19) closely links discipleship (following Jesus) with shepherding (taking care of Jesus' sheep).[50] The interchange between Jesus and Peter at the end of Jesus' earthly ministry prior to his ascension emphasizes the full restoration of Peter, but also denotes a clear delegation of responsibility from God's eschatological Good Shepherd to human undershepherds to carry on the activity of the Chief Shepherd until he returns at which time he will personally shepherd God's flock. At that time, "the Lamb in the midst of the throne will be their shepherd, and he will guide them to springs of living water, and God will wipe away every tear from their eyes" (Rev. 7:17).

SHEPHERDING AND PASTORAL LEADERSHIP IN THE TWENTY-FIRST CENTURY

This final section will explore three dimensions of the shepherding motif in the Gospels that are relevant to pastoral leadership in the twenty-first century. First, the shepherding motif in the Gospels is primarily *Christocentric*—demonstrating how Jesus is God's promised eschatological shepherd of his people. As mentioned, this Christological shepherding activity is explicitly extended to Peter (and, by extension, to other apostles and church leaders) in John 21:15–17. Second, during Jesus' ministry he involved his disciples in his shepherding activity—providing for the

---

49. Cf. Raymond E. Brown, *The Gospel according to John XIII–XXI*, AB 29B (Garden City, NY: Doubleday, 1970), 1105; Rudolf Schnackenburg, *The Gospel according to St. John*, 3 vols., trans. C. Hastings et al (New York: Crossroad, 1990), 3:363.

50. Laniak makes a similar point: "The element that is most germane to our discussion of this passage is the conceptualization of discipleship in terms of shepherd functions. As we have seen in all the Gospels, 'following' Jesus ultimately entails 'shepherding' his sheep. John's epilogue makes this most explicit. While Jesus had placed an enormous emphasis on the disciples' relationship with him, this final scene demonstrates the intended outcome of that intimacy. Verbs convey the emphasis on action; three times Peter is told to 'feed/shepherd my sheep'" (*Shepherds after My Own Heart*, 222).

physical and spiritual needs of the flock (Matt. 10:5–6; Mark 6:34). Third, Jesus' teaching and shepherding set the example for his undershepherds to follow—particularly in regard to compassion for the sheep, feeding and sacrificing for the sheep, and seeking the sheep who are lost (Matt. 9:36; 18:10–14; Mark 6:34; Luke 15:4–7; John 10:11, 15, 17–18).

A major caution must be registered before attempting to apply principles from Gospel narratives to the present life of the church. With Jesus' exaltation and the outpouring of the Spirit, a new salvation-historical era was inaugurated, marked by the pouring out of the Holy Spirit at Pentecost and the birth of the church. The book of Acts, among other things, narrates the replacement of Judas (Acts 1:15–26), the early church's devotion to the apostles' teaching (Acts 2:42), the appointment of elders throughout the churches as part of Paul's Gentile mission (Acts 14:23; cf. Titus 1:5), and the Jerusalem council (Acts 15). Paul's letters and some of the other letters found in the New Testament provide stipulations regarding qualifications for church leaders. The Gospels cannot be removed from their place in salvation history and be made wholesale into a normative leadership training manual for the modern church.[51] That said, I propose the following implications from the Gospels' teaching about shepherding for church leadership today.

The Shepherd Mandate: "Feed My Sheep"

Although Jesus' explicit commands to "feed my sheep" are directed toward Peter in John 21:15–19, Peter rightly extends the meaning to all those who would shepherd God's flock as undershepherds. In 1 Peter 5:1–4, he commands elders to willingly "shepherd the flock of God that is among you," not for financial gain or in a domineering way, but as "examples to the flock," in anticipation of being rewarded by the "chief Shep-

---

51. See my critique of this approach as advocated by Robert E. Coleman, *The Master Plan of Evangelism* (Old Tappan, NJ: Fleming H. Revell, 1963), and *The Mind of the Master* (Old Tappan, NJ: Fleming H. Revell, 1977). "[T]hese approaches seem to be based on the underlying, but rarely explicitly stated, assumption that Jesus' principles of training his disciples have normative character. . . . The model of a Jewish rabbi who gathers around himself a group of disciples who leave their own surroundings to share their teacher's lifestyle, travel with him on his journeys, and depend on others' support for their sustenance should not be seen as paradigmatic for all times. There is no indication that the Scriptures present this model as normative" (Köstenberger, *Missions of Jesus and the Disciples,* 218).

herd" when he appears. These instructions in 1 Peter explicitly apply and extend Jesus' command to "feed my sheep" to all the elders of God's flock, the church. They make clear that human leaders, as in the Old Testament, are but undershepherds to the Chief Shepherd. They are responsible to carry on the activities of the Chief Shepherd and must give an account for how well they performed their shepherding duties.

The extension of Jesus' shepherding activity to that of his followers, in turn, fits the broader mission theme in the Gospels. As I have argued more extensively elsewhere, John "conceived of the mission of the Christian community as ultimately the mission of the exalted Jesus carried out through his followers."[52] Jesus is the Chief Shepherd who ultimately provides for, feeds, protects, and guides his flock, while he also commissions undershepherds to work alongside him, through the Spirit, in his shepherding activity.

This mandate from Jesus to Peter is extended by Peter to all the elders of God's flock and therefore applies to modern pastors, elders, and leaders as well. As an outworking of our personal discipleship ("follow me"), we are obligated to feed, tend, and care for God's people as we take our place in the biblical trajectory of good shepherds (Moses, David, Jesus) rather than joining the ranks of the bad shepherds who were motivated by self-interest and personal gain and had no care for the sheep. The mandate to shepherd God's flock is not an optional activity for leaders in which to engage only if they feel that they have the right personality or inclination. Pastors will no doubt shepherd in different ways based on individual gifting and temperament, but the obligation to shepherd cannot and must not be delegated to others, and no matter how construed contains a personal dimension. Remote or absentee shepherding is not an option.

Shepherd Training: The Disciples' Involvement

During his earthly ministry, Jesus intentionally involved his disciples in his shepherding activity. This is most obvious in the sending out of disciples in Matthew 9:36–42 and the return of the Twelve from their two-by-two ministry in Mark 6:30–44.

---

52. Köstenberger, *Missions of Jesus and the Disciples*, 210.

Matthew 9:36–38 provides Jesus' assessment of the present situation in Israel: he is filled with compassion because the people are desperate and needy in the absence of proper shepherds. The harvest is plentiful, but the laborers are few. Jesus responds to this situation by sending out his followers to cast out unclean spirits, to heal every disease and affliction, and to proclaim the coming of the kingdom of heaven (Matt. 10:1, 7). The connection between these chapters is evident from the fact that Jesus sends his disciples to "the lost sheep of the house of Israel" (Matt. 10:6), the very people who were "harassed and helpless, like sheep without a shepherd" (Matt. 9:36). Jesus thus sends out his undershepherds to meet the needs of the sheep—a delegated fulfillment of his own role as the shepherd of his people Israel (Matt. 2:6).

The context of Mark 6:34 places this statement of Jesus at a time when the twelve apostles had just returned from their two-by-two ministry (Mark 6:7–13), and Jesus had led them away to rest for a while because the mass of people prevented them from being able even to eat (Mark 6:31). The crowds, however, followed Jesus and his disciples, preventing them from getting the rest they sought and needed (Mark 6:33–34). Within this context, the condition and need of the people ("like sheep without a shepherd") motivated Jesus, who involved his disciples (Mark 6:37), to fulfill the functions of a shepherd and to meet their spiritual and physical needs, teaching them (Mark 6:34) and providing for them (Mark 6:41–42).

It is important to note here that the disciples are involved in the shepherding activities of both teaching and feeding. They helped meet people's spiritual needs by participating in Jesus' teaching through their proclamation of the need to repent (Mark 6:12), and they helped meet people's physical needs by participating in Jesus' feeding ministry (Mark 6:37–43). As evangelicals, we are often very good at fulfilling the shepherding function of teaching, which pastors rightly consider their primary duty (e.g., Acts 6:2; Eph. 4:11; 2 Tim. 4:2), but not so good at meeting people's physical needs. Jesus was concerned with both (though doubtless considering meeting spiritual needs primary), in light of the fact that these cannot be easily divided in effective shepherding.[53]

---

53. This is made clear in what is very likely an extension of Jesus' teaching on shepherding in 1 John 3:16–17: "By this we know love, that he laid down his life for us, and we ought to lay

Jesus' compassion for the sheep motivated him to meet their needs even in the midst of weariness when he and his disciples were actively seeking solitude and rest. The text does not record whether or not the disciples grumbled over the interruption of their rest as many of us likely would have done. Modern-day shepherds of God's flock must be prepared to meet the needs of the sheep even in the midst of personal weariness and strain (though there are certainly times when they must rest as well).

Shepherd Modeling: Jesus' Example

Jesus set a clear example for his undershepherds to follow in at least three areas: (1) compassion for the sheep (Matt. 9:36; Mark 6:34); (2) feeding and sacrificing for the sheep (John 10:11, 15, 17–18); and (3) seeking the sheep that are lost (Matt. 18:10–14; Luke 15:4–7). Both texts that describe Jesus seeing the crowds of people as sheep without a shepherd emphasize the compassion that he felt for them (Matt. 9:36; Mark 6:34). Jesus' compassion for the crowds and those in need made such an impression upon his disciples that it is recorded multiple times across the synoptic Gospels (Matt. 14:14; 15:32; 20:34; Mark 1:41; 8:2; Luke 7:13). Jesus deeply cared for others, and each text that highlights his compassion also describes how he took concrete action to meet people's spiritual and physical needs.

Genuine compassion is a characteristic that is sadly lacking in many leaders of God's flock today. It is comparatively easier for us to confront sin and heresy and to teach correct doctrine, but it is often much harder to have genuine compassion for those to whom we are ministering—to actually care deeply for their needs, concerns, and problems. We are often far too easily preoccupied with our own needs, concerns, and problems. I have heard more than one pastor say in jest that church ministry would not be so bad if it were not for having to deal with people. While there is certainly an element of truth in this assertion, this attitude is far removed from that demonstrated by Jesus as he modeled for his followers what a good shepherd is truly like.

---

down our lives for the brothers. But if anyone has the world's goods and sees his brother in need, yet closes his heart against him, how does God's love abide in him? Little children, let us not love in word or talk but in deed and in truth."

The second characteristic of good shepherding that Jesus modeled for his undershepherds, particularly in John's shepherd discourse, is that of being willing to sacrifice.[54] Jesus' sacrifice of his life on the cross was a non-repeatable, decisive salvation-historical event, but a willingness and readiness to sacrifice for the sheep should characterize all of Christ's undershepherds (see esp. John 13, esp. vv. 12–17).[55] God's flock does not need undershepherds who flee when they see a wolf coming (John 10:12), nor does it need undershepherds who are in the ministry only or primarily for self-interest and personal gain (cf. Ezekiel 34) and will not sacrifice because this requires prioritizing the needs of the sheep over self. Sacrifice is not popular, nor is it easy. As we saw in our discussion of John 10, Jesus' willingness to sacrifice for the sheep in many ways defined what it meant for him to be a "good" shepherd—a correlation that applies to his undershepherds as well.[56]

Sacrifice for the sheep should set Christian leaders of God's flock apart from any secular models of leadership—it is certainly not displayed by CEOs who fill their own bank accounts while the company slides into bankruptcy or politicians who only care about reelection in order to maintain their social and financial status rather than actually serving their country. Which (if any) secular models of leadership have genuine self-sacrifice as a key component? In many ways, this is counter-intuitive, but such a sacrificial disposition makes sense in God's upside-down world where the last will be first and the first last (Matt. 20:1–16).

Finally, Jesus' parable of the lost sheep, as told by both Matthew and Luke, sets forth the shepherd who diligently sought for the sheep that was

---

54. Laniak argues that *kalos* ("good") should be translated as "model" in John 10:11, 14: "First, 'good' might imply nothing more than a moral quality. While Jesus is certainly contrasting malevolent thieves, bandits and hirelings with a benevolent shepherd, he might have used the more common term *agathos*. *Kalos* implies an attractive quality, something noble or ideal. 'Model' captures these connotations, but also implies a second nuance that is important in this context: Jesus should be emulated. John makes it clear elsewhere that Jesus is ultimately training his followers to be like him in his life and death (4:34–38; 14:12; 17:20; 20:21–23; 21:15–19). They will eventually take care of his flock and risk their lives like their master (21:15–23)" (*Shepherds after My Own Heart*, 211).

55. On the way in which Jesus' footwashing of his disciples epitomizes his disposition that is ultimately displayed by his death on the cross, see Andreas J. Köstenberger, *A Theology of John's Gospel and Letters*, BTNT (Grand Rapids: Zondervan, 2009), chap. 13.

56. In concluding his discussion of Mark 6:34, Laniak notes, "Self-sacrificing service is the hallmark of the Lord's deputy shepherds (10:45)" (*Shepherds after My Own Heart*, 179).

lost as a model for his disciples to follow (Matt. 18:10–14; Luke 15:4–7). As we saw above, the stress in Matthew falls on seeking those members of the community who had strayed or fallen away while Luke emphasizes the search for sinners and their need to repent.[57] The seeking shepherd exemplifies deep concern for the lost, a complete focus on the search, and great joy over the find. These are not passive shepherds who leave it all up to the sheep ("If it wants to come back, it knows where to find me"), nor lazy shepherds ("This terrain is too difficult, I'm going home"), nor shepherds prone to give up ("This is taking too long, I'm going back to the sheep who haven't strayed"). The example of the seeking shepherd stands against the practice of sitting back and simply hoping the backslidden and lost will show up for Sunday services.

The figure of the "seeking shepherd" also makes clear that the dichotomy between pastoring God's flock of those already saved and evangelizing those who are still lost is an unfortunate and unbiblical one. The seeking shepherd combines both functions in one. He cares for the sheep who are already in the flock and provides for them spiritually (and if need be, physically) and keeps them safe, but he is also concerned for those in the world who are lost in their sin. Not only does he lead by example in reaching out to the lost, he also seeks to mobilize the church to be moved with compassion for the lost and to take the gospel to them. This calls for wisdom and discernment, and wise shepherds, guided by the Holy Spirit, will strike the right balance between caring for the saved and seeking to reach the lost.

CONCLUSION

The Old Testament's presentation of God as Israel's shepherd, the delegation of his shepherding activity to the leaders of Israel, the fulfillment of this shepherding activity by some leaders (notably Moses and David), the bad exercise of it by other leaders who preyed on the flock and fed only themselves, and the expectation that God would send an eschatological shepherd to redeem, guide, and protect Israel provide

---

57. Laniak observes, "While Matthew's interest is in the restoration of a believer, the parable in Luke is integral to his portrait of Jesus' compassionate, 'evangelistic' ministry as 'the Son of Man [who] came to seek out and to save the lost' (19:10 NRSV)" (*Shepherds after My Own Heart*, 204).

the conceptual background for the development of shepherding motifs in the Gospels. Jesus is presented in the Gospels as the eschatological Good Shepherd whom God had sent to rule and shepherd his people. He performed this eschatological shepherding role by taking care of the sheep during his earthly ministry—teaching, healing, and feeding—and by dying for the eternal salvation of God's flock composed of repentant sinners from all places and all times, and commissioning undershepherds to continue shepherding God's flock in the power of the Spirit until his return.

Christ's undershepherds in the twenty-first century must recognize that they share the mandate to tend God's flock which Christ originally extended to Peter. This shepherding mandate involves sacrificially meeting the spiritual and physical needs of the flock and diligently seeking after those who have strayed and are lost. This shepherding activity should be motivated not only by love for the Chief Shepherd, but also by genuine compassion for the sheep. May we faithfully fulfill Christ's shepherding mandate given to us in the trajectory of Moses, David, and Jesus rather than following in the vein of Israel's bad shepherds who lived to serve and please only themselves.

CHAPTER 3

The Pattern of Leadership in Acts and Paul's Letters to Churches[1]

Benjamin L. Merkle[2]

There seem to be three extremes when it comes to studying the pattern of leadership in the early church. One extreme is to claim that the early church did not have any set leaders but each church was led as the Spirit moved upon various individuals to serve. This view is dangerous because it ignores the fact that God gifts and calls individuals to serve as appointed leaders in the church and because it forces an artificial separation between gift (or *charisma*) and office. A second extreme is to claim that although the New Testament church followed certain patterns, these patterns are nearly irrelevant since what the church has done throughout history is just as authoritative as what the church did during the time of the twelve apostles. This view is dangerous because it ignores the fact that in his wisdom God has established certain principles in his word related to church government that should be followed today. A third extreme is to view the New Testament as a handbook for church polity that assumes every church was organized identically. This view is dangerous because it ignores the differences and nuances between churches and tends to artificially flatten out and synchronize divine revelation. As we study the pattern of leadership as

---

1. Most of the material in this chapter is a revised version of Benjamin L. Merkle, *The Elder and Overseer: One Office in the Early Church* (New York: Peter Lang, 2003), 67–119, 121–35.
2. Benjamin L. Merkle (PhD, The Southern Baptist Theological Seminary) is Professor of New Testament and Greek at Southeastern Baptist Theological Seminary in Wake Forest, North Carolina.

found in the book of Acts and Paul's letters to churches, we shall seek to avoid all three extremes. In Acts we will focus on the authority, the appointing, and the activity of both the elders in Jerusalem as well as the elders in the churches planted by Paul and his co-workers. In addition, we will also consider the role of the Seven appointed in Acts 6. The second part of this chapter will cover the relevant material regarding Paul's correspondence with the churches in Rome, Corinth, Galatia, Ephesus, Philippi, Colossae, and Thessalonica.[3] Although some scholars and theologians have maintained that Paul's churches were led by the direct guidance of the Holy Spirit and not by office-holders, we will show this dichotomy to be false. In each of the churches to which Paul writes, he mentions designated leaders who are gifted and appointed to help shepherd the church under the authority of Jesus Christ.

THE PATTERN OF LEADERSHIP IN ACTS

The Authority of the Jerusalem Elders (Acts 11:30; 15:2–6, 22–23; 21:17–26)

The first mention of Christian elders in Acts occurs in 11:30 where the church in Antioch commissioned Barnabas and Paul to deliver famine-aid to the elders in Jerusalem. Luke does not provide any background information concerning the origin of these elders but simply introduces them assuming his readers will know who they are. As is apparent, these elders had some authority in the church since they were in charge of the money given by the church in Antioch. Strauch notes, "The fact that money was placed into their care reveals that they were the church's official representatives."[4] One might expect Barnabas and Paul to have given the money to the Jerusalem apostles since they were in charge of an earlier relief effort (Acts 6:1–6). This apparent change suggests that some authority was beginning to shift away from the apostles toward the elders.[5]

---

3. Paul's letters to churches include all his letters except the Pastoral Epistles (1–2 Timothy and Titus) and Philemon. Because Philemon was written during the time of Paul's earlier writings, it will also be considered under Paul's letters to churches.
4. Alexander Strauch, *Biblical Eldership: An Urgent Call to Restore Biblical Church Leadership*, 3rd ed., rev. and exp. (Littleton, CO: Lewis & Roth, 1995), 124.
5. Lightfoot maintains that the persecution following the martyrdom of the Apostle James "was the signal for the dispersion of the Twelve on a wider mission. Since Jerusalem would

The Jerusalem elders again appear in Acts 15 in connection with the so-called "Apostolic Council." Disturbed by those who came from Judea teaching, "Unless you are circumcised according to the custom of Moses, you cannot be saved" (v. 1), Paul and Barnabas were appointed to go to Jerusalem to discuss this issue with the "apostles and elders." Unlike Acts 11:30, here the elders are consistently mentioned with the apostles and are always referenced second, most likely demonstrating that the apostles were viewed as having more authority than the elders. Yet, at this "Apostolic Council" the apostles were not the only ones deliberating on this important matter. Luke records that the elders were also intimately involved (Acts 15:6).[6] "The elders' close association with the apostles demonstrates their significant position and role in the church at Jerusalem."[7] It is likely that as the apostles began to gradually leave Jerusalem, the responsibility of spiritual leadership was transferred into the hands of the elders.[8]

Although the Jerusalem elders did not possess direct authority over the church at Antioch, they did hold an important leadership position in the church at Jerusalem.[9] Luke's report indicates that the elders in Jerusalem were intimately involved in responding to this doctrinal conflict.[10]

The final appearance of the Jerusalem elders occurs in Acts 21:17–26. Paul returned to Jerusalem after his third missionary journey to bring the Gentiles' offering to the "poor" there. Luke states that Paul

---

no longer be their home . . . it became necessary to provide for the permanent direction of the Church there" (J. B. Lightfoot, *St. Paul's Epistle to the Philippians* [London: Macmillan, 1881], 193). It should also be noted that the use of the term "apostle" is used more frequently in the beginning of Acts, then fades out.

6. It should also be noted that this "Council" was not like later councils, which had delegates from churches throughout the world. Fitzmyer therefore comments that the title "Apostolic Council" is "a misnomer, because the meeting as described is not a solemn assembly of authorities from all over the church" (Joseph A. Fitzmyer, *The Acts of the Apostles*, AB 31 [New York: Doubleday, 1998], 543). It may have been the case, however, that at this relatively early date many of the apostles were still in Jerusalem.

7. Strauch, *Biblical Eldership*, 127.

8. The leadership of the elders (or apostles), however, did not eclipse the voice of the church as a whole. According to Acts 15:22, "the whole church" was also involved with the proceedings. Also cf. v. 12 which mentions that "all the assembly" kept silent.

9. It should be noted that the decision of the apostles and elders, although authoritative, did not contain any claim to their authoritative positions but rather was an appeal for Gentile churches to follow certain restrictions.

10. Strauch asserts that "the elders' role . . . was absolutely essential in combating any legalistic error that might emanate from Jerusalem" (*Biblical Eldership*, 127).

went to see "James, and all the elders" (Acts 21:18; cf. Gal. 1:19). The singling out of James, the brother of Jesus, indicates his leadership position among the elders (Acts 15:13; cf. Acts 12:17). The apostles are no longer mentioned, most likely indicating that they are no longer in Jerusalem.[11] James, however, is not the central person in Luke's account. The passage is taken up with the dialogue between the elders and Paul, which is indicated by the use of the plural throughout the text.

According to Luke's account, James and the elders rejoiced concerning Paul's work among the Gentiles but they had a pressing problem related to Paul's reputation. Many believing Jews who were zealous concerning the law were told that Paul taught the Christian Jews in the Diaspora to forsake the Law of Moses and to abandon the practice of circumcision. Therefore, James and the elders urged Paul to prove these rumors false by going through a rite of purification and paying for the sacrifices of four others' Nazarite vows in the temple (cf. Num. 6:1–21). Paul willingly agrees to this plan, which ends up in his arrest. Again, this text demonstrates the elders' authoritative role in the life of the church. They sought harmony in the church and therefore wanted to resolve this potentially disastrous conflict.

The Appointing of Elders (Acts 14:23)

According to the narrative of Acts, on their first missionary journey Barnabas and Paul established churches in the cities of Pisidian Antioch, Iconium, Lystra, and Derbe. Before returning to Antioch in Syria, they revisited these newly founded churches and appointed leaders. In Acts 14:23 Luke states, "And when they had appointed elders for them in every church, with prayer and fasting they committed them to the Lord in whom they had believed." This passage has been notoriously difficult due to the fact that in his undisputed letters Paul never mentions "elders." Because of this omission, some scholars accuse Luke of reading back the later ecclesiastical development of his own day into this earlier account. For example, Haenchen writes, "Luke has simply taken for granted that

---

11. It is likely that Paul considered James an apostle, though not one of the Twelve (see Gal. 1:19; 2:9). For although he was not a believer until after the resurrection, he certainly had the apostolic qualification of seeing the risen Christ (Acts 1:21–22). See Thomas R. Schreiner, *Galatians*, ZECNT (Grand Rapids: Zondervan, 2010), 110–11.

the ecclesiastical constitution of his own day already existed in the time of Paul."[12] Marshall, admitting the apparent discrepancy, maintains that although the precise term "elders" may not have been used by Paul on this occasion, "The most . . . that we may deduce from these facts is that Luke has used a term current in his own time to refer to leaders who may possibly have been known by other designations in the earlier period."[13] What separates Marshall's statement from Haenchen's is that Marshall believes that Barnabas and Paul actually appointed leaders (whether originally called "elders" or not), while Haenchen is not convinced the account has any historical foundation. Yet, there does not seem to be any compelling reason to deny that these earlier leaders were indeed called elders by Paul himself. This is especially true when one considers that elders were common in both the Old Testament and in Jewish leadership (though there is not a one-to-one correspondence between Jewish elders and Christian elders; see chap. 1).

Although Luke mentions Barnabas and Paul appointing "elders" only in Acts 14:23, it is likely that this was Paul's customary procedure.[14] We read in Acts 14:23 that the apostles appointed elders "in every church" (*kat ekklēsian*) in a particular region. Apparently, each church had its own apostolically appointed leaders who were called "elders" or given another title (e.g., "overseers" or "pastors").

The Activity of Elders (Acts 20:17–38)

While returning from his third missionary journey, Paul's ship harbored at Miletus for a few days. Fearing that he would not return to Asia, Paul sent word to Ephesus in order to summon the elders of the Ephesian church. In his "farewell address," Paul exhorts the elders: "Be on guard for yourselves and for all the flock, among which the Holy Spirit has made you overseers to shepherd the church of God, which he purchased with his own blood" (Acts 20:28 NASB). Accord-

---

12. Ernst Haenchen, *The Acts of the Apostles*, trans. Basil Blackwell (Philadelphia: Westminster, 1971), 436.
13. I. Howard Marshall, *The Acts of the Apostles*, TNCT, vol. 5 (Leicester, England: InterVarsity Press; Grand Rapids: Eerdmans, 1991), 241.
14. So William M. Ramsay, *St. Paul the Traveller and the Roman Citizen*, 2nd ed. (New York: G. P. Putnam's Sons; London: Hodder & Stoughton, 1896), 121; Lightfoot, *Philippians*, 193.

ing to Paul, the work of the elders was to guard themselves and their congregation from false teachings and false teachers that will inevitably come. They are also commanded "to shepherd" the church of God (cf. John 21:16; 1 Peter 5:1–2; Eph. 4:11) and to "be alert" (20:31). It is also stated that the Holy Spirit has made or appointed them as overseers. This is not necessarily inconsistent with Acts 14:23 where the apostles appoint elders since Luke would not have regarded human participation as being excluded. The Holy Spirit gifted the men, thus making them fit for appointment (cf. Acts 13:2–3).[15] Furthermore, in Acts 14:23 the appointment of elders was accompanied by prayer and fasting—signs of dependence on the Holy Spirit. It should also be noted that in this passage the terms "elders" (*presbyteros*) and "overseers" (*episkopos*) are used interchangeably. In verse 17, Paul summons the "elders," but in verse 28 we read that the Holy Spirit has made them "overseers."

Who were these elders? It is unlikely that the term "elders" merely refers to old men or even those who were respected in their communities.[16] Paul summons those who were the designated leaders in the church, which is evident from his admonition to them. Since the text mentions the church of Ephesus in the singular (*ekklēsias*), this evidence suggests that there was only one body of believers in Ephesus that was governed by a plurality of leaders.[17] Strauch writes, "The natural reading of the passage, then, indicates that there is one church in Ephesus and one body of elders to oversee it."[18] This position is also affirmed by Acts 14:23 which states that Paul and Barnabas appointed elders "in every church."

---

15. So F. F. Bruce, *The Book of Acts*, NICNT (Grand Rapids: Eerdmans, 1980), 416; John B. Polhill, *Acts*, NAC 26 (Nashville: Broadman, 1992), 426–27.
16. This is the thesis of R. Alastair Campbell's work *The Elders: Seniority within Earliest Christianity*, Studies of the New Testament and Its World (Edinburgh: T&T Clark, 1994).
17. Also note the singular use of "flock" in verse 28. Contrast the use of the singular in this passage with Galatians 1:2 where Paul writes to the "churches" of Galatia.
18. Strauch, *Biblical Eldership*, 143. Marshall states, "The picture that emerges from relevant passages (Phil. 1:1; Acts 20.17, 28; 14.23; 16.4) suggests a plurality of leaders in a church" (I. Howard Marshall, *A Critical and Exegetical Commentary on the Pastoral Epistles*, in collaboration with Philip H. Towner [Edinburgh: T&T Clark, 1999], 153). Even if there were a number of house churches in Ephesus which constituted the "church" in that city, Luke did not consider them separate local bodies but one congregation which had a plurality of elders.

The Addition of a New Order (Acts 6:1–7)

Although many assume that the Seven appointed in Acts 6 were the first deacons, the term itself is not used. Only the related verb *diakoneō* ("to serve") is found (Acts 6:2). This does not rule out the strong possibility that the Seven did at least serve as the prototype for the New Testament deacon. In other words, Acts 6 does provide a pattern or paradigm that seems to have continued in the early church. Thus, it is necessary to investigate this passage in more detail.

> Now in these days when the disciples were increasing in number, a complaint by the Hellenists arose against the Hebrews because their widows were being neglected in the daily distribution. And the twelve summoned the full number of the disciples and said, "It is not right that we should give up preaching the word of God to serve tables. Therefore, brothers, pick out from among you seven men of good repute, full of the Spirit and of wisdom, whom we will appoint to this duty. But we will devote ourselves to prayer and to the ministry of the word." And what they said pleased the whole gathering, and they chose Stephen, a man full of faith and of the Holy Spirit, and Philip, and Prochorus, and Nicanor, and Timon, and Parmenas, and Nicolaus, a proselyte of Antioch. These they set before the apostles, and they prayed and laid their hands on them. (Acts 6:1–6)

The need for the Seven to be chosen arose from growth in the church. As the church grew, there arose more spiritual and physical needs among the new converts. Widows, for example, were usually dependent on others for their daily needs. One problem that emerged in the early church was that the Greek-speaking Jewish widows were being neglected. When the twelve apostles received news of this problem, they knew that something must be done. They understood the importance of providing for the physical needs of the people. They understood that allowing this problem to continue could cause division in the church.

But there was another problem. Although the apostles realized the gravity of the situation before them, they also realized that for them to get distracted with serving tables would divert them from their primary calling of preaching the word of God. The apostles were not indicating that it would be too humiliating for them to serve widows. Jesus had already taught them that being a leader in His kingdom is different than worldly leaders (Matt. 20:25–27). He had already washed their feet to demonstrate servant leadership (John 13:1–18). Rather, they wanted to remain faithful to the calling and the gifts they received from God. For them to leave the preaching of the word to serve tables would have been a mistake. Instead, they proposed a better solution to this problem.

The apostles decided to call all the disciples together and present a solution to the problem. The disciples were to choose seven men to be appointed with the task of overseeing the daily distribution of food. The congregation, however, was not to simply choose anyone who was willing to serve; they had to select men who had a good reputation and were Spirit-filled. By appointing these men to help with the daily distribution of food, the apostles took this need seriously and, at the same time, did not get distracted from their primary calling. With the Seven appointed to take care of this problem, the apostles were able to devote themselves "to prayer and to the ministry of the word" (v. 4).

In the earliest period of the church, the primary spiritual leaders of the congregation were the apostles. They were appointed to a "ministry of the word." As the church grew, the number of problems grew with it. As a result, other factors began to distract them from their calling. The Seven were needed to allow the apostles the freedom to continue with their work. This is a similar paradigm to what we see with the offices of elder/overseer and deacon. Like the apostles, the elders' primary role is one of preaching the word of God (Eph. 4:11; 1 Tim. 3:2; 5:17; Titus 1:9). Like the Seven, deacons are needed to serve the congregation in whatever needs may arise. Thus, although the term "deacon" does not occur in the Acts 6 passage, it provides a helpful model of how godly servants can assist those who are called to preach the word of God.[19]

---

19. Grudem comments, "It seems appropriate to think of these seven men as 'deacons' even though the name *deacon* had perhaps not yet come to be applied to them as they began this

Conclusion

The purpose of this section has been to highlight some important characteristics related to the Christian elders in the book of Acts. The authority of the Jerusalem elders was seen in their handling of the famine-relief money (Acts 11:30), their intimate involvement with the Jerusalem Council (Acts 15), their participation in refuting false teachings (Acts 15), and their leadership in resolving conflicts in the church (Acts 21:17–26). It was also concluded that in Acts 14:23, Barnabas and Paul appoint elders in every church which signifies that these leaders were set apart with a special task within the church. This appointing also implies the elements of permanency of position, recognition by others, and authority within the community. In Acts 20:17–38 Paul charges the Ephesian elders to be engaged in the activity of guarding and shepherding the flock which has been put under their care. The elders are to be alert always protecting the congregation against false teachings and false teachers. Finally, the Seven chosen in Acts 6 provide an early model for the New Testament office of deacon. That is, just as the Seven were appointed to allow the apostles the freedom to fulfill their calling of the ministry of the word and prayer, so deacons are needed to allow the elders (who eventually assumed the role of shepherding and teaching the congregation) to fulfill their primary calling.

PATTERNS OF MINISTRY IN PAUL'S LETTERS TO CHURCHES

Did Paul Endorse or Establish Organized Ministries?

For more than a century and a half, theologians and historians have vigorously disputed the organizational structure of the earliest Christian communities. With the advent of biblical criticism, the discovery and availability of new sources, and the freedom to challenge the status quo, scholars began to posit new theories related to the development of ecclesiastical structures in the primitive church. It was assumed that since the

---

responsibility" (Wayne Grudem, *Systematic Theology: An Introduction to Biblical Doctrine* [Leicester: InterVarsity Press; Grand Rapids: Eerdmans, 1994], 919).

books of the New Testament could be accurately dated, the comparison of later New Testament documents with earlier ones demonstrated a historical and theological evolution. A reconstruction of the early church was then proposed based on the relevant data. This reconstruction usually stated that the earliest churches had no officers or formal ecclesiastical organization but were led by those divinely gifted by the Spirit to serve and lead. Thus, the church was led by the free movements of the Spirit and not by static, legal codes. Jesus had no office and warns his disciples not to seek positions and titles, as is typical among the heathen rulers. Furthermore, when comparing Paul's earliest writings (Romans, 1 and 2 Corinthians, Galatians, Philippians, and 1 Thessalonians) with later Pauline Epistles (2 Thessalonians, Colossians, Ephesians, 1 and 2 Timothy, and Titus), many noted a marked difference in organizational structure. In the later epistles, the community was no longer led by divinely appointed apostles, prophets, teachers, and other gifted charismatics, but was led by humanly appointed church officials. The functional, fluid references of those who serve (e.g., co-worker, servant, or overseer) gave way to official, permanent roles. The church's embracing of such formal, hierarchical structures was seen as a later addition and even corruption, causing the church to spiral into formalism.

Although the new consensus offered some important correctives (such as affirming the priesthood of all believers and thereby rejecting a clergy-laity distinction), it still distorted the New Testament evidence. All of Paul's letters to churches contain elements of organized ministries. For Paul, church offices are not the center of the church, but neither are they are an unnatural intrusion.[20]

Organized Ministries in Paul's Letters to Churches

Is it correct that in his early letters Paul speaks much of spiritual gifts and little, if anything, about office? Is it true that the early churches were led by Christians endued with certain spiritual gifts and not by those appointed or elected to some office? Is it accurate to maintain that Paul did not establish offices in the churches under his oversight? Answering these questions positively, Käsemann notes that "the New Testament

---

20. For a thorough overview of this topic, see Merkle, *Elder and Overseer,* 67–94.

seems of set purpose to have avoided the technical conception of office which could have been expressed by such words as [*leitourgia, timē,* and *archē*]."[21] Käsemann's assessment, however, is not completely accurate since the terms he names were not likely to be used for an ecclesiastical office by the earliest church. The term *leitourgia* occurs six times in the New Testament but is never used as the title of an office-holder.[22] It usually refers to the service one performs to God.[23] Only later did *leitourgia* come to be used as a technical term for a church office (e.g., *1 Clem.* 44:2–3, 6). Therefore, one would not expect this term to be used as an official designation in the early church. The second term, *timē,* is also an unlikely term to be used for a New Testament church office. This term is primarily used to signify (1) price, value or (2) honor, reverence. Under the second meaning it can take on the added quality of "place of honor" or "(honorable) office," although it is used as such only once in the New Testament. In Hebrews 5:4, it refers to the high priest's (official) dignity, a dignity which now belongs only to Christ. As a result, when this term is used with a more technical sense, it is reserved for the honor of Christ alone. The last term, *archē,* can be used to signify a "ruler" or "authority." In the Septuagint and the New Testament the term is used to refer to government officials, religious officials, the rule of angels and demons, and the rule of Christ.[24] Again, it is questionable whether this term is an appropriate title for a servant-leader in the church (cf. Mark 10:42–44). Christ alone is the *archē* of the Church.[25] It appears that the nature of the

---

21. Ernest Käsemann, "Ministry and Community in the New Testament," trans. W . J. Montague, in *Essays on New Testament Themes,* SBT 41 (Philadelphia: Fortress, 1964), 63. Similarly, Dunn contends that "the word 'office' is best avoided completely in any description of the Pauline concept of ministry" (James G. D. Dunn, *Jesus and the Spirit* [Philadelphia: Westminster, 1975], 291). According to Dunn, authority in the early Pauline churches lay primarily with the Spirit and not in any official position in the Church. He states that "*authority was essentially charismatic authority: only he who ministered could have authority and that only in the actual exercise of his ministry*" (ibid., emphasis original).
22. Luke 1:23; 2 Corinthians 9:12; Philippians 2:17, 30; Hebrews 8:6; 9:21. *Leitourgos* occurs five times: Romans 13:6 (the *service* rendered by the government); 15:16 (Paul calls himself a *minister* of Christ Jesus); Philippians 2:25 (Epaphroditus is called a *minister*); Hebrews 1:7 (angels are called *ministers*); 8:2 (Jesus is a *minister* in the true tabernacle).
23. In the LXX it is often used for the ceremonial service performed by the priest.
24. Government officials (Gen. 40:13, 21; 41:13 [Pharaoh's court official]; Luke 12:11; Titus 3:1 [Roman and Jewish officials]); religious officials (1 Chron. 26:10 [levitical doorkeeper]; 2 Macc. 4:10; 4 Macc. 4:17 [high priest]); rule of angels and demons (Rom. 8:38; Eph. 3:10; 6:12; Col. 1:16; 2:15); rule of Christ (1 Cor. 15:24; Eph. 1:21; Col. 2:10).
25. Küng makes a similar assessment. He states that the New Testament avoided such terms

New Testament ministry demanded other terms for those selected to be the leaders of the church.

Nevertheless, it is true to some extent that more technical terms for office could have been used in various passages. This omission, however, is not proof that the *concept* of office, or more broadly, organized ministry, does not exist. Thus, it will be shown that even though Paul does not use the word "office" in his writings, it is clear that he endorsed and established organized ministries in the churches and even sometimes mentions official titles.[26] That is, in every one of the churches to which he writes, Paul affirms organized ministries. We will now examine each of these references in order to help understand the leadership structure of the various churches.[27]

Galatians 6:6

In Galatians 6:6, Paul states, "Let the one who is taught the word share all good things with the one who teaches." In the previous section (6:1–5) Paul admonishes his readers to bear one another's burdens. He then relates that theme to teachers in the church. Those who are being taught are to share with their teachers. Paul makes a distinction between the "teacher" (*katēchōn*) who gives instruction and the "one taught" (*katē choumenos*) who receives instruction. This verse suggests that there was a class of instructors or catechizers who taught the word

---

as *archē* and *timē* because "despite the varieties of area they cover, they have one common factor: all express a relationship of rulers and ruled. And it is precisely this which makes them unusable" (Hans Küng, *The Church*, trans. Ray and Rosaleen Ockenden [New York: Sheed & Ward, 1967], 389).

26. The following elements are often considered to be constitutive for office: (1) permanency; (2) recognition by others (possibly by a title); (3) authority or dignity; (4) payment; and (5) appointment (probably including the laying on of hands). Of course, all these elements do not have to be present. For example, one can serve in an official capacity without receiving payment or without having been officially appointed. When those elements are present, however, it adds to the seriousness and solemnity of the position. The first three elements (permanence, recognition, and authority) may be regarded as representing the essential qualities of "office" and are naturally bound up with one another (See Ulrich Brockhaus, *Charisma und Amt: Die paulinische Charismenlehre auf dem Hintergrund der frühchristlichen Gemeinde funktionen* [Wuppertal: R. Brockhaus, 1972], 24–25 n. 106, 123; Bengt Holmberg, *Paul and Power: The Structure of Authority in the Primitive Church as Reflected in the Pauline Epistles* [Philadelphia: Fortress, 1980], 109–12).

27. We will treat Paul's letters to the churches in their probable chronological order.

to such an extent that they needed to be financially supported.[28] Some have noted that such a teaching role was at an incipient stage since Paul admonishes "the one who is taught" to share with the teacher rather than charging the congregations as a whole to recompense those who teach. On the other hand, it is also possible that Paul is speaking generically and does not have only individuals in mind, thereby emphasizing the benefit received and implicitly exhorting the entire congregation. Some have suggested that the Galatian Christians were refusing to pay their teachers because of the negative influence of the Judaizing agitators.[29] Another explanation is that since the Galatian churches were newly established, and therefore any type of ministry was at an incipient stage, Paul needed to encourage the body to begin paying their leaders. It is possible that these leaders were also known as "elders" (cf. 1 Tim. 5:17; Titus 1:5) or "overseers" (cf. Phil. 1:1; 1 Tim. 3:2; Titus 1:7) but in this context Paul focuses on the function of the leaders and not their title. Schreiner comments, "Perhaps this dimension of the leader's role is highlighted because false teachers had disturbed the Galatians."[30] Whatever the reason, Paul commands the Galatian Christians to make sure their teachers are supported. Obviously these teachers were recognized by Paul not only to be gifted to teach "the word" (*ton logon*, i.e., the Christian message),[31] but also to have the right to receive support for their labors (cf. Rom. 15:26–27).[32]

---

28. See Ernest Burton, *A Critical and Exegetical Commentary on the Epistle to the Galatians* (Edinburgh: T&T Clark, 1921), 335; H. W. Beyer, "κατηχέω," in *TDNT*, 3:639.
29. So Timothy George, *Galatians*, NAC 30 (Nashville: B&H, 1994), 420.
30. Thomas R. Schreiner, *Galatians*, ZECNT (Grand Rapids: Zondervan, 2010), 367.
31. Cf. 1 Corinthians 1:18; 2 Corinthians 5:19; Ephesians 1:13; Philippians 1:14; Colossians 1:25; 4:3; 1 Thessalonians 1:6; 2:13; 2 Timothy 4:2. Burton suggests that the elements taught probably included (a) the doctrine of a living and true God; (b) narratives and teachings of Jesus, especially his death, resurrection, and return; (c) the way of salvation; and (d) the fundamental principles of Christian ethics (*Galatians*, 337–38).
32. There are good reasons for maintaining that Paul is referring to physical or financial support (Burton, *Galatians*, 336; Richard N. Longenecker, *Galatians*, WBC 41 [Dallas: Word, 1990], 279). First, in Philippians 4:15, *koinōneō* clearly refers to material goods (cf. Rom. 12:13). Also, in Romans 15:26 and 2 Corinthians 9:13 the noun *koinōnia* likewise refers to a material gift. Second, Luke 1:53 and 12:18 demonstrate that the term *agathos* can be used to refer to material goods. Third, in 1 Corinthians, Paul unequivocally states the principle that the one who devotes himself to the gospel should be supported by those to whom he ministers. Although Paul personally renounced the right to such financial support (1 Cor. 9:15–18; 1 Thess. 2:9; Acts 20:33–35), he indicates in several places that the normal model is for those who are taught to pay their teachers (1 Cor. 9:9; 1 Tim. 5:18).

The implication, then, is that these teachers were to be recognized by the congregations as holding distinct positions by virtue of their gifts.[33] Fung summarizes the implications of this verse: "Paul's exhortation indicates that the 'teacher' had a fixed status; even if the teacher was not a full-time instructor in the faith, his work of teaching and preparation for teaching must have taken enough of his time that the community had to be responsible for his material support."[34]

Longenecker mentions seven inferences one can make from this text:

1. Formal Christian instruction was going on in the churches of Galatia.
2. Teachers were called as a class *ho katēchōn* (= the one who catechizes).
3. Those instructed were called as a class *ho katēchoumenos* (= the one who receives catechetical instruction).
4. The content of what was instructed and learned was the Christian message.
5. Christian teaching was then a full-time—or at least a heavily time-consuming—occupation that deserved material and/or financial compensation.
6. For some reason Christian teachers were not being adequately compensated materially in some or all of the churches of Galatia.
7. Paul thought it incumbent on those who received instruction to take the initiative to rectify this wrong.[35]

1 Thessalonians 5:12–13

To the church at Thessalonica Paul writes, "We ask you, brothers, to respect those who labor among you and are over [or 'who lead'] you

---

33. It is possible that the "instructor" here is to be identified with the "teacher" in 1 Corinthians 12:28 and Ephesians 4:11 (so Beyer, "κατηχέω," 3:639; Ronald Y. K. Fung, *The Epistle to the Galatians*, NICNT [Grand Rapids: Eerdmans, 1988], 292; Herman Ridderbos, *The Epistle of Paul to the Churches of Galatia*, NICNT [Grand Rapids: Eerdmans, 1956], 217 n. 3).

34. Fung, *Galatians*, 293. He continues, "Here, then, we have probably the earliest extant evidence for a form of full-time or nearly full-time ministry supported by the congregation in the early Church" (ibid.). Gehring writes that "we can conclude from all this that we are dealing with a somewhat formal, ongoing, and more or less full-time function in the church" (Roger W. Gehring, *House Church and Mission: The Importance of Household Structures in Early Christianity* [Peabody, MA: Hendrickson, 2004], 204–5).

35. Longenecker, *Galatians*, 279.

in the Lord and admonish you, and to esteem them very highly in love because of their work. Be at peace among yourselves" (1 Thess. 5:12–13). In this passage Paul makes an appeal to the Thessalonian Christians that they "respect" (or "recognize") their leaders. It is important to note that this text makes a distinction between the "brothers" and those whom they are to recognize. Apparently, not every believer was to be honored and respected in the same way. Some, because of their gifts and function in the community, were to be considered worthy of special recognition.

Three participles describe these leaders who are to be esteemed very highly. The use of only one definite article governing the three participles (*touskopiōntas . . . kaiproistamenous . . . kainouthetountas*) indicates that it is one group of people who perform all three functions, and not three distinct groups.[36] It is possible that the first participle ("laboring") is a general description and the two following participles ("leading" and "admonishing") are specific functions of the type of work they perform.[37] First, they are said to "labor" or "work hard" (*kopiōntas*) in the church. This verb indicates strenuous work that results in fatigue. Although not a technical term, it is often used to describe the labor involved with Christian service.[38] For example, 1 Timothy 5:17 states, "Let the elders who rule well be considered worthy of double honor, especially those who labor [*hoi kopiōntes*] in preaching and teaching."

Second, these leaders are characterized as "those who are over" or "those who lead" (*proistamenous*) others in the church. The verb *proistēmi* can mean (1) lead, rule, direct, manage or (2) show concern for, care for, give aid.[39] Regardless of how the verb is best translated in 1 Thessalonians 5:12, it should be noted that these leaders are singled out

---

36. See Daniel B. Wallace, *Greek Grammar Beyond the Basics: An Exegetical Syntax of the New Testament* (Grand Rapids: Zondervan, 1996), 283.
37. So James E. Frame, *A Critical and Exegetical Commentary on the Epistle to the Thessalonians*, ICC (Edinburgh: T&T Clark, 1979), 191; Leon Morris, *The First and Second Epistle to the Thessalonians*, NICNT (Grand Rapids: Eerdmans, 1991), 166; Gene L. Green, *The Letters to the Thessalonians*, PNTC (Grand Rapids: Eerdmans; Leicester: Apollos, 2002), 248; G. K. Beale, *1–2 Thessalonians*, IVPNTCS (Downers Grove, IL: InterVarsity Press, 2003), 159. The *kai . . . kai* construction could then be translated "both" . . . "and."
38. See John 4:38; Acts 20:35; Romans 16:6, 12; 1 Corinthians 4:12; 15:10; 16:16; Galatians 4:11; Philippians 2:16; Colossians 1:29; 1 Timothy 4:10; 2 Timothy 2:6.
39. See BDAG, 870. Reicke states that this verb "has in the NT the primary senses of both 'to lead' and 'to care for'" (Bo Reicke, "προΐστημι," in *TDNT*, 6:702).

from the rest of the believing community. This verb is used seven other times in the New Testament, all in the Pauline corpus.[40] In Romans 12:8 it is used to describe the gifts (*charismata*) given to various members of the church. In the Pastoral Epistles the term is used three times in reference to the overseer or deacon who is to "manage" or "rule" his own house well (1 Tim. 3:4, 5, 12). In 1 Timothy 5:17 it is "the elders who rule well" (*hoi kalōs prestōtes presbyteroi*) who are worthy of double honor. It is worth noting that 1 Timothy 5:17 provides the closest parallel with 1 Thessalonians 5:12 since the duty of the elders is to rule or lead the people and that they too are to be honored for their hard work. Morris states that although this term "is not an official description of a technical order of ministry . . . it is difficult to understand who could be meant other than office bearers in the church."[41]

The third characteristic of these leaders is that they "admonish" (*nouthetountas*) those they lead. This verb is found seven other times in the New Testament, only in the Pauline Epistles and in Paul's speech to the elders of Ephesus (Acts 20:31). While it is true that admonishing was not reserved for only a few as 1 Thessalonians 5:14 indicates,[42] here it is clear that some have a special task of admonishing that is not given to all since the context distinguishes the leaders from the brothers (i.e., the rest of the congregation).[43] Thus, the leaders had the responsibility to correct the moral and doctrinal errors of those under their care.

Paul instructs the believers to "esteem [their leaders] very highly in love because of their work." Although the verb translated "esteem" (*hēgeomai*) usually means "to deem," the context seems to favor the above reading. The adverb "very highly" (*hyperekperissou*) is an emphatic compound. This appreciation is to flow from the love the Christians have for their leaders "because of their work." Respect and honor due to a leader is not based on personality or an office but on the hard work that the individual performs. Green aptly comments, "What legitimized this leadership was not their status or social rank, as was

---

40. Romans 12:8; 1 Timothy 3:4, 5, 12; 5:17; Titus 3:8, 14.
41. Morris, *First and Second Epistles to the Thessalonians*, 166. Likewise, Beale states, "This is merely another way of referring to elders" (*1–2 Thessalonians*, 160). Gehring suggests that those described as leaders "were, at least in part, householders and leaders of house churches" (*House Church and Mission*, 200).
42. Cf. Romans 15:14; Colossians 3:16; 2 Thessalonians 3:15.
43. Cf. 1 Corinthians 4:14; Colossians 1:28.

commonly the case in both Greek and Roman society, but the labor they undertook among members of the congregation."[44] This respect, however, is not to be out of duty's sake but done "in love." The following imperative to be at peace with one another is probably best taken as related to the previous section. Paul, then, is commanding the leaders and non-leaders to work together and not cause division or tension within the church.

To summarize, Paul exhorts the congregation to recognize those who are performing leadership tasks (such as laboring, leading, and admonishing) and to esteem such people highly because of the importance of their work. Although the term "elders" is not used, it is clear that those whom Paul is referring to were the spiritual leaders of the congregation, performing elder-like functions. Simply because Paul does not use the term "elders" in this context does not rule out the possibility that these leaders were also known by that title.[45]

1 Corinthians 16:15–16

Included in Paul's final remarks to the Corinthians are these words: "Now I urge you, brothers—you know that the household of Stephanas were the first converts in Achaia, and that they have devoted themselves to the service of the saints—be subject to such as these, and to every fellow worker and laborer" (1 Cor. 16:15–16). As Paul exhorts his readers, he reminds them of two things concerning the household of Stephanas. First, they were the "first converts" (lit. "firstfruits," *aparchē*) in the province of Achaia. Paul's use of the term *aparchē* almost certainly means that those in Stephanas' household were the first converts in a particular region. In Romans 16:5 Paul writes, "Greet my beloved Epaenetus, who was the first convert [lit. 'firstfruit,' *aparchē*] to Christ in Asia" (cf. 2 Thess. 2:13). This word not only has the idea of "first con-

---

44. Green, *Thessalonians*, 248. Strauch notes, "Leaders are not to be loved or esteemed because they are older men, hold special religious titles, have received an apostolic appointment, or have winning personalities" (*Biblical Eldership*, 172).

45. So, Morris, *First and Second Epistles to the Thessalonians*, 165; Beale, *1–2 Thessalonians*, 160. Beale argues, "Many scholars mistakenly think that the office of elder is not being referred to, since church offices purportedly did not evolve until later when the church had more time to develop." See Acts 19:29; 20:4; 27:2; Colossians 4:10 and Philemon 24 where Aristarchus and Secundus were leaders in the Thessalonian church.

vert" but also the firstfruits in relation to the promise of more to come.[46] Based on this description, and the fact that Paul states that he did not baptize anyone in Corinth except Stephanas' household (1 Cor. 1:16), it is likely that they were the founding members of the church.

Paul, therefore, exhorts the Corinthians to submit to the household of Stephanas not only because they were the first converts but also because they "devoted themselves" to serving in the church. It is clear that Stephanas was to be viewed as a leader by those in the church.[47] Paul then commands the church to "be subject to" (*hupotassēsthe*) Stephanas and such that are like him. Interestingly, this verb is used only here in the New Testament to refer to the relationship the community of believers has to those who labor among them. Consequently, the church at Corinth was to be led not only by the free movement of the Spirit, but also by those who diligently labored in the church. The Pauline usage of the words "to every fellow [*sunergounti*] worker and laborer [*kopiōnti*]"[48] almost certainly refers to the ministry of the gospel.

Although not every detail is spelled out, we do know that Paul urges his readers to submit to the leadership of certain individuals—those who are apparently more mature in their faith and who are committed to working and laboring among God's people. Although he is not given a formal title, Paul goes out of his way to make sure that others recognize Stephanas as a leader in the church and that they submit to his leadership.[49] While acknowledging that no formal language is used, Fee comments, "The language of v. 16 further makes certain that he [i.e., Stephanas] is a leader in the church."[50]

---

46. See Anthony C. Thiselton, *The First Epistle to the Corinthians*, NIGTC (Grand Rapids: Eerdmans; Carlisle: Paternoster, 2000), 1338.

47. Unfortunately, we do not know the precise nature of Stephanas' ministry. Fee speculates that his ministry might have included (1) preaching and teaching, (2) owning one of the houses where the church met, and/or (3) serving as one of the "patrons" of the Lord's Supper, but Fee ultimately acknowledges that we cannot be certain (Gordon D. Fee, *The First Epistle to the Corinthians*, NICNT [Grand Rapids: Eerdmans, 1987], 830).

48. For uses of *sunergos* (the noun related to the verb *sunergeō*), see Romans 16:3, 9, 21; 1 Corinthians 3:9; 2 Corinthians 1:24; 8:23; Philippians 2:25; 4:3; Colossians 4:11; 1 Thessalonians 3:2; Philemon 1:1, 24. For uses of *kopiaō*, see John 4:38; Acts 20:35; Romans 16:6, 12; 1 Corinthians 4:12; 15:10; 16:16; Galatians 4:11; Philippians 2:16; Colossians 1:29; 1 Timothy 4:10; 2 Timothy 2:6.

49. Elsewhere in 1 Corinthians Paul also makes a distinction between the leaders of the church and those who are led (e.g., 1 Cor. 3:5–9).

50. Fee, *First Epistle to the Corinthians*, 829.

How does this interpretation fit with the view of the church presented in Romans 12 and 1 Corinthians 12 and 14? For example, if the Corinthian church was experiencing such disorder, why did Paul neglect to call on leaders like Stephanas in order to solve the church's dilemma? Raising this same objection Dunn comments, "The absence of an appeal to or rebuke of established leaders is very hard to explain, were there such in Corinth."[51]

In response to this objection the following rejoinder is offered. First, the apostles, prophets, and teachers mentioned in 1 Corinthians 12:28 seem to represent a special class of recognized leaders.[52] Second, it is possible that Paul's authoritative presence (in person and in his writings) limited the immediate need for church officials. Third, Paul's normal custom of writing letters to churches and dealing with problems in the churches was to appeal to the whole congregation. Although Paul recognized leaders within the local churches, he also believed that all parts of the body were essential and therefore appealed to all the people of God, not just the leaders, to solve difficulties in the church. Strauch rightly notes this emphasis.

> Disorder and sin in the church at Corinth had to be dealt with, yet in Paul's letter to the church, he calls upon no one person or group to resolve the problems. Does this mean there was no one to call upon? Not at all! Paul could have called upon the dedicated Stephanas (1 Cor. 16:15–18); Gaius, in whose home the church met (Rom. 16:23); Erastus, the city treasurer (Rom. 16:23); Crispus, a converted chief ruler of the synagogue (Acts 18:8); or a number of other gifted men and prophets (1 Cor. 1:5, 7). He could easily have asked one of these men to help the congregation resolve its problems, but, as always, he addresses the entire gathering of holy saints (1 Cor. 1:2).[53]

---

51. James D. G. Dunn, *Theology of Paul the Apostle* (Grand Rapids: Eerdmans, 1998), 584.
52. Based on the central importance Paul placed on the office of apostle, Gehring maintains that "the suggestion that, because there is no indication of institutionalization in Corinth, Paul left everything up to the free working of the Spirit is inadmissible and finds no support in the text" (*House Church and Mission*, 197).
53. Strauch, *Biblical Eldership*, 163.

Finally, it is possible that some of the church leaders were themselves among the charismatic contingency and therefore were in no position to control the overly enthusiastic element of which they were a part. As Holmberg states, "If the problem in Corinth consisted of lack of unity, self-discipline, love and wisdom, primarily situated in the leading stratum it is no wonder that Paul cannot appeal to them to set all this aright except by a letter addressed to *all* Christians in Corinth, where he impresses on them that they are one body and must act as such."[54]

Romans 16:1–2

In his conclusion of the letter to the Roman Christians, Paul writes, "I commend to you our sister Phoebe, a servant of the church at Cenchreae, that you may welcome her in the Lord in a way worthy of the saints, and help her in whatever she may need from you, for she has been a patron of many and of myself as well" (Rom. 16:1–2). There is much debate concerning the nature of Phoebe's role. Was she a "deacon" or simply a "servant" of the church at Cenchreae? The term *diakonos* can be used generally of every believer since a Christian is a "servant" of Christ and other believers. Given this interpretation, Paul is simply emphasizing the fact that Phoebe has effectively "served" the church in Cenchreae.[55] The term *diakonos*, however, does not appear to be used here as a general reference to service in the church. In the New Testament the term is applied to governments (Rom. 13:4), Christ (Rom. 15:8; Gal. 2:17), and Christians who are in some sort of leadership position. Besides referring to Phoebe and himself as a *diakonos*,[56] Paul also names Apollos (1 Cor. 3:5), Tychicus (Eph. 6:21; Col. 4:7), Epaphras (Col. 1:7), and Timothy (1 Tim. 4:6). Based on this data it would appear that Paul refers to Phoebe as a *diakonos* because, like Apollos, Tychicus, Epaphras, and Timothy, she had some leadership responsibilities among the people of God.

It is also possible that Phoebe was more than a servant-leader of the church, but that she actually held the office of deacon.[57] Three points

---

54. Holmberg, *Paul and Power*, 113.
55. KJV, NKJV, NASB, NIV[84], ESV, and HCSB translate *diakonos* "servant." The TEV renders it "who serves the church."
56. 1 Corinthians 3:5; 2 Corinthians 3:6; 6:4; Galatians 2:17; Ephesians 3:7; Colossians 1:23, 25.
57. NRSV, NLT, NIV translate *diakonos* as "deacon."

are usually given. First, Paul uses the masculine *diakonos* to refer to a woman. Thus, it can be argued that Paul is not referring to the general usage of servant-leader but has a specific "office" in mind. The masculine form of *diakonos* used of a woman suggests that the term became standardized when referring to an office. Second, Paul states that Phoebe is a *diakonos* "of the church at Cenchreae." This is the only place Paul speaks of someone being a *diakonos* of a local church. Tychicus is called a "servant in the Lord," Epaphras is named a "servant of Christ," and Timothy "a servant of Jesus Christ." Since only Phoebe is specifically said to be a servant of a local congregation, it is likely that she was a "deacon" of her church. Third, Phoebe is sent to perform an official task on behalf of the apostle Paul and her church. Paul urges the Romans to aid her since she is about the important business of the church. Thus, it is argued that such an official task requires an official office.[58]

Phoebe's service to the church is described in verse 2 where she is said to be a "patron" (*prostatis*) of many, including Paul. The precise meaning of *prostatis* is also debated. The word occurs only here in biblical Greek and is sometimes translated "benefactor." Since the word is related to the verb *proistēmi*, some have argued that Phoebe was a "leader" (or "president") of the church.[59] She is said, however, to be the leader "of many" (including Paul) rather than the leader "of the church" (cf. v. 1). Therefore, it is unlikely that *prostatis* denotes an official position and most likely has the meaning found in secular Greek of "benefactor" or "patron." Moo notes, "A 'patron' was one who came to the aid of others, especially foreigners, by providing housing and financial aid and by representing their interests before local authorities."[60] Since Cenchreae was a port city only eight miles from Corinth, it is easy to see how Phoebe, a wealthy Christian, would have been able to help Paul and many others.

In conclusion, although there is simply not enough information to make a dogmatic claim, it is likely that Phoebe was the letter-carrier of Romans and was sent on an official task by the church in Cenchreae. What is not clear is whether she actually held the office of deacon in her church.[61]

---

58. It is also likely that Phoebe was in fact the bearer of the letter of Romans.
59. So Ray R. Schulz, "A Case for 'President' Phoebe in Romans 16:2," *LTJ* 24 (1990): 124–27.
60. Douglas J. Moo, *The Epistle to the Romans*, NICNT (Grand Rapids: Eerdmans, 1996), 916.
61. It is also debated as to whether Andronicus and Junia were well-known "among the apos-

Philippians 1:1

Paul's greeting in Philippians 1:1 is perhaps the clearest indication of a distinction between church members and church leaders in Paul's early writings. He greets not only the church as a whole but also the "overseers" (*episkopoi*) and "deacons" (*diakonoi*).[62] Some immediately object to the idea that Paul is referring to any organized church office arguing that the terms refer to function and not office since no definite article is given in the Greek. They maintain that Paul is not referring to officers but those who are merely engaged in watching over others and serving. It is noted that these terms are often used functionally to designate those who are ministering to the saints. Furthermore, there is a danger of reading later nuances into a term (e.g., translating *episkopos* as "bishop" can be misleading).

There is a problem with the above analysis, however. If Paul is merely greeting all of those who serve freely and spontaneously, why is it necessary for him to greet those people separately? Is Paul merely addressing those who sometimes function as overseers or perform acts of service, or does he have a definite group of individuals in mind? Hawthorne rightly notes, "Paul mentions the ['overseers and deacons'] in such a way as to distinguish them from the congregation. This implies that he considered them to be persons with some kind of official status."[63] It is simply not convincing to argue that Paul is naming any-

---

tles" or well-known "by the apostles" (Rom. 16:7). The later interpretation, which does not recognize them as apostles, is to be preferred (see Daniel B. Wallace and Michael H. Burer, "Was Junia Really an Apostle?" *NTS* 47 [2001]: 76–91. The same article also appeared in the *Journal for Biblical Manhood and Womanhood* 6, no. 2 [2001]: 4–11).

62. It is possible to take the *kai* as epexegetical, forming a hendiadys ("bishops who are deacons" or "overseers who serve"). Paul is then speaking of one group and not two (so Gerald F. Hawthorne, *Philippians*, WBC 43 [Waco, TX: Word, 1983], 9–10). Ephesians 4:11 does have a reference to "pastors who are teachers" *(tous de poimenas didaskalous)* but this construct is governed by one article. In Philippians 1:1, however, the article is omitted. Also, it would have been clearer for Paul to use a participle to modify the overseers. I agree with Holmberg who asserts, "The two titles probably designate two groups of persons which consequently cannot have identical functions" (*Paul and Power*, 100).

63. Hawthorne, *Philippians*, 7. Best affirms this position with even stronger words when he writes, "I say 'officials' because [*episkopos*] at any rate could not have been used in any other way than as a designation of an office. The word was widely employed for officers in different types of societies and organisations including religious groups, and for (though less widely) civil officials; a first century Greek could not have used it in a purely functional sense without suggesting that the person who exercised oversight held 'official' status" (E. Best, "Bishops and Deacons: Philippians 1,1," in *SE*, ed. F. L. Cross, TU 102 [Berlin:

one who might function as a supervisor or servant without referring to some definite group of people.[64] Therefore, the absence of the definite articles does not prove that these groups are indefinite since the context suggests otherwise.

Some scholars object to the notion that Paul is singling out specific leaders in the church based on the fact that he does not mention these leaders in the rest of the letter. For example, Ralph Martin states, "The apostle writes to a whole church, and there is no suggestion of a small group which held ecclesiastical office as in the later 1 Clement 42."[65] But as we have noted above, Paul's normal method of communicating to his churches was to address the entire congregation, not simply the leaders.

Therefore, apart from the introductory greeting in Philippians 1:1, we would have no indication of church leaders and an organized ministry in the Philippian church. Nevertheless, the presence of such leaders does not change Paul's writing style of addressing the entire congregation.[66] Paul links the overseers and deacons with all the saints since they are not to be treated as believers on a higher level. Yet, they are, for reasons unknown, distinguished within the greeting. A. T. Robertson aptly comments:

> Paul does not ignore the officers of the saints or church, though they occupy a secondary place in his mind. The officers are important, but not primary. The individual saint

---

Akademie-Verlag, 1968], 4:371). Gehring likewise states, "[T]his function is unmistakably designated as an office. Paul uses ἐπίσκοποι and διάκονοι as technical terms. He assumes that the church knows what they mean and that he therefore does not need to explain them. . . . Hence in Philippi . . . we have concrete reference to a formal, ongoing leadership function and an obviously special position for those who carry out the function" (*House Church and Mission*, 206). Gehring affirms that those who held such positions "were overseers of the churches that met in their homes" and that "as a group such overseers could have formed the leadership team or council for the whole local church in that city" (206).

64. So Peter T. O'Brien, *The Epistle to the Philippians*, NIGTC (Grand Rapids: Eerdmans; Carlisle, England: Paternoster, 1991), 48; H. W. Beyer, "ἐπίσκοπος," in *TDNT*, ed. Gerhard Kittel, trans. Geoffrey W. Bromiley (Grand Rapids: Eerdmans, 1964), 2:616; Holmberg, *Paul and Power*, 99; Strauch, *Biblical Eldership*, 176.

65. Ralph P. Martin, *The Epistle of Paul to the Philippians*, rev. ed., TNTC 11 (Leicester, England: InterVarsity Press; Grand Rapids: Eerdmans, 1987), 59.

66. Paul does address specific people in 4:2–3 (Euodia and Syntyche), but this is necessary since he is addressing a specific problem.

> is primary. Church officers are made out of saints. . . . Paul
> does not draw a line of separation between clergy and la-
> ity. He rather emphasizes the bond of union by the use of
> "together with."[67]

Therefore, simply because Paul does not mention church "officers"
in other letters to churches, this does not mean that these leaders did
not exist. It is also worth pointing out that both groups are referred to
in the plural. There does not seem to be any evidence for a single leader
as the head of the local congregation in any of the Pauline churches (cf.
Ign. *Smyrn.* 8:1–2; 9:1).

Colossians 1:7; 4:12, 17

In the epistle to the church at Colossae, there are two men of importance
relating to organized ministry in the early Pauline writings—Epaphras
and Archippus. Epaphras is mentioned in 1:7 and 4:12. Paul writes,
"Just as you learned [the gospel] from Epaphras, our beloved fellow
servant. He is a faithful minister of Christ on your behalf. . . . Epaphras,
who is one of you, a servant of Christ Jesus, greets you, always strug-
gling on your behalf in his prayers, that you may stand mature and fully
assured in all the will of God." Paul indicates that the Colossian church
learned the gospel from Epaphras. It is likely that Epaphras was a native
of Colossae (*ho ex humōn*, Col. 4:12) and was probably converted during Paul's long stay in Ephesus (cf. Acts 19:8–10). Paul usually speaks of
the gospel's acceptance in terms of "believing," "hearing," or "obeying"
but here he speaks of the congregation "learning" it. The term "learned,"
states O'Brien, "probably indicates that Epaphras had given them systematic instruction in the gospel."[68] Epaphras is called a "minister" or
"servant" (*diakonos*) of Jesus Christ. Fung states that this verse possibly
indicates "Epaphras's having a special ministry, and possibly holding
a special office, in the church at Colossae."[69] Since we do not know the
exact nature of Epaphras' ministry, we cannot assume that Paul's use of

---

67. A. T. Robertson, *Paul's Joy in Christ: Studies in Philippians* (New York: Revell, 1917), 42–43.
    Also see Hawthorne, *Philippians*, 7–8; Gordon D. Fee, *Paul's Letter to the Philippians*, NIC-
    NT (Grand Rapids: Eerdmans, 1995), 67.
68. Peter T. O'Brien, *Colossians, Philemon*, WBC 44 (Waco, TX: Word, 1984), 15.
69. Fung, "Charismatic versus Organized Ministry," 198.

diakonos refers to an official position. We can be more confident, however, that Epaphras was a leader in the church and was recognized by others as such. Paul refers to him as "our beloved fellow servant" (Col. 1:7), "a faithful servant of Christ" (Col. 1:7), "a servant of Christ Jesus" (Col. 4:12), and "my fellow prisoner" (Philem. 23). O'Brien comments that these references "state significantly that he is Paul's representative in Colossae who has worked and who will continue to work in his place within the congregation."[70]

Archippus is also singled out because of his ministry in the church. Paul comments, "And say to Archippus, 'See that you fulfill the ministry that you have received in the Lord'" (Col. 4:17). Fung notes, "The fact that Archippus ["received his ministry from the Lord"] and is now to be solemnly charged . . . with the responsibility of fully discharging it . . . would seem to point to some definite, recognized ministry in the church."[71] In Philemon 2, Paul refers to him as a "fellow soldier." Paul reserves the use of this term for his co-workers who played an important role in his missionary labors (cf. Epaphroditus in Phil. 2:25).

Although the examples Epaphras and Archippus are somewhat vague, they demonstrate that Paul often singles out certain individuals as having particularly important ministries in the life of the church. It may be possible that they served freely without being formally recognized by the church, but it is also consistent with what we have seen in Paul's writings that official positions are not out of the ordinary. Each church was led by a group of men who were the recognized leaders of that congregation.

Ephesians 4:11

In Ephesians 4:11 Paul lists various "gifts" which Christ has given to the church. While in 1 Corinthians 12–14 Paul speaks of a variety of *charismata*, here the word for gifts is *domata*, which is quoted from the Septuagint.[72] Interestingly, the gifts given in this text are not abilities allocated to individuals for the purpose of ministry, but the people themselves given by the ascended Christ to the church. Paul lists four categories of workers:

---

70. O'Brien, *Colossians, Philemon*, 15.
71. Fung, "Charismatic versus Organized Ministry," 197.
72. Ephesians 4:8, quoted from Psalm 68:18 (LXX 67:19).

apostles, prophets, evangelists, and pastors and teachers. In 1 Corinthians 12:28, Paul lists three of the named "gifts" in order of precedence: "first apostles, second prophets, third teachers." In Ephesians 4:11, evangelists are placed between prophets and teachers, and teachers are given the two-fold designation "pastors and teachers" (*poimenas kai didaskalous*).[73]

Apostles are listed first in time and importance. According to Ephesians 2:20, the apostles and prophets were viewed as foundational gifts of the church. The prophets were those who proclaimed divine words to the community.[74] Evangelists (*euangelistas*) are not mentioned elsewhere in the Pauline corpus except in 2 Timothy 4:5, where young Timothy is exhorted to "do the work of an evangelist."[75] Bruce postulates that evangelists are not mentioned in 1 Corinthians 12 because they do not exercise special ministries inside the church but outside, in the world.[76] Yet, he acknowledges that while the ministry of the evangelist is not *in* the church it is still *for* the church. The noun "pastor" (*poimēn*, "shepherd") does not occur elsewhere in the New Testament as a reference to a leader in the church but the derivative verb and the noun "flock" are found occasionally.[77] The pastor is also given the title "teacher," which together with "pastor" denote one order of ministry. Similarly, in 1 Timothy 3:2 we read that an overseer should be "able to teach" (*didaktikos*).

Although Paul is not listing various "offices" in the church per se, he clearly mentions specific categories of gifted people. Each group or

---

73. Although the Granville Sharp rule does not apply here since we are dealing with plural nouns, the two concepts should be seen as overlapping. That is, "pastors" is a subset of "teachers" because all pastors were also teachers, but not all teachers were pastors (see Wallace, *Greek Grammar*, 284; Peter T. O'Brien, *The Letter to the Ephesians*, PNTC [Grand Rapids: Eerdmans; Leicester: Apollos, 1999], 300; Harold W. Hoehner, *Ephesians: An Exegetical Commentary* [Grand Rapids: Baker Academic, 2002], 544–45).

74. See, for example, 1 Corinthians 13:2; 14:22, 29; Ephesians 3:5; 2 Peter 1:19–2:1.

75. In Acts 21:8, Philip is called "an evangelist."

76. Bruce writes, "The church is the community of those who have heard the preaching of the gospel and responded to it in faith; they do not need to be evangelized further" (F. F. Bruce, *The Epistles to the Colossians, to Philemon, and to the Ephesians*, NICNT [Grand Rapids: Eerdmans, 1984], 347). It should be noted, however, that Paul states that he was eager to preach the gospel (*euangelisasthai*) to the church in Rome (Rom. 1:15).

77. The verb *poimainō* is used by Paul in 1 Corinthians 9:7 but refers to the shepherding of animals. The following uses are found in the context of shepherding people: Matthew 2:6; John 21:16; Acts 20:28; 1 Peter 5:2; Jude 1:12; Revelation 2:27; 7:17; 12:5; 19:15. The noun *poimēn* refers to a group of people in Matthew 26:31 and John 10:16. In Luke 12:23; Acts 20:28–29 and 1 Peter 5:2–3 the diminutive *poimnion* is used.

individual has a different function in the community. The evangelists would win people to the faith and the apostles would start new churches. The prophets would bring a particular divine word for specific situations, and the pastor-teachers would perform the daily ministry of instructing the believing community in the word of God. This is not to say, however, that those described as "pastors and teachers" did not possess a designated and regular position in the church.[78] While Paul is addressing gifted people who perform specific functions, those who perform such functions could also be said to hold an "office."[79] Furthermore, the comparison with 1 Corinthians 12:28 shows us that Paul does not always give us a complete list of those who performed ministries in the church.

CONCLUSION

It has been demonstrated that specific, organized ministries are found in every one of the churches to which Paul writes. The notion that the early Pauline churches were led merely by the voluntary service of people who were willing to serve is based on a romanticized view of 1 Corinthians. Although it is true that Paul normally addresses the function and not the office of these particular leaders, this does not imply that offices are foreign to Paul or his churches. Rather, it suggests that Paul was concerned more about the function or duty of the leaders than the particular office or title they might hold.[80] It is the one who *teaches* the word who receives some sort of compensation (Gal. 6:6). It is those who *labor, lead,* and *admonish* who are to be respected *because of their work* (1 Thess. 5:12). The church is to be subject to those who *devote themselves to ministry* (1 Cor. 16:15–16). Epaphras is called a

---

78. Fung states that this verse "does not preclude the possibility that there were church officers in the communities being addressed" ("Function or Office," 25).

79. O'Brien rightly notes, "To suggest . . . that the listing in v. 11 'has to do with *function*, not with office' is to introduce a false antithesis" (*Ephesians*, 301).

80. For example, Holmberg states, "The general impression we get when reading Paul's letters is that the local offices were rather unimportant. . . . even if the apostle seems to appreciate them" (*Paul and Power*, 112). Some reasons for this phenomenon are (1) Paul's own authority was still preeminent; (2) the presence of prophets and teachers limited the need for other leaders; (3) the young churches were not in a position to be self-governed; and (4) Paul normally addressed his letters to whole congregations, not simply the leadership.

faithful *servant* who has *labored earnestly* for the gospel (Col. 1:7; 4:12). Archippus is exhorted to fulfill his *ministry* (Col. 4:17). Paul first speaks of their functions since these new leaders needed to be instructed as to how they should serve. Although at times Paul more specifically speaks of office (Rom. 16:1–2 [?]; Phil. 1:1; Eph. 4:11), his main concern is that the gospel is advanced. Yet, for that advancement to take place it is often necessary that others recognize and respect those in leadership positions. Thus, the Pauline churches had a definite organizational structure even at the earliest stage.[81] The testimony of the non-Pauline writings also supports the notion that organized ministries were not foreign to the early church (e.g., see Heb. 13:7, 17, 24; 1 Peter 5:1–5; James 5:14). Although not fully developed, elements of office are already seen in Paul's day.[82]

From the earliest state, the New Testament churches were led, not only by apostles, but also by mature leaders from among the congregations. As was evident in Paul's strategy, he did not seek to permanently lead the churches that he planted but appointed indigenous leaders for each congregation. These leaders were sometimes referred to as "elders" (Acts 14:23) and at other times are called "overseers" (Phil. 1:1) or "pastors" (Eph. 4:11). They were responsible for shepherding the congregation (Eph. 4:11; Phil. 1:1; 1 Thess. 5:12), which included teaching the word of God (Gal. 6:6; Eph. 4:11; Col. 1:7; 1 Thess. 5:12). Because of their labor in the church, they were to be highly respected by the congregation (1 Cor. 16:15; 1 Thess. 5:12–13), which involved the congregation submitting to their lead-

---

81. Fung summarizes, "From the above evidence, it may legitimately be concluded (a) that in some of the Pauline communities there was some kind of public or specialized ministry (e.g. the teachers in Galatia, Epaphras and Archippus at Colossae), with a rudimentary form of official organization (elders in Galatia, and possibly also in Thessalonica), and (b) that at Philippi there appears to have been a comparatively more advanced system with its twofold division of overseers and deacons. There is thus ample evidence to show that the Pauline communities, like the primitive Church as a whole, were by no means amorphous associations run on more or less haphazard lines" ("Charismatic versus Organized Ministry," 200).

82. Holmberg concludes, "[There existed] permanent acknowledged functions in local churches filled by stable groups of persons who lead and serve and take responsibility for their congregations in different ways, in some cases even having a designation or title and some form of material support. The conclusion must be that we can rightly speak of offices in Paul's churches, even if they are not yet fully developed or legally authorized" *(Paul and Power,* 111–12).

ership (1 Cor. 16:16) and sometimes supporting them financially (Gal. 6:6). A second type of leader that is referenced is the "deacon" (Rom. 16:1[?]; Phil. 1:1; cf. 1 Tim. 3:8, 12). Based on the pattern established in Acts 6, these servant-leaders were called to assist the church so that the elders could devote themselves to their main task of shepherding the congregation.

Chapter 4

Overseeing and Serving the Church in the Pastoral and General Epistles

Thomas R. Schreiner[1]

The aim of this essay is to trace the character and duties of those who oversee and serve the churches in the Pastoral and General Epistles. The essay is limited, therefore, to texts in these epistles that address those who lead and serve in churches. I will divide the chapter into two major parts. First, most of the essay will be devoted to what the Pastoral Epistles teach about overseeing and serving the church, for the Pastorals have much to say on the matter before us. Second, I will glean the contribution of the General Epistles on the subject. The General Epistles do not expend much attention on church leaders, but there are scattered texts in Hebrews, James, 1 Peter, and 3 John that relate to our investigation. I will conclude the essay with a brief summary of what has been found in the study.

OVERSEEING AND SERVING CHURCHES IN THE PASTORAL EPISTLES

Instructions about Elders in 1 Timothy and Titus

The letters of 1 and 2 Timothy were addressed to Timothy and the letter titled Titus was written to a person of the same name. Clearly, both

---

1. Thomas R. Schreiner (PhD, Fuller Theological Seminary) is the James Buchanan Harrison Professor of New Testament Interpretation and the Associate Dean for the Scripture and Interpretation Division at The Southern Baptist Theological Seminary in Louisville, Kentucky.

Timothy and Titus functioned as leaders in the churches addressed since Paul directed them to convey and implement his instructions to the churches. Some scholars have identified Timothy and Titus as overseers/elders/pastors of the churches.[2] Certainly they were leaders, but it is a mistake to conclude that they were pastors. Timothy and Titus are better designated as apostolic delegates or representatives.[3] They stood in for Paul in his absence, giving the instructions Paul would have given if he were present. Just as Paul as an apostle appointed elders in newly established churches on his first missionary journey (Acts 14:23), so Titus was to appoint elders in Crete (Titus 1:5–9), and Timothy was to teach the church the qualifications for elders and deacons (1 Tim. 3:1–13; 5:17–25). Timothy and Titus were not permanent leaders of the congregation as are elders.[4] Their task was temporary. They communicated and applied Paul's apostolic instructions before rejoining Paul or before traveling to another place of ministry. The ministry of elders is settled and ongoing, whereas Timothy and Titus had itinerant ministries in which they taught Pauline directives.

Even though Timothy and Titus were not elders/overseers/pastors, some of the instructions given to them apply to elders as well. Later, we will sketch the responsibilities of elders, and there we shall see that they have a particular responsibility for godly living and for right doctrine. In that sense, their duties overlap with what Timothy and Titus are instructed to do. Hence, Paul's admonitions to Timothy and Titus regarding godliness and orthodox teaching and his warnings against false teaching apply in principle to elders as well.

Often Paul exhorts Timothy and Titus regarding the importance of right doctrine. Such doctrine is never abstracted from life, as if Paul wanted his associates to spin out arcane teachings for churches. Quite the contrary. It is false doctrine that detracts from godly living.

---

2. All these terms refer to the same office. In this essay I will use the different terms interchangeably. For a sustained and convincing defense for the idea that elders and overseers refer to the same office, see Benjamin L. Merkle, *The Elder and Overseer: One Office in the Early Church* (New York: Peter Lang, 2003). Cf. also William D. Mounce, *Pastoral Epistles*, WBC 46 (Nashville: Thomas Nelson, 2000), 161–63.

3. Philip H. Towner, *The Letters to Timothy and Titus*, NICNT (Grand Rapids: Eerdmans, 2006), 242.

4. Rightly Mounce, *Pastoral Epistles*, 387; Benjamin L. Merkle, *40 Questions about Elders and Deacons* (Grand Rapids: Kregel, 2008), 101–5.

Timothy must not yet depart from Ephesus, for false teachers must be commanded to desist from teaching "different doctrine" and from promulgating "myths and endless genealogies" (1 Tim. 1:3–4). Their teaching swerves away from what is central (1 Tim. 1:6), for the "aim of our charge is love that issues from a pure heart and a good conscience and a sincere faith" (1 Tim. 1:5). Orthodox doctrine, Paul insists, leads to love, and hence orthodoxy is immensely practical. Part of what it means for Timothy to "wage the good warfare" (1 Tim. 1:18) is to give proper instructions to the churches, which means that one preserves a "good conscience" and "faith" (1 Tim. 1:19).[5]

False teachers infiltrated the church in Ephesus just as was predicted, banning marriage and the eating of certain foods (1 Tim. 4:1–3). Their teaching is not a minor deviation, but is demonic in character since it denies God's good creation (1 Tim. 4:4–5). Timothy must be a "good servant," as one "trained in the words of the faith and of the good doctrine" (1 Tim. 4:6), warning and instructing believers about such "irreverent silly myths" (1 Tim. 4:7). The myths distract from and lead away from "godliness" (1 Tim. 4:7–8). They are so dangerous because they end up denying the saving work of God (cf. 1 Tim. 1:1, 15; 2:3, 4, 15; 4:10, 16). Timothy is commanded to teach the centrality of salvation and the godliness that accompanies it (1 Tim. 4:11), and hence he must feature in his ministry the public reading of Scripture since it is God's authoritative word. He must also teach and explain the Scriptures, and apply the word fervently to the lives of those listening (1 Tim. 4:13). The pressures of life and persecutions may provoke Timothy to neglect his gift (4:14, 16).

Timothy must apply what he teaches to himself, for he must serve as "an example in speech, in conduct, in love, in faith, and in purity" (4:12). He must continue to live a godly life (4:15–16), for if his life contradicts his teaching, he becomes like the false teachers whose "teaching" does not accord "with godliness" (1 Tim. 6:3), for they are proud and quarrelsome, provoking dissension and conflict wherever they go (1 Tim. 6:4–5). Hence, Paul reminds Timothy that he must seek after "righteousness, godliness, faith, love, steadfastness, gentleness" (1 Tim.

---

5. Cf. here 2:1 which functions as the introduction for the remaining instructions in the letter.

6:11). Like Jesus he must "keep the commandment unstained and free from reproach" (1 Tim. 6:14). So, Paul closes the letter by instructing Timothy to "guard the deposit entrusted to you" and to repudiate the false teaching (1 Tim. 6:20–21).

Paul writes to Timothy with instructions about orthodoxy and orthopraxy, but since elders are to teach correct doctrine and to live a life pleasing to God, it follows that the words to Timothy function as a paradigm for elders. What it means fundamentally to be an elder is to teach in accord with orthodoxy, to counter false teaching, and to live in a way that pleases God. A very similar pattern emerges in 2 Timothy. Timothy is "to fan into the flame the gift" God has given him (2 Tim. 1:6). Even when suffering comes, he must "not be ashamed of the testimony about our Lord" (2 Tim. 1:8). He is called upon to "guard the good deposit" (2 Tim. 1:14), and to adhere to "the pattern of the sound words" he heard from Paul (2 Tim. 1:13). The things Paul taught him are to be "entrust[ed] to faithful men who will be able to teach others also" (2 Tim. 2:2). Certainly these faithful men include the elders who are in turn to transmit the good deposit to others. And like Timothy, they must endure suffering and work hard in the ministry (2 Tim. 2:3–6). Timothy must "present" himself to God as an "approved" "worker" (2 Tim. 2:15), resisting and countering the words of the false teachers (2:15–18). That means Timothy must "preach the word" (4:2), being ready to do so when people are eager to hear and also when the audience is hostile (4:2–5). Again, Paul calls upon Timothy to suffer, just as Paul did.

As we saw in 1 Timothy, godly character is a priority for Timothy. He must "flee youthful passions and pursue righteousness, faith, love, and peace" (2 Tim. 2:22), not becoming embroiled in disputes which lead to dissension and breed hatred (2 Tim. 2:23–26). The foolishness of unbelievers could provoke anger, but Timothy should desist from anger and gently and patiently teach, realizing that only God can grant repentance. The challenge is great, for there are many who are self-absorbed and have given themselves over to evil (2 Tim. 3:1–9). Paul summons Timothy to follow his example by being devoted to God in the midst of his sufferings and persecutions (2 Tim. 3:10–13). Again, the instructions given to Timothy apply particularly to those who are called to be elders, to those who serve as leaders of God's flock.

Titus follows the same pattern observed in 1–2 Timothy, though on a briefer scale. Titus must "teach what accords with sound doctrine" (Titus 2:1). As we saw in 1–2 Timothy, sound doctrine is intertwined with a godly life, for healthy teaching is carried out when older and younger men, older and younger women, and slaves live godly lives (Titus 2:2–10). Indeed, Titus is "to be a model of good works" (Titus 2:7). Such good works are founded on the saving work of Christ (Titus 2:11–14) and are to be taught with confidence and authority (Titus 2:15). The importance of good works surfaces in the last chapter as well (Titus 3:8). At the same time, "foolish controversies, genealogies" and fruitless disputes are to be avoided (Titus 3:9). The divisive person should be warned, and if he refuses to repent then "have nothing more to do with him" (Titus 3:10). The paradigm for elders is not difficult to perceive. They, like Titus, are to be an example of good works and to teach the truth boldly and confidently, reproving those who fall into error. Perhaps the connection is even clearer in Titus, for after giving instructions on appointing elders, Paul immediately gives a reason why elders are needed ("for," *gar*) in Titus 1:10–16, warning about the presence of rebellious "empty talkers" (Titus 1:10). Paul says they "must be silenced" (Titus 1:11), and surely this is one of the responsibilities of the elders. They need to be rebuked and reproved since they are promulgating "Jewish myths" (Titus 1:13–14).

To sum up, it is clear that Timothy and Titus were not pastors/overseers/elders. They were temporary delegates for the churches. At the same time, Paul calls upon both Timothy and Titus to teach the word faithfully, to resist false teachers, and to live a godly life. Such commands were not limited to Timothy and Titus but also applied to elders, for elders, as we shall see below, were also instructed to teach, to refute unhealthy teaching, and to live a life pleasing to God.

Are Elders and Overseers Two Different Terms for the Same Office?
The question as to whether elders and overseers designate the same office has been examined carefully and convincingly by Merkle elsewhere.[6] A few comments will suffice here to indicate that the office is

---

6. See note 2. See also Marshall, *Pastoral Epistles*, 170–80. Against Fee who thinks overseers and deacons are both subsumed under elders (Gordon D. Fee, *1 and 2 Timothy, Titus*

the same. First, Paul glides from "elders" (*presbyterous*) to the "overseer" (*episkopos*) in Titus 1:5 and 1:7. It is doubtful that the reference to the overseer in 1:7 refers to a new office, for the text is joined by a connecting "for" (*gar*).[7] Furthermore, v. 5,which clearly addresses elders, is stitched to v. 7 in another way. Both verses say that the person appointed must be "above reproach" (*anenklētos*), using the very same word on both occasions. The repetition of the same term joins the verses together, indicating that the same office is referenced. The singular "overseer" (v. 7) does not signify that a separate office is in view, for the singular is generic. The one stands for the many, just as we say "worker" when we have in mind many workers (cf. 1 Tim. 5:18). The word "elder" denotes the status and the office, while the word "overseer" denotes the function, supervising and caring for God's flock.

Second, Paul's speech to the elders in Miletus supports the same conclusion. He summons "the elders (*presbyterous*) of the church" (Acts 20:17), but later in the speech he identifies them as "overseers" (*episkopous*), indicating that the terms are two different words for the same office. Third, in 1 Peter 5:1, Peter gives directives to "the elders" (*presbyterous*), but in v. 2 he describes their work with the participle "exercising oversight" (*episkopountes*), which is from the same root as the word "overseer," suggesting again that the two terms describe the same office. In fact, in both Acts 20:28 and 1 Peter 5:2, the elders are called upon to "shepherd" (*poimainein* and *poimanate* respectively) God's people. The verb "shepherd" is from the same root as the noun "pastor" (cf. *poimenas* in Eph. 4:11), and thus we have grounds for concluding that elders/overseers/pastors all refer to the same office.

Instructions about Overseers/Elders in 1 Timothy

First Timothy was written so that believers would "know" how they "ought to behave in the household of God" (1 Tim. 3:15). Part of this instruction relates to overseers/elders. The most significant text on overseers is found in 1 Timothy 3:1–7. Paul immediately commends the desire to be an elder (v. 1), for such a desire for the work is one in-

---

[NIBC; Peabody: Hendrickson, 1988], 78). Towner proposes a single overseer with a plurality of elders (*The Letters to Timothy and Titus*, 247).

7. Cf. also Marshall, *Pastoral Epistles*, 160.

dication that one is called to serve as an overseer. Obviously, one could desire the position of overseer for the wrong reasons and have base motives. Or, one might long for the office but lack ability to serve as such. On the other hand, some might think *any* longing to be an overseer proves selfishness and pride. We might be tempted to think that those who aspire to be an overseer are guilty of sin, thinking that the scriptural pattern is to be *selected* by others as an overseer without any desire to serve as such. Of course, a selection must take place. And a yearning to be an elder does not mean one *should* be an elder. Still, the aspiration to be an elder may represent a longing to serve the church and to glorify God, and this aspiration should be commended and encouraged.

What stands out in the list is the emphasis on character qualities instead of skills. The fundamental requirement for elders is that they lead a godly life. This is scarcely surprising and fits, as discussed above, with the exhortations given to Timothy and Titus. The overarching requirement is that an elder "be without reproach" (*anepilēmptos*, v. 2; cf. 1 Tim. 5:7; 6:14). To be above reproach should not be confused with sinlessness or perfection. The term means that sin should not have dominion in the life of an overseer. There is no blatant transgression that stains his life, which causes others to wonder why this man functions as an elder. In 1 Timothy, this requirement is bracketed by having a good reputation with outsiders (1 Tim. 3:7).[8] The rest of the character qualities explain what it means "to be without reproach." Some have even complained that the requirements here are rather banal and even dull. Johnson rightly responds that we do not have here "virtues of excitement and dynamism, but of steadiness, sobriety, and sanity."[9] He goes on to say, "Fidelity to one spouse, sobriety, and hospitality may seem trivial virtues to those who identify authentic faith with momentary conversion or a single spasm of heroism. But to those who have lived longer and who recognize how the administration of a community can erode even the strongest of characters and the best of intentions, finding a leader who is truly a lover of peace and not a lover of money can be downright exciting."[10]

---

8. Towner, *The Letters to Timothy and Titus*, 250.
9. Luke Timothy Johnson, *Letters to Paul's Delegates: 1 Timothy, 2 Timothy, Titus* (Valley Forge, PA: Trinity Press International, 1996), 148.
10. Ibid., 148–49.

Before I briefly examine the various character qualities, a couple of comments should be made about the list in vv. 1–7, and the comments apply to the list in Titus as well. First of all, the list is representative, not exhaustive. The general requirement is covered in the obligation "to be without reproach," but there is no attempt here to list all the positive qualities necessary or to specify all the sins that exclude someone from being an overseer. Indeed, the character qualities noted here are *expected of all Christians*.[11] Paul does not have one set of expectations for ordinary believers and a second set for pastors. Pastors, of course, must meet the requirements noted here, but it does not follow from this that the obligations are extraordinary. Second, in my experience, some over-read the instructions, interpreting them in a hyper-literal fashion. This mistake is made in part because they fail to see that what is mandated here applies to all believers. Paul is not *requiring* that an overseer be married or have children to serve as a leader. He addresses these matters since most men are married and have children, and their married life and conduct as fathers must be assessed to determine whether they should be overseers. It is quite improbable that Paul thought that he could not be an overseer or that Jesus could not serve as such since both Paul and Jesus were unmarried.[12] The requirements found here are to be applied with wisdom and understanding and maturity. In the hands of the untutored and unwise they could be wielded as clumsily as someone swinging an axe in the kitchen.[13]

We will look at the character requirements one by one and devote a bit more attention to those which are controversial. The overseer must be "the husband of one wife" (v. 2). We immediately land in controversy, for the interpretation of what is said here is disputed, sometimes quite fiercely. Of course, all the issues cannot be examined here, for one's understanding of divorce and remarriage in the rest of the Scriptures impinges on how the phrase here is interpreted. I will list the various interpretations, beginning with the interpretation that I

---

11. So Marshall, *Pastoral Epistles*, 148. I am not saying that if one does not meet these qualifications, then one is not a believer. It is one thing to say that character qualities are expected of all believers, but it would be a mistake to conclude from such a statement that someone is, necessarily, an unbeliever if some of these qualities are lacking.

12. See Mounce, *Pastoral Epistles*, 158–59.

13. See the wise comments of Towner, *The Letters to Timothy and Titus*, 684–85.

think is least probable and concluding with the reading I think is correct.[14] First, some, especially in the early church, understood this to say that overseers should never remarry, even if their first wife died. Such a reading is almost certainly wrong. It falls into the mistake already mentioned of thinking that Paul has extraordinary requirements for leaders. Elsewhere, it is quite clear that remarriage is permitted when one's spouse dies (Rom. 7:1–3; 1 Cor. 7:39), and there is no reason to think that such a permission would be denied to overseers. Second, others think the prohibition has to do with polygamy. In a sense this view is correct, for a husband of one wife excludes those who have more than one wife from serving as an elder. On the other hand, Paul probably does not have polygamy specifically in mind.[15] After all, polygamy was quite rare in the Greco-Roman world. More decisive, is the parallel in 1 Timothy 5:9 "the wife of one husband." It is important to observe that the phrases are the same: "husband of one wife" (*mias gynaikos andra*, 1 Tim. 3:2) and "wife of one husband" (*henos andros gynē*, 1 Tim. 5:9). Since the phrases are the same, they should probably be interpreted similarly, for we know that polyandry was virtually non-existent in the Greco-Roman world. Since the phrases are parallel and since polyandry was clearly not in Paul's mind in 1 Timothy 5:9, it is unlikely that he refers to polygamy in 1 Timothy 3:2.

Thirdly, Paul prohibits divorce *and* remarriage. Divorce would not necessarily disqualify one on this view, for it may be read as permitting divorce (as the innocent party) as long as the pastor does not remarry. This interpretation is certainly possible, and it depends in turn on how one reads the other divorce and marriage texts in the Scriptures, especially in the NT. I believe divorce and remarriage are permissible in some situations and, therefore, conclude that this interpretation should be rejected.[16] That leads to the fourth view. One is qualified to serve as

---

14. For an excellent and convincing discussion, see Merkle, *40 Questions about Elders and Deacons*, 124–29. See also Towner, *The Letters to Timothy and Titus*, 250–51.

15. Rightly George W. Knight, *The Pastoral Epistles: A Commentary on the Greek Text*, NIGTC (Grand Rapids: Eerdmans, 1992), 158.

16. See especially Craig L. Blomberg, "Marriage, Divorce, Remarriage, and Celibacy: An Exegesis of Matthew 19:3–12," *TrinJ* 11 (1990): 161–96; Andreas Köstenberger with David Jones, *God, Marriage, and Family: Rebuilding the Biblical Foundation*, 2nd ed. (Wheaton, IL: Crossway, 2010), 239–48.

an overseer if one is "a one-woman man."[17] In other words, one must have a significant and observable track record of being a faithful husband before one is appointed as an elder.[18] If a person has been divorced, the circumstances may be such to preclude such a man from serving as an overseer for a long time. On the other hand, there are situations where an elder has been divorced and remarried in which the circumstances of his divorce, the time that has lapsed since the divorce, and the quality and length of the new marriage warrant a man serving as an elder.

Two other observations support this reading. Paul says in 1 Timothy 3:3 (cf. Titus 1:7) that an overseer must not be a drunkard. Paul does not mean by this that a man cannot be an overseer if he got drunk once, nor is a person excluded from being an overseer if he was a drunkard for a number of years, as long as he has a significant track record of being sober so that he no longer has a reputation of being a drunkard. So too, a previous divorce doesn't disqualify a man if he has lived as a faithful husband for some years. It seems that this view is supported by the parallel already mentioned in 1 Timothy 5:9. A widow should receive financial support if she is over sixty years old and "a one man woman." It seems doubtful that a widow would be excluded from the list if she was divorced and remarried many years previously and had lived a godly life a number of years with her husband before he died. More likely, Paul asks whether the widow was known for being a faithful and godly wife in her marriage, if she had a good reputation as a wife. To sum up, what the church examines in this instance is the quality of the man's marriage.

The other character qualities in v. 2 can be handled in shorter compass. The prudence and level-headed nature of the pastor is addressed. The overseer must be "sober-minded, self-controlled, and respectable." He must think and act in a sane and reasonable manner so that he represents the character of God and Christ well, both to the church and to the world. His behavior should be both sensible and honorable. He

---

17. See Sidney Page, "Marital Expectations of Church Leaders in the Pastoral Epistles," *JSNT* 50 (1993): 105–20; Mounce, *Pastoral Epistles*, 170–73; Marshall, *Pastoral Epistles*, 155–57; Fee, *1 and 2 Timothy, Titus*, 80–81.

18. Knight, therefore, is too specific in tracking this to one's conversion (*The Pastoral Epistles*, 159).

must also be "hospitable." Hospitality was essential in the ancient world where inns were expensive and notorious for sin. Those who are overseers must love people and be glad to serve others.

Verse 3 addresses the passions of an elder, insisting that he must have control over his desires and his behavior. The pleasures of this world must not dominate the life of an elder, and hence he must not be a "drunkard" (v. 3). Abstinence from alcohol is not mandated, but an overseer must not surrender himself to the control of wine or any other substance. The elder must not be a "violent" person who gives into rages of temper which he takes out on others, which would result in "bullying, verbal abuse, angry pushing and shoving."[19] Such fits of anger demonstrate that a man is not qualified to serve as an overseer. Instead, the overseer should be "gentle" and "not quarrelsome." Overseers are not wimps, but their demeanor should be gentle and kind. Some people are prone to fighting and arguing and debating, but the inclination of an overseer should be to avoid conflict if possible. If it means standing up for the truth, he must join the battle. But he must not be known as a person who is always itching for a battle. Controlling his passions also means conquering the love of money. His goal in the ministry should be to serve others, not to make his life comfortable by indulging in what is costly and expensive.

The overseer's responsibility relative to the household will be picked up shortly when I consider the skill overseers must have to serve. Here the contents of vv. 6–7 will be explored. The churches in Ephesus had been established for some time, and hence recent converts should not be selected as leaders.[20] Recent converts are naturally prone to pride and conceit and, therefore, should not be appointed or set forth as examples for others too soon. The condemnation here refers to the judgment the devil faced for his pride.[21] Whatever one makes of the role of the devil, one of the great dangers of serving as a leader is pride. C. S. Lewis rightly identifies pride as "The Great Sin,"[22] and both believers

---

19. Towner, *The Letters to Timothy and Titus*, 253.
20. Interestingly, as will be discussed below, this requirement is not included in Titus.
21. In support of the objective genitive where the devil receives judgment, see Johnson, *Letters to Paul's Delegates*, 144; Knight, *The Pastoral Epistles*, 164. Cf. Towner who supports a subjective genitive (*The Letters to Timothy and Titus*, 257–58).
22. C. S. Lewis, *Mere Christianity* (New York: Macmillan, 1960), 108–14.

and unbelievers have a hard time looking at Christ if overseers are arrogant, condescending, and haughty.

Finally, an overseer should not be appointed if he has a bad reputation with outsiders (v. 7). Appointing such a person as an elder would lead one into the devil's trap and would bring reproach upon the person and the gospel. Towner rightly notes relative to both elders and deacons that our values are often inverted today so that we apply "the sort of criteria applied in the corporate setting, where education, innovation, and a youthful, energetic image (not to mention attractive, fashionable outward appearance) govern the 'professional' profile. This is a power profile that, however applicable to corporate life with its high esteem for mobility and innovation, is drastically superficial and at odds with the kind of values that frame leadership in these texts."[23]

Clearly the most important requirement for overseers is their character. Some ability, however, is needed for the task as well. Paul emphasizes two skills in 1 Timothy: the ability to teach and the ability to lead. Paul says in 1 Timothy 3:2 that overseers must be "apt to teach" (*didaktikon*). The emphasis on teaching accords with 1 Timothy 5:17 where those who "labor in preaching and teaching" (*en logo kai didaskalia*) should be granted double honor. Such an emphasis on teaching is scarcely surprising, for the crucial role teaching plays was sketched above relative to Timothy and Titus.[24] In examining the Pastorals as whole, it is clear that the elders have a particular responsibility to teach. False teaching threatens the churches, as all the Pastorals indicate, and thus elders are not only to teach positively but must also warn against doctrine that is contrary to the gospel. One may only serve as an elder if he has a good grasp of biblical teaching and is able to teach it clearly and accurately.

The second skill required for elders is leadership. They must be able to "rule well" (1 Tim. 5:17). Their ruling, as this very verse demonstrates, is tied to their teaching, for it is in teaching that elders particularly exercise their leadership and direction over the congregation. Parenthetically, nothing in this verse justifies a two-tiered eldership split

---

23. Towner, *The Letters to Timothy and Titus*, 269.
24. Cf. Mounce, *Pastoral Epistles*, 159.

between teaching and ruling elders.[25] The verse recognizes that some elders are particularly gifted in and devoted to teaching, but there is no warrant for the conclusion that some elders only rule while others only teach. Those who engage in the toilsome task of preaching and teaching should be accorded "double honor." Double honor means that they should both be highly regarded and paid for their teaching.[26]

I return to the main point: overseers are not only teachers but are also leaders. This is reflected in 1 Timothy 3:4–5 as well. Elders must "manage" their households well (1 Tim. 3:4). The word translated "manage" (*proistamenon/prostēnai*, 1 Tim. 3:4–5) is from the same verb which is translated "rule" (*proestōtes*) in 1 Timothy 5:17. The "managing" of the house, therefore, has to do with leadership. The household "initially exceeds issues of parenting and husbanding to include management of slaves, property, business interests, and even maintenance of important relationships with benefactors/patrons or clients."[27] It certainly includes one's family as well. If his children are out of control, rebellious, and disobedient, it is an indication he is not leading his home well. What this means practically with respect to children will be investigated briefly when considering the instructions to elders in Titus. Paul's point here is that one can hardly lead the church if one cannot manage one's household.

We have another hint that the leadership in view focuses fundamentally and primarily on godly character, for it is the latter quality that is essential for leadership in the home. The use of the word leadership could be misread. Paul matches "managing" one's house with "caring" "for God's church" (1 Tim. 3:5). The word "care" (*epimelēsetai*) indicates that the leadership is not imperious and dictatorial. The word "implies both leadership (guidance) and caring concern. In the home and church neither has validity without the other."[28] The same word is used to describe the Good Samaritan's care for the man who was left half-dead (Luke 10:34–35). The leadership and management of the

---

25. Rightly Merkle, *40 Questions about Elders and Deacons*, 84–88.
26. So also Fee, *1 and 2 Timothy, Titus*, 129; Knight, *The Pastoral Epistles*, 232. Less probable is Marshall's view that they receive twice what members of the congregation get at the church meal (*Pastoral Epistles*, 614–15).
27. Towner, *The Letters to Timothy and Titus*, 254.
28. Fee, *1 and 2 Timothy, Titus*, 82.

church is compared to a man's tending of his family. There is to be a compassion, a tenderness, a deep love that informs the leading of the church. Now this is not to deny that there is leadership involved. Just as a father may have to make tough and unpopular decisions, so overseers need to lead and guide the church even if the course taken is not always popular. Of course, such leadership must be grounded in the Scriptures, not the selfish will of the pastor.

First Timothy 5:17–25 also addresses the matter of elders, though the text is not as central as 1 Timothy 3:1–7.[29] We have already addressed 1 Timothy 5:17 where elders who "labor in preaching and teaching" are to be accorded "double honor."[30] Verse 18 supports the notion that elders who invest in teaching should be paid sufficiently by citing a verse from the OT, which says that an ox that treads out grain should not be muzzled (Deut. 25:4). And Paul cites a saying from Jesus which was first given to the seventy-two when they went out on mission (Luke 10:7). The one who works in proclaiming the gospel should be paid so that he can devote himself full time to teaching and preaching. Congregations, then, should direct their funds particularly to those who preach and teach the word of God. If a congregation suffers financially, it should, if at all possible, try to pay at least one person so he can devote himself full-time to preaching and teaching.

How should churches handle accusations against elders? Paul addresses this matter in vv. 19–21. Churches must be on guard, for accusations may be leveled against elders which lack any foundation. They may be motivated by hatred, envy, or bitterness. Hence, charges against an elder should not be considered unless there are "two or three witnesses" (v. 18). The instructions here "protect elders from malicious and unsubstantiated accusations."[31] Such a requirement fits with the

---

29. In support of seeing one unit of thought addressing elders in 1 Timothy 5:17–25, see Mounce, *Pastoral Epistles*, 304–6.

30. The word "especially" (*malista*) here does not mean "namely" (so e.g., T. C. Skeat, "'Especially the Parchments': A Note on 2 Timothy iv. 13," *JTS* 30 [1979]: 173–77; R. A. Campbell, "KAI MALISTA OIKEIWN—A New Look at 1 Timothy 5:8," *NTS* 41 [1995]: 157–60; Marshall, *Pastoral Epistles*, 612), but "especially" or "particularly" (Vern Sheridan Poythress, "The Meaning of μάλιστα in 2 Timothy 4:13 and Related Verses," *JTS* 53 [2002]: 523–32; Hong Bom Kim, "The Interpretation of μάλιστα in 1 Timothy 5:17," *NovT* 46 [2004]: 360–68).

31. Mounce, *Pastoral Epistles*, 311.

OT where punishments for crimes should not be imposed apart from "two or three witnesses" (Deut. 17:6; 19:15). Neither the OT nor Paul means by this that if two people can be found to agree on any charge then it should be investigated. What this means is that charges should be accepted against an elder only if there is substantial and convincing evidence against him. Personal vendettas should be ignored, and the elder should be presumed innocent until proven guilty.

If an elder is guilty of sin, then he should be rebuked "in the presence of all." The "all" here likely refers to the whole congregation instead of being limited to the rest of the elders.[32] Because the congregation pays the elders (vv. 17–18), members of the congregation may bring charges against elders (v. 19). Hence, the "all" in v. 20 probably refers to the congregation.[33] The translation "persist in sin" *(tous hamartanontas)* presses the tense of the participle unduly. Participles do not in and of themselves denote the time of the action, and whether it refers to ongoing action must be deciphered from the context. There is no indication here to support the idea that the only sins worthy of censure are ongoing or persistent.[34] Elders may need to be reproved and removed from their position for even one sin if the sin is egregious enough.[35] All believers sin daily and must solicit forgiveness for their sins as the Lord Jesus instructed us (Matt. 6:12), and such a daily battle with sin does not warrant public reproof. Paul thinks here of extraordinary situations. If overseers fall into sins that bring reproach upon the church (cf. 1 Tim. 3:2), such as significant sexual sin or financial impropriety or speech that is slanderous or false etc., then public reproof and removal are fitting. Whether the sins committed warrant public reproof is a matter of wisdom and prudence that must be deliberated upon by the elders. Some sins are so serious that they warrant reproof and removal if committed once. In other cases, a pattern of sin must be discerned before a public censure is given.

Public reprimand and even removal of an overseer has a purifying function. When "the rest" see the open rebuke they "stand in fear" (v.

---

32. Rightly Knight, *The Pastoral Epistles*, 236; Towner, *The Letters to Timothy and Titus*, 371.
33. Rightly Mounce, *Pastoral Epistles*, 313–14; Marshall, *Pastoral Epistles*, 618.
34. Knight argues that the issue is "present guilt" not ongoing sin (*Pastoral Epistles*, 236).
35. Marshall says that the participle probably "refers to persistent sinners [among the elders] who did not respond to the private exhortation that was the first stage of church discipline" (*Pastoral Epistles*, 618). The part in brackets is my addition, but Marshall says on the same page that elders are addressed here.

20). Who are "the rest" (*ho loipoi*)? It is difficult to be sure. The reference may be to the whole congregation which fits with the "all" in the verse.[36] It seems more likely, however, since the reproof is directed at an elder that those who fear are the other elders.[37] Censure and rebuke for significant sin reminds the elders of the awesome responsibility of serving as leaders of the congregation. Their leadership is severely compromised if they fall into sin that brings reproach, and hence they must fear lest their lives cause others to be scandalized.

The urgency of Paul's instructions is underscored in v. 21. The "instructions" (*tauta*) probably focus on vv. 19–20.[38] The Pauline commands are given "in the presence of God and Christ Jesus and of the elect angels." Clearly, the godliness of the elders is an awesomely serious matter; what Paul says here cannot be dismissed as trivial. If sin begins to take root among the leaders of the church, the church will suffer inevitable corruption and ultimate dissolution. Therefore, what is mandated must be discharged without "prejudging" (*prokrimatos*) and without "partiality" (*prosklisin*). Two different words are used for partiality, which emphasizes the solemnity of the instructions.[39] What this means practically is that an elder should not be spared from public censure and rebuke because he is favored or popular. Nor should unwarranted charges against an elder be tolerated.

Paul's concern about the holiness and fair treatment of elders is scarcely surprising, for as the leaders go so goes the church. The instructions of v. 22 fit with this theme, "Do not be hasty in the laying on of hands, nor take part in the sins of others; keep yourself pure." The "laying on of hands" in this context refers to the appointing of someone for a leadership position (cf. 1 Tim. 4:14; 2 Tim. 1:6).[40] In context it is quite likely that the reference is to the appointment of elders. If we wish to use the language of ordination, here is where we find it. When elders are appointed to serve as such in their congregations, then they are "ordained." Paul cautions that elders are not to be installed too quickly,

---

36. So Knight, *The Pastoral Epistles*, 236–37; Marshall, *Pastoral Epistles*, 619; Towner, *The Letters to Timothy and Titus*, 371–72.

37. So Mounce, *Pastoral Epistles*, 314.

38. Knight, *The Pastoral Epistles*, 237.

39. The weightiness of the instructions is also conveyed by the verb "I charge" (*diamartyromai*, s. v. *BDAG*).

40. For a fuller discussion, see Marshall, *Pastoral Epistles*, 620–22.

which fits with the admonition earlier not to appoint someone who is a recent convert (1 Tim. 3:6). Haste must be avoided, for if an ungodly elder is put into the job, then those who appoint him "to some degree" are "responsible for their ministry and the sins they may commit."[41] Those who appoint him are held responsible for not being wiser or at least slower about putting an unqualified man into a position of leadership. A man must be tested and examined before being granted more responsibility. By exercising wisdom and caution before installing one as an overseer, those who do the appointing keep themselves pure.

The remainder of the verses here can be handled quickly given the subject before us. In an aside, Timothy is admonished not to take purity too far (v. 23). Purity does not mean abstention from all wine, for wine brings relief for Timothy's stomach problems. Verse 23 is parenthetical, and vv. 24–25 provide the reason for v. 22. What vv. 24–25 mean in detail is disputed, and I shall not linger over the particulars here but shall concentrate on the main point. Care should be taken (v. 22) in appointing elders, for the character of a person is often evident, though in some cases their character will not be apparent immediately. Timothy should not become overly scrupulous about whom he selects since infallible judgment of the character of others is not possible. Hence, leaders should not worry if they make some mistakes, for God will sort out everything at the last judgment.[42]

Instructions about Elders in Titus

The churches in Crete, in contrast to the churches in Ephesus, were recently established.[43] Johnson suggests that the churches in Crete were a bit more raw, rough-hewn, and primitive than the churches in Ephesus, which may account for some of the differences in the letters.[44] The instructions about elders in the letter are found in Titus 1:5–9. The text

---

41. Mounce, *Pastoral Epistles*, 317.
42. So Marshall, *Pastoral Epistles*, 624–26; Towner, *The Letters to Timothy and Titus*, 376–78. The point, then, is not that leaders should wait until hidden sins become evident (so Knight, *The Pastoral Epistles*, 240–41; Mounce, *Pastoral Epistles*, 322), for Paul's very point here is that such sins will not be revealed until "the final judgment" (Towner, *The Letters to Timothy and Titus*, 378, n. 94).
43. Marshall says they were "in a less developed state" (*Pastoral Epistles*, 146).
44. Johnson, *Letters to Paul's Delegates*, 213, 223. So also Towner, *The Letters to Timothy and Titus*, 688.

overlaps with 1 Timothy 3:1–7 in many respects, and I will keep comments to a minimum where there is overlap. As was noted above, the shift from "elders" (*presbyterous*, v. 5) to "overseer" (*episkopon*, v. 7) does not signify the shift to a new subject, but instead supports the notion that elders and overseers were two different terms for the same office.[45] The mandate to "appoint elders in every town" (v. 5) repeats in writing what Titus was told orally. The repetition underscores the importance of the admonition. Apparently, the installation of elders is the most practical way to set things in order in the Cretan cities. It is also likely that there was a plurality of elders in each church, for each town in Crete likely had only one church, and Paul instructs Titus to appoint *elders* in each town.[46] This fits with Acts 14:23, for on their first missionary journey Paul and Barnabas "appointed *elders* for them *in every church*" (Acts 14:23).[47]

As we saw in 1 Timothy 3:1–7, the crucial requirement for elders is being "without reproach" (1 Tim. 3:2). Titus uses a different term (*anenklētos*) than Timothy,[48] but it has the same meaning ("without reproach"). The importance of the term is signified by it being repeated twice in Titus (1:6–7). Some of the character qualities are repeated from 1 Timothy 3:1–7: "husband of one wife" (Titus 1:6); not a "drunkard" (v. 7); not "violent" (v. 7); "hospitable" (v. 8); "self-controlled" (v. 8). All of these should be interpreted in the same way that we saw in 1 Timothy 3. Elders must not be "arrogant" (*authadē*, Titus 1:7), which matches the requirement that overseers should not be "puffed up with conceit" (1 Tim. 3:6). As noted above, both Titus and Timothy say that an overseer/elder should not be "violent." Titus adds that he must not be "quick-tempered" (*orgilon*, v. 7), emphasizing that an elder must not be a person who "blows his top" and yells at others. He must be a person who exercises "self-control" (v. 8). Titus particularly emphasizes that an elder must be "self-controlled" and "disciplined" (v. 8). His life must be "upright" and "holy" (v. 8). Timothy says an overseer must not be "a lover of money," and Titus says that he must not be "greedy for gain" (Titus 1:7).

---

45. Elders here refers to office, not to old men (so Marshall, *Pastoral Epistles*, 153).
46. So also Knight, *The Pastoral Epistles*, 288.
47. Italics mine.
48. I am referring to the book, not the author, in saying "Titus" or "Timothy" in instances like these.

Titus adds a few other character qualities that are not found in 1 Timothy 3, though the expectations are not remarkably different, confirming the idea that the lists are representative rather than exhaustive.

Interestingly, Paul omits in Titus the mandate from 1 Timothy 3:6 that only a new convert should be appointed as an elder.[49] Presumably the requirement is lacking in Titus because there were not any old converts. Recognizing the distinctiveness of Titus confirms what was said earlier about how the lists should be interpreted. Mature Christians should be installed as elders, but there was some flexibility, for mature Christians in Titus were by definition relatively new Christians. We are reminded again that the character qualifications must be applied with wisdom and insight.

One of the more debatable qualifications is found in v. 6, "his children are believers and not open to the charge of debauchery or insubordination." In 1 Timothy 3:4 the overseer manages his house "with all dignity keeping his children submissive." The ESV, as cited above, interprets Titus 1:6 to say that the children of elders must be believers. The word used here (*pista* from *pistos*) certainly means "believers" in some of the texts in the Pastoral Epistles (1 Tim. 4:3, 10, 12; 5:16; 6:2 [2 uses]). The term also means "faithful" (1 Tim. 1:12, 15; 3:1, 11; 4:9; 2 Tim. 2:2, 11, 13; Titus 1:9; 3:8). The word is ambiguous, therefore, and can be read to mean that the children of elders must be "faithful" or that they must be "believers."

It is more likely that the reference is to faithful children rather than to believers.[50] This fits with the parallel in 1 Timothy 3:4 where children are to be submissive (*hypotagē*) and obedient to their parents and to the father in particular. Thus in Titus 1:6 children are to be faithful, which is explained in terms of being free from "insubordination" (*anupotakta*) and dissipation. The conceptual link between "insubordination" (Titus 1:6) and "submissive" (1 Tim. 3:4) suggests that both texts require the same behavior in children. What is mandated is that the children are obedient,

---

49. See the helpful comments here of Mounce, *Pastoral Epistles*, 181. He says, "The application of this rule would depend upon the relative age of the local church, its speed of growth, and many other factors that would vary from place to place and from time to time" (181). Cf. also Fee, *1 and 2 Timothy, Titus*, 172.
50. Rightly Merkle, *40 Questions about Elders and Deacons*, 141–44.

that they are "faithful" children, not that they are believers.[51] Another link with 1 Timothy 3:4–5 seems to be present. In 1 Timothy 3:4–5, managing one's household well serves as an indication that one can serve as a leader in the church. In Titus, the requirement that children be obedient and controlled and "faithful" (v. 6) is joined in v. 7 (see the "for," *gar*) with the need for the elder to be "without reproach" as "God's steward" (*oikonomon*). In both 1 Timothy and Titus, elders cannot steward or manage the church if their children are running out of control.

It also seems probable that Paul has in mind, in the culture of the first century, children who have not reached maturity, which roughly speaking covers the years before one becomes a teenager.[52] As Knight says, "The implication is that Paul is talking only about children who are still rightfully under their father's authority in his home."[53] When children reach the teenage years they begin to form their own identity. This is not to deny the influence of parents. Still, parents are not responsible for whether their children become believers. This is not to deny that parents exert a tremendous influence over children and have a weighty responsibility. I am merely saying that Paul has in mind younger children in the context, those who are still under the protection and care of their parents. If younger children are not obedient and compliant (I am speaking of what is generally true here, not perfection!), it signals a serious problem with parenting. It is possible, of course, that what I am proposing is wrong, that Paul requires children to be believers. Even if this is the case, the meaning of the text does not change dramatically. Paul is still talking about younger children, and younger children naturally believe what their parents believe. If they disagree with their parents when they are younger, this is an indication of a serious problem. So, even if Paul speaks of children believing, he is not saying that they will believe for their entire lives, nor is he saying that parents are ultimately responsible for the adult faith of their children. So, if one adopts the idea that children must be believers, then the requirement is that children confess the same faith as their parents.[54]

---

51. Rightly Knight, *The Pastoral Epistles,* 289–90. Others, however, think the reference is to believers (Marshall, *Pastoral Epistles,* 158; Towner, *The Letters to Timothy and Titus,* 255, 682–84).
52. Knight says it refers to children "not yet of age" (*The Pastoral Epistles,* 161).
53. Ibid., 289.
54. Paul is speaking phenomenologically, and hence the requirement should not be pressed to demand that children necessarily have persevering faith.

We saw in 1 Timothy that the focus is on character requirements rather than skill, and the same is apparent in Titus. But Titus, in accord with 1 Timothy, also specifies the two skills necessary to serve as an elder: leadership and teaching. He says that elders are "God's steward[s]" (*oikonomon*). The word "steward" implies both service and responsibility to lead. Those who are leaders are "stewards of the mysteries of God" (1 Cor. 4:1). Elders exercise leadership particularly in their teaching. Hence, Titus must appoint elders who "hold firm to the trustworthy word as taught, so that he may be able to give instruction in sound doctrine and also to rebuke those who contradict it" (v. 9). Elders must be stable doctrinally, knowing the truths of the Scriptures and faithfully abiding by them. They must be able to build up the saints with their teaching and be able to counter those who teach what is false.

Instructions about Deacons in 1 Timothy

First Timothy is the only letter in the literature surveyed here that also includes a reference to and discussion of deacons (3:8–13). Male deacons are discussed in vv. 8–10 and 12–13, and there is a dispute over whether female deacons or wives are in view in v. 11. Before looking at the lists in particular, a couple of general remarks will be made about the topic. How do deacons differ from elders? Two of the qualities required to serve as an elder or an overseer are not mentioned with deacons.[55] Overseers must be gifted in teaching and have gifts of leadership, but nothing is said about deacons having such gifts. I conclude from this that deacons did not engage in leadership or teaching but served the church in various ways.[56] Their service was probably multifaceted, and probably included caring for the sick and superintending finances. In the same way, deacons should continue to serve the church and to assist the elders/overseers today. Many churches today give deacons a governing role and do not even have elders, and thus in effect

---

55. So also Knight, *The Pastoral Epistles,* 167. Against this, see Marshall, *Pastoral Epistles,* 487–88. Marshall does say, with respect to female deacons teaching, that it is likely that "the author simply forbade women deacons from doing all that the men did" (494).
56. Towner suggests deacons were subordinate to the elders, but wrongly concludes that their service may have included instruction (*The Letters to Timothy and Titus,* 261–62). The requirement for doctrinal fidelity (1 Tim. 3:9) and household management does not signify that they functioned as teachers and preachers.

put deacons in the role of elders. In the Scriptures, however, the elders were the leaders and teachers in the church, and the deacons served the church and the elders and did not occupy positions of leadership.

There is no indication that the qualifications for deacons are less rigorous than those for elders. The character qualities noted here, which are representative and not exhaustive, indicate that deacons must be just as godly as the elders. Deacons have different responsibilities than elders, which focus on serving rather than leading, but churches must not take deacons for granted and should appoint those who are godly.

When examining the qualifications for deacons, the same kinds of things demanded of overseers are included. Deacons must "be without reproach" (*anenklētoi*, v. 10).[57] As we saw with overseers, this is the general behavioral prerequisite for one to serve as an elder/overseer or a deacon. Other stipulations duplicate what was mandated for elders. Deacons must not be "addicted to much wine" (1 Tim. 3:8; cf. 1 Tim. 3:3; Titus 1:7), nor "greedy for dishonest gain" (1 Tim. 3:8, *aischrokerdēs*), which is the same word found in Titus 1:7. Like overseers, they must be "the husband of one wife" and rule their households well (1 Tim. 3:12; cf. 1 Tim. 3:4; Titus 1:6). Deacons must also be "dignified" and not "double-tongued" (v. 8). Their godly behavior must accord with the office to which they are called. Deacons are not called to teach, and yet they must be orthodox in their theology, and are to "hold the mystery of the faith with a clear conscience" (v. 9).[58] Those who meet all the character qualities should not be appointed as deacons if there are questions about their doctrinal fidelity or if they deny tenets of the faith.

The character and doctrinal requirements for deacons indicate that they should be examined before being appointed (v. 10).[59] Are those being considered as deacons truly living in accord with the gospel and do they confess and hold to the apostolic deposit of faith? Only those who meet such prerequisites should be appointed to serve. Finally, serving as a deacon brings great blessing. Actually, the blessing does not belong to those who merely serve as deacons but to those who serve

---

57. My translation. For some reason, the ESV translates the term as "blameless" here but as "above reproach" in Titus 1:6–7 when elders are addressed.
58. Paul has in mind doctrinal fidelity here (so Mounce, *Pastoral Epistles*, 200).
59. Knight says that "the testing is to be a thoughtful and careful evaluation of a man's life by a congregation aware of these needed qualifications" (*The Pastoral Epistles*, 170).

"well" (v. 13). Those who serve unto Christ and in a godly way will "gain a good standing for themselves" and "great confidence in the faith which is in Christ Jesus" (v. 13). Those who commit themselves to the church and give their time and energy in helping fellow believers will be rewarded.

Whether women can serve as deacons (v. 11) is disputed. The ESV, for instance, sees those described as "wives."[60] I will argue here, however, that Paul refers to women deacons rather than wives for the following reasons.[61] First, the Greek word used *gynaikas* may mean either women or wives. It is more likely that female deacons are described, for if wives were in view, Paul could have easily made this clear by adding the word "their" (*autōn*) or "their own" (*idias* or *heautōn*), as he does in other texts when addressing husbands or wives (cf. 1 Cor. 14:35; Eph. 5:22, 28, 33; Titus 2:5; cf. 1 Peter 3:1, 5). Second, the discussion of women comes in the midst of a section which gives qualifications for church office and is linked with the requirements for male deacons with the word "likewise" (*hōsautōs*). Third, if wives were intended, Paul would probably have also listed requirements for the wives of overseers, for elders, as argued above, teach and lead in the church while deacons have a serving ministry. It would be quite odd for Paul to say nothing about the wives of elders and restrict himself to wives of deacons, particularly since elders govern the church. But it makes perfect sense if Paul refers to female deacons for him to omit a reference to women in relation to elders since he does not believe women can serve as elders. Fourth, Paul forbids women "to teach or exercise authority over a man" (1 Tim. 2:12).[62] As argued above, teaching and ruling are the two dimensions of the eldership which distinguish elders from deacons. Hence, women serving as deacons does not contradict the notion that women should not teach or exercise authority, for deacons function as servants, not as leaders. Fifth, the character qualities for women ("serious, not slanderers, but temperate, faithful in all things") fit with what is demanded

---

60. For this view, see Knight, *The Pastoral Epistles*, 170–72; Mounce, *Pastoral Epistles*, 203–4. See especially the arguments supporting this view in Merkle, *40 Questions about Elders and Deacons*, 244–58.
61. Cf. also Towner, *The Letters to Timothy and Titus*, 265–67 (see esp. n. 28); Fee, *1 and 2 Timothy, Titus*, 88.
62. So also Johnson, *Letters to Paul's Delegates*, 153.

elsewhere of overseers or deacons (cf. 1 Tim. 3:2, 8). It seems most likely, then, that qualifications for an office are prescribed. Women deacons must meet the same character qualities required for male deacons and elders. Sixth, Romans 16:1 most likely should be interpreted to say that Phoebe served as a deacon "of the church at Cenchreae."[63] Seventh, the letter from Pliny the Younger to the Roman emperor Trajan confirms this view, for Pliny speaks of interrogating and "torturing two female slaves who were called deaconesses" (Pliny, *Letters* 10.96). This letter is dated near AD 111, and it seems quite unlikely that women would be called "deaconesses" (*quae ministrae dicebantur*) here if they had not served as such from an earlier period.[64] Eighth, J. N. Collins disputes what is argued for here, maintaining that the *diakonia* word group does not refer to lowly service but designates an authoritative emissary and mediator and go-between.[65] Clarke shows, however, that Collins's interpretation is questionable, and that the notion of service is most likely.[66]

OVERSEEING AND SERVING CHURCHES IN THE GENERAL EPISTLES

1 Peter and Elders

Peter in his first letter exhorts elders in 1 Peter 5:1–4.[67] One of the interesting dimensions in this exhortation is that Peter identifies himself as "a fellow elder" (v. 1), indicating that Peter was not only an apostle but also an elder. Peter also identifies himself as a "witness" of Christ's sufferings as well as a recipient of the glory that is coming (v. 1). Since

---

63. See Thomas R. Schreiner, *Romans*, BECNT (Grand Rapids: Baker Academic, 1998), 786–87.
64. The word *ministrae* is the Latin translation of the Greek word "deacon."
65. John N. Collins, *Diakonia: Re-interpreting the Ancient Sources* (New York: Oxford University Press, 1990).
66. Andrew D. Clarke, *Serve the Community of the Church: Christians as Leaders and Ministers* (Grand Rapids: Eerdmans, 2000), 233–45.
67. The term refers here to leaders, not just to those who were older. So Paul J. Achtemeier, *1 Peter: A Commentary on First Peter*, Hermeneia (Minneapolis: Augsburg Fortress, 1996), 322; Peter H. Davids, *The First Epistle of Peter*, NICNT (Grand Rapids: Eerdmans, 1990), 175. For a different view, see Karen H. Jobes, *1 Peter*, BECNT (Grand Rapids: Baker Academic, 2005), 302.

these words are addressed to elders, they serve as a reminder that leadership in the churches brings suffering. Glory is an eschatological promise, not a present reality. Elders should expect that their labor will be hard and often painful. Hence, Peter concludes his admonition to the elders by reminding them that "when the chief Shepherd appears, you will receive the unfading crown of glory" (v. 4). The reward, given at Christ's coming, will not fade and pass away, whereas every joy in this world is evanescent and temporary.

Another notable feature of this text is that the leaders are identified as "elders" (v. 1), are summoned to "shepherd the flock" (v. 2; cf. John 21:15) by "exercising oversight" (v. 2).[68] The word "shepherd" comes from the word "pastor," and hence Peter includes in these two verses the concept that elders are those who are involved in pastoring and overseeing, suggesting that all three terms designate one office.[69] Whatever one makes of the above observation, the main point is that elders are called upon to shepherd and care for the flock and exercise oversight over it. They are not to be like the shepherds criticized in Ezekiel 34 who tended their flock "with force and harshness" (34:4), who cared only for themselves (34:8). The flock belongs to God ("shepherd the flock of God"), but elders are to care for the flock allotted to them.

The text concentrates on how elders should shepherd the flock with three admonitions, containing a negative and positive element. First, elders should serve gladly and willing, "not under compulsion" (5:2). God's will for elders is that they serve with joy instead of serving under constraint. There are certainly days in which elders will desire to quit, for the intensity of the work and persecution could dim their desire for the ministry.[70] Michaels says, "Peter knows that the human ego is a severe and unhealthy taskmaster and that ministry all too often becomes a compulsive act of self-gratification. He wants it instead to be a free and joyous response to God's love."[71] If, however, elders do their work unto God and to please him, he will fan into a flame again their desire to serve (cf. 2 Tim. 1:6–7). He will give joy where it was lacking. Sec-

---

68. For the grammar, see Achtemeier, *1 Peter*, 325. For the text-critical issue, see Jobes, *1 Peter*, 310.
69. So also Wayne Grudem, *1 Peter*, TNTC (Grand Rapids: Eerdmans, 1988), 187.
70. Davids, *First Peter*, 178–79.
71. J. Ramsey Michaels, *1 Peter*, WBC 49 (Waco, TX: Word, 1988), 284.

ond, elders must not serve "for shameful gain, but eagerly" (v. 2). The word translated "shameful gain" (*aischrokerdōs*) is also found in Titus relative to elders (Titus 1:7), where Paul instructs Titus not to appoint elders who desire dishonest gain (cf. also 1 Tim. 3:3). In the NT, the mark of false teachers is often love of money (cf. 2 Cor. 2:17; 11:7–15; 1 Tim. 6:5–10; 2 Peter 2:3,14–15; Jude 11). Elders are to serve eagerly, as those who work to please the Lord. Serving as an elder is not just "another job," for those who serve have the joy and awesome responsibility of caring for God's flock.

Finally, elders must not lord it over those who assigned to them by lot *(tōn klērōn)*. The latter idea probably refers to the congregation under their charge.[72] Serving as an elder does not mean that overseers enjoy the privilege of getting their way. Elders must not view their leadership as an opportunity for advancing their selfish will where they rule imperiously over the congregation. The word "domineering" (*katakyrieuō*) alludes to the teaching of Jesus where he commanded his disciples not to follow the pattern of unbelievers, who use their authority to dominate others and advance their own interests (Matt. 20:25; Mark 10:42).[73] Followers of Jesus are to use their position of authority to serve and edify others, imitating the example of Jesus (Matt. 20:28; Mark 10:45). Elders should not view their position as a path to rule over others but as a calling to live as an example to others. Grudem rightly says, "academic excellence and administrative or financial skills do not automatically qualify one for leadership in the church."[74] Their desire must be to please God and Christ, and thereby they demonstrate to the congregation what it means to follow Christ.

Sound Bites from Hebrews, James, and 3 John

The other general epistles have a smattering of comments about leaders in the churches. Two verses in Hebrews address the matter of lead-

---

72. So Achtemeier, *1 Peter*, 328; Michaels, *1 Peter*, 285–86; Jobes, *1 Peter*, 306.
73. So R. H. Gundry, "'*Verba Christi*' in I Peter: Their Implications concerning the Authorship of I Peter and the Authenticity of the Gospel Tradition," *NTS* 13 (1967): 344; cf. Gerhard Maier, "Jesustradition im1. Petrusbrief?" in *The Jesus Tradition outside the Gospels*, vol. 5 of *Gospel Perspectives*, ed. David Wenham (Sheffield: JSOT Press, 1984), 93–95.
74. Grudem, *1 Peter*, 190.

ers (Heb. 13:7, 17; but cf. also Heb. 13:24). In Hebrews those guiding the church are not called overseers or elders or pastors but "leaders" (*hēgoumenoi*), though Attridge is probably correct in conjecturing that they were elders.[75] The term derives from the LXX where it is also used to designate leaders (Deut. 1:13; 5:23; Josh. 13:21; Judg. 9:51; Ezek. 23:6). The term used here is "not technical" but is "broadly descriptive of the role certain men played in the life of the community in its formative period."[76] The two verses in Hebrews confirm three observations made about leaders in the Pastoral Epistles. First, they have the primary responsibility to teach the truth of the gospel to the church. The author of Hebrews notes that they "spoke to you the word of God" (13:7),[77] signifying that their fundamental role was to instruct the church in the Scriptures.[78] Second, the godly behavior of leaders is crucial. Hence, the recipients of the letter are summoned to "remember" not only the word the leaders proclaimed, but also to "consider the outcome of their way of life, and imitate their faith" (v. 7). The leaders of the church lived in an exemplary manner warranting imitation. The call to imitation is a call to discipleship and perseverance.[79] The Pastoral Epistles focus upon the godly character of elders/overseers, and Hebrews 13:7 confirms the importance of such.

Thirdly, the responsibility to govern the church is clear from both Hebrews 13:7 and 13:17, for those who direct the church are called "leaders" and the church is called upon to "obey" and "submit" to their leaders (13:17), for the leaders have a particular responsibility to keep watch over the lives of their flock. They will give an account to God on the last day for their leadership and for their care for the flock. Leaders must not use their authority for their own benefit but must think and pray and labor to shepherd and care for the flock. They watch over the flock with vigilance

---

75. Harold W. Attridge, *The Epistle to the Hebrews*, Hermeneia (Philadelphia: Fortress, 1989), 391.

76. William L. Lane, *Hebrews 9–13*, WBC 47B (Dallas: Word, 1991), 526.

77. Lane remarks that the author "brings to light a remarkable theology of the word that informs the function and authority of former leaders" (*Hebrews 9–13*, 527). Cf. also Peter O'Brien, *The Letter to the Hebrews*, PNTC (Grand Rapids: Eerdmans, 2010), 515–16.

78. Most commentators agree that the leaders in 13:7 were deceased, while those in 13:17 were the current leaders. So F. F. Bruce, *The Epistle to the Hebrews*, NICNT (Grand Rapids: Eerdmans, 1964), 395; Philip E. Hughes, *A Commentary on the Epistle to the Hebrews* (Grand Rapids: Eerdmans, 1977), 569; O'Brien, *Hebrews*, 516; Lane, *Hebrews 9–13*, 527.

79. So Lane, *Hebrews 9–13*, 527–28.

because they are concerned with the salvation of each member.[80] As Lane says, "Although there is clear interest in v. 17 in strengthening a respect for the authority of the leaders, this is a consequence of the word that undergirds v. 7. No other grounding and safeguarding of the position of the community leaders is provided than the authority that derives from the word of preaching."[81] And members of churches should be inclined to follow the leadership of those in charge of the congregation. The submission of the congregation is not a light matter. In the context of Hebrews, where apostasy is the danger, not following the leaders who proclaimed the gospel would lead to judgment and destruction.[82] Clearly there are exceptions in which leaders should not be followed, but the inclination should be to follow the directions of those who govern the church, for submission to leaders will bring great joy.

Only two verses in James pertain to our topic, but they substantiate again what was proposed in the Pastoral Epistles. First, in James 3:1, leaders are called "teachers" (*didaskaloi*), corroborating that one of the fundamental roles of those who lead was teaching and instruction in the word of God. Moo defines teaching as "expounding of the truth of the gospel on the basis of the growing Christian tradition."[83] The weightiness of the responsibility is underscored by the admonition that not many should serve as teachers since they will be judged more strictly.[84] Teachers must faithfully teach the word of God instead of promulgating their own opinions and judgments. They minister in God's presence and for his glory, and hence they must always remember that they are servants of their master with the responsibility to be trustworthy ambassadors. James also mentions "the elders of the church" in 5:14. It is probably the case that those who functioned as "teachers" (3:1) were also elders. This verse substantiates the notion that each church had a plurality of elders, for it is almost certainly the case that

---

80. Ibid., 555. Lane speaks here of "eschatological vigilance."

81. Ibid., 554.

82. So Attridge, *Hebrews,* 402. Attridge observes that "unprofitable" means harmful, and in this context the harm relates to final judgment.

83. Douglas J. Moo, *The Letter of James,* PNTC (Grand Rapids: Eerdmans, 2000), 149. Cf. also Sophie Laws, *A Commentary on the Epistle of James,* HNTC (San Francisco: Harper & Row, 1980), 142–43.

84. Laws says this involves a stricter scrutiny on the last day (*James,* 144).

elders from a local church would pray for a sick person.[85] We also see the role of the elders in caring for the flock, for they attended to the sick by praying and supplicating the Lord for him.

Finally, 3 John warns about the abuse of authority that can arise among leaders in the case of Diotrophes. Diotrophes was apparently a leader in a church and was drunk with power, for he did not submit to the authority of the apostle John and "like[d] to put himself first" (v. 9). Indeed, he engaged in slander against John (v. 10) and kicked out of the church those who disagreed with him (v. 10). Leaders face the danger of abusing their power, of using their authority as a form of self-worship. Clearly, Diotrophes had fallen into this error, reminding us that those who lead churches, though they are to lead and direct, must use their leadership to serve the church.

CONCLUSION

Even though I have covered a lot of ground, the results of the investigation can be summed up rather quickly. The fundamental requirement for both elders/overseers/pastors and deacons is godliness. Those who are stable, sensible, and righteous, who have a good reputation both inside and outside the church should be appointed as elders and deacons. In the case of overseers they are to particularly concentrate on the ministry of the word. They lead the church on the basis of the word of the gospel which they are to proclaim faithfully. Elders must be vigilant and prepared to fend off the errors of false teachers, and hence they must be able to explain clearly where false teachers have swerved off course. Healthy teaching will support growth in love (1 Tim. 1:5) and the church will function as "the pillar and support of the truth" (1 Tim. 3:15).

---

85. Against Luke Timothy Johnson, *The Letter of James*, AB (New York: Doubleday, 1995), 330–31.

CHAPTER 5

The Development and Consolidation of the Papacy

Michael A. G. Haykin[1]

Among the texts at the very fountainhead of theological reflection regarding the governance of the church is the apostle Paul's (died *c.*67) maxim that "whoever aspires to the office of an overseer/bishop (*episkopos*), desires a beneficial task" (1 Tim. 3:1).[2] When the monastic leader John Cassian (*c.*360–*c.*435) reflected on the nature of the Christian life three and a half centuries later, however, his opinion about bishops could not have been more different than Paul's: "a monk"—that is, one striving to live a holy life for the benefit of other believers—"must by all means flee from women and bishops"![3] A substantial monograph would be needed to detail the way that the church moved from Paul's positive endorsement of the desire to be an overseer to the negative perspective of Cassian about episcopal leadership—such leaders are a danger to the monk's soul, and presumably their office endangers their own souls as well. This essay has a much more modest goal: it seeks to elucidate the development of ecclesial oversight in the western church, particularly as it relates to the papacy, a development that, for some, more than justifies Cassian's pessimism. First, though, we look at the emergence of monepiscopacy—necessary soil for the papal plant.

---

1. Michael A. G. Haykin (ThD, Wycliffe College and University of Toronto) is Professor of Church History and Biblical Spirituality at The Southern Baptist Theological Seminary in Louisville, Kentucky.
2. Author's translation.
3. *The Institutes* 11.18, trans. Boniface Ramsey, *John Cassian: The Institutes*, Ancient Christian Writers, no. 58 (New York/Mahwah, NJ: Newman Press, 2000), 247.

"Monarchy Is Superior": The Rise of Monepiscopacy

According to the witness of the New Testament, along with the authority of the apostolic band there are two distinct groups of residential
ministers in the churches of that time: the bishops or overseers (*episkopoi*), who are described elsewhere in the New Testament as elders
(*presbyteroi*), and the deacons (*diakonoi*).[4] While this two-tier model
of ministry remained a live option throughout the second century, a
shift towards three offices—a bishop, elders, and deacons—appeared
immediately after the New Testament era in the church at Antioch-on-
the-Orontes (Syrian Antioch). In his correspondence, Ignatius (died
c.107), bishop of the congregation in what was then the third largest
city in the Roman world, seems to have assumed a three-tier model to
be normative,[5] though it is noteworthy that in his letter to the church at
Rome, he makes no mention of a bishop.[6] Ignatius' view of the ministry
turned out to be the wave of the future, for by the close of the second
century it had been all but universally embraced by the church within
the Roman *Imperium*. It also bears noting, as Philip Schaff once wisely
observed, "this primitive catholic Episcopal system must by no means
be confounded with the later hierarchy" of bishops in the Middle Ages.[7]

Recognizing that any explanation for the development of the episcopate during the second and third centuries is complex,[8] at least six

---

4. See Philippians 1:1; 1 Timothy 3:1–13. For the identification of the *episkopos* and *presbyteros*, see Acts 20:17 and 28, as well as Titus 1:5–7. See also *Didache* 15 that seems to equate
   bishops and elders since it mentions only "bishops and deacons." As Philip Schaff noted:
   the "undeniable identity of presbyters and bishops in the New Testament" is a fact "con-
   ceded even by the best interpreters among the church fathers, by Jerome, Chrysostom, and
   Theodoret" (*History of the Christian Church* [New York: Charles Scribner's Sons, 1889],
   2:139).
5. See, for example, Ignatius, Letter to Polycarp 6.1 and his Letter to the Smyrnaeans 8.1.
6. John Knox, "The Ministry in the Primitive Church" in H. Richard Niebuhr and Daniel D.
   Williams, eds., *The Ministry in Historical Perspectives* (New York, NY: Harper & Brothers,
   1956), 23.
7. *History of the Christian Church*, 1:144. See also Kenneth A. Strand, "The Rise of the Monarchical Episcopate," *Andrews University Seminary Studies* 4 (1966): 70–71.
8. For a listing of these various factors, see Schaff, *History of the Christian Church*, 1:132–54;
   Adolf von Harnack, *The Mission and Expansion of Christianity in the First Three Centuries*,
   trans. and ed. James Moffatt (1908 ed.; repr. New York: Harper & Brothers, 1962), 439–86;
   John Knox, "Ministry in the Primitive Church," 24–25; Strand, "Rise of the Monarchical
   Episcopate"; Henry Chadwick, *The Early Church*, rev. ed. (London: Penguin Books, 1993),
   49. Seeking to understand this development is fraught not only with issues that relate to

key factors should be identified. First, in the midst of their life-and-death struggles with the heresy of Gnosticism and persecution from the Roman state, churches learned that it was profoundly helpful to have one main preaching elder, the bishop, as the focal point of church unity.[9] Then, by the time of Cyprian (*c.*200–258), correspondence between one church and another was being handled by the bishop in his own name, which was a shift from the previous century when such correspondence was directly between churches, with the bishop, if involved, acting as a secretary.[10] Furthermore, when an individual was ordained, it was not often possible for every presbyter from neighboring churches to attend. It came to be considered sufficient if simply the bishops from the other churches were present. There is also evidence that the presidency of the Lord's Supper facilitated the acceptance of the pre-eminence of one elder, namely, the one who came to be called the bishop.[11] The complexity of organization in some of the urban churches—for example, at Rome, Alexandria, and Antioch—also pushed these churches in the direction of monepiscopacy. For instance, Cornelius mentions in a letter during his episcopate at Rome—he was bishop from 251–253—that the church in the imperial capital had "46 presbyters, 7 deacons, 7 sub-deacons, 42 acolytes, [and] 52 exorcists,

---

the history of the ancient church, but that also have to do with the interpretive horizon of the one seeking to trace this historical phenomenon. Roman Catholic, Eastern Orthodox, and Anglo-Catholic authors have generally argued that the single-bishop model arose because it was put in place by the apostles. Protestant scholars, on the other hand, have usually maintained that the episcopacy emerged out of an original Presbyterian or even Congregational model. And in more recent days—roughly paralleling the rise of the Pentecostal and Charismatic movements in the late nineteenth and twentieth centuries—there have been those who have argued for an earlier charismatic and more "fluid" situation with regard to ministry that gave way to more formal structures as the initial fervor of the apostolic era waned. See Strand, "Rise of the Monarchical Episcopate," 67–68. To cite one example of authorial convictions shaping an argument's direction, see Everett Ferguson on the congregationalism of the apostolic era: "The 'Congregationalism' of the Early Church" in D. H. Williams, eds., *The Free Church and the Early Church: Bridging the Historical and Theological Divide* (Grand Rapids/Cambridge, UK: Eerdmans, 2002), 129–40.

9. Henry Chadwick, "The Role of the Christian Bishop in Ancient Society" in his *Heresy and Orthodoxy in the Early Church* (Aldershot, Hampshire: Variorum, 1991), no. 3:3.

10. Ferguson, "'Congregationalism' of the Early Church," 132–34. See, for example, *The Shepherd of Hermas,* Vision 2.4.3, where an individual named Clement (is this Clement of Rome?) seems to serve the churches in Rome as a secretary. See also Allen Brent, "Was Hippolytus a Schismatic?" *Vigiliae Christianae* 49 (1995): 218–19.

11. George H. Williams, "The Ministry of the Ante-Nicene Church (*c.*125–325)" in Niebuhr and Williams, eds., *Ministry in Historical Perspectives,* 27–28.

readers and door-keepers."[12] Finally, there was the ideological ambience of a larger culture that made anything but hierarchical structures appear less than credible. As Eusebius of Caesarea (*c.*260–*c.*340) commented in the sermon he gave at the celebration of Constantine's thirtieth anniversary as emperor:

> Monarchy is superior to every other constitution and form of government. For polyarchy, where everyone competes on equal terms, is really anarchy and discord. This is why there is one God, not two, three, or even more.[13]

Eusebius is, of course, defending Constantine's monarchical rule and his elimination of imperial colleagues, but the same reasoning was used to defend monepiscopacy.[14]

"The Chair of Peter": Two Early Claims for the Primacy of Rome

Claims for the primacy of the bishop of Rome over fellow bishops go back to Victor I (189–198). Drawing upon archaeology and a variety of literary sources, Peter Lampe has persuasively argued that, prior to Victor's episcopate, the governance of the various house-churches in Rome was through a collegial presbyterate with each house-church having its own presiding elder. Victor sought to change this, however, and impose himself as a monarchical bishop.[15] Victor's convictions regarding his authority were on full display during the Quartodeciman controversy in the early 190s. Victor threatened the churches in Asia Minor with excommunication if they did not give up their adherence to the Jewish

---

12. Cited in Eusebius, *Ecclesiastical History* 6.43.11, trans. Hugh Jackson Lawlor and John Ernest Leonard Oulton, *Eusebius: The Ecclesiastical History and the Martyrs of Palestine* (London: SPCK, 1954), 1:211–12. See the comments of Walter Ullmann, *A Short History of the Papacy in the Middle Ages* (2nd ed.; London/New York, NY: Routledge, 2003), 5.

13. *Oration in Honour of Constantine on the Thirtieth Anniversary of his Reign* 3, in Maurice Wiles and Mark Santer, eds., *Documents in Early Christian Thought* (Cambridge: Cambridge University Press, 1975), 234.

14. Chadwick, "Role of the Christian Bishop in Ancient Society," 3.

15. *From Paul to Valentinus: Christians at Rome in the First Two Centuries* (Minneapolis: Fortress Press, 2003), especially, 397–408.

calendar in their celebration of Christ's resurrection, for this entailed these churches not confining their celebration of this central Christian festival to the Lord's Day as was done at Rome and in numerous other centers.[16] Victor's desire to impose the custom of celebrating the resurrection solely on the Lord's Day, however, provoked a storm of protest from a number of bishops, including Irenaeus of Lyons (*c.*130–*c.*200), who together appear to have persuaded him to desist from an imprudent use of authority.

In the century that followed, Cyprian, who fully embraced the idea that there can be only one legitimate bishop within a given geographical area, found himself embroiled in a bitter controversy with Stephen, the bishop of Rome (254–257) over whether or not heretics and schismatics who returned to the Catholic church were to be baptized or not.[17] This controversy is usually described as a controversy about rebaptism, though, in many ways, the real issue at stake had to do not so much with baptism as with the Holy Spirit.[18] Was the Spirit present within heretical or schismatic assemblies? If not, then, as Cyprian argued, the only valid baptism that the Spirit would honor as a true baptism is that given within the church that he indwelt; thus heretics and schismatics were to be baptized.[19] Stephen disagreed, and argued that the laying on of hands would suffice as the rite of reception into the church if the person had already undergone baptism into the Triune name. It is noteworthy that he appealed at one point to his "occupancy of the chair

16. Eusebius of Caesarea, *Ecclesiastical History* 5.23–25. Allen Brent ("Was Hippolytus a Schismatic?" 220) and John M. Rist (*What Is Truth? From the Academy to the Vatican* [Cambridge: Cambridge University Press, 2008], 227) interpret Victor's threat of excommunication as being "aimed at those Asian Christians in the city of Rome itself who followed their native practice." In other words, this is not a claim by the bishop of Rome to a wider primacy.

17. The bitterness of this controversy can be seen, for example, in Stephen's last word about Cyprian, cited by Firmilian of Caesarea (died *c.*269), that the African bishop was "a bogus Christ, a bogus apostle, and a crooked dealer" (Cyprian, *Letter* 75.25.4, trans. G. W. Clarke, *The Letters of St. Cyprian of Carthage*, Ancient Christian Writers, no. 47 [New York/Ramsey, NJ: Newman Press, 1989], 4:94).

18. Michel Réveillaud, "Note pour une Pneumatologie Cyprienne" in F. L. Cross, ed., *Studia Patristica*, Texte und Untersuchungen, vol. 81 (Berlin: Akademie-Verlag, 1962), 6:181–82.

19. Allen Brent, "Introduction" to his trans., *St Cyprian of Carthage, On the Church: Select Treatises*, Popular Patristics Series, no. 32 (Crestwood, NY: St Vladimir's Seminary Press, 2006), 32–33.

of Peter (*cathedram Petri*)"[20] to support his argument. This is a clear reference to Matthew 16:16–18 and it appears to have been the first occasion that a bishop of Rome used what would become a standard argument in the fourth and fifth centuries.[21]

By the time of the Council of Nicaea (325), monepiscopacy had largely triumphed throughout the church in the Roman world, as is clearly seen in the focus of some of the canons of this first ecumenical council upon the proper working of the episcopate.[22] Canon 6 specifically recognized the authority of the bishops of Alexandria, Rome, and Antioch—and by implication the bishops of other important cities like Carthage—over the bishops of churches in smaller towns located near these major urban centers, evidence of a further level of hierarchy within the governance of the church. The Nicene canons distinguished the bishops of these significant cities by the term "metropolitan" (*ho mētropolitēs*), though it is striking that there is no privileging of the bishop of Rome over his fellow metropolitan bishops.[23]

"Make Me Bishop of Rome": The Episcopate of Damasus I

Critical for what R. A. Markus has called "the creation of the papacy with jurisdictional rights acknowledged" by most other bishops in the West were the Roman episcopates between Damasus I (366–384) and Leo I (440–461).[24] Relatively little is known about Damasus' early years until his appointment as a deacon in the church at Rome during the episcopate of Liberius (352–366) in the early 350s.[25] Liberius had been a firm

---

20. *Letter* 75.17.2, trans. Clarke, *Letters of St. Cyprian of Carthage*, 4:89.
21. Walter Ullmann, "Leo I and the Theme of Papal Primacy," *JTS* 11 (1960): 29–30; J. N. D. Kelly, *The Oxford Dictionary of Popes* (Oxford/New York: Oxford University Press, 1986), 21; Hanns Christof Brennecke, "Papacy" in Hans Dieter Betz *et al.*, eds., *Religion Past & Present: Encyclopedia of Theology and Religion* (Leiden/Boston, MA: Brill, 2011), 9:490.
22. See especially Canons 2–8, 15. For the text of the canons, see "Canons of the Council of Nicaea," *Fourth-Century Christianity* (http://www.fourthcentury.com/index.php/nicaea-325-canons; accessed December 8, 2013).
23. For an overview of the fourth- and fifth-century conciliar canons dealing with the episcopate, see George H. Williams, "The Ministry in the Later Patristic Period (314–451)" in Niebuhr and Williams, eds., *Ministry in Historical Perspectives*, 60–66.
24. "Papacy and Hierarchy" in his *From Augustine to Gregory the Great: History and Christianity in Late Antiquity* (London: Variorum Reprints, 1983), no. 17:17.
25. For a positive evaluation of the life and career of Damasus, see Stanley Morison, "An Unacknowledged Hero of the Fourth Century, Damasus I 366–384" in Charles Henderson,

opponent of Arianism and supporter of the principled stand of Athanasius of Alexandria (c.299–373) for Nicene Trinitarianism. He also had undergone exile in Thrace for these convictions from 355 to 358.[26] During Liberius' exile, the clergy in Rome had elected Felix II (355–365), who had distinct sympathies for Arianism, as their bishop. In 358 the Arian emperor Constantius II, at whose behest Liberius had been exiled, brought significant pressure to bear upon the exiled bishop to renounce his previous allegiances. Liberius eventually agreed to give up his support of Athanasius and sign a creedal statement in which he confessed the Son to be merely "like (*homoios*)" the Father, a clear rejection of the Nicene Creed's affirmation of the oneness of being of the Father and the Son. Satisfied that Liberius now shared his Arianism, Constantius allowed him to return to Rome, where he expected him to work with Felix as his co-bishop. The congregations in Rome, however, rejected this arrangement and compelled Felix to relocate to the suburbs of the city, where he had a church built for his ministry. Constantius died in 361, whereupon Liberius felt the freedom once again to declare his support for the Nicene Creed. At Liberius' death in 366, a group of his closest supporters elected a deacon by the name of Ursinus (died c.385) to succeed him, but Felix's followers—Felix having died the previous year—contested the election and nominated Damasus as bishop. The rivalry between these two groups was so intense that it led eventually to sanguinary conflict on three distinct occasions, one of which, according to the pagan historian Ammianus Marcellinus (325/330–after 391), left 137 dead in the Christian basilica of Santa Maria Maggiore. It is noteworthy that Marcellinus traced this violence back to the "superhuman desire" each man had to "seize the bishopric" (*supra humanum modum ad rapiendam episcopi sedem ardentes*) of Rome.[27]

Jr., ed., *Classical, Mediaeval, and Renaissance Studies in Honor of Berthold Louis Ullman* (Rome: Edizioni di storia e letteratura, 1964), 241–63. Also see the overview by Kelly, *Oxford Dictionary of Popes*, 32–34.

26. For what follows regarding Liberius' episcopate, I am indebted to the masterly summary by Kelly, *Oxford Dictionary of Popes*, 30–31. For more extensive studies, see James Barmby, "Liberius (4)" in William Smith and Henry Wace, eds., *A Dictionary of Christian Biography* (London: John Murray, 1882), 3:717–24; and J. Zeiller, "La question du pape Libère," *Bulletin d'ancienne littérature et d'archéologie chrétienne* 3 (1913): 20–51.

27. *History* 27.3.12–13, trans. John C. Rolfe, *Ammianus Marcellinus*, LCL, rev. ed. (Cambridge, MA: Harvard University Press; London: William Heinemann, 1952), 3:19, altered. For help obtaining this text I am indebted to Mr. Kevin Hall of Louisville, KY.

Damasus emerged the victor from this shameful conflict, but at a fright-
ful cost to his credibility. In the early 370s a charge of homicide was also
leveled against Damasus, though it was never proven.[28] Christian critics
were scandalized by the opulent lifestyle he adopted—possibly to reach the
Roman aristocracy, one of the last bastions of paganism—and the impact
of his sermons upon upper-class Roman women in particular led to his
being called derisively "the ladies' ear-tickler"![29] No wonder the prominent
pagan aristocrat Vettius Agorius Praetextatus (c.315–384), mocking the
whole idea of Christian conversion, is said to have told Damasus: "Make
me bishop of Rome and I will become a Christian immediately."[30]

Help in understanding Damasus' thought about the Roman episcopate is actually found in a letter written to him in 375 by one of his pro-
tégés, namely Jerome (c.345–420), who had been baptized as a believer
in Rome in the mid-360s and had served subsequently as Damasus'
secretary in the 380s. Jerome is reflecting on the havoc that Arianism
had wrought in the churches of the east:

> Since the East . . . is tearing piecemeal the undivided tunic
> of Christ, woven from the top throughout, and foxes are
> destroying the vineyard of Christ, so that among the bro-
> ken cisterns that have no water it is difficult to locate the
> fountain sealed and the garden enclosed, I have consid-
> ered that I ought to consult the chair of Peter (*cathedram
> Petri*), and the faith praised by the mouth of the Apostle.
> I now ask for food for my soul, from the place whence I
> received the garment of Christ.
>
> Neither the vast expanse of ocean, nor all the breadth of
> land which separates us could keep me from seeking the
> pearl of great price. "Wherever the body is, there will the
> eagles be gathered together." Now that evil children have

28. Henry Chadwick, *The Church in Ancient Society: From Galilee to Gregory the Great* (Ox-
    ford: Oxford University Press, 2001), 316–18.
29. Chadwick, *Early Church*, 160–62; idem, *Church in Ancient Society*, 317; Bernard Green,
    The Soteriology of Leo the Great (Oxford: Oxford University Press, 2008), 10–11.
30. Cited in Jerome, *Against John of Jerusalem* 8 (*Patrologia Latina* 23.377C–D). For a discus-
    sion of this remark of Praetextatus, see Burton L. Visotzky, "Hillel, Hieronymus and Prae-
    textatus," *Journal of the Ancient Near Eastern Society* 16–17 (1984–1985): 217–24.

squandered their patrimony, you alone keep your heritage intact. There the fertile earth gives back a hundredfold the pure seed of the Lord. Here the corn, cast into the furrows, degenerates into darnel or wild oats. It is now in the West that the sun of righteousness arises; whilst in the East Lucifer, who had fallen, has set his throne above the stars. "You are the light of the world." "You are the salt of the earth." You are vessels of gold and silver. Here the vessels of clay or wood await the iron rod and eternal fire.

... I am speaking with the successor of the fisherman, with the disciple of the cross. Following none in the first place but Christ, I am in communion with your holiness, that is with the chair of Peter (*cathedrae Petri*). I know that upon this rock the Church is built. Whoever shall eat the Lamb outside this house is profane. If any be not with Noah in the ark, he shall perish in the flood.[31]

Here Jerome uses a variety of biblical images to describe the church. There is, for example, "the sealed fountain and the enclosed garden" from Song of Songs 4:12—a verse that had been interpreted ecclesiologically since at least the time of Cyprian[32]—as well as Noah's ark. Interwoven among these images are at least two allusions to Matthew 16:16–18: Damasus sits on the "chair of Peter," which is the rock on which the church is built, and therefore, by implication, has a primacy over other episcopal sees. This emphasis on the apostle Peter as the source of Damasus' authority is what Walter Ullmann has called "the basic petrinological theme," which turns out to have been a key feature of Damasus' thinking.[33]

In 380, the Emperor Theodosius I issued the Edict of Thessalonica, which declared the "religion which the divine Peter the Apostle is said to have given to the Romans, and which it is evident that the Pontiff

---

31. Jerome, *Letter* 15 (*Patrologia Latina* 22.355B–D), trans. E. Giles, ed. *Documents Illustrating Papal Authority, A.D. 96–454* (London: SPCK, 1952), 148–49, modernized and slightly altered.
32. See Cyprian, *Letter* 69.2.1; 74.11.2. In the first of these texts Cyprian also uses Noah's ark as a type of the church. For Cyprian's exegesis of Song of Songs 4:12, see especially Giuseppe Nicotra, "Interpretazione di Cipriano al Cap. IV, Vers. 12, della Cantica," *La Scuola Cattolica* 68 (1940): 380–87.
33. *Short History of the Papacy*, 11.

(*pontificem*) Damasus and Peter, Bishop of Alexandria, a man of apostolic holiness, follow,"[34] to be the only legal religion of the Empire. Damasus must have been deeply gratified by this public recognition of the authority of the Roman bishop and the link to the apostle Peter. The following year, after the Niceno-Constantinopolitan Creed, which effectively closed the debate on the nature of the Godhead in the Arian controversy, had been drawn up at the Council of Constantinople (381), Theodosius issued an edict on July 30, 381, to confirm the council's doctrinal conclusions. Eleven bishops were explicitly named as the guarantors of the orthodox faith contained in the creedal statement.[35] Damasus was not among them. By way of response, a synod in Rome in 382 issued a formal statement that explicitly grounded the primacy of the bishop of Rome on Jesus' words to Peter in Matthew 16:17:

> . . . though all the catholic churches diffused throughout the world are but one bridal chamber of Christ, yet the holy Roman church has been set before the rest by no conciliar decrees, but has obtained the primacy by the voice of our Lord and Saviour in the gospel: "you are Peter, and on this rock I will build my church . . . ." There is added also the society of the most blessed apostle Paul, . . . who was crowned on one and the same day, suffering a glorious death, with Peter in the city of Rome, under Caesar Nero; and they alike consecrated the above-named Roman church to Christ the Lord, and set it above all others in the whole world by their presence and venerable triumph.[36]

Since Peter, along with Paul, had planted the church in Rome, whatever privileges and responsibilities were accorded to Peter were the Roman bishop's by inheritance.[37]

---

34. *Codex Theodosianus* 16.1.2, trans. The Library of Original Sources, ed. Oliver J. Thatcher (New York: University Research Extension, [1907]), 70, altered.
35. *Codex Theodosianus* 16.1.3.
36. Damasus, *Post has omnes* (*Patrologia Latina* 13.374B–C) in Giles, ed. *Documents Illustrating Papal Authority*, 131. For a discussion of this text, see Ullmann, *Short History of the Papacy*, 10–11; Chadwick, *Church in Ancient Society*, 321–22.
37. The belief that Peter and Paul founded the church in Rome goes back to Irenaeus; see his *Against Heresies* 3.3.1–2.

It was probably to further buttress his authority and influence that Damasus penned an epigram around the time of this Synod of Rome that recalled an old belief that originally Peter and Paul had been buried together on the Via Appia after their martyrdoms:

> Whoever you may be that seek the names of Peter and Paul should know that the saints dwelt here once. The East sent the disciples; that we readily admit. But on the account of the merit of their blood (they have followed Christ through the stars and attained to the ethereal bosom and the realms of the holy ones) Rome has gained a superior right to claim them as her citizens. Damasus would thus tell of your praises as new stars.[38]

Here, Damasus claimed that although Peter and Paul had journeyed from the orient, their dwelling at and especially their dying in Rome gave the church there "a superior right" to claim them as their very own. Damasus could thus refer to Rome as an "apostolic see (*sedes apostolica*)."[39] In other words, Damasus was asserting that apostolic authority had been transferred from the east to the west, from early Christian centers like Jerusalem and Antioch, where Peter and Paul had been active, to Rome, where they had died together.

"So Great Is Our Authority": From Siricius to Zosimus

A letter of Damasus' successor, Siricius (384–399), to Himerius of Tarragona, written in the year after Siricius became bishop of Rome, continued this vein of interpretation.[40] He informed Himerius that

---

38. Cited in Chadwick, *Church in Ancient Society*, 324. For a discussion of this epigram, see Henry Chadwick, "St. Peter and St. Paul in Rome: The Problem of the Memoria Apostolorum ad Catacumbas," *JTS* 8 (1957): 34–35; idem, "Pope Damasus and the Peculiar Claim of Rome to St. Peter and St. Paul" in his *History and Thought of the Early Church* (London: Variorum Reprints, 1982), no. 3; and idem, *Church in Ancient Society*, 324–25. For the dating of this epigram, see Chadwick, *Church in Ancient Society*, 325.
39. Ullmann notes that the term "apostolic see" is first consistently used by Damasus: "Leo I and the Theme of Papal Primacy," 43, n. 2 and *Short History of the Papacy*, 10.
40. On Siricius, see Kelly, *Oxford Dictionary of Popes*, 35–36 and Chadwick, *Church in Ancient Society*, 325–28; for Himerius of Tarragona, see Mary Augusta Ward, "Himerius (3)" in Smith and Wace, eds., *Dictionary of Christian Biography*, 3:83–84.

as the bishop of Rome he had a responsibility to bear "the burdens of all who are heavily laden," though actually it was "the blessed Apostle Peter [who] bears them" in Siricius. Moreover, the bishop of Rome stated his belief that Peter "protects and watches his heir (*haeredes*) in all the cares of his office," an allusion to Paul's words of apostolic care in 2 Corinthians 11:28.[41] In this letter there is also the assertion that in the person of each bishop of Rome, who is now said to be the heir (*haeres*) of Peter, the apostle continues to lead the church.[42] Here then we have a fairly distinct claim to Roman primacy. It is also noteworthy that this letter is modeled after imperial decrees: in it Siricius gives instructions as to various practical issues and problems. In time, these decretals, as they would come to be known, would amount to a sizable body of "case law."[43]

Along with the claim of historical succession to Peter was the argument that the bishop of Rome had been granted the juridical powers of the apostle to bind and to loose according to Matthew 16:18–19.[44] One sees this authority in a letter of Innocent I (401–417) to Decentius of Gubbio, written in 416:

> Who is unaware or does not observe that what was handed down to the Roman church by the Prince of the Apostles, Peter, and is still kept up to now, must be observed by all; further, that nothing is to be brought in or introduced which does not have authority or seems to have other origins? This is even more obvious when you realize that no church was ever founded in all of Italy, Gaul, Spain, Africa, Sicily or any of the islands unless the venerable Apostle Peter or his successors appointed bishops for them. See if, in any of these provinces, there is any mention of another

---

41. Siricius, *Letter to Himerius of Tarragona* 1.1 (*Patrologia Latina* 13.1133A), trans. Robert B. Eno, *Teaching Authority in the Early Church*, Message of the Fathers of the Church, v. 14 (Wilmington, DE: Michael Glazier, 1984), 154.
42. Eno, *Teaching Authority in the Early Church*, 153. According to Walter Ullmann, this is the first occasion when a bishop of Rome described himself as an heir of Peter: "Leo I and the Theme of Papal Primacy," 30–31.
43. Robert Louis Wilken, *The First Thousand Years: A Global History of Christianity* (New Haven, CT/ London: Yale University Press, 2012), 167–68.
44. Chadwick, *Early Church*, 239–40.

> Apostle teaching there or even being there. If they do not
> discover any, as indeed they cannot, then they must follow
> the practice of the church of Rome. . . .[45]

According to this theoretical reflection by Innocent, all of the churches in the Western Roman Empire ultimately trace their origins to Rome, and as such, must conform in both teaching and praxis to the pattern in the Roman church. In actual practice, however, Roman episcopal jurisdiction was limited to disciplinary matters in a number of the western provinces such as Gaul and Spain, and definitely did not include North Africa, as Innocent's successor Zosimus (417–418) would discover.[46]

During the latter years of Innocent's episcopate, the mid-410s, the teaching of a British monk, Pelagius (375/380–423/429), had become a major issue of controversy. He argued that the human will was sufficiently free to obey God and his commands without the aid of divine grace and therefore a person was potentially able to lead a sinless life.[47] In the words of J. N. L. Myres, Pelagianism encouraged an "attitude of self-reliance" and emphasized "the saving quality of a virtuous life."[48] Innocent had formally condemned this perspective on the Christian faith. Zosimus, however, came close to reversing his predecessor's condemnation of Pelagius as he was deeply impressed by the moral seriousness of the Pelagians and their profound respect for his authority as the bishop of Rome. Having held a synod in Rome to discuss the matter of Pelagianism, in September 417, Zosimus informed the African bishops—including the man who would become Pelagius' main opponent, Augustine (354–430)—that their view of Pelagius did not accord with reality. If Pelagius were judged on the basis of what had been at the heart of the main theological controversies in the previous century, namely, the doctrine of the Trinity, he must be regarded as

---

45. Innocent I, *Letter to Decentius of Gubbio* (*Patrologia Latina* 20.552A–B), trans. Eno, *Teaching Authority in the Early Church*, 155.

46. B. Studer, "Papacy" in Angelo Di Berardino, ed., *Encyclopedia of the Early Church*, trans. Adrian Walford (New York: Oxford University Press, 1992), 2:461, cols.1–2.

47. Gerald Bonner, "Pelagianism" in Trevor A. Hart *et al.*, eds., *The Dictionary of Historical Theology* (Grand Rapids: Eerdmans, 2000), 422–24.

48. "Pelagius and the End of Roman Rule in Britain," *The Journal of Roman Studies* 50 (1960): 28–29.

orthodox. The African bishops were outraged and informed Zosimus that Innocent I's ruling must be upheld. They sent Alypius of Thagaste (died *c.*430), a close friend of Augustine, to plead their position with imperial authorities at Ravenna. The upshot of Alypius' trip was an imperial edict issued at the end of April 418 by the Western Roman Emperor Honorius (384–423) banishing the Pelagians from Rome as a threat to civic and ecclesial peace.[49]

Humiliated by these events, Zosimus eventually wrote the African bishops to reassure them that he had no intention of reversing Innocent's condemnation of the Pelagians.[50] But he was obviously deeply disturbed by the Africans' "lack of docility" and that they were not fully on board with the understanding of the Roman see that had been developing in Rome since Damasus.[51] He thus took the opportunity to reaffirm his authority as the bishop of Rome. Here is the relevant portion of that letter written in 418:

> The tradition of the Fathers attributed such great authority (*auctoritatem tantam*) to the Apostolic see that no one would dare dispute its judgment and has preserved this for all time by canonical rules. Up to the present, through these laws, ecclesiastical discipline gives due honor to the name of Peter from whom it also derives. The ancient canons assigned this great power to the Apostle from the very promise of Christ our God so that he might loose what was bound and bind what had not been bound. A like condition of power has been given to those who have merited the inheritance of this see with his assent.
>
> For he has, along with the care of all the churches, above all the care of this see where he sat. He permits no wavering of its privileges or its teachings because he has made its foundations firm by his name. It cannot be shaken; no one may assault it except at his own peril. Since therefore Pe-

---

49. Chadwick, *Church in Ancient Society*, 456–58.
50. For a discussion of these events, see Ullmann, "Leo I and the Theme of Papal Primacy," 32–33; Chadwick, *Early Church*, 230; Green, *Soteriology of Leo the Great*, 17–18.
51. The words of "lack of docility" are Chadwick's; see his *Church in Ancient Society*, 457.

ter is the source of such great authority (*tantae auctorita-tis*), he has confirmed the zeal of all our predecessors who came after him so that the Roman church is strengthened by all laws and discipline both human and divine. . . . So great is our authority that no one can reconsider our decision (*tamen cum tantum nobis esset auctoritatis, ut nullus de nostra possit retractare sententia*).[52]

As Walter Ullmann has pointed out, this letter marks a key step forward on the road to the papacy.[53] The episcopal power of the bishop of Rome—the phrase "such great authority" occurring no less than three times in this short text—stems ultimately from the apostle Peter, which he derives from Christ's promise to him in Matthew 16:16–18 to "loose what was bound and bind what had not been bound." Such juristic power comes to the bishop of Rome since he is the heir of Peter—it being understood that Peter founded the church at Rome—and since in Roman law there is a "juristic continuity between the deceased and the heir," Peter is still living, acting, and exercising solicitude in the person of the bishop. What this entails is this: due to the "Petrinity" of the apostolic see of Rome, no one can question decisions made by its holder.[54]

Leo (d. 461)

Zosimus' letter was taken to North Africa by an acolyte named Leo, who is most probably the Leo I (440–461) who became the bishop of Rome twenty-two years later.[55] Remembered for his important Christological contribution to the Council of Chalcedon and his saving Rome from the ravages of Attila and the Huns, Leo also drew together the assertions of his predecessors about the bishopric of Rome and through

---

52. Zosimus, *Letter 12 to Aurelius of Carthage* (*Patrologia Latina* 20.676A–B), trans. Eno, *Teaching Authority in the Early Church*, 156–57, altered.
53. Ullmann, "Leo I and the Theme of Papal Primacy," 32–33.
54. For the neologism "Petrinity," see Ullmann, *Short History of the Papacy*, 15.
55. Green, *Soteriology of Leo the Great*, 18–19, n. 72. For Leo's thought and career, see especially T. G. Jalland, *The Life and Times of St. Leo the Great* (London: SPCK, 1941); Philip A. McShane, *La Romanitas et le pape Léon le Grand* (Tournai: Desclée, 1979); Susan Wessel, *Leo the Great and the Spiritual Rebuilding of a Universal Rome* (Leiden/Boston: E. J. Brill, 2008); Bronwen Neil, *Leo the Great* (London/New York: Routledge, 2009).

the exegesis of a number of familiar Petrine texts created the theoretical foundations of the medieval papacy.[56] In a sermon that he preached on the third anniversary of his election as bishop, he exegeted Matthew 16:16–19 thus:

> When . . . the Lord had asked the disciples whom they believed him to be amid the various opinions that were held, and the blessed Peter had replied, saying, "You are the Christ, the Son of the living God," the Lord says, "Blessed are you, Simon Bar-Jona, because flesh and flood has not revealed this to you, but my Father, who is in heaven. And I say to thee, you are Peter, and upon this rock I will build my church, and the gates of Hades shall not prevail against it. And I will give you the keys of the kingdom of heaven. And whatever you will have bound on earth, shall be bound in heaven; and whatever you shall loose on earth, shall be loosed also in heaven."

> The dispensation of truth therefore abides, and the blessed Peter persevering in the strength of the rock, which he has received, has not abandoned the helm of the Church, which he undertook to control. For he was ordained before the rest in such a way that from his being called the Rock, from his being pronounced the Foundation, from his being constituted the Doorkeeper of the kingdom of heaven (*regni coelorum janitor*), from his authority as the Umpire to bind and to loose, whose judgments shall retain their validity in heaven—from all these mystical titles we might know the nature of his association with Christ. And still to-day he more fully and effectually performs what is entrusted to him, and carries out every part of his duty and charge in him and with him, through whom he has been glorified. And so if anything is rightly done and rightly decreed by us, if anything

---

56. Here I follow Walter Ullmann, "Leo I and the Theme of Papal Primacy"; William Dennis Lindsey, "Christology and Roman Primacy at Chalcedon," *Toronto Journal of Theology* 1 (1985): 37–38; Wessel, *Leo the Great*, 285–321.

is won from the mercy of God by our daily supplications, it is of his work and merits whose power lives and whose authority prevails in his see. For this, dearly-beloved, was gained by that confession, which, inspired in the Apostle's heart by God the Father, transcended all the uncertainty of human opinions, and was endued with the firmness of a rock, which no assaults could shake.[57]

According to Leo's reading of Matthew 16:16–19, Peter's faith in declaring Jesus to be the Messiah merited his being appointed the foundation of the church, the doorkeeper of the kingdom of heaven and the judge whose earthly decisions are guaranteed heavenly confirmation. Critical to Leo's application of Matthew 16 is the Roman law of inheritance, which made its appearance in Zosimus' letter to the African bishops cited above. According to this legal perspective, a true heir replaces the deceased person, stepping into their shoes, as it were, and inheriting not only their possessions and wealth, or debts, but also taking over their responsibilities and duties in society. As Ullmann puts it: "Legally . . . there is no difference between the heir and the deceased: the latter is literally continued in the former."[58] It is obvious that Leo had this Roman understanding of inheritance in mind when he emphasized that Peter's ministry was still ongoing. It was such because he lived and acted through his heir, the bishop of Rome.[59] As Leo declared in a sermon preached two years later: "not only the apostolic but also the episcopal dignity of blessed Peter . . . has not ceased to preside over his see . . . for the solidity which he, having been made Peter the rock, received from Christ the rock, he has passed on to his heirs."[60]

So as to defend his right of primacy over all other bishops, Leo also

---

57. Leo, *Sermon* 3.2–3 (*Patrologia Latina* 54.146A–C), trans. C. L. Feltoe in Philip Schaff and Henry Wace, eds., *A Select Library of Nicene and Post-Nicene Fathers*, 2nd series (1895 ed.; repr. Edinburgh: T&T Clark; Grand Rapids: Eerdmans, 1997), 12:117, cols.1–2, modernized and slightly altered.

58. "Leo I and the Theme of Papal Primacy," 34.

59. A little later in the sermon Leo describes himself as "an unworthy heir (*indigno haerede*)" (*Sermon* 3.4 [*Patrologia Latina* 54.147A]). On this term, see Ullmann, "Leo I and the Theme of Papal Primacy," 34–36; Michael M. Winter, *Saint Peter and the Popes* (London: Darton, Longman and Todd; Baltimore: Helicon Press, 1960), 179.

60. *Sermon* 5.4 (*Patrologia Latina* 54.155A), trans. Eno, *Teaching Authority in the Early Church*, 162, altered.

emphasized that Peter's primacy was exercised even during the lifetime of the other apostles. Taking his cue from Luke 22:31–32, he argued:

> As his passion drew near, an event that was going to shake the fidelity of his disciples, the Lord said, "Simon, Simon, Satan has asked for you, to sift you like wheat. But I have prayed for you, that your faith may never fail. You in turn must strengthen your brothers, lest you enter into temptation." The danger from the temptation to fear was common to all the Apostles and all had equal need of the aid of divine protection since the Devil wished to upset them all and cause them to fall.

> And yet the Lord shows a special care for Peter and prays in particular for the faith of Peter, as if the future situation would be more secure for the others if the spirit of the leader remained unconquered. Thus in Peter the courage of all is fortified and the aid of divine grace is so arranged that the strength which comes to Peter through Christ, through Peter is transmitted to the Apostles.[61]

As Leo reads the Lukan text, he asks, "What does this passage say about Peter's authority among the apostolic band?" The answer seems obvious: just as the grace of fortitude at the time of the passion of the Lord Jesus came from Christ to the apostles through Peter, so it was the apostles derived their authority not directly from the Lord, but from him by means of Peter. If Peter had such a primacy among the apostles, should not his heir, the bishop of Rome, hold such a primacy among his fellow bishops? For Leo all ecclesial power ultimately stems from the heir of Peter.[62] As he put it quite plainly: "Through Peter, the holy prince of the apostles, the Roman Church possesses the sovereignty over all the churches in the whole world."[63] With such far-reaching claims for papal authority, it is no surprise that Leo's words to his fellow

---

61. *Sermon* 4.3 (*Patrologia Latina* 54.151B–152A), trans. Eno, *Teaching Authority in the Early Church*, 161–62, altered.
62. Ullmann, "Leo I and the Theme of Papal Primacy," 44.
63. Leo, *Letter* 65.2 (*Patrologia Latina* 54.881B).

bishops are so frequently terms of governance and obedience to the statues issued by the apostolic see.[64] In essence, Leo has established that communion with Rome is a necessary condition for communion with Christ and God.

Two Other Historical Reasons for the Development of the Papacy

There were two other critical reasons, non-theological ones, for the emergence of the papacy. The total collapse of Roman rule in Western Europe removed the Church of Rome from its patristic context and its vital relationship with other ancient Christian centers like Alexandria, Antioch, and Constantinople that rejected the claim of Rome's primacy. Then, the advent of Islam in the seventh century and the loss of North Africa to the Christian world further isolated the Church of Rome, on the one hand, and, on the other, enabled her to argue her claims with more vehemence as she was now the mother church for so much of Europe.[65] North Africa had been a principal source of spiritual and intellectual vitality in the Latin-speaking western church and was, in R. A. Markus' words, "the only area in the western church which could look Rome in the face."[66] If neither of these events had taken place, it is extremely doubtful if Rome's claims for universal obedience to her bishop could have succeeded to any extent at all. But these events did happen—and down to the present-day there have been and are multitudes for whom the Pope was and is the "blessed gatekeeper of heaven,"[67] to use words that Hilary of Poitiers (*c.*315–367/368) once used to describe the apostle Peter.

Postscript: An Evangelical Reflection

Roman Catholic historiography often regards the development of the papacy detailed above as being providentially ordered. Thus, John Rist, though very conscious of the failings of the papal theocracy of

---

64. Ullmann, "Leo I and the Theme of Papal Primacy," 25.
65. Markus, "Papacy and Hierarchy," 21–25.
66. Ibid., 22–23.
67. *Commentary on Matthew* 16.7 (*Patrologia Latina* 9.1010A).

the Middle Ages, has argued that the development of the papacy was essential to "the maintenance of theological purity" as well as for "the possibility of an expanding culture which in all its ramifications was to remain Catholic, that is, universal."[68] R. A. Markus (1924–2010), a Roman Catholic layman, however, regarded the development of the papacy in late Antiquity as fraught with problems. Writing in the wake of Vatican II, he emphasized that the dominant idea of Christian ministry during its early centuries was "loving service rendered to the community of believers." Markus stressed that among the early Fathers, Augustine definitely knew this. As the North African bishop reminded his congregation on the anniversary of his ordination: "For you, I am a bishop; with you I am a Christian. The former is the name of an office undertaken, the latter, a name of grace; the former means danger, the latter salvation."[69] Like Cassian, who was cited at the outset of this essay, Augustine was well aware of the dangers of episcopal office; yet, he deemed such an office as necessary for the good of the church. Markus stressed, however, that this concept of ministry was overlaid by another concept in the patristic era, namely, that of hierarchy: the bishop was *over* the rest of the Christian community, and in the case of the bishop of Rome, he was over the entirety of the episcopate. In this idea of ministry, the bishop became a mediatorial figure and the conduit of God's grace to the community, an idea clearly seen in Leo I's exegesis of Luke 22:31–32.[70] Markus wanted to differentiate between the papacy in late antiquity, where the biblical concept of ministry as service has not been completely lost, and the later medieval institution, where one has a full-blown papal monarchy or theocracy and "obedience has become the fundamental ecclesiastical virtue."[71] But, the roots of the papal monarchy of the Middle Ages lie clearly in the soil of the papal primacy worked out by the bishops of Rome from Damasus to Leo I. One cannot have the former without the latter, and the latter was rooted in distinct historical circumstance and tendentious exegesis.

---

68. *What Is Truth?*, 232, 254–257 (quote from page 232).
69. *Sermon* 340.1 (PL39.1483), trans. Michael A. G. Haykin. Cited in Markus, "Papacy and Hierarchy," 4. As Ray van Neste has noted, this whole sermon is "a beautiful portrait of pastoral ministry" (*Oversight of Souls* [http://rayvanneste.com/?p=1434; accessed December 16, 2013]).
70. See Markus, "Papacy and Hierarchy," 6–13, 26–28.
71. See ibid., 26–37 (quote from page 37).

Leadership is indeed critical for the *esse* of the church, as is apparent from a quick overview of the earliest of Christian texts, the letters of the apostle Paul. In Paul's letter to the Galatians, for instance, the earliest book in the New Testament next to James' letter, Paul states that the "one who is taught the word must share all good things with the one who teaches" (Gal. 6:6). Again, in 1 Thessalonians, also a very early text, Paul encourages his readers: "We ask you, brothers, to respect those who labor among you and are over you in the Lord and admonish you" (1 Thess. 5:12). And in Philippians 1:1, Paul and Timothy greet not only "all the saints in Christ Jesus who are at Philippi," but also the "overseers and deacons." The key question for the early Christians was not whether they should have leaders or not. Leadership was a given. Rather, the key questions were: What model of leadership was to be promoted? And how should the church relate to her leaders? Standing in the tradition of Puritanism and eighteenth-century Evangelical Nonconformity, which respectfully listened to the Fathers but refused to read the New Testament solely through their colored spectacles, I heartily affirm what P. T. Forsyth once said about the confidence of that tradition: "Out of village Bethels God is always, by the word of his Gospel, raising up children to Abraham and successors to Peter and Paul, though bishops be ignorant of them and priests acknowledge them not."[72]

---

72. *The Church and the Sacraments*, 3rd ed. (London: Independent Press, 1949), 46. The phrase "colored spectacles" comes from Forsyth on the same page. "Bethel" was a favorite name for many eighteenth-and nineteenth-century Nonconformist chapels.

CHAPTER 6

The Papacy from Leo I to Vatican II

Gregg R. Allison[1]

A s recounted by in the preceding chapter, the position of the
bishop of Rome gained increasing importance during the first
four centuries of the Christian church. This elevation of the Roman
bishopric was due to several factors, including the development of the
monoepiscopalian church government structure, accompanied by the
emergence of the authority of the bishops of the five key cities of Christendom (Jerusalem, Antioch, Alexandria, Constantinople, and Rome);
the importance of Rome as a political and commercial city, especially
as the rise of Constantinople as the new (Eastern) capital of the Roman
Empire created a power vacuum in the Western part of the Empire; the
consistent orthodoxy of the Roman bishops, attended by the increasingly important role they played in the doctrinal controversies of the
fourth and fifth centuries; the tradition of Peter's burial in Rome; and a
biblical argument focusing on the incipient idea of an inchoate papacy
in Matthew 16:13–20.

With this religious and cultural background, I will trace the development of the papacy from Leo I, also known as Leo the Great, to Vatican
Council II, with a brief treatment of the post-conciliar popes up to the
current Pope Benedict XVI. Given space limitations, this survey will necessarily be brief, highlighting only the major people, events, and writings.
It should also be duly noted that I will not present a history of the Catholic Church in general but will focus on the development of the papacy

---

1. Gregg R. Allison (PhD, Trinity Evangelical Divinity School) is professor of Christian Theology at The Southern Baptist Theological Seminary in Louisville, Kentucky.

in particular. This account, which will surely be discouraging for many readers because of the moral corruption, spiritual bankruptcy, worldly kingdom-building, and the like of these leaders of the church, necessarily must leave untold the progress of the gospel and the advancement of the faith among common Christians and even lower-level shepherds of the church. At the conclusion of the chapter, I will offer applications for church leadership for evangelical churches today.[2]

THE PAPACY FROM THE FIFTH THROUGH THE NINTH CENTURY

Leo I, Roman bishop from 440 to 461, elevated the apostle Peter to a position of great height, thereby increasing the authority of the Church of Rome. Ever since the heated debate (254–256) over ultimate church authority between Stephen, bishop of Rome, and Cyprian, bishop of Carthage (North Africa), appeal was made to the important text of Matthew 16:13–20. Upon Peter's confession of the identity of Jesus— "You are the Christ, the Son of the Living God" (v. 16)—the One confessed made the following promise: "And I tell you, you are Peter, and on this rock I will build my church, and the gates of hell shall not prevail against it. I will give you the keys of the kingdom of heaven, and whatever you bind on earth shall be bound in heaven, and whatever you loose on earth shall be loosed in heaven" (vv. 18–19). Stephen claimed this text supported the notion that the bishop of Rome—represented in this text by Peter—exercised ultimate authority. By way of contrast, Cyprian claimed the passage supported his position that all of the bishops of the church—represented in this text by the twelve apostles (v. 13)—were equal in authority.[3]

Advancing two centuries, the bishop of Rome, Leo I, argued from this text that the apostle Peter is the key to everything that Christ does in his church:

---

2. Several books on the history of the papacy have served as the foundation for this chapter and provide excellent resources for further study of the topic: Eamon Duffy, *Saints and Sinners: A History of the Popes*, 3rd ed. (New Haven, CT: Yale University Press, 2006); J. N. D. Kelly, *The Oxford Dictionary of the Popes* (Oxford and New York: Oxford University Press, 1986).

3. Cyprian, *Treatise* 1.4 "On the Unity of the Church" (*ANF* 5:422); *Letter* 51.21(*ANF* 5:332); *Letter* 71.3 (*ANF* 5:379); *Letter* 70.3 (*ANF* 5:377).

The most blessed apostle Peter was watered with very abundant streams from the very fountain of all graces that, while nothing has passed to others without his participation, yet he received many special privileges of his own. Out of the whole world, one—Peter—is chosen. He presided both at the call of the Gentiles and over all the apostles and collected fathers of the church. Thus, though there are many priests and many shepherds among God's people, still Peter especially rules all whom Christ also originally rules. It is a great and wonderful sharing of his own power that the divine honor gave to this man, and—if he wished that other rulers should be in common with him—yet he never gave except through him what he did not deny to others.[4]

The singular power and authority granted to Peter thus became a point of focus. Specifically, Peter was the one through whom Christ transferred his authority to the apostles. As Leo commented on Matthew 16:19: "'I will give you the keys . . . loosed in heaven.' The right of this power did indeed pass on to the other apostles, and the order of this decree passed on to all the chiefs of the church. But it was not in vain that what was imparted to all was entrusted to one. In Peter the strength of all is fortified, and the help of divine grace is so ordered that the stability that is given to Peter through Christ is conveyed to the apostles through Peter."[5] Moreover, Peter continues to exercise this mediating role in the church through the bishop of Rome:

There is a further reason for our celebration—not only the apostolic but also the episcopal dignity of the most blessed Peter, who does not cease to preside over his See [the administrative center, Rome] and obtains an abiding partnership with the eternal priest. For the stability that the rock himself was given by that Rock—Christ—he also

---

4. Leo the Great, *Sermon* 4, 2, in *Documents Illustrating Papal Authority*, ed. E. Giles (London: SPCK, 1952), 279.
5. Ibid., 4, 3, in Giles, *Documents Illustrating Papal Authority*, 279.

conveyed to his successors [the bishops of Rome]. Who
so ignorantly or grudgingly estimate the honor of blessed
Peter as not to believe that all parts of the church are ruled
by his care and enriched by his help?[6]

Leo I advocated the ongoing supremacy of Peter expressed through
his successors, the Roman bishops.[7]

Gelasius, bishop of Rome from 492 to 496, was the first to be referred to as "the vicar of Christ," meaning that the bishop of Rome
stands in the place of Christ as his earthly representative. As a tangible
expression of such responsibility, Gelasius claimed that the decisions
of the general or ecumenical councils of the church (of which up to
this point there had been four—Nicea, Constantinople I, Ephesus, and
Chalcedon) receive their authority from the bishop of Rome.

Importantly, Gelasius formulated the relationship between ecclesiastical authority and imperial authority in a letter to Emperor Anastasius. At
stake was the extent of the authority of the state in relation to the church:

There are two powers by which this world is chiefly ruled,
that is, the sacred authority of priests and the power of
kings. Of these, the responsibility of the priests is the
weightier in that in the divine judgment, they will have
to give an account even for kings. For you know, most
dear son [the Emperor Anastasius], that you are permitted
rightly to rule the human race, yet in divine matters you
devoutly bow your head before the principal clergy and
ask of them the means of salvation. . . . In these matters, as
you know, you are dependent on their judgment, and you
have no desire to compel them to do your will.[8]

---

6. Ibid., 5, 4, in Giles, *Documents Illustrating Papal Authority*, 282.
7. A source of friction for Leo I was the Council of Chalcedon's decision, enshrined in Canon
   28, granting equal status to Constantinople and Rome and thus to the bishops of the respective churches in those two imperial cities. Leo dissented from this decision, justifying
   his opposition by appealing to Canons 6 and 7 of the Council of Nicea, which officially
   acknowledged the patriarchies of Alexandria (Egypt), Antioch, Rome, and Jerusalem, with
   no mention of Constantinople.
8. Gelasius, *To the Emperor Anastasius*, in *The Church: Its Changing Image Through Twenty
   Centuries*, vol. 1: *The First Seventeen Centuries*, ed. Eric G. Jay (London: SPCK, 1977), 98.

To this affirmation of the authority of the clergy, Gelasius appended his view of the authority of the Church of Rome: "And if it is proper that the hearts of the faithful are in submission to all priests everywhere who exercise their divine ministry aright, how much more is obedience to be given to the bishop of that See [the administrative center, Rome] whom the most high God willed to be preeminent over all other bishops?"[9] Again, Gelasius contributed to the growing preeminence of the Church of Rome and its bishops.

Theologically, the bishop of Rome grew in importance; two examples will suffice. Regressing for the moment to Leo I, this Roman bishop played a decisive role in the development of what came to be called Chalcedonian Christology. In his *Tome* (June 13, 449), Leo affirmed that the Son of God was equal in all ways—eternity, power, glory, and essence—to God the Father. In the incarnation the Son of God took on human nature, resulting in one person with two natures:

> Thus the properties of each nature and substance were preserved entire, and came together to form one person . . . true God in the entire and perfect nature of true man, complete in his own properties, complete in ours.[10]

Through his *Tome*, Leo paved the way for the Chalcedonian Creed, which echoed the bishop's theological formulation in affirming "our Lord Jesus Christ, at once complete in Godhead and complete in manhood, truly God and truly man, consisting also of a reasonable soul and body; of one substance with the Father as regards his Godhead, and at the same time of one substance with us as regards his manhood; like us in all respects, apart from sin."[11] Furthermore, the Chalcedonian Creed explicitly denounced the heresies of Apollinarianism, Nestorianism, and Eutychianism. This theological precision and fight against heresy underscored the orthodoxy of the bishop of Rome and contributed to the developing importance of that office.

---

9. Ibid.
10. Leo I, "The Tome of Leo," in *Documents of the Christian Church*, 3rd and new ed., ed. Henry Bettenson and Chris Maunder (Oxford/New York: Oxford University Press, 1999), 54–55.
11. "The Definition of Chalcedon," in Bettenson, *Documents of the Christian Church*, 56.

A second example of the growing theological influence of the bishop of Rome is Hormisdas, (514–523). Confronting the anti-Chalcedonian theology of many church leaders in the Eastern part of the Roman Empire—a theological position that had incurred the excommunication of Acacius, the Patriarch of Constantinople, resulting in the thirty-five-year Acaian schism (484–519) between the church in the East and the church in the West—Hormisdas rallied the support of the pro-Chalcedonian emperor Justin I (518–527). The "Formula of Hormisdas" set forth the abiding theological orthodoxy of the Church of Rome, tied it to Jesus' promise to Peter, and established the Roman bishop as the one who is responsible to condemn heresies:

> The first condition of salvation is to keep the norm of the true faith and in no way to deviate from the established doctrine of the Fathers. For it is impossible that the words of our Lord Jesus Christ, who said, "You are Peter, and upon this rock I will build my Church" [Matthew 16:18], should not be verified. And their truth has been proved by the course of history, for in the apostolic See [the administrative center, Rome] the catholic religion has always been kept unsullied. From this hope and faith we by no means desire to be separated and, following the doctrine of the Fathers, we declare anathema all heresies. . . .[12]

This "Formula of Hormisdas" was signed by both Emperor Justin and the Patriarch of Constantinople, along with two hundred Eastern bishops, thus ending the Acacian schism and underscoring submission to the theologically orthodox bishop of Rome.[13] The "Formula" would become an important consideration in later discussions and promulgation of the doctrine of papal infallibility.[14]

---

12. This affirmation is followed by a list of heretics condemned by Rome, including Nestorius, Eutychus, and Acacius.
13. When Hormisdas's successor, John I, travelled to Constantinople, he was warmly received by Emperor Justin and accorded higher honor than the Patriarch of Constantinople. A later pope, Agapitus (535–536), succeeded in securing the excommunication of his contemporary Anthimus, Patriarch of Constantinople, on the grounds that he was heretical. In the Patriarch's place, Agapitus consecrated Menas (536–552), who affirmed the Formula of Hormisdas.
14. See later discussion.

Such affirmation of the theological robustness of the bishop of Rome must be tempered by other realities, as exemplified by Pope Vigilius (537–555). More or less a pawn of the Empress Theodora,[15] who had promised him the bishopric if he would denounce the Council of Chalcedon, Vigilius was forced by pressure from Emperor Justinian to condemn the so-called "Three Chapters." This theological document, which denounced the person and writings of Theodore of Mopsuestia and certain writings of Theodoret of Cyrrhus and Ibas of Edessa, was a blatant attempt on the part of Justinian to appease the anti-Chalcedonian Eastern church leaders. By denouncing these three theologians, who appeared to the Eastern bishops as egregiously affirming the heresy of Nestorianism, the Emperor hoped to bring back the East into unity with the West. Vigilius wrote his *Iudicatum* (*Verdict*) condemning the "Three Chapters" without prejudice to the Council of Chalcedon, but this compromise was rejected by many bishops of the West, leading to their excommunication of him. Retracting his *Iudicatum*, a move that brought reconciliation with the Western clergy, Vigilius fell into disfavor with Justinian. The proposed way out of this catastrophe was the convening of the fifth general council, the Council of Constantinople II (553), which condemned the "Three Chapters." Under house arrest, Vigilius was forced to (1) retract his earlier support of the "Three Chapters" and (2) affirm the council's condemnation of it. While mitigating factors must be considered as strongly influencing the Roman bishop in this matter, Vigilius's wavering on the issue was disconcerting. The bishop of Rome's reputation was sullied.

During the tenure of Gregory I, also known as Gregory the Great, as bishop of Rome (590–604), the term "pope" was applied exclusively to the Roman bishop. Gregory himself argued that the bishop of Rome exercised supreme authority in the church throughout the world: "Certainly Peter, the first of the apostles, himself a member of the holy and universal church, Paul, Andrew, John—what were they but heads of particular communities? . . . Was it not the case . . . that the leaders of this apostolic See [the administrative center, Rome], which by the providence of God I serve, had the honor offered them of being called universal by the

---

15. The Empress was known for her sexual immorality and support of monophysitism (see later discussion).

venerable Council of Chalcedon?"[16] Furthermore, according to Gregory, "without the authority and the consent of the apostolic See, nothing that might be passed [by a church council] would have any [binding] force."[17]

Such declarations were particularly targeted against the continuing and often disruptive influence of the bishop of Constantinople, whose title "ecumenical [or universal] patriarch" was a constant sore spot with Gregory. Ever since Canon 28 of the Council of Chalcedon had granted equal privileges to the Church of Constantinople and the Church of Rome, bishops of Rome had chaffed under this decision and even considered it invalid. Following in this line of protest, Gregory argued that the Church of Constantinople, like all the other churches in the world, was subject to Rome. Indeed, Gregory complained to the bishops of Alexandria and Antioch about the use of the title:

> This name of "universality" [i.e., as it appears in the title "universal [ecumenical) patriarch"] was offered by the holy synod of Chalcedon to the pontiff of the apostolic See [the administrative center, Rome] which by the providence of God I serve. But no one of my predecessors has ever consented to use this so profane a title because, consequently, if one patriarch is called "universal," the name of patriarch in the case of the rest is derogated [disparaged]. . . . Therefore let not your Holiness in your letters ever call anyone "universal," lest you detract from the honor due to yourself in offering to another what is not due.[18]

At the same time, Gregory seemed to envision papal authority as being distributed in three locations—Rome, Alexandria, and Antioch (but not Constantinople)—as he wrote to Eulogius, bishop of Alexandria, explaining the "chair of Saint Peter":

> For who can be ignorant that holy church has been made firm in the solidity of the prince of the apostles, who de-

---

16. Gregory the Great, *Book 5, Letter* 18 (*NPNF²* 12:167).
17. Gregory the Great, *Book 9, Letter* 68 (*NPNF²* 13:19).
18. Gregory the Great, *Book 5, Letter* 43 (*NPNF²* 12:179). The text has been rendered clearer.

rived his name from the firmness of his mind, so as to be called *Petrus* from *petra* [adapted from "you are *Peter*, and on this *rock*" (Matt. 16:18). And to him it is said by the voice of the Truth [Jesus], "To you I will give the keys of the kingdom of heaven" [Matt. 16:19]. . . . Therefore, though there are many apostles, yet with regard to the principality itself, the See [the administrative center, Rome] of the prince of the apostles alone has grown strong in authority, which in three places is the See of one. . . . Since then it is the See of one, and one See, over which by divine authority three bishops now preside, whatever good I hear of you, this I impute to myself.[19]

Accordingly, it appears that Gregory's main point of contention was the overextended reach of the Church of Constantinople, which threatened the primacy of the "Petrine" church (which included Rome, Alexandria, and Antioch). Such a development could not be permitted, for biblical and historical reasons (even if Canon 28 of the Council of Chalcedon had erroneously ascribed an equal place of honor to the Church of Constantinople).[20] Because of this development, the Roman church became increasingly characterized by its hierarchical structure with the bishop of Rome—now called the "pope"—at the top of its government.

Gregory used his authority in benevolent ways. For example, he utilized the vast property holdings of the Church of Rome (to which he himself, as part of a very wealthy family that owned vast estates in Italy and Sicily, contributed) to feed the poor through a well-organized welfare system competently run by the church rather than the state. Additionally, probably prompted by the sight of young Anglo-Saxon slave boys in Rome (when they were identified as *Angles*, Gregory rejoined, "they are *angels* of God"), he commissioned a group of forty monks, led by Augustine (not the bishop of Hippo from an earlier time), to evangelize Britain, an endeavor that constituted the first missional out-

---

19. Gregory the Great, *Book 7, Letter* 40 (*NPNF*[2] 12:228–29). The text has been rendered clearer.
20. It appears that Gregory disparaged this Canon in his letter to Count Narses, in which he opined, "the synod of Chalcedon was in one place falsified by the Constantinopolitan Church" (Gregory the Great, *Book 6, Letter* 14[*NPNF*[2] 12:192]).

reach to pagan lands beyond the Roman Empire (Britain had been lost to the Empire, of which it had formerly been a part). The fruit of this initial missionary foray would increase over the next centuries, as English missionaries would export the gospel to northern Europe. Furthermore, Gregory was the first monk to be elected as pope. His encouragement of monasticism, together with his employment of monks as his advisors, elevated monasticism to a level of great importance in the church and set a trajectory of its highest leaders being taken from the monastic ranks in the upcoming centuries. Indeed, monasticism would become one of the chief characteristics of the church and its hierarchy.

Pope Honorius I (625–638) continued Gregory's trend of appointing monks as his associates and furthered the missionary endeavors in Britain, which included the conversion of Edwin of Northumbria (627) and the commissioning of Birinus for the mission to the West Saxons. Importantly, Honorius took an improper theological position in the ongoing debate about the nature(s) of the incarnate Son of God. Honorius sided with monophysitism (Gr. μονο, *mono* = one; φυσις, *physis* = nature), affirming the description of Christ as possessing "two distinct natures but one operation,"[21] which meant that the incarnate Son had only one will (thus, technically, Honorius affirmed monothelitism (Gr. μονο, *mono* = one; θελημα, *thelēma* = will), an offshoot of monophysitism. Though Honorius was dead when the sixth general council of the church, the Council of Constantinople III (680–681), was convened, it declared him a heretic, anathematizing his "one will" perspective and affirming instead that the incarnate Christ possessed two wills (dyothelitism; Gr. δυο, *dyo* = two; θελημα, *thelēma* = will), the one being the divine will of the eternal Son, the other being the human will of the man Jesus of Nazareth. This anathema was ratified by Leo II (682–683), thus creating the embarrassing situation of one pope condemning another pope. Its specter would come to haunt the Catholic Church after the Protestant Reformation and especially when the dogma of paper infallibility was promulgated in the nineteenth century.

In the middle of Honorius's reign, an event seemingly far removed from the development of European Christianity took place that would have a profound impact on the church for centuries to come (and which

---

21. The proposal was put forth by Patriarch Sergius I of Constantinople.

has renewed importance for the worldwide church today). The Prophet Mohammed, whose revelations are recited in the Qur'an, died in 632, and the movement that was launched by him spread rapidly. Indeed, within ten years Islam had conquered Antioch and Alexandria, and other locations in which Christianity had originally flourished would later fall to the Arab conquerors and their religion. In less than a century, Arab armies had taken Spain and were threatening the southern part of Gaul (modern day France). Stemming the tide of this incursion into central Europe was Charles Martel, the first Frankish king of the Merovingian Dynasty, whose help was then sought by Pope Zacharias (741–752) to ward off Rome's constant threat, the barbarian tribe called the Lombards.

One of the key elements in cementing the pope's claim to ecclesial authority and predominance was a document entitled the "Donation of Constantine." In 754, Rome came under attack by the Lombards. Pope Stephen II (752–757) appealed to Pepin the Short, son of Martel and king of the Franks, to help stave off the Lombardian invasion; indeed, Stephen asked to place Rome under Pepin's protection. In response, Pepin fought to recover much of northern and central Italy from the Lombards and, having completed his conquest, he donated those lands to the pope.

But why such a move on the part of the Frankish king? Stephen presented Pepin a document written by Constantine in which the Roman Emperor had described his conversion, baptism, and miraculous healing from leprosy through the ministry of Pope Sylvester I, the bishop of Rome (314–335).[22] The document continued that, out of gratitude, Constantine had bequeathed "all provinces, palaces and districts of the city of Rome and Italy and of the regions of the West . . . as a permanent possession to the holy Roman Church," specifically to Sylvester and "to the pontiffs, his successors, who to the end of the world shall sit in the seat of blessed Peter."[23] Moreover, Constantine had decreed that the earthly, imperial authority "shall venerate and honour his most holy Roman Church and that the sacred see [the administrative center, Rome] of blessed Peter shall be

---

22. According to the Donation, the apostles Peter and Paul appeared to Constantine in a dream, instructing him how to be cleansed of his leprosy through the intervention of bishop Sylvester.
23. "The Donation of Constantine," in Bettenson, *Documents of the Christian Church*, 110, 109 [the first half of the quote is from p. 110; the continuation of it is from p. 109].

gloriously exalted above our empire and earthly throne."[24] Furthermore, the Emperor had ordained that the Church of Rome "shall have rule as well over the four principal Sees, Antioch, Alexandria, Constantinople, and Jerusalem, as also over all the churches of God in all the world."[25] Accordingly, when Pepin donated the conquered Lombardian lands to Pope Stephen, he was fulfilling the explicit terms of this imperial document. The "Donation of Constantine" paved the way for the bishop of Rome to become a powerful and extensive landowner (the future Papal States developed out of this land grant) and the single most important leader in the West. It also fortified the position of the Church of Rome with the pope at its head as supreme above all other churches.

In the fifteenth century, Lorenzo Valla, employing the discipline of textual criticism, exposed linguistic and historical errors in the writing and so proved the "Donation of Constantine" to be a forgery.[26] It had been written by someone—perhaps even Stephen himself—as the pope travelled to enlist Pepin's intervention, with the purpose of demonstrating to the Frankish king the authority of the bishop of Rome. Despite being one of the greatest forgeries of all times, the "Donation of Constantine" was one of the foundational elements in the emergence of the papacy in the eighth century.

The relationship between Pepin's son Charlemagne (Charles the Great; he assumed the Frankish kingship in 771) and Pope Hadrian I (772–795) resulted in an even closer cooperation between the Frankish kings and the Roman popes. Charlemagne confirmed the Donation of Constantine, thereby sanctioning the vast landownership of the Church of Rome, and the pope in turn provided the king with religious unity for his vastly expanding kingdom. But Charlemagne envisioned more for himself in relation to the pope, as he articulated in a letter to Hadrian's successor, Leo III (795–816):

> I desire to make with you an inviolable treaty of mutual fidelity and love; that, on the one hand, you [the pope] shall

---

24. Ibid., 109.
25. Ibid., 109.
26. Lorenzo Valla, *De falso credita et ementita Constantini donation declamatio* (Mainz, 1518). Others before Valla had recognized the document as a forgery, but it was he who demonstrated its spurious nature.

pray for me [the king] and give me the apostolic benediction, and that, on the other, with the aid of God I will ever defend the most holy See of the most holy Roman church. For it is our part to defend the holy church of Christ from the attacks of pagans and infidels from without [externally], and within [internally] to enforce the acceptance of the Catholic faith. It is your part, most holy father, to aid us in the good fight by raising your hands to God as Moses did, so that by your intercession the Christian people under the leadership of God may always and everywhere have the victory over the enemies of his holy name, and the name of the Lord Jesus Christ may be glorified throughout the world.[27]

Charlemagne clearly envisioned an asymmetrical relationship between his reign and the church's realm, claiming imperial responsibility for both the protection and expansion of the Christian faith. Despite this disproportionate vision, the relationship was formalized in Rome on Christmas Day, 800, when Pope Leo III crowned Charlemagne the Christian emperor—in the image of Constantine—of what would later be called the Holy Roman Empire. This papally endorsed coronation, which emphasized the important role of the pope in establishing the emperor, would be repeated by the successive popes.[28]

While papal relationships with the Empire improved, they soured with respect to the Church of Constantinople and its patriarch. Exemplifying this deterioration was the papacy of Nicholas I/the Great (858–867), which featured his excommunication of Patriarch Photius (858) and his scolding of Byzantine Emperor Michael III. When Photius reciprocated his excommunication by excommunicating Nicholas, the initial split between the two great churches of the East and the West occurred. At the same time, the might of the Holy Roman Empire was waning, and the Roman church was plunged into a bleak period. The papacy did not escape

---

27. Andrea Overfield, *The Human Record: Sources of Global History*, vol. 1, 4th ed. (Boston: Houghton, Mifflin, Harcourt, 2012), 348.

28. This authority was enhanced by the appearance of a collection of canon laws, including the so-called "False Decretals of Pseudo-Isidore" and the *Donation of Constantine*, which attempted to legitimize papal control of the appointment of bishops in the Frankish church.

this darkness, as numerous popes—increasingly chosen from the Italian aristocratic class or appointed by the German emperor and acting as sacred/secular rulers—between the middle of the ninth century to the middle of the eleventh century met their unfortunate demise through bludgeoning, strangulation, suffocation, mutilation, exile, and imprisonment.

THE PAPACY FROM THE TENTH THROUGH THE FIFTEENTH CENTURY

Significantly, this dark age yielded to a flowering of the church and a reform of the papacy in the middle part of the medieval period. One of the decisive factors in this development was the initiation of new monastic orders. The Cluny monastic order, founded 909/910 in Cluny (modern-day France), did away with the work aspect of earlier monastic orders (e.g., the Benedictine order) so that the monks could wholeheartedly give themselves to the religious life (e.g., prayer, observing the rules of the order, and celebration of the mass in highly decorated and adorned churches). It also became free of control by the local bishop, depending solely on the pope, and free of control by the king. The Cistercian monastic order was founded about 1100 in Citeaux (modern-day France); its most illustrious member was Bernard of Clairvaux, who promoted mysticism, championed the moral reform of the papacy, and attracted thousands into the Cistercian movement.

Such monastic orders encouraged reform of the church and its hierarchy, specifically in four areas: (1) lay investiture, or appointment of church leaders by secular rulers; (2) simony, the payment of large sums of money for church offices; (3) heresy, among which were simony and wrongful ideas about the presence of Christ in the Eucharist (exemplified by Berengar of Tours, who opposed the identification of the bread and the wine with the historical body and blood of Christ); and (4) clerical marriage and concubinage, despite the church's call for its leaders to be celibate. Pope Leo IX (1049–1054) led a number of synods aimed at the reform of the church against these four transgressions.[29]

---

29. Leo IX also contributed to the furthering split (seen earlier) between the Eastern and Western churches in 1054 when his legate excommunicated the Patriarch of Constantinople, who in turn excommunicated the pope.

Leo's successors, Victor II (1055–1057) and Nicholas II (1058–1061), shared his zeal for church reform. Nicholas crafted a new process for the election of the popes, limiting it to the choice of the seven cardinal bishops of Rome, with the affirmation of the twenty-eight cardinal priests of the five papal churches in Rome and the nineteen deacons of Rome. This procedure, along with the four reforms mentioned above, was confirmed by the Lateran synod of 1059.

As could be anticipated, this move to expel "outside" influence over the papacy by the emperor was not well received by the German court. Indeed, Emperor Henry IV attempted to invest the archbishop of Milan with the signs of his clerical office. This blatant disregard for papal prerogative was countered by the reform-minded Hildebrand, who as Pope Gregory VII (1073–1085), excommunicated the Emperor. Moreover, in his *Memorandum* (*Dictatus Papae*; 1075), Gregory articulated twenty-seven principles as the basis of papal authority, including the following: the pope alone can be called universal; he alone can depose, reinstate, and transfer bishops; secular princes must kiss his feet; he can depose emperors; his order is necessary for the convening of a general council of the church; he may be judged by no one; the Church of Rome has never erred nor will it ever err;[30] the pope is certainly made a saint (supported by an appeal to Matt. 16:18–19).[31] Henry IV did not take this rebuff well and deposed Gregory from the papal office. The uneasy relationship between the church and the secular reign came to the forefront, as the balance seemed to be tipping in favor of the papacy.

The king's move to depose the pope was not taken well; the leading German powers, both bishops and princes, even though loyal to the king, could not support this breach of imperial authority and demanded that Henry retract his deposition and swear allegiance to Gregory. Travelling to meet Henry, Gregory sought shelter in a castle at Canossa where he was approached by the king who, standing barefoot in the snow, pleaded with the pope to absolve him of excommunication. The difficult and fragile balance of power between the papacy and the empire had to be maintained. On the one hand, the king could not just

---

30. Gregory's *Memorandum* overlooked the case of Pope Honorius.
31. Considering the widely known moral and spiritual bankruptcy of the preceding popes, this claim must have seemed both shocking and preposterous.

do as he pleased in religious matters; on the other hand, the pope had to respect the divine right of the king to rule. So, for example, when Gregory later deposed Henry (1080), public opinion turned against the pope for his blatant grab for power over the imperial realm, a move that damaged the centuries-old relationship between the two spheres of authority.

Gregory dissented from this view, however, and was the first in a series of popes to champion the supremacy of the papacy over the secular realm. In a letter written in 1081, the pope explained his perspective. Beginning with Matthew 16:18–19, Gregory underscored the "universal concession of the power of binding and loosing" to St. Peter and noted that the imperial authority falls under this papal authority: "Shall not an authority founded by laymen . . . be subject to that authority which the providence of God Almighty has for his own honor established and in his mercy given to the world?" He then rehearsed the pagan and demonic roots (for support, he cited Satan's temptation of Christ; Matt. 4:9) of the imperial realm: "Who does not know that kings and leaders are sprung from men who were ignorant of God, who by pride, robbery, perfidy [treachery], murders—in a word, by almost every crime at the prompting of the devil, who is the prince of this world—have striven with blind cupidity [lust, greed] and intolerable presumption to dominate over their equals, that is, over mankind?" In terms of the supremacy of the spiritual realm, his argument focused on the privileges and prerogatives of the church that are not shared by the secular realm:

> Every Christian king, when he comes to die, seeks as a pitiful suppliant the aid of a priest, that he may escape hell's prison, may pass from the darkness into the light, and at the judgment of God may appear absolved from the bondage of his sins. Who, in his last hour (what layman, not to speak of priests), has ever implored the aid of an earthly king for the salvation of his soul? And what king or emperor is able, by reason of the office he holds, to rescue a Christian from the power of the devil through holy baptism? . . . Who of them can by his own words make the body and blood of our Lord—the greatest act in the

Christian religion? Or who of them possesses the power of binding and loosing in heaven and on earth? From all of these considerations it is clear how greatly the priestly office excels in power.[32]

Accompanying this development, and fueled by the new reformed-minded monastic movements, proponents of church renewal looked to Rome for support. What the papacy had to offer was a growing bureaucratic organization, legal system, stability, and international flavor. It was also busy leading general church councils. For example, within the ninety-year period between 1123 and 1215, four ecumenical councils—Lateran I (1123), Lateran II (1139), Lateran III (1179),and Lateran IV (1215)—were convened to treat such disparate matters as the ongoing threat of investiture and imperial intrusion into church matters, the continuing problem of clerical marriage, the healing of schisms, the denunciation of heretical movements (e.g., the Waldensians and the Cathari), appeals for the Eastern church to reunite with the Western church, and the reiteration of the primacy of the Church of Rome (followed, in successive order, by the churches of Constantinople, Alexandria, Antioch, and Jerusalem). Importantly, the Fourth Lateran Council (1215) promulgated the doctrine of transubstantiation, the church's position regarding the eucharistic presence of Jesus Christ, "whose body and blood are truly contained in the sacrament of the altar under the forms of bread and wine. The bread is transubstantiated into the body and the wine into the blood by the power of God, so we may receive from him what he has received from us."[33] This council also established the law that people should participate in the sacrament at least once a year after the confession of sins.[34] The important con-

---

32. Gregory VII, "Letter to the Bishop of Metz," in Bettenson, *Documents of the Christian Church*, 115–17.

33. Fourth Lateran Council, Canon 1, in *A History of Christianity: Readings in the History of the Church*, ed. Ray C. Petry, vol. 1: The Early and Medieval Church (Grand Rapids: Baker, 1990), 322–23. Later that century, Thomas Aquinas would provide the philosophical and theological underpinnings for the doctrine (Thomas Aquinas, *Summa Theologica*, part 3, q. 75, art. 4).

34. Fourth Lateran Council, Canon 21, in Petry, *History of Christianity*, 323. Though proclaimed by this council, the rule stipulating participation in communion at least once a

tributions of these general councils would later lead to the conciliar movement challenging papal supremacy.

Other important developments at this time included the increasing authority of the cardinals of the church and the compilation and formation of canon law. The cardinals met regularly with the pope in the Consistory, and were gradually viewed as collaborators with him, not just as mere advisors. Indeed, the pope increasingly used the cardinals as his legates, or papal representatives, who travelled widely to enforce papal decisions, raise money, grant papal privileges, and the like, thus increasing the visibility of papal authority. Moreover, beginning in the middle of the twelfth century, clerics with legal training were chosen to be popes (e.g., Alexander III, 1159–1181), thus introducing a legal cast to the papacy. Not only were old canon laws compiled (e.g., in 1140, Gratian's *Decretum*, or *Concordia Discordantium Canonum* [Harmony of Discordant Laws], systematized almost 3,800 texts about church discipline and regulation, laying the foundation for the *Corpus Juris Canonici*), but new canon laws were written, thereby rendering the papacy a vast juridical system and establishing canon law as one of the church's characteristics. Indeed, the administration of the papacy began to be called the "Curia," or court. Of course, such a growing operation was desperately in need of finances, and huge sums of money were brought into the Curia's coffers as cardinals charged for their services, the papacy exacted taxes, simony continued to be rampant, and secular kingdoms paid their dues.

Much of this money began to be directed toward financing the Crusades. A combination of pilgrimage and holy war, the Crusades redirected the internecine fighting between Christians in Europe to combating the enemies of Christianity in the Islamic-controlled Middle East. For involvement in liberating Jerusalem from the Muslims, crusaders were promised a plenary indulgence, or pardon from all punishment due to sin. Religious zeal for salvation, combined with fascination for holy war, produced a fever pitched enthusiasm for the

---

year was not followed by other councils in the thirteenth century. For example, the Council of Toulouse in 1229 and the Council of Albi in 1254 ruled that the faithful should participate in the Eucharist at least three times a year—Christmas and Pentecost, in addition to Easter (George Park Fisher, *History of Christian Doctrine* [New York: Charles Scribner's Sons, 1896], 101).

papally endorsed Crusades. Pope Urban II (1088–1099) launched the First Crusade; by the last year of his papacy Jerusalem had been liberated and its Muslim inhabitants decimated. While the Second Crusade (1145–1149; launched by Pope Eugenius III [1145–1153]) failed in its attempt to wrest back control of the Holy Land, which had been recaptured by Muslim armies under Saladin, the Third Crusade (1189–1192; called by Gregory VIII [1187]) resulted in a truce between the Crusaders and Saladin without securing Jerusalem for the Christians. The Fourth Crusade (1202–1204; convened by Innocent III [1198–1216]), which was allegedly launched to retake Jerusalem, detoured to Constantinople and conquered the city, establishing the Latin Empire and thus further alienating the Eastern and Western churches.

At the same time, influential spiritual movements arose within the church. Francis of Assisi and his mendicant *Ordo Fratum Minorum* (Order of Little Brothers; the Franciscans) received approbation from Pope Innocent III (1198–1216) for his original monastic rule in 1209. Dominic Guzman and his *Ordo Praedicatorum* (Order of Preachers; the Dominicans) was endorsed by Pope Honorius III (1216–1227) in 1216. These two movements—characterized by mendicancy (begging for money), chastity, and obedience—contributed to the flowering of spirituality among the masses through preaching the gospel, helping the poor, stamping out heresy, and exhibiting lifestyles opposed to the wealth and ostentatiousness of the church's hierarchy.

As these developments continued and expanded, the rise of papal authority meant not only that the pope was the supreme ruler over the church; he was also seen as ruler over the entire world. This summary by the medieval theologian/philosopher James of Viterbo (1255–1308) demonstrates the pope's vast authority:

> The definition of the church as a kingdom was "the most correct, the truest, and the most fitting" definition for it, and it was "more proper" to refer to it as a kingdom than to use any of the other possible terms. Thence it followed that "just as the church is called the kingdom of Christ, so it may truly be called the kingdom of his vicar [earthly representative], that is, of the supreme pontiff, who is truly called a king and is one." Not only was he "the king

of all spiritual kings" and "the pastor of pastors," but he as "the king both of secular and of spiritual kings." For "because Christ is both king and priest, therefore his vicar has both royal and priestly power, and it is through him that royal power is instituted, ordered, sanctified, and blessed."[35]

Such overarching claims reached their apex with Pope Innocent III, who expressed the superiority of the papacy over the emperor in his fanciful commentary on Genesis 1:14–18:

> The creator of the universe set up two great luminaries in the firmament of heaven; the greater light to rule the day, the lesser light to rule the night. In the same way for the firmament of the universal Church, which is spoken of as heaven, he appointed two great dignities; the greater to bear rule over souls (these being, as it were, days), the lesser to bear rule over bodies (those being, as it were nights). These dignities are the pontifical authority and the royal power. Furthermore, the moon derives her light from the sun, and is in truth inferior to the sun in both size and quality, in position as well as effect. In the same way the royal power derives its dignity from the pontifical authority: and the more closely it cleaves to the sphere of that authority the less is the light with which it is adorned; the further it is removed, the more it increases in splendor.[36]

The pope's power was exemplified in his excommunication of King John of England in 1209, a factor that contributed to emboldening the English barons to force the king to agree to their demands for certain liberties. This event resulted in the document known as the Magna

---

35. James of Viterbo, *On Christian Government*, 1.1; 2.5, 2.3, in Jaroslav Pelikan, *The Christian Tradition: A History of the Development of Doctrine*, vol. 4, Reformation of Church and Dogma (1300–1700) (Chicago and London: University of Chicago Press, 1984), 82.
36. Innocent III, "Letter to Acerbius" (1198), in Bettenson, *Documents of the Christian Church*, 123 (in which the document is entitled "The Moon and the Sun").

Carta, but Innocent III declared it invalid when John surrendered to the pope's demands.[37]

Such allegiance, expressed as dependence upon the papacy, was enjoined on all secular authorities, yet these latter powers began to express reluctance to submit to the church's hierarchy. This boldness was heightened as northern European monarchies replaced the once-powerful empire and established their own authority. Less than a century after Innocent III, Pope Boniface VIII (1294–1303) sought to intervene in national affairs to halt the kings of England and France (countries locked in incessant warfare with each other) from taxing the clergy in their lands to raise money for the war.[38] The Pope threatened the kings with excommunication should they persist in this illegal taxation, but Edward I of England and Philip IV of France would not be deterred from their course of action.

Boniface countered with a restatement of papal authority, supported by various biblical passages and images.[39] By far the most interesting argument he offered was an allegorical interpretation of the two swords brandished when Jesus was captured at the garden of Gethsemane (Luke 22:38; John 18:11):

> And we learn from the words of the gospel that in this church and in her power are two swords, the spiritual and the temporal. For when the apostles said, "Behold, here" (that is, in the church, since it was the apostles who spoke) "are two swords"—the Lord did not reply, "It is too much," but "It is enough" [Luke 22:38]. Truly he who denies that the temporal sword is in the power of Peter, misunderstands the words of the Lord, "Put up your sword into the sheath" [John 18:11]. Both are in the power of the church, the spiritual and the material. But the latter is to be used for the church, the former by it; the former by the priest, the latter by kings and captains but at the will and the permission of

---

37. Such authority was not only wielded against secular rulers. Innocent III also launched the Albigensian Crusade against the heretical Cathari, or Albigensians, resulting in the massacre of 20,000 inhabitants of the town of Béziers (1209), a stronghold of the heretics.
38. Boniface VIII, "Clericis Laicos" (1296), in Bettenson, *Documents of the Christian Church*, 124–25.
39. Song 6:9; the ark of Noah; Ps. 22:20; John 10:16; 19:23; 21:16.

the priest. The one sword, then, should be under the other, and temporal authority subject to spiritual. For when the apostle says, "there is no power but of God, and the powers that be are ordained by God" [Rom. 13:1], they would not be so ordained were not one sword made subject to the other. . . . Furthermore, we declare, state, define and pronounce that it is altogether necessary to salvation for every human creature to be subject to the Roman pontiff.[40]

Through this blatantly fanciful interpretation of the two swords, Pope Boniface hoped to settle the dispute over rightful authority in the world. Beyond this, he underscored "that there is one Holy Catholic and Apostolic Church, and that outside this church there is neither salvation nor remission of sins," concluding "that it is altogether necessary to salvation for every human creature to be subject to the Roman pontiff."[41]

The Pope's claim that the state must be in submission to the church with its papacy would not go unchallenged, however; Boniface was forced to resign by the emissary from Philip IV and shortly thereafter died. This debacle paved the way for one of the most bleak periods in the existence of the papacy. The first part of this era featured the so-called "Babylonian Captivity of the Church,"[42] a nearly seventy-year period (1309–1377) in which the papacy was hijacked from Rome to Avignon (modern-day France) and characterized by

---

40. Boniface VIII, "Unam Sanctam" (1302) in Bettenson, *Documents of the Christian Church*, 126–27. Boniface cemented his case by appealing to a prophecy of Jeremiah, Paul's instructions, and Jesus' words: "Thus, concerning the church and her power, is the prophecy of Jeremiah fulfilled, 'See, I have this day set you over the nations and over the kingdoms' [Jer. 1:10], etc. If, therefore, the earthly power err, it shall be judged by the spiritual power; and if a lesser power err, it shall be judged by a greater. But if the supreme power err, it can only be judged by God, not by man; for the testimony of the apostle is 'The spiritual man judges all things, yet he himself is judged by no man' [1 Cor. 2:15]. For this authority, although given to a man and exercised by a man, is not human, but rather divine, given at God's mouth to Peter and established on a rock for him and his successors in him whom he confessed, the Lord saying to Peter himself, 'Whatsoever you shall bind,' etc. [Matt. 16:19]. Whoever therefore resists this power thus ordained of God, resists the ordinance of God [Rom. 13:2]."

41. Ibid.

42. This disparaging title was a reference to the seventy-year captivity suffered by the people of Israel in Babylon from 605 to 537 BC. Martin Luther would pick up on this disastrous period in the church's history in this polemical anti-Catholic writing *The Babylonian Captivity of the Church* (1520).

nepotism (the granting of church offices to family members), luxurious living, extravagant spending, partying, capitulation to secular political theory, and immorality, as the popes became little more than puppets in the hands of the French kings. The second part was the so-called "Great Schism" (1378–1417) during which the Catholic Church was led by two popes, one in Rome and one in Avignon, resulting in almost hopeless division as the various nations of Europe sided with one pope or the other.[43] The low point in this schism arrived when the Council of Pisa (1409) deposed both popes—the Roman Pope Gregory XII (1406–1415) and the Avignon Pope Benedict XIII (1394–1417)—and elected Pope Alexander V (1409–1410; succeeded by John XXIII, 1410–1415) in their place, only to find that neither the pope in Avignon nor the pope in Rome accepted its decision. Thus, instead of two popes, the church had three, a situation that would not be rectified until the Council of Constance in 1415.

Of course, significant people other than secular leaders strongly objected to this accumulation of power, wealth, and prestige by the church and its leaders. Two such radical critics of the decrepit state of the church were the Englishman John Wycliffe and the Bohemian (now Czech) Jan Hus. In his treatise *On the Pastoral Office*, Wycliffe sought to rectify the current dismal state of church leadership by proposing an alternative model for the pastors of the church. His basic thesis was straightforward: "There are two things that pertain to the status of pastor: the holiness of the pastor and the wholesomeness of his teaching."[44] As for pastoral holiness, Wycliffe was hardly novel, arguing that pastors should live frugally, supported exclusively by the giving of their church members. Concerning the teaching ministry of the pastor, Wycliffe urged:

---

43. The schism began when Pope Gregory XI (1370–1378), who had transferred the papacy back to Rome in 1377, died in 1378. The conclave of mostly French cardinals that was to elect the next pope was overrun by a Roman mob, which exercised pressure to choose an Italian rather than a Frenchman. Urban VI (1378–1389) was selected but proved to be an arrogant and dangerous pope. The cardinals retracted their choice and elected Pope Clement VII (1378–1394) to replace him, but both men held tightly to their claim to the papacy, excommunicating each other and ruling as two popes, Urban VI in Rome and Clement VII in Avignon.
44. John Wycliffe, *On the Pastoral Office*, 1.1, in *The Library of Christian Classics*, vol. 14: Advocates of Reform, ed. Matthew Spinka (Philadelphia: Westminster, 1953), 32.

The first condition of the pastor is to cleanse his own spring, that it may not infect the Word of God. And as for the second condition, which is very manifold, the first and particular function of the pastor remains to be seen. The pastor has a threefold office: first, to feed his sheep spiritually on the Word of God, that through pastures ever green they may be initiated into the blessedness of heaven. The second pastoral office is to purge wisely the sheep of disease, that they may not infect themselves and others as well. And the third is for the pastor to defend his sheep from ravening wolves, both sensible and insensible. In all these the special office of the pastor seems that of sowing the Word of God among his sheep.[45]

Wycliffe returned to this emphasis on teaching the Word, making a startling statement: "It is evident that preaching the gospel is the special work of the [pastor], for Christ advances more in his apostles by preaching to the people than by doing any miracle which in his own person he did in Judea. . . . Preaching the gospel exceeds prayer and administration of the sacraments, to an infinite degree. . . . Spreading the gospel has far wide and more evident benefit; it is thus the most precious activity of the church."[46] Wycliffe's call for the reform of the pastoral office, when wedded to a denouncement of the current church and its pastor/pope, would lead to his condemnation.

Following a similar course, Jan Hus denounced certain church doctrines and practices, including its administration of the Eucharist (serving the laity the bread only—communion in one kind—and not both the bread and the cup—communion in two kinds), its sale of indulgences, its involvement in the political realm, and its claim that the papacy was established by divine right. Hus added his voice to that of Wycliffe in demanding reformation of the church.

Such cries for renewal of the church became more and more pronounced. As we have seen, some movements within the heart of the church succeeded in bringing about renewal, but other voices like those

---

45. Ibid., 2.1, in *The Library of Christian Classics*, 48.
46. Ibid.,2.2, in *The Library of Christian Classics*, 49.

of Wycliffe and Hus would ultimately be silenced. But a more immediate crisis loomed large: how to heal the Great Schism and reunite the church? The answer to this question was the conciliar movement. Beginning in the twelfth century, the popes had regularly convened general councils to denounce deeply entrenched clerical sins, promulgate sound doctrine, confirm papal supremacy over imperial rulers, and the like. Now, the church looked to a council to bind up its wounds and restore order by deposing the two existing popes and electing a new one in their place. Though the earlier Council of Pisa (1409) had failed, a newly convened Council of Constance (1414–1418) first deposed John XXIII (successor to the Pisa-elected Pope Alexander V) and the Avignon Pope Benedict XIII, then persuaded the Roman Pope Gregory XII to abdicate his office, and finally elected Martin V (1417–1431) as the sole pope. Though Benedict XIII persisted in his belief that he continued to be pope, he lacked any significant support; accordingly, the Council succeeded in binding up the Great Schism.

The Council of Constance not only succeeded in ending the church's internal problem; it also dealt with external threats to its doctrine and practice. It condemned forty-five articles of belief held by John Wycliffe and thirty articles held by Jan Hus, whom the council closely associated with Wycliffe. Tragically, some of the reforms voiced by these two men echoed the measures of renewal for which the church had called for centuries. Still, the council took action against Wycliffe, announcing that it "decrees that the said John Wycliffe was a notorious and obstinate heretic who died in heresy, and it anathematises him and condemns his memory. It decrees and orders that his body and bones are to be exhumed, if they can be identified among the corpses of the faithful, and to be scattered far from a burial place of the church. . . . "[47] As for Hus, though he was granted a promise of safe conduct to the Council, he was imprisoned, condemned, excommunicated, and handed over to the authorities to be burned at the stake as a heretic.

Having resolved the problem of heresy and healed the church's internal schism, it would appear that the Council of Constance was a success. In reality, however, the Council's solution to the schism cre-

---

47. Proceedings from the Council of Constance, session 8 (May 4, 1415), http://www.papalencyclicals.net/Councils/ecum16.htm.

ated another problem: if a general council of the church could depose popes and elect a new pope in their place, what does this prerogative mean for the primacy of papal authority? Was it the case that a council could only exercise its authority in a desperate situation, to depose a heretical pope(s), or was it the case that a council has authority over the pope himself, that is, the papal office, regardless of who holds it? Some theologians and church leaders backed the former view, others the latter view.

The Council of Constance itself, in a decree justifying its own existence, had taken the latter view: "This holy Council of Constance . . . declares, first that it is lawfully assembled in the Holy Spirit, that it constitutes a general council, representing the Catholic Church, and that therefore it has its authority directly from Christ; and that all men, of every rank and condition, including the pope himself, is bound to obey it in matters concerning the faith, the abolition of the schism, and the reformation of the Church of God in its head and its members."[48] This position envisioned the authority of a general council as residing in the church as a whole and not in the papacy; indeed, the highest authority of the church, the pope, is to submit to the decisions of the church itself as expressed by a general council of its members. To ensure that general councils would exercise the highest authority in the church, the Council issued the decree "Frequens" (1417) calling for a frequent convening of councils (the first council after Constance was to follow in five years, the second one in seven years, leading to a regular scheduling of a general council every ten years).

Conciliarism was met with both support and opposition. Those in favor appealed to Marsilius of Padua and William of Ockham, church leaders who had formulated the theory that ecclesial authority is vested in the church primarily and in the papacy derivatively. But this theory also attracted strong opponents, not the least of whom was the pope himself. The Council of Basel (1431–1439), convened by Pope Martin V according to the schedule prescribed by "Frequens," was attended only reluctantly by his successor, Pope Eugenius IV (1431–1447), after an attempt to disband it failed (December, 1431). Among the Council's

---

48. Decree of the Council of Constance, "Sacrosancta" (April, 1415), in Bettenson, *Documents of the Christian Church*, 149. The document is also entitled *Haec sancta*.

actions were fresh attempts to provide relief from heavy taxation by the Curia, to rectify the perpetual problems of simony and clerical marriage/concubinage, and to curb abuses of papal authority. These and other proceedings disturbed the pope and those loyal to papalism.

Accordingly, in September, 1437, Eugenius IV issued another decree, *Doctoris Gentium*, that transferred the Council from Basel to Ferrara (1438–1445); the move resulted in another schism with two popes—Eugenius (deposed by the Council of Basel) and Felix V (elected by the Council of Ferrara in 1439)—in charge of the church. The Council of Ferrara succeeded in temporarily healing the split between the East and the West through acceptance of the *Filioque* clause ("the Holy Spirit proceeds from the Father *and the Son*") and papal supremacy on the part of the Byzantine emperor and the Patriarch of Constantinople. The success of the Council of Ferrara (later transferred to Florence in 1439), the growing suspicion of the anti-papalism of the Council of Basel, and the healing of the schism in 1449 by Pope Nicholas V (1447–1455) contributed to the discrediting of conciliarism. The death knell for this movement was sounded with the publication of "Execrabilis" in 1460 by Pope Pius II (1458–1464): "There has sprung up in our time an execrable abuse, unheard of in earlier ages, namely that some men, imbued with the spirit of rebellion, presume to appeal to a future council from the Roman pontiff. . . . Anyone who is not wholly ignorant of the laws can see how this contravenes the sacred canons and how detrimental it is to Christendom. . . . We condemn appeals of this kind and denounce them as erroneous and detestable."[49] This decree was echoed at the Fifth Lateran Council (1512–1517). The conciliar movement, which for a time had rescued the church from its internal problems, was put to rest.

The lingering effects of the weakening of the papacy by the conciliar movement were felt not only within the church; papal political power among the nations of Europe also waned. The solution was for the popes to sign concordats with monarchs, agreements that regulated church matters in their nations. This loss of influence was accompanied by an acute financial crisis in the church; it no longer had the income from

---

49. Pius II, "Execrabilis" (January, 1460), in Bettenson, *Documents of the Christian Church*, 150.

European nations on which it once depended. It appeared that the high point of the papacy was succeeded by an irreversible downward spiral.

Such proved not to be the case. With the flourishing of the Renaissance, the papacy was restored to its former splendor. Contributing to this thriving was humanism, an educational renewal that rediscovered the ancient sources (classical Greek and Roman literature and philosophy, the Hebrew Bible and Greek New Testament, the writings of the early church Fathers) and an artistic revival that resulted in massive new building projects and a fresh flowering of painting and sculpturing. Within the church, humanist popes, drawn from the wealthiest of Italian families, became patrons of the Renaissance, with the city of Rome especially being benefited.

Pope Nicholas V initiated this revival with his commissioning of the reconstruction of St. Peter's and his restoration of the many dilapidated structures in Rome. His motivation was clearly expressed: "if the authority of the Holy See were visibly displayed in majestic buildings, imperishable memorials and witnesses seemingly planted by the hand of God himself, belief would grow and strengthen like a tradition from one generation to another, and all the world would accept and revere it."[50] Funding for these many envisioned projects came from an immense influx of pilgrims to Rome, beginning with Nicholas's proclamation of the year of Jubilee in 1450. His enthusiasm for the Renaissance restoration of Rome was continued by the popes Pius II (1458–1464), Paul II (1464–1471), Sixtus IV (1471–1484), and Julius II (1503–1513). Restoration projects undertaken included the Pantheon and the Arch of Titus. New projects included the Hospital of the Holy Spirit, the Church of Santa Maria del Popolo, and the Sistine Chapel in the Vatican. Tragically, these same popes were also involved in constant skirmishes to resist foreign takeover of the Papal States and other regions (e.g., Sicily, Milan) of the Italian landmass. These wars were directed against Florence, Ferrara, Venice, and Naples, and for their funding the popes were required to court the favor of leading families (e.g., the Medici of Florence) and continue the centuries-long crimes of simony and nepotism. New concordats were signed, thus guaranteeing income from nations such as France. Additionally, the sale of indul-

---

50. Ludwig Freiherr von Pastor, *History of the Popes: From the Close of the Middle Ages*, 40 vols. (London: Routlege, and Kegan Paul, 1891–1953), 2:30.

gences to finance Renaissance projects became a major money-maker for the papacy. The church, plunged into desperate measures, becoming again the target of cries for reform, was about to encounter its greatest challenge ever.

THE PAPACY FROM THE SIXTEENTH THROUGH THE EIGHTEENTH CENTURY

On October 31, 1517, an unknown monk nailed his "Ninety-five Theses" to the door of the church in Wittenberg, thereby announcing his desire to debate the use and sale of indulgences. With this act, Martin Luther set into motion what would later be called the Protestant Reformation, a complex of several reforming movements (Lutheran, Zwinglian, Calvinist, Anglican, Anabaptist) that would split the church once again. The Medici pope, Leo X (1513–1521), at first reacted to Luther's disturbance with a dismissive attitude, deeply underestimating the widespread longing for a renewed church that would refuse compromise and not tolerate moral laxity and spiritual bankruptcy. Only as Luther's 1520 writings—*A Treatise on Good Works, On the Papacy in Rome, The Open Letter to the Christian Nobility of the German Nation, The Babylonian Captivity of the Church*, and *The Freedom of the Christian Man*—gained immense public support did Pope Leo X act seriously with his papal bull, "Exsurge, Domine," charging Luther with forty-one heresies, thus excommunicating him:

> Arise, O Lord, and judge your own cause. Remember your reproaches to those who are filled with foolishness all through the day. Listen to our prayers, for foxes have arisen seeking to destroy the vineyard whose winepress you alone have trod. When you were about to ascend to your Father, you committed the care, rule, and administration of the vineyard, an image of the triumphant church, to Peter, as the head and your vicar and his successors. The wild boar from the forest seeks to destroy it and every wild beast feeds upon it.[51]

---

51. Leo X, "Exsurge, Domine," http://www.papalencyclicals.net/Leo10/110exdom.htm.

Fueled by anti-papal sentiment, the German princes from whom Luther sought protection would not carry out the pope's orders of excommunication. The Reformation was well under way and receiving support from various quarters. Never again would the church in the West be the same.

While Protestantism was being launched, the Catholic Church was as always embroiled in its own affairs. The sack of Rome in 1527 traumatized the city. Cool papal relationships with Emperor Charles V meant that no united front between church and empire would be marshaled as a military response against the Protestant heretics. Indeed, the Peace of Augsburg (1555) called for the irenic coexistence of Lutherans and Catholics in Germany.[52] In England, King Henry VIII was not satisfied with the pope's handing of his request for an annulment of his marriage to Catharine of Aragon and thus forged a breakaway *Chiesa Anglicana*—the Church of England—spelling the papacy's loss of that nation.[53]

With calls for its renewal increasing in urgency, with the threat of Protestantism looming large, and with a desperate need for administrative reform, the church's response was a call for a new general council. After several failed attempts to agree on its location, Pope Paul III (1534–1549) finally succeeded in convening the Council of Trent (modern-day northern Italy) in 1545. The most illustrious of its participants included Gasparo Contarini (an important humanist voice for ecclesial reform), Reginald Pole (the future Archbishop of Canterbury under Queen Mary), and Gian Pietro Caraffa (who would later become Pope Paul IV). These three had been members of the Oratory of Divine

---

52. The basic principle was that the religion of the ruler is the religion of the realm, meaning that where a Catholic prince ruled, his subjects would be Catholic, and where a Lutheran prince ruled, his subjects would be Lutheran (The Peace of Augsburg [1555], in Bettenson, *Documents of the Christian Church*, 238–39).

53. The Supremacy Act of 1534 proclaimed Henry VIII and his successors "the only supreme head in earth of the Church of England, called *Anglicana Ecclesia*" ("The Supremacy Act of 1534," in Bettenson, *Documents of the Christian Church*, 252–53). Under the reign of Queen Elizabeth, this proclamation was modified as The Supremacy Act of 1559, affirming that the English monarch "is the only supreme governor of this realm . . . as well in all spiritual or ecclesiastical things or causes, as temporal, and that no foreign . . . prelate [i.e., the Pope] . . . has, or ought to have, any jurisdiction, power, superiority, preeminence, or authority ecclesiastical or spiritual, within this realm ("The Supremacy Act of 1559," in Bettenson, *Documents of the Christian Church*, 260–61).

Love, a confraternity of clergy and laity of deep devotion and ability who met frequently in Rome to pray and work for the renewal of the church. Additionally, the three had been members of Pope Paul III's 1536 Commission for the Reform of the Church. In its *Consilium de Emendenda Ecclesia* (Plan for Reforming the Church, 1537), the Commission listed a wide-ranging litany of papal and clerical abuses: simony, the sale of indulgences, immorality, disorganization of monastic orders, and the like. Though the pope would not act decisively on this report, its reform measures would later be incorporated into the Council of Trent. In the meantime, an illegal publication of the report found its way to Luther, and Protestants turned it as evidence of Catholicism's corrupt state and heartily ridiculed the church for its own frank admission of its many failures.

The Council of Trent met in three sessions: 1545–1547, 1551–1552, and 1562–1563. Different currents and cross currents jockeyed for supremacy: some participants (e.g., members of the papal Curia) resisted any reforms that would interfere with their extravagant lifestyle; others (e.g., the French and Spanish clerics), still championing the ideal of conciliarism, wanted a stronger, more independent role for the hierarchy; some like the Emperor Charles V dreamed of a council that would reunite divided Europe; others (e.g., Contarini and Pole, who had participated at Regensburg in 1541 in a failed attempt to negotiate a compromise with the Protestant representatives) hoped for some type of doctrinal rapprochement with Protestantism; still others (e.g., Caraffa, the Jesuits) sought the outright condemnation of the Protestant heresy leading to its destruction.

This latter group carried the day in terms of setting the agenda for Trent: Catholic dogmas were explicitly articulated over and against Protestant doctrines; the convictions of the Protestants were clearly labeled as heresies rather than debate points; and concrete steps for the thoroughgoing moral, spiritual, and administrative reform of the Catholic Church were enacted, with the hope that such changes would lead to a renewed, more organized, and more vibrant church. From a Protestant perspective, in the aftermath of the Council, Luther's suspicions that the church was irreformable were confirmed.

The church instituted several new measures in an attempt to destroy—or at least diminish—the Protestant Reformation. One such means was the censorship of books, which took various permutations: (1) in 1559, the Index of Prohibited Books (also called the Index of Pope Paul IV), established by Gian Pietro Caraffa as Pope Paul IV (1555–1559); (2) in 1564, the Tridentine Index, established by an act of the Council of Trent under the direction of Pope Pius IV (1559–1565); (3) in 1571, the Congregation of the Index, created by Pope Pius V (1566–1572) for the periodic updating of the list.[54]

Another measure aimed at stamping out the Protestant threat was the revival of the Inquisition. Originally constituted in the thirteenth century and used to wipe out the heretical Cathari in southern Gaul (modern-day France), it was also used powerfully in the fifteenth century under Ferdinand and Isabella in Spain to ensure that Jews and Muslims would convert to the Catholic faith. This Inquisition was revived in 1542 by Pope Paul III and reorganized under the leadership of Gian Pietro Caraffa. Its philosophy was simple and reflected the position of Thomas Aquinas on heretics:

> They deserve not only to be separated from the Church by excommunication, but also to be severed from the world by death. For it is a much graver matter to corrupt the faith that enlivens the soul, than to forge money, which supports temporal life. Therefore if forgers of money and other evil-doers are immediately condemned to death by the secular authority, much more reason is there for heretics, as soon as they are convicted of heresy, to be not only excommunicated but even put to death.[55]

The Inquisition tortured and threatened thousands of Protestants with death if they did not "convert," and in the case of "heretics"—Protestants who would not recant and embrace again the Catholic faith—the death penalty was pronounced (though the secular authorities had to carry out the execution). Such tactics were especially effective in Italy, Spain, and Portugal, and to a lesser extent in France. In these areas the Inquisition became the major deterrent to the further spread of Protestantism.

---

54. In one form or another, these lists would continue until 1966.
55. Thomas Aquinas, *Summa Theologica*, 2nd part of part 2, q. 11, art. 3.

Still another means to combat Protestantism was a new monastic order. The Society of Jesus, also known as the Jesuits, was founded by Ignatius of Loyola and approved by Pope Paul III in 1540. Under papal supervision the Jesuits would seek to win back Protestants to Catholicism.

Most importantly, a stronger papally dominated church emerged from the Council. The papacy was responsible for the enactment of the moral reforms and administrative reorganization called for by Trent, it minimized the authority and responsibilities of the cardinals, it directed the zealous new monastic orders in their missionary work to return all of Europe to the Catholic faith, it suppressed heresy by the use of force (e.g., during the St. Bartholomew's Day Massacre on August 23–24, 1572, in Paris, at least five thousand, and possibly tens of thousands of Huguenots [French Protestants], were killed), it dispatched papal nuncios to secure the cooperation of secular leaders, and it continued the rebuilding of Rome as the glorious center of Catholicism (e.g., St. Peter's was remodeled to include the dome; Michelangelo worked on that project as well as the Last Judgment in the Sistine Chapel). The papacy became, once again, a very powerful force in ecclesial and secular matters in the latter part of the sixteenth century.

This triumphalism turned to defeat for the papacy in the seventeenth and eighteenth centuries. The Thirty Years War (1618–1648), undertaken with great confidence that Catholicism would ultimately defeat Protestantism, failed to achieve the envisioned victory; rather, it established the legitimacy of the Protestant cause throughout European nations. Indeed, the three major Western branches of Christendom—Catholicism, Lutheranism, and Calvinism—were acknowledged, as the Peace of Westphalia (1648), going beyond the Peace of Augsburg (1555) and its accord between Lutherans and Catholics, made several new provisions: "Subjects whose religion differs from that of their prince are to have equal rights with his other subjects. . . . The Reformed [Calvinists] are to have equal rights in religion and other matters with the other states and subjects."[56] When Pope Innocent X (1644–1655) issued a papal bull—*Zelo Domus Dei* (November 26, 1648)—declaring the Peace of Westphalia null and void because it was antithetical to the Catholic

---

56. The Peace of Westphalia (1648), in Bettenson, *Documents of the Christian Church*, 240–41.

Church, the startling disregard for his position underscored just how marginalized the papacy had become in European affairs.

Other developments contributed to the demise of the papacy at this time. Pope Urban VIII (1623–1644) left the papacy in ruins through his disastrous conflict with Venice, Tuscany, and Modena, a war that ruined the Papal States and left the church with an immense debt. French anti-papalism reached a near crescendo when Louis XIV encouraged the French Assembly of the Clergy to pass the "Four [Gallican] Articles" (1682): (1) secular rulers are not "subject to any ecclesiastical power in temporal matters;" (2) papal authority must be wielded in accordance with and in subjection to general councils (specifically, the Council of Constance); (3) papal authority must be regulated by the canons of the church; and (4) papal pronouncements on matters of faith are "not unalterable unless the consent of the church is given."[57] These "Four Articles" were a direct repudiation of the authority of Pope Innocent XI (1676–1689). Still more radical principles of anti-papal Gallicanism appeared in Germany under the ecclesial-political system known as Febronianism (1763; condemned by Pope Clement XIII [1758–1769] in 1764), which championed the idea of conciliarism; limited papal authority to administrative matters; and denounced the overreaching universal authority of the papacy to condemn heresies, appoint bishops, establish new dioceses, change canon laws, and make infallible dogmatic pronouncements apart from a general council or universal Church approbation. Even the church's most faithful monastic orders were not secure from secular attack. Under extreme pressure from the rulers of Spain, Portugal, France, and Austria—monarchies whose extensive financial interests in South America were challenged by the Jesuits—Pope Clement XIV (1769–1774) dissolved the Society of Jesus, thereby highlighting the impotence of the papacy and the ability of secular rulers to manipulate it for their own devious purposes. "By the 1780s, every Catholic state in Europe wanted to reduce the Pope to a ceremonial figurehead, and most had succeeded."[58]

---

57. The Gallican Declaration (1682), in Bettenson, *Documents of the Christian Church*, 285–86.
58. Duffy, *Saints and Sinners*, 247.

The apex of anti-papalism came with the demise of the Catholic Church during the French Revolution. In 1789 the Estates General enacted certain extreme measure to confront the French national crisis. French payment of tithes to the church was ended, all property belonging to the church was confiscated (with this wealth being used to pay off the national debt), the taking of religious vows was prohibited and persecution of the existing orders was instituted, the clergy came under the control of the civil authorities and were constrained to swear an oath in support of the Civil Constitution (1790; those who refused to comply were imprisoned or executed by guillotine), and a thoroughly secularized Constitutional Church was established that arrogantly mocked the former Catholic Church through its pagan rituals. Pope Pius VI (1775–1799), though horrified at the demise of the French Church, stood by idly, not wanting to align himself with the European Coalition that was forming to halt the French Revolution, out of fear of alienating the French and thus inviting their invasion of the Papal States. Yet, this annexation of some of the papal lands was precisely what Napoleon did; Rome was spared from his conquest only through a costly armistice reluctantly agreed to by Pius VI. Napoleon's attempts to convince the pope of the compatibility of democracy/republicanism and Christianity—which, at least in its Catholic form, was a monarchy with the pope as its king—were unsuccessful and unnecessary, as papal capitulations to the new emperor's demands meant that the church was well on its way to submitting completely to the absolute state.

THE PAPACY IN THE NINETEENTH CENTURY

Napoleon made an abrupt about-face in 1800 as he sought accommodation with the Catholic Church (for various political reasons, not the least of which was to secure peace in France and the French-occupied lands). The Emperor expressed "the feelings which I entertain for the Catholic Apostolic Roman religion:"

> I am convinced that this religion is the only one that can bring true happiness to a well-ordered community, and lay firm the foundations of government. I assure you that I shall strive to guard and defend it at all times, and by all

means. . . . It is my intention that the Christian Catholic Roman religion in its entirety shall be maintained and publicly exercised, and that it shall have as full, as extensive, and as inviolable an exercise, as it had at the time when I first entered this happy country. . . . France . . . has her eyes at last opened; she has recognized that the Catholic religion is the only anchor that can give her stability amidst the surges and save her from the storm.[59]

A religious reason also prompted Napoleon's move toward accommodation: he desired to remove all the bishops of the secularized Constitutional Church and replace them with clerics of his own choosing, but he needed papal approval of his actions. Pius VII (1800–1823), despite many reservations, signed the new concordat with France (July, 1801). This accord (which would remain in force for a century) acknowledged that "Catholicism was the religion of the vast majority of the French" but also required the church to forfeit all claims to its French property confiscated after 1790 and to recognize the Emperor's appointments of French bishops (who would swear an oath of loyalty to the government and be paid by the state). In one fell swoop, the Catholic Church in France was completely remade. Still, Napoleon sensed that he had overly capitulated to the pope, so in 1802 the publication of the concordat was joined with seventy-seven "Organic Articles," new ecclesial restrictions that sought to recover what the Emperor felt he had given away. The European monarchs were incensed with this development, but with no power to reverse course, Pius VII signed the concordat; two years later (December, 1804), he crowned Napoleon as Emperor of France. The first imperial coronation in France by a pope in over a thousand years, this event surprisingly underscored that papal authority was still a force in the world. Shortly thereafter, however, Napoleon turned on Pius VII, made the pope his prisoner, and took over Rome and the Papal States.

As the Napoleonic Empire faded away over the next decade, the Congress of Vienna (1815) returned almost all of the confiscated lands

---

59. Napoleon Bonaparte, speech to the clergy of Milan (June 5, 1800), http://www.cristoraul.com/ENGLISH/readinghall/MODERN-HISTORY/XIXTH_CENTURY_PAPACY/Book/9-CONCORDAT.html.

to the church, including the Papal States. This restoration created a problem for nationalistic aspirations for the unification of Italy, but also highlighted a key element of the papacy: Essential to the authority of the pope was a temporal holding—an "earthly kingdom," if you will. Within Catholicism itself, it became nearly impossible to conceive of the papacy apart from some temporal power. Outside of the church, however, the demise of papal temporal power was a goal that seemed well within reach. Indeed, as concordats—more than two dozen in the nineteenth century—between the popes and secular leaders were signed, more and more papal control over the church in these lands was yielded to the states.

A conservative reaction to this development arose. Some argued that the only hope for overcoming the disasters of the modern world— exemplified by the fallout from the Protestant Reformation and the horrors of the French Revolution—was a fully restored papacy as the absolute foundation for all authority. Joseph De Maistre's *Du Pape* (1819) championed the cause of a revived Catholic Church with an infallible pope authoritatively guiding it. De Maistre asserted that the pope is sovereign in the church; as sovereign, the pope makes decisions that are not patient of any appeal. The doctrinal pronouncements of the pope, which cannot be appealed, are binding on everyone. Therefore, papal teachings are infallible, as they are the means by which he exercises his sovereignty. De Maistre's ultramontanism (*ultra*, beyond; *montes*, mountains; from the perspective of most of Europe, the pope with his authority is on *the other side of the Alps*) not only provided a vision for a conservative political reality, but his ideas of papal authority linked to infallibility struck a religious chord as well.

In concert with this sentiment, Pope Gregory XVI (1831–1846), fully convinced of the monarchical nature of the papacy, condemned and sought to suppress the Risorgimento (the "Young Italy" liberation movement). Accordingly, he found himself on the wrong side of the growing tide of Italian nationalism and further alienated the church from the populace. Additionally, in reaction to Felicité de Lamennais's call for freedom of conscience (the newspaper he launched, *L'Avenir* ["The Future"], had for its motto "God and Liberty"), Gregory XVI published the papal encyclical *Mirari Vos* (August 15, 1832), lamenting: "Depravity exults; science is impudent; liberty, dissolute. The holiness of the sacred is despised; the majesty of divine worship is not only disapproved by evil men, but defiled and held up to ridicule. Hence sound doctrine is perverted and errors of all kinds spread boldly. The laws of the sacred, the rights, institutions, and discipline—none are safe from the audacity of those speaking evil."[60] He condemned indifferentism (the "claim that it is possible to obtain the eternal salvation of the soul by the profession of any kind of religion, as long as morality is maintained"), freedom of conscience, freedom of the press ("freedom to publish any writings whatever and disseminate them to the people"), resistance to authority, and the separation of church and state. Once again, a papal stance was at odds with growing popular sentiments. Gregory's successor, Pius IX (1846–1878) further alienated the Italian people when he refused to participate in a war against Austrian forces to liberate the Papal States for inclusion in the Italian confederation, and denounced "those who would have the Roman Pontiff to be the head and to preside over the formation of some sort of novel republic of the whole Italian people."[61] After failed attempts by Giuseppe Garibaldi and Giuseppe Mazzini, King Victor Emmanuel II succeeded in unifying Italy as a nation that included most of the former papal lands. Unsurprisingly, the new premier Camillo Cavour enacted strong anti-papal measures while marginalizing the church.[62]

Still, ultramontanism retained its vitality, at least in the religious sphere. Popular religious piety was revived, as evidenced by renewed liturgical life and a growing interest in the saints and the Virgin Mary. For example, in 1830 Catherine Labouré received the vision of Our Lady of the Miraculous Medal; the Virgin Mary, appearing to her, communicated a design according to which a medallion was to be made, promising that "all who wear this medal will receive great graces."[63] In 1848, two shepherd children—Mélanie Calvat and Maximin Giraud—reported apparitions of Our Lady of La Salette (France), who bemoaned swearing, blasphemy, drunkenness, and the desecration of

---

60. Pope Gregory XVI, *Mirari Vos* (August 15, 1832), http://www.papalencyclicals.net/Greg16/g16mirar.htm#par14.
61. Pope Pius IX, "Papal Allocution 29 April, 1848," http://www.age-of-the-sage.org/history/1848/papal_allocution. html.
62. Cavour served as premier from March to June of 1861, as gluttony and alcoholism caused his premature death at the age of fifty-one.
63. St. Catherine Labouré, http://www.fatima.org/essentials/requests/weapons3.asp.

Sunday. As pilgrims flocked to the location of these appearances, miraculous healings were reported. In 1858 a fourteen-year-old shepherd girl, Bernadette Soubirious, announced that she had received a vision in the grotto of Massabielle, near the town of Lourdes (France). Later on, in subsequent visions (there were eighteen in all), the young girl who appeared identified herself: "I am the Immaculate Conception." Pope Pius IX himself attributed his cure from epilepsy to the intercession of Mary. Interest in the cult of Mary increased substantially.

Several crucial papal actions accompanied these mid-nineteenth-century developments. Pius IX promulgated the Dogma of the Immaculate Conception of Mary in *Ineffabilis Deus* (December 8, 1854; four years prior to Lourdes): "We declare, pronounce, and define that the doctrine which holds that the most Blessed Virgin Mary, in the first instance of her conception, by a singular grace and privilege granted by Almighty God, in view of the merits of Jesus Christ, the Savior of the human race, was preserved free from all stain of original sin, is a doctrine revealed by God and therefore to be believed firmly and constantly by all the faithful."[64] Appealing to Scripture (e.g., Gen. 3:15; Luke 1:28), the parallelism between Eve and Mary (thus, setting up Mary as the second Eve), long-standing church practice (e.g., the Feast of the Conception of Mary), earlier dogmatic pronouncements (e.g., Pope Alexander VII, *Sollicitudo*, 1661), and tradition, the Dogma of the Immaculate Conception cemented papal authority to define church doctrine.

On the tenth anniversary of this dogmatic pronouncement, Pius IX issued the encyclical *Quanta Cura* (December 8, 1864) as an expression of his ultramontane sympathies, targeted especially against the clamor for a "Free Church in a Free State" as voiced by such notables as the Italian patriot Cavour and the liberal Catholic Charles le Compte de Montalembert.[65] The most important aspect of the encyclical, however, was its appendix, the Syllabus of Errors, containing the condemnation of eighty propositions. These denunciations included certain modern theological and political movements like pantheism, naturalism, rationalism, indifferentism and latitudinarianism (types of soteriological

---

64. Pius IX, *Ineffabilis Deus* (December 8, 1854), http://www.papalencyclicals.net/Pius09/p9ineff.htm.
65. In the 1830s in France, Felicité de Lamennais had involved Montalembert in the editorial production of *L'Avenir*.

pluralism), socialism, communism, and liberalism. Included also were condemnations of errors concerning the church and its prerogatives, civil society in itself and in relationship to the church, natural and Christian ethics, Christian marriage, and the civil authority in relationship to papal authority. The last condemnation summed up the spirit of *Quanta Cura* and the Syllabus of Errors: "The Roman Pontiff can, and ought to, reconcile himself, and come to terms with, progress, liberalism, and modern civilization."[66] The nineteenth-century church and its papacy refused any and all such modern developments.

Such obscurantism and lack of toleration was not lost on liberal Catholics and the wider European and American audience. Unsurprisingly, then, a shockwave disturbed this same group when Pius IX convened a new general council, Vatican I (1870). Its initial purpose was to continue the denunciations of the Syllabus, but a new agenda came quickly to the forefront: papal infallibility. Ever since the "Formula of Hormisdas" (519) had highlighted the consistent theological orthodoxy of the Church of Rome, linked it to Matthew 16:18–19, and established the papal See as being responsible for the preservation of apostolic truth, some notion of freedom from error had circulated in the church. Scholars and ecclesial leaders had engaged in debates about whether such doctrinal soundness resides in the pope alone, the pope in conjunction with the bishops, the office of the papacy, a general council of the church, or the church itself, but nothing had been defined; only a general sense had been present and believed. Certainly, a general council of the church in 1870 seemed an unusual venue to address the issue, but ultramontane pressure and papal feelings of being besieged contributed to moving infallibility to the front and center.

Vatican Council I carefully and restrictively defined the infallibility of the pope. This authority has to do with defining true Catholic doctrine that has always been recognized in the church, through Scripture and tradition:

---

66. Pius IX, *Quanta Cura* (December 8, 1864), with the Syllabus of Errors, http://www.archive.org/stream/QuantaCuraTheSyllabusOfErrors_247/pius_ix_pope_quanta_cura_and_the_syllabus_of_errors_djvu.txt.

From time to time, the Roman popes defined as to be affirmed those things that with the help of God they had recognized as conformable with the sacred Scriptures and apostolic traditions. For the Holy Spirit was not promised to the successors of Peter so that by his revelation they might make known new doctrine, but that by his assistance they might inviolably keep and faithfully expound the revelation or deposit of faith delivered through the apostles. All have fully known that this See of holy Peter remains always free from all blemish of error, according to the divine promise the Lord our Savior made to the prince of his disciples: "I have prayed for you that your faith may not fail, and when you are converted, confirm your brothers" (Luke 22:32).[67]

The Council affirmed several benefits that flow from this infallible authority: "This gift, then, of truth and never-failing faith was conferred by heaven on Peter and his successors in this chair (*cathedra*). This was done in order that they might perform their high office for the salvation of all people; that the whole flock of Christ, kept away by them from the poisonous food of error, might be nourished with the pasture of heavenly doctrine; and with opportunity for division being removed, that the whole church might be kept united and, resting on its foundation, might stand firm against the gates of hell."[68] Finally, the Council announced the exact doctrine that it was defining—the infallibility of the pope speaking *ex cathedra*:

We teach and define that the following is a doctrine divinely revealed: The Roman pope, when he speaks *ex cathedra*, that is, when discharging the office of pastor and doctor of all Christians, by virtue of his supreme apostolic authority, he defines a doctrine regarding faith or morals

---

67. Vatican Council I, First Dogmatic Constitution on the Church of Christ, session 4, 4, in Creeds of Christendom, 3 vols., ed. Philip Schaff (New York: Harper, 1877–1905), 2.266–67. For an outline of this definition from a Catholic source, see http://www.papalencyclicals.net/Councils/ecum20.htm#papal infallibility-defined.
68. Ibid., 2.269–70.

to be held by the universal church, by the divine assistance promised to him in blessed Peter, is possessed of infallibility. It is the infallibility with which the divine Redeemer willed that his church should be endowed for defining doctrine regarding faith or morals. Therefore, such definitions of the Roman pope are irreformable of themselves and not from the consent of the church.[69]

Key elements to be noted (thus, preventing much of the misunderstanding associated with this dogma) include the following: infallibility applies to pronouncements of the pope speaking *ex cathedra* (*from the chair* [of Peter]; hence, on a solemn occasion) on a matter of *faith or morals* (thus, it does not pertain to papal statements about science, economics, politics, and the like) that is to be *universally believed* by all Catholics; such dogmatic or moral declarations *cannot be changed of themselves* (i.e., immutability is not conferred on them by the *church's consent*).

Paradoxically, the day after Vatican Council I proclaimed this dogma of papal teaching authority, the Franco-Prussian War broke out and the Council was halted. Within two months, Pius IX imprisoned himself in the Vatican, and Rome fell (it would be reconstituted within a year as the capital of Italy). In terms of a temporal realm, the papacy was left with the Vatican, the Basilica of St. John Lateran (in Rome), and Castel Gandolfo (the pope's summer residence, outside of Rome). Yet, Pius IX had also overseen a vast missional enterprise, having approved new religious orders and launched massive Catholic missionary efforts outside of Europe, contributing to a nearly unprecedented expansion of the church.

Pius IX's death ended the longest pontificate in history, and his successor, Pope Leo XIII (1878–1903), loosened up the church's stance toward the modern world while still holding tightly to an overall conservative vision as set forth in the Syllabus of Errors and Vatican Council I. As the author of eighty-six encyclicals during his twenty-five year rule, he presented himself as the authoritative teacher of the church. He also set the trajectory for future Catholic biblical scholarship in his *Providentissimus Deus* (November 18, 1893), an encyclical that both

---

69. Ibid., 2.270–71.

affirmed the traditional stance of the church toward Scripture while at the same time calling for Catholic scholars to master the biblical languages and textual criticism. Leo XIII also elevated the teachings of Thomas Aquinas. In *Aeterni Patris* (August 4, 1879), the pope sought a restoration of Christian philosophy—which, in his view, would offset philosophical trends such as Kantianism and Hegelian dialecticism—by championing Thomistic philosophy, calling the works of the Angelic Doctor "immortal" and urging Catholics to thoroughly imbibe them.[70]

THE PAPACY IN THE TWENTIETH CENTURY

The twentieth century would embroil the papacy in some of the most difficult circumstances it had ever faced. Coming out of the nineteenth century, the papacy, decrying the erosion of society and religion through the insidious "isms" of the day—e.g., liberalism, modernism, socialism, indifferentism, Kantianism—and fueled by ultramontane sentiments, had set itself resolutely on a conservative course. This trajectory was picked up by the first of the twentieth-century popes, Pius X (1903–1914). For centuries, the church had become characterized by canon law; Pius X brought together all of these divergent collections into one volume, *Codex Iuris Canonici* (the Code of Canon Law), thus enforcing the legal cast of the papacy and leading to a large increase in centralization at the Vatican. Furthermore, he demanded complete submission to papal authority, exemplified in Canon 329 of the new Code assigning the appointment of all bishops to the pope. Moreover, through various initiatives, the pope exercised a conservative crackdown on Catholic biblical scholarship. For example, the Pontifical Biblical Commission addressed several important topics between 1905 and 1915 that included apparent historical narratives, the authenticity of Mosaic authorship of the Pentateuch, the authorship and historical truth of John's Gospel, the historical nature of Genesis 1–3, and the synoptic problem.[71] Indeed, Pius X's motu proprio *Praestantia Sacrae Scripturae* (November 18, 1907), attacking the acceptance

---

70. Leo XIII, *Aeterni Patris*, http://www.vatican.va/holy_father/leo_xiii/encyclicals/documents/hf_l-xiii_enc_04081879_aeterni-patris_en.html.
71. Pontifical Biblical Commission, http://www.vatican.va/roman_curia/congregations/cfaith/pcb_doc_index.htm.

of the results of the historical critical method by a growing number of Catholic scholars, urged submission "to the decisions of the Biblical Commission relating to doctrine, which have been given in the past and which shall be given in the future."[72] Additionally, the 1907 encyclical *Lamentabili Sane Exitu* (July 3, 1907)[73] and its more comprehensive sequel *Pascendi Dominici Gregis* (September 8, 1907)[74] decried scores of modernist interpretations of Scripture and novel views of the development of doctrine. Reaction to these papal initiatives was quite divided, with conservatives feeling that the pope's position legitimated and fueled their agenda and progressives lamenting what they saw as a reactionary drift toward a Catholic form of fundamentalism. Certainly, the latter group had much to fear when Pius X published "The Oath against Modernism" (September 1, 1910), with these instructions: "To be sworn by all clergy, pastors, confessors, preachers, religious superiors, and professors in philosophical-theological seminaries." There followed an introductory oath ("I . . . firmly embrace and accept each and every definition that has been set forth and declared by the unerring teaching authority of the church") followed by five professions (general revelation as a source of the knowledge of God, miracles confirming divine revelation, the establishment of the church by "the real and historical Christ" followed by apostolic succession, the non-evolution of doctrine, and the nature of true faith) and a vow to submit to the two papal encyclicals *Pascendi Dominici Gregis* and *Lamentabili Sane Exitu* and all they reject.[75]

Pope Benedict XV (1914–1922) continued his predecessor's position. In *Spiritus Paraclitus* (Sept. 15, 1920), he complained about scholars who thought that Leo XIII's *Providentissimus Deus* allowed for errors in Scripture and chastised their appeal to Leo's principle that the biblical authors wrote according to the appearance of natural phenomena. Tragically, Benedict XV's pontificate was absorbed with the Great War (World War I). He sought to maintain neutrality in the conflict,

---

72. Pius X, *Praestantia Sacrae Scripturae*, http://www.papalencyclicals.net/Pius10/p10prasc. htm.

73. Pius X, *Lamentabili Sane Exitu*, http://papalencyclicals.net/Pius10/p10lamen.htm.

74. Pius X, *Pascendi Dominici Gregis*, http://www.vatican.va/holy_father/pius_x/encyclicals/ documents/hf_p-x_enc_19070908_pascendi-dominici-gregis_en.html.

75. Pius X, "The Oath against Modernism," http://www.papalencyclicals.net/Pius10/ p10moath.htm.

reasoning that only with that stance could the church exercise its powers of persuasion to get both sides to agree to a negotiated peace. The strategy failed, however, as both sides considered the pope as favoring the other; consequently, when diplomatic talks for peace began, Benedict was excluded from them. His political endeavors after the war, however, proved fruitful and included the establishment of good relations with the state of Italy. Moreover, his post-war encyclical *Maximum Illud* (November 30, 1919) on Catholic missions emphasized the identification and training of indigenous clergy, and called upon missionaries not "to busy themselves with the interests of their terrestrial homeland" (i.e., European colonization or empire building) but to dedicate themselves to "those [interests] of their homeland in heaven." He also insisted on adequate linguistic training for cross-cultural missionaries, and the like, setting the agenda for expanding Catholic missional endeavors.

The fruit of this missional direction was born during the papacy of Pius XI (1922–1939), who consecrated the first indigenous bishops in China, Japan, India, and Southeast Asia, thereby rectifying the situation he inherited in which no missionary diocese was led by an indigenous bishop. Pius XI also continued Benedict XV's diplomatic success by signing new concordats with post-war European nations. Significantly, the concordat between the Pope and Mussolini permitted the papacy to maintain the small temporal holdings agreed to in the concordat of Pius IX: the Vatican, St. John Lateran, and Castel Gondolfo. It also recognized the legitimacy of canon law, provided for the teaching of Catholic doctrine in public schools, and gave an immense amount of money to the church in recompense for its forfeiture of the Papal States. But any agreement between the church and a totalitarian state would prove to be unsatisfactory to both sides. As Italian democracy suffered under Fascism, it condemned the accord and denounced the church—which had never favored the ideology of democracy—as being sympathetic to Mussolini's regime. Moreover, the state failed to live up to its agreement with the church, provoking the pope's condemnation (in the encyclical *Non abbiamobisogno*; June 29, 1931) of "a true, a real pagan worship of the state—the 'Statolatry.'"[76]

---

76. The main thrust of this encyclical was a defense of the organization Catholic Action as

Similar conflicts developed with the concordat between Pius XI and Hitler. The pope believed that Nazism was the best hope as a deterrent against Communism, yet he was distressed by reports of the growing number and severity of atrocities committed by the Nazis. Emboldened by the concordat, Hitler turned against the church; once again, Pius XI issued an encyclical (*Mit Brennender Sorge*; March 14, 1937) excoriating the Third Reich for breaking the treaty, engaging in a "war of extermination," substituting "a dark and impersonal destiny for the personal God," idolizing the state, distorting religious language and concepts (e.g., immortality, original sin, grace) for profane use and to repudiate Christianity, compelling German youth to be involved in organizations that promote the state and attack religion, and persecuting priests and religious orders.[77]

This encyclical was quickly followed by another one condemning Communism. In *Divini Redemptoris* (March 19, 1937), Pius XI attacked the barbarism of "bolshevistic and atheistic communism, which aims at upsetting the social order and at undermining the very foundations of Christian civilization." His denunciation was specifically aimed at the Communist regimes in Russia, Mexico, and Spain. Specific evils condemned included "a false messianic idea;" "a pseudo-ideal of justice, of equality, and fraternity in labor;" "a deceptive mysticism" that allures and entraps with "delusive promises;" a false sense of economic progress; dialectical materialism; anti-authoritarianism; collectivism; the devastation of marriage and family life; poisonous propaganda, state control of the press, fierce persecution of the church, and atheism. The pope then presented a vision for a church-led and church-fostered human society and called for a "spiritual renovation" particularly promoted by "detachment from earthly goods and the precept of charity" infused with a concern for justice.[78] While certainly not a proponent of democracy, Pope Pius XI stationed himself firmly against all forms of totalitarian systems—Italian

---

being "outside and above all party politics" and not associated with the Popular Party and its opposition to Fascism; thus, the pope repudiated fascist persecution of Catholic Action. Pius XI, *Non abbiamobisogno* (June 29, 1931), http://www.vatican.va/holy_father/pius_xi/encyclicals/documents/hf_p-xi_enc_29061931_non-abbiamo-bisogno_en.html.

77. Pius XI, *Mit Brennender Sorge* (March 14, 1937), http://www.vatican.va/holy_father/pius_xi/encyclicals/documents/hf_p-xi_enc_14031937_mit-brennender-sorge_en.html.

78. Pius XI, *Divini Redemptoris* (March 19, 1937), http://www.vatican.va/holy_father/pius_xi/encyclicals/documents/hf_p-xi_enc_19031937_divini-redemptoris_en.html.

Fascism, German Socialism, and Communism—yet attempted to wield spiritual authority across this wide gamut of ideologies.

Pope Pius XII (1939–1958) inherited this precarious balancing act and hopelessly attempted to stave off international conflict. During World War II he tried to remain neutral in order to be a prophetic voice directed at and heard by all. Such cautious diplomacy, however, satisfied no one. The Allies sought papal condemnation of German atrocities, but the pope's response was limited to rescuing the Jews of Rome from deportation. He believed that any denunciation would not significantly aid the Jews and would only increase Nazi persecution of the church in the lands that Hitler had conquered. Yet, even papal neutrality could not stand before the growing tide of Nazi brutality. In his Christmas address of 1942, Pius XII finally denounced the slaughter of the Jews, a measure that angered the Germans but that the Allies still considered as falling far short of the kind of condemnation demanded by such genocide. The external authority of the church seemed to be compromised.

Within the church itself, however, new currents were swirling that eventually would lead to a new conceptualization of its nature and mission. In part this development was due to the prolific writings of Henri deLubac, who directed the church back to its Patristic roots (specifically in his Patristic translation series, *Sources chrétiennes*, started in 1942) and medieval exegesis (*Exégèse médiévale*; 1956–1965). His theological acumen and resourcefulness would contribute greatly to Vatican Council II. The institutional nature of the church became less emphasized and its spiritual character highlighted. A greater openness in biblical studies, including a lessening of resistance toward historical criticism, followed in the wake of Pius XII's encyclical *Divini Afflante Spiritu* (September 30, 1943). Published on the fiftieth anniversary of *Providentissimus Deus* (1893) and reminding its audience of that encyclical's condemnation of the error that "restricts the truth of Sacred Scripture solely to matters of faith and morals," *Divini Afflante Spiritu* encouraged Catholic biblical scholars to "seek the aid of profane sciences [e.g., archaeology, philology, Ancient Near Eastern studies, textual criticism] which are useful for the interpretation of the Scriptures." The pope assured these scholars that no conflict exists between the Council of Trent's decree that the Latin Vulgate is the official version of Scripture for the church, and the study of the original Hebrew and

Greek texts of the Old Testament and New Testament, respectively. Indeed, Pius XII insisted that "this authority of the Vulgate in matters of doctrine by no means prevents—nay, rather today it almost demands—either the corroboration and confirmation of this same doctrine by the original texts or the having recourse on any and every occasion to the aid of these same texts, by which the correct meaning of the Sacred Letters is everywhere daily made more clear and evident." The encyclical also called for serious recognition of the human character of Scripture—the "personal traits" of each biblical author—and the careful use of historical-cultural studies, source criticism, genre sensitivity, and authorial intent in order to achieve a proper interpretation.[79]

Even with these developments, the church remained strongly conservative. Toward the end of his papacy, Pius XII took a more hard line stance against progressive initiatives that claimed justification from his earlier openness. Papal sternness was at its height in political matters, as the pope openly condemned Communism and its deleterious effect on Catholics in the Soviet Union and Eastern European countries. Indeed, in the face of a growing Communist influence in Italy, he encouraged an alliance between Italian Christian Democrats and neo-Fascist movements. Theologically, papal conservatism led to the *ex cathedra* pronouncement of the Dogma of the Bodily Assumption of Mary (*Munificentissimus Deus*; November 1, 1950):

> . . . immaculate in her conception, a most perfect virgin in her divine motherhood, the noble associate of the divine Redeemer who has won a complete triumph over sin and its consequences, [Mary] finally obtained, as the supreme culmination of her privileges, that she should be preserved free from the corruption of the tomb and that, like her own Son, having overcome death, she might be taken up body and soul to the glory of heaven where, as Queen, she sits in splendor at the right hand of her Son, the immortal King of the Ages.[80]

---

79. Pius XII, *Divini Afflante Spiritu* (September 30, 1943), http://www.vatican.va/holy_father/
pius_xii/encyclicals/documents/hf_p-xii_enc_30091943_divini-afflante-spiritu_en.html.
80. Pius XII, *Munificentissimus Deus* (Nov. 1, 1950), http://www.vatican.va/holy_father/pius_xii/
apost_constitutions/documents/hf_p-xii_apc_19501101_munificentissimus-deus_en.html.

The next pope, John XXIII (1958–1963), is best known for his convening of the most recent general council of the church, Vatican Council II (1962–1965). Though conservative elements attempted to prepare for and dominate the Council—especially by drafting the original *schema* of the constitutions, declarations, and decrees—these voices were largely overruled by the Pope's agenda that Vatican II would not be about condemnations but about an *aggiornamento* (updating) of the church.

Several highlights of the Council must suffice. In terms of the nature of the church, *Lumen Gentium* (Dogmatic Constitution of the Church; November 21, 1964) redefined the people of God. It insisted that all Christians constitute a priesthood of the faithful: "The baptized, by regeneration and the anointing of the Holy Spirit, are consecrated to be a spiritual house and a holy priesthood, that through all the works of Christian people they may offer spiritual sacrifices and proclaim the perfection of him who has called them out of darkness into his marvelous light (1 Peter 2:4–10)."[81] While certainly not doing away with the traditional priesthood, nor rendering it less important, Vatican II closely tied this "common priesthood" to the ordained ministry of the church:

> Though they differ essentially and not only in degree, the common priesthood of the faithful and the ministerial or hierarchical priesthood are nonetheless ordered one to another; each in its own proper way shares in the one priesthood of Christ. The ministerial priest, by the sacred power that he has, forms and rules the priestly people; in the person of Christ he effects the eucharistic sacrifice and offers it to God in the name of all the people. The faithful indeed, by virtue of their royal priesthood, participate in the offering of the Eucharist. They exercise that priesthood, too, by the reception of the sacraments, prayer and thanksgiving, the witness of a holy life, abnegation and active charity.[82]

---

81. Vatican Council II, *Dogmatic Constitution on the Church*, 2.10.
82. Ibid.

Such mutuality was also highlighted in the cooperative authority exercised by the pope and the cardinals at the highest level of leadership in the church. While certainly not doing away with papal authority, nor diminishing its importance, Vatican II called for a greater exercise of ruling authority by the pope in conjunction with the College of Cardinals:

> Just as in accordance with the Lord's decree, St. Peter and the rest of the apostles constitute a unique apostolic college, so in like manner the Roman Pope, Peter's successor, and the bishops, the successors of the apostles, are related with and united to one another. There is a collegial character and structure to the episcopal order. The college or body of bishops has for all that no authority unless united with the Roman Pope, Peter's successor, as its head, whose primary authority, let it be added, over all—whether clergy or lay people—remains in its integrity. For the Roman Pope, by reason of his office as Vicar of Christ, namely, and as pastor of the entire Church, has full, supreme and universal power over the whole Church, a power that he can always exercise unhindered. The order of bishops is the successor to the college of the apostles in their role as teachers and pastors, and in it the apostolic college is perpetuated. Together with their head, the Supreme Pope, and never apart from him, they have supreme and full authority over the universal Church. But this power cannot be exercised without the agreement of the Roman Pope. In this college the bishops, while loyally respecting the primacy and pre-eminence of their head, exercise their own proper authority for the good of their faithful, indeed even for the good of the whole Church.[83]

The Council even extended the doctrine of infallibility to include this episcopal college when it proclaims matters of faith and morals in conjunction with the Pope:

---

83. Ibid., 3.17.

Although the bishops, taken individually, do not enjoy the privilege of infallibility, they do, however, proclaim infallibly the doctrine of Christ on the following conditions: namely, when, even though dispersed throughout the world but preserving the bond of communion among themselves and with Peter's successor, in their authoritative teaching concerning matters of faith and morals, they are in agreement that a particular teaching is to be held definitively and absolutely. This is still more clearly the case when, assembled in an ecumenical council, they are, for the universal Church, teachers of and judges in matters of faith and morals. Their decisions must be adhered to with the loyal and obedient assent of faith.[84]

Lumen Gentium also clouded the church's stance on salvation outside of the church, insisting that whereas the fullness of salvation belongs to Catholics, Protestants "in some real way . . . are joined with us [the Catholic Church] in the Holy Spirit, for to them too he gives his gifts and graces whereby he is operative among them with his sanctifying power." So too is the plan of salvation related to Jews and Muslims, and to others as well:

Nor is God remote from those who in shadows and images seek the unknown God, since he gives to all men life and breath and all things (cf. Acts 17:25–28) and since the Savior wills all men to be saved (cf. 1 Tim. 2:4). Those who, through no fault of their own, do not know the gospel of Christ or his Church, but who nevertheless seek God with a sincere heart, and, moved by grace, try in their actions to do his will as they know it through the dictates of their conscience—those too may achieve eternal salvation. Nor shall divine providence deny the assistance necessary for salvation to those who, without any fault of theirs, have not yet arrived at an explicit knowledge of God, and who, not without grace, strive to lead a good life.[85]

---

84. Ibid., 3.25.
85. Ibid., 2.16.

Other traditional church stances were significantly modified by Vatican II. For example, the historical position on the inerrancy of Scripture was modified in *Dei Verbum* (Dogmatic Constitution on Divine Revelation; November 18, 1965). Whereas the original draft of this Constitution affirmed the inerrancy of all of Scripture, its final form limits the extent of scriptural truthfulness to salvific matters: "we must acknowledge that the books of Scripture firmly, faithfully and without error, teach that truth which God, for the sake of our salvation, wished to see confided to the sacred Scriptures."[86] *Gaudiumet Spes* (Pastoral Constitution on the Church in the Modern World; December 7, 1965), rather than furthering the time-worn opposition of the church to the world, called upon the church to "recognize and understand the world in which we live, its explanations, its longings, and its often dramatic characteristics. . . . to decipher authentic signs of God's presence and purpose in the happenings, needs and desires" of humanity.[87] It affirmed the dignity of all human beings as created in the image of God; the innate natural law/ conscience to which all people are to yield obedience; the divine purpose for humanity; the partial responsibility of believers for the denial of God by atheism; the call of believers and unbelievers "to work for the rightful betterment of this world in which all alike live," especially through "sincere and prudent dialogue;"[88] the working of grace in "an unseen way" in the hearts of "all men of good will;"[89] the community of all mankind; universal human rights; and the like. This openness to the world at large was a far cry from the hostility toward and condemnation of the world so prevalent in the church and its papacy throughout its history.

Additionally, *Sacrosantum Concilium* (Constitution on the Sacred Liturgy; December 4, 1963) reversed the long-standing practice of saying the Mass in Latin by calling for its celebration in the vernacular of the people, who were also to become more active participants in the Mass. *Unitatis Redintegratio* (Decree on Ecumenism; November 21, 1964) and *Nostra Aetate* (Declaration of the Relation of the Church to Non-Christian Religions; October 28, 1965) were the Council's forays into ecumenism and

---

86. Vatican Council II, *Dogmatic Constitution on Divine Revelation*, 3.11.
87. Vatican Council II, *Pastoral Constitution on the Church in the Modern World*, introduction 4; 1.11.
88. Ibid., 1.21.
89. Ibid., 1.22.

dialog with non-Christians, momentous steps taken to reverse the church's previous suspicion and rejection of everything non-Catholic. Indeed, the banner of religious liberty for all human beings was raised in *Dignitatis Humanae* (Declaration on Religious Liberty; December 7, 1965), reversing the church's previous denial of such a right. Most certainly, Vatican Council II was an aggiornamento of the church that thrust it, even if ill-prepared because of its former positions, into the modern world.

FROM VATICAN II TO THE PAPACY TODAY: A BRIEF SEQUEL

Though convened by Pope John XXIII, the Council was concluded by Pope Paul VI (1963–1978), to whom also fell the initial responsibility to enact the changes it proposed. Such reform faced stiff opposition: from conservatives, who saw the Council's vision as a betrayal of the irreformable traditional church, which consequently experienced whole scale defections within its ranks; from liberals, who chaffed under the pope's attempt at a balancing act to appease both conservative and progressive factions in the church and his obstructionist maneuvers to try to neutralize some of the most radical reforms called for by the Council. His progressive-conservative equilibrium can be illustrated by his policy of easing tensions between the church and Communist regimes and his condemnation of artificial birth control (in his encyclical *Humanae Vitae*; July 25, 1968).

Paul VI also dedicated himself to international affairs, establishing the trajectory for future popes as worldwide ambassadors for the church. Indeed, his travels took him to Jerusalem to meet with Patriarch Athenagoras of the Greek Orthodox Church (1964), to the United Nations to advance the cause of world peace (1963), to Geneva for a meeting with the World Council of Churches for ecumenical dialog with Protestants and Orthodox (1969), and to Africa (1969), the Philippines (1970), and Australia (1970), countries never before visited by a pope. Paul VI's missional concerns were also front and center in his encyclical *Evangelii Nuntiandi* (December 8, 1975), a manifesto on evangelization in the modern world.

His successor, Albino Luciani, took the names of the two popes who had conducted Vatican Council II, John XXIII and Paul VI, becoming

Pope John Paul. His tragedy-shortened pontificate lasted only thirty-three days (August 26 to September 28, 1978) as he died of a coronary embolism.

In honor of his predecessor, Karol Wojtyla took the papal name John Paul II (1978–2005), becoming the first non-Italian pope in over 450 years. Growing up in Communist-held Poland, he was familiar with persecution and thus well prepared to support the Solidarity movement and help the country transition to a stable government as the Communist regime fell. He also played a crucial role in the downfall of Communism and the reestablishment of the church in the Soviet Union and Eastern Europe. He continued the worldwide reach of his predecessor, visiting 129 countries. His theological profundity, philosophical acumen, and moral judgment were manifested in the various themes treated in his encyclicals and addresses: the endorsement of a culture of life over against a culture of death (with an accompanying condemnation of abortion, birth control, euthanasia, and capital punishment; e.g., *Evangelium Vitae*; March 25, 1995); a theology of the body (dovetailing with the promotion of legitimate human sexuality); Marian devotion (*Redemptoris Mater*; March 25, 1978); encouragement of Eucharistic adoration (e.g., *Ecclesia de Eucharistia*; April 17, 2003); and the relationship between faith and reason (expressed especially through philosophy; *Fides and Ratio*, September 14, 1998). The breadth of Pope John Paul II's teachings established him as a leading figure beyond the walls of the church, yet he was staunchly situated within its traditional confines as well. Accordingly, he could extend hope for reconciliation with the Orthodox churches yet avoid all overtures toward unity with the Protestant churches (*Ut Unum Sint*; May 25, 1995), and he could pray with Muslims, Jews, Buddhists, Hindus, Sikhs, Baha'is, Zoroastrians, Shintoists, and animists,[90] yet neutralize the Jesuits for their spearheading of liberation theology.

After the death of Pope John Paul II, Joseph Aloisius Ratzinger was elected pope and took the name Benedict XVI (2005–2013). He was

---

90. The Pope organized the first World Day of Prayer for Peace on October 27, 1986, in Assisi (repeated January 24, 2002), in which representatives from scores of Christian churches (Catholic, Orthodox, and Protestant) and non-Christian religions participated.

the former Prefect of the Congregation for the Doctrine of the Faith (appointed 1981) and the main author of the Catechism of the Catholic Church (1994). He was elected in (unrealized) anticipation that his papacy would be short and transitional (he was seventy-eight years old when selected) and was noted for his advocacy and defense of traditional Catholicism. In February 2013 he resigned, becoming the first pope since Pope Gregory XII in 1415 to do so. As of the time of the writing of this chapter, my history of the papacy ends with the reign of Pope Francis (March 2013). Born Jorge Mario Bergoglio, he was appointed Archbishop of Buenos Aires in 1998 and made a cardinal by Pope John Paul II in 2001. He is the first Jesuit pope, the first pope from the Americas, the first pope from the Southern Hemisphere, and the first non-European pope since Gregory III (741). He is known for his humility, concern for the poor, and simple lifestyle, and though it is difficult to describe the trajectory of his papacy, initial signs indicate that Pope Francis will be known for opening up the Catholic Church through ecumenical dialog and an inclusivistic theology.

APPLICATIONS

As evangelicals we often find it very difficult to conceive of and understand the highest level of church leadership in terms of the papacy with its temporal authority exercised together with or over emperors and monarchs, and its kingdom-building that amassed vast amounts of territory and huge sums (and deficits) of money while mounting armies for international wars and patronizing the artistic flourishing of an entire city like Rome—all with a religious twist. Yes, we must seek to conceptualize most of the history of the papacy in terms of a dominant world (or at least European) power, the likes of which we do not see today. Though it is very difficult to do, we should attempt to evaluate papal history from this perspective and not just dismiss it.

At the same time, if you are like me, we as evangelicals we often look in vain for biblical support for such a notion of the papacy. On the contrary, our thoughts are turned to Jesus' affirmation before Pilate: "My kingdom is not of this world. If my kingdom were of this world, my servants would have been fighting, that I might not be delivered over to the Jews" (John 18:36). We then wonder, what does the church and its leadership have to do with lay investiture, the Crusades, the Inquisition, concordats, and the like? Most of us will respond in the negative; the church has nothing to do with such matters.

Accordingly, we conceive of church leadership in very different terms. We acknowledge that Jesus Christ is the supreme head of the church, which is his body and which manifests itself in local congregations. These assemblies are cared for by pastors or elders, to whom are given four responsibilities: teaching, or the communication of sound doctrine (1 Tim. 3:2; 5:17); leading at the highest level of authority (1 Tim. 3:5; 5:17; 1 Thess. 5:12); praying, especially for the sick (James 5:13–15); and shepherding, involving the exercising of oversight (1 Peter 5:2) and modeling stellar Christian conduct (1 Peter 5:3; Heb. 13:7, 17). Deacons and deaconesses serve Jesus Christ through the various ministries of their local churches (1 Tim. 3:7–13; e.g., Phoebe, Rom. 16:1–2). For many evangelicals, the congregation also plays an important role in church leadership (Matt. 18:15–20; Acts 6:1–6; 15:1–34).[91] This polity, with its many permutations, is a far cry from the papacy.

At the same time, we need to be reminded that the church, as a spatio-temporal/eschatological reality,[92] is responsible to engage the world at large. Specifically, one of its ministries is being for and against the world: "the church is *for* the world—encouraging its members to faithfully obey the cultural mandate to build civilization while loving neighbors and making disciples—and *against* the world, helping its members to be compassionately critical of and justly opposed to all that in this fallen world is tainted by sin and in rebellion against Jesus Christ, head of the world and head of the church."[93] As evangelicals we are rightly suspicious of and indeed reject the historical papacy with its temporal power and kingdom-building authority. Yet, we need to consider carefully and seriously our engagement with this world as sojourners on earth and citizens of heaven.

---

91. For further discussion, see Gregg R. Allison, *Sojourners and Strangers: The Doctrine of the Church*, Foundations of Evangelical Theology, gen. ed. John S. Feinberg (Wheaton, IL: Crossway, 2012), especially chapters 7–8.
92. Ibid., 148–57.
93. Ibid., 463.

CHAPTER 7

The Rule of Elders:
The Presbyterian Angle on Church Leadership

Nathan A. Finn[1]

Like many folks who were raised in Christian families, I have a "home church": the Central Baptist Church of Waycross, Georgia. In 1986, Central Baptist relocated from the outskirts of downtown into new facilities located next door to the First Presbyterian Church. Over the years, I became fairly familiar with our Presbyterian neighbors. Two of my cousins were members of First Presbyterian at different times, so I occasionally participated in their church's youth group activities. I knew that the folks at First Presbyterian sprinkled babies, believed in predestination, never held revival services, and were less concerned about moderate consumption of alcohol than we Baptists were. Their pastor during my middle school and high school years, Dr. Norman McCrummen, was the most educated clergyman in town (he had earned a PhD in Middle Eastern Studies). On Saint Andrews Sunday every summer, all the men wore kilts to church, which I thought was very cool. I also knew that First Presbyterian had both deacons and elders, and that besides Dr. McCrummen, all of the other elders were laypeople who did not receive a paycheck from the church.

First Presbyterian Church holds to presbyterian polity, which is that view of church government that places the final earthly ecclesiastical authority in the hands of groups of elders.[2] The name "presbyterian" is

1. Nathan A. Finn (PhD, Southeastern Baptist Theological Seminary) is Associate Professor of Historical Theology and Baptist Studies at Southeastern Baptist Theological Seminary in Wake Forest, North Carolina.
2. Throughout this chapter, I periodically make a distinction between presbyterian polity and

taken from the Greek word *presbyteros*, which is translated into English as the word "elder." Self-described Presbyterian churches and denominations embrace presbyterian polity and place governing authority into the hands of their elders. In America, the largest presbyterian groups include the Presbyterian Church in the USA (PC-USA), the Presbyterian Church in America (PCA), and the Evangelical Presbyterian Church (EPC).

In addition to these self-designated Presbyterian groups, presbyterianism is also the most common form of polity among Reformed churches that do not use "Presbyterian" in their denominational name. This includes such groups as the Reformed Church in America (RCA), the Christian Reformed Church in North America (CRC), and the United Reformed Churches in North America (URCNA). These latter denominations trace their roots to Continental Reformed traditions rather than the Presbyterian movements in the British Isles. Though the terminology varies at times, each of these groups argue that groups of elders make binding decisions on behalf of the churches they serve.

The purpose of this chapter is twofold. First, I hope to summarize the basics of presbyterian polity. This includes describing the biblical rationale presbyterians use for their position as well as tracing the historical development of presbyterian government. Second, I hope to offer a brief, friendly critique of presbyterianism from a baptistic perspective. My own convictions will become clear when I critique presbyterian polity, but it seems appropriate for me to lay my cards on the table before proceeding any further. It is only fair that readers understand my biases, since I am not a part of the tradition I am interacting with in this chapter.

I am a convictional Baptist who advocates a plural-elder-led form of congregational polity. I believe that this position represents the best application of New Testament polity to our contemporary milieu. I argue that elders, pastors or shepherds, and bishops or overseers are all different names for the same church office. All elders, whether paid or unpaid, are tasked with the responsibility of leading their congregations through

---

self-designated Presbyterian denominations. For the sake of clarity, I refer to presbyterian polity with a lowercase "p" and denominations with a capital "P."

the ministries of teaching, prayer, and shepherding.[3] In addition to my responsibilities as a seminary professor, I serve as a non-staff elder in a Southern Baptist congregation that embraces the view of polity that I have described, the First Baptist Church of Durham, North Carolina. For a document that briefly summarizes my views on the nature of elder ministry and its relationship to the congregation, see the FBC Durham bylaws, which are available online at the church's website.[4]

ELDERS IN PRESBYTERIAN POLITY

Christians who affirm presbyterianism or congregationalism share several key beliefs about church government. First, both traditions argue unequivocally that the ultimate authority in any church is the Lord Jesus Christ.[5] The question is to whom within a church King Jesus delegates his authority. Second, both traditions reject the episcopal belief that bishops exercise any form of apostolic authority over groups of local congregations. This was a point of contention between the pro-episcopal Anglicans in the Church of England and the Puritans (mostly presbyterians) and Separatists (mostly congregationalists) who challenged the Elizabethan status quo during the later English Reformation.[6] Third, presbyterians and congregationalists affirm the priesthood of all believers more consistently than episcopal traditions. According to this idea, all believers comprise a "holy priesthood" (1 Peter 2:5) that offers spiritual sacrifices of worship to the Lord (Rom. 12:1), builds up the body of Christ (1 Thess. 5:11), and proclaims the gospel to all peo-

---

3. For other Baptist authors who affirm elder-led congregational polity, see Mark Dever, *Nine Marks of a Healthy Church*, new ed. (Wheaton, IL: Crossway, 2004), 219–43; John S. Hammett, *Biblical Foundations for Baptist Churches: A Contemporary Ecclesiology* (Grand Rapids: Kregel Academic, 2005), 135–89; Phil A. Newton, *Elders in Congregational Life: Rediscovering the Biblical Model of Church Leadership* (Grand Rapids: Kregel Academic, 2005); Benjamin L. Merkle, *40 Questions about Elders and Deacons* (Grand Rapids: Kregel Academic, 2008); Benjamin L. Merkle, *Why Elders? A Biblical and Practical Guide for Church Members* (Grand Rapids: Kregel Academic, 2009).
4. See http://www.fbcdurham.org/fbc-life/bylaws/ (accessed January 3, 2012).
5. For example, see Sean Michael Lucas, *What Is Church Government? Basics of the Faith* (Phillipsburg, NJ: P&R, 2009), 6–13; R. Stanton Norman, *The Baptist Way: Distinctives of a Baptist Church* (Nashville: B&H Academic, 2005), 33–46.
6. See Agha Uka Agha, "Puritan Presbyterian Polity in Elizabethan England, 1559–1593" (PhD diss., Drew University, 1985); B. R. White, *The English Separatist Tradition* (Oxford, UK: Oxford University Press, 1971).

ples (Matt. 28:19–20).[7] Finally, both groups argue that the two biblically ordained officers in a local church are elders and deacons. The debate rests with the nature of the eldership.

Two Types of Elders

Presbyterians argue for two types of elders: *teaching elders* and *ruling elders*. In presbyterian polity, the former is comprised of vocational ministers while the latter are laypersons. Presbyterians believe that all of the elders are elected by the congregation, ordained to the eldership, and share in the governance of the church. Nevertheless, only the teaching elders are expected to be gifted to preach and teach the Scriptures. Thus, the distinction between elders is based upon giftedness; ruling elders are not required to possess the ability to teach. Robert Reymond summarizes this distinction:

> These designations are simply current conventions to mark respectively the distinction between the church's ministers of the Word and the church's other elders, all of whom, laboring together, govern the church, a distinction that Presbyterians believe the Holy Scripture itself endorses.... "Ruling elders" then is a term descriptive of the non-ministerial elders in the church; "teaching elders" are those that have been set apart for the ministry of the Word.[8]

This twofold view of the eldership is characteristic of virtually all contemporary presbyterians. This approach to church leadership is also common among many non-presbyterian churches, though the specific

---

7. For a helpful articulation of the priesthood of all believers from a congregationalist perspective, see Malcolm B. Yarnell III, "The Priesthood of Believers: Rediscovering the Biblical Doctrine of Royal Priesthood," in *Restoring Integrity in Baptist Churches*, ed. Thomas White, Jason G. Duesing, and Malcolm B. Yarnell III (Grand Rapids: Kregel Academic, 2008), 221–43. The doctrine of the royal priesthood is foundational to congregationalism. While presbyterian theologians normally give this doctrine a brief treatment, it would be fair to say it is assumed more than it is defended. For example, see Louis Berkhof, *Systematic Theology*, new ed. (Grand Rapids: Eerdmans, 1996), 560.

8. Robert L. Reymond, "The Presbytery-Led Church: Presbyterian Church Government," in *Perspectives on Church Government: Five Views on Church Polity*, ed. Chad Owen Brand and R. Stanton Norman (Nashville: B&H Academic, 2004), 121.

terminology of ruling elder and teaching elder is not necessarily embraced.[9]

The Biblical Evidence

In advocating a place for both teaching and ruling elders in local churches, presbyterians believe they are recovering apostolic polity. They cite two key New Testament texts. The first is Ephesians 4:11–13, which argues for a variety of church officers during the apostolic period.

> And he gave the apostles, the prophets, the evangelists, the shepherds and teachers, to equip the saints for the work of ministry, for building up the body of Christ, until we all attain to the unity of the faith and of the knowledge of the Son of God, to mature manhood, to the measure of the stature of the fullness of Christ.

Presbyterians argue that this list of officers can be divided into groups: offices that ceased at the end of the apostolic era, and offices that continue to the present day. Apostles, prophets, and evangelists are considered temporary offices that were accompanied by miraculous gifts and helped to establish the Christian movement during the first century. Shepherds (or pastors) and teachers are permanent offices that endure to the present day.[10] Early presbyterians argued that shepherds and teachers were different offices, whereas most modern presbyterians argue that these are two roles associated with the same office.[11]

---

9. Many congregations make a distinction between pastors and elders, with the former being paid staff and the latter being laypeople who make governing decision, sometimes in conjunction with the staff and sometimes exercising authority over the staff. This approach to elders is common among nondenominational churches and Bible churches. It is also a minority view in some Baptist churches. For example, a Southern Baptist church not far from where I live makes a general distinction between elders and pastors. Elders are mostly laymen who function like a church board, while most of the pastors are ministry program directors. The one exception is the senior pastor, who is the only paid staff member to also serve as an elder. Some of my critiques in this chapter apply as much to these "semi-presbyterian" arrangements as they do to intentionally presbyterian congregations.

10. John Calvin, *Institutes of the Christian Religion*, vol. 2, ed. John T. McNeill, trans. Ford Lewis Battles (Philadelphia: Westminster-John Knox, 1960), 4:3:4 and 4:3:5. See also Thomas Smyth, *The Name, Nature, and Functions, of Ruling Elders* (New York: Mark R. Newman et al, 1845), 2–3.

11. This historical development is discussed below.

The second key biblical text for presbyterians is 1 Timothy 5:17: "Let the elders who rule well be considered worthy of double honor, especially those who labor in preaching and teaching." For presbyterians, this verse establishes the distinction between teaching elders and ruling elders. As Sean Lucas notes, "This text suggests that all elders rule, but some elders also labor in preaching and teaching God's Word as a focus."[12] Lucas then expounds on this interpretation based upon the *Book of Church Order of the Presbyterian Church in America*. Ruling elders are to be godly individuals who are "entrusted with the administration of order and discipline in a particular church." Teaching elders, sometimes called "ministers of the Word," also share in the general oversight of the congregation. But unlike ruling elders, teaching elders also "have the function of feeding the flock by reading, expounding, and preaching the Word of God and administering the sacraments."[13]

Based upon 1 Timothy 5:17, most presbyterians believe that a *presbyteros* is always a ruler or governor, but is not always a teacher or preacher. In arguing this point, James Henley Thornwell contends, "Preachers, accordingly, are Elders, not because they preach or administer the sacraments, but because they are governors."[14] Furthermore, Thornwell argues, "The inference is unavoidable that they [Paul and Timothy] regarded *Presbyter* as synonymous, not with *Preacher*, but *ruler*, and as properly descriptive of all who are called to administer government in the house of God."[15] Charles Hodge agrees, arguing that in the New Testament churches, all elders ruled, but the vast majority of elders were not pastors and many did not have a permanent relationship with a particular congregation. According to Hodge, "Presbyterians do not believe that Timothy was the pastor of Ephesus, or Titus the bishop of Crete."[16] John Murray agrees, suggesting that Timothy and

---

12. Lucas, *What Is Church Government?*, 21.
13. Ibid. Lucas is referring to *The Book of Church Order of the Presbyterian Church in America*, 6th ed. (Lawrenceville, GA: The Committee for Christian Education and Publication, 2012), chapters 8–5 and 8–9.
14. James Henley Thornwell, "The Ruling Elders," in *The Collected Writings of James Henley Thornwell, Volume Four: Ecclesiastical*, ed. John B. Adger and John L. Girardeau (1873; reprint, Birmingham, AL: Solid Ground Christian Books, 2005), 105.
15. Ibid., 106.
16. Charles Hodge, *The Church and Its Polity* (New York: Charles Scribner and Sons, 1878), 268. For a dissenting position from one of Hodge's and Thornwell's contemporaries, see Smyth, *The Name, Nature, and Functions, of Ruling Elders*, 33. Smyth affirms the ministry

Titus might have been evangelists who represented the Apostle Paul rather than elders or bishops in the New Testament churches.[17]

Interestingly, presbyterian exegetes are less uniform in arguing that 1 Timothy 5:17 teaches a twofold eldership. Some argue for the traditional presbyterian view. For example, William Hendricksen argues that 1 Timothy 5:17 demonstrates that "already in Paul's day a distinction began to be made between those whom today we call 'ministers' and those whom we still call 'elders.'"[18] Others, however, demur, or at least are ambivalent about the passage. George Knight argues the likelihood that Paul "is speaking of a subgroup of the 'overseers' that consists of those who are *especially* gifted by God to teach, as opposed to other overseers, who must all 'be *able* to teach' (1 Tim. 3:2)."[19] Brian Chappell makes no reference to the twofold eldership, but focuses instead on the importance of honoring and remunerating gifted preachers by setting them apart as full-time, paid pastors.[20]

Historical Development

Based on their interpretation of the aforementioned texts, presbyterian denominations have historically placed significant emphasis on their polity. Most presbyterian groups produce books of church order or church discipline or forms of government (the terminology varies) that elaborate their polity. The twofold eldership is always codified in these polity manuals. For example, the PCA's *Book of Church Order* makes this distinction clear:

> The ordinary and perpetual classes of office in the Church are elders and deacons. Within the class of elder are the two orders of teaching elders and ruling elders. The elders

---

of ruling elders, but argues that the biblical term *presbyteros* was always used only for teachers or bishops in the churches.

17. John Murray, "The Government in the Church," in the *Collected Writings of John Murray, Volume 2: Select Lectures in Systematic Theology* (Carlisle, PA: Banner of Truth, 1996), 342.

18. William Hendricksen and Simon J. Kistemaker, *New Testament Commentary: Exposition of Thessalonians, Pastorals, and Hebrews* (Grand Rapids: Baker, 2002), 180.

19. George W. Knight, *The Pastoral Epistles: A Commentary on the Greek Text*, NIGTC (Grand Rapids: Eerdmans, 1999), 233 (emphasis original).

20. Bryan Chappell, *To Guard the Deposit: 1 & 2 Timothy and Titus*, Preach the Word (Wheaton, IL: Crossway, 2000), 130–32.

jointly have the government and spiritual oversight of the Church, including teaching. Only those elders who are specially gifted, called and trained by God to preach may serve as teaching elders.[21]

The twofold understanding of ruling elders and teaching elders is also maintained among other presbyterian bodies, including the Presbyterian Church in the USA and Reformed Church in America.[22]

The presbyterian view of elders finds its genesis with the Reformed traditions that arose in Europe and the British Isles during the sixteenth and seventeenth centuries. In Reformation Strasbourg, Martin Bucer developed a fourfold view of the ministry that included teachers, pastors, elders, and deacons. Following his time in Strasbourg from 1538–1540, John Calvin adopted Bucer's position and further developed it in Geneva.[23] By the time Calvin had written his final edition of *Institutes of the Christian Religion*, he was arguing that the teachers, pastors, and "governors," Calvin's term for ruling elders, were all various types of elders or bishops; the latter two terms were considered biblical synonyms. Teachers and pastors shared in the teaching ministry of the church, but teachers had no disciplinary or sacramental responsibilities. Pastors and governors shared in the disciplinary and sacramental ministries, but governors had no teaching responsibilities.[24] The fourfold ministry was also advocated by Heinrich Bullinger in the Second Helvetic Confession (1562), which was widely adopted throughout Europe and Scotland in the 1560s and 1570s.[25]

---

21. *Book of Church Order of the Presbyterian Church in America*, Chapter 7–2.

22. The PC-USA adopted a new Form of Government at their 2011 General Assembly. The distinction between ruling elders and teaching elders is clearly maintained. See *The Session and the New Form of Government: Building a Community of Faith, Hope, Love and Witness*, 1 (not paginated), available online at http://www.pcusa.org/media/uploads/oga/pdf/nfog-session.pdf (accessed December 19, 2012). For the RCA's affirmation of a twofold eldership, see *The Book of Church Order* (New York: Reformed Church Press, 2012), 4, available online at http://images.rca.org/docs/bco/2012BCO.pdf (accessed December 19, 2012).

23. Bruce Gordon, *Calvin* (New Haven, CT: Yale University Press, 2011), 89.

24. Calvin, *Institutes of the Christian Religion*, 4:3:4 and 4:3:8. See also Joseph H. Hall, "John Calvin's View of Church Government," in *A Theological Guide to Calvin's Institutes: Essays and Analysis*, ed. David W. Hall and Peter A. Lillback (Phillipsburg, NJ: P&R, 2008), 393–97.

25. "The Second Helvetic Confession," Chapter 18: Of the Ministers of the Church, their Institution, and Offices, cited in *Paradigms in Polity*, ed. David W. Hall and Joseph H. Hall (Grand Rapids: Eerdmans, 1994), 113.

Around this same period, Reformed theologians began to collapse pastors and teachers into a single elder office, though they maintained the distinction between teaching and ruling elders. On the Continent, Guido de Brès and others drafted the Belgic Confession (1561). The Belgic Confession articulated a threefold ministry of ministers, elders, and deacons. The ministers were equivalent to teaching elders while elders were governing laymen who worked alongside the ministers.[26] The Belgic Confession was subsequently adopted by the Synod of Dort (1618), and along with the Canons of Dort and the Heidelberg Catechism, it became one of the Three Forms of Unity adopted by the Dutch Reformed Church. The Belgic Confession continues to inform the polity of American denominations such as the Christian Reformed Church and the Reformed Church in America.

A similar trend was taking root in the British Isles. Following his exile to the Continent during Mary Tudor's reign, John Knox returned to Scotland in 1559, where he became the leading reformer in the Church of Scotland and the founder of the Presbyterian tradition. In his *Book of Discipline* (1560), Knox argued that Scottish churches should select both ministers and elders; the former were equivalent to teaching elders, while the latter were ruling elders.[27] Knox's *Book of Discipline* was not approved by crown or parliament, leading to ongoing conflicts between presbyterians and episcopals in the Church of Scotland until the Act of Union in 1707 guaranteed presbyterian polity in the Kirk.[28] Throughout, those Protestants who most closely identified with the Reformed tradition advocated presbyterianism.

Presbyterian views proved decisive at the Westminster Assembly of the Divines, which met from 1643–1649. Though the meeting originally included congregationalists and episcopals, the presbyterian point of view prevailed in the documents produced by the Westminster Assembly. In 1645, the delegates adopted a Directory for Church

---

26. "The Belgic Confession, 1561," Article 31: The Ministers, Elders, and Deacons, cited in *Paradigms in Polity*, 173–74.
27. "The Book of Discipline, 1560," Chapter VII (3). Persons Subject to Discipline, The Eighth Head, touching the Election of Elders and Deacons, & c., cited in *Paradigms in Polity*, 224–25.
28. See Philip Benedict, *Christ's Churches Purely Reformed: A Social History of Calvinism* (New Haven, CT: Yale University Press, 2002), 164–72.

Government, which argued that the two offices in the church are pastors and elders. These two offices rule the church together, though the pastors are ministers and the elders are laymen. Teachers or doctors were ordained pastors who served in a university setting.[29] The Directory for Church Government became part of the Westminster Standards, which also included the Westminster Confession of Faith, the Westminster Larger Catechism, the Westminster Shorter Catechism, and the Directory of Public Worship. The Westminster Standards became authoritative for Presbyterians in the English-speaking world, including in matters of polity.

As presbyterians relocated to North America, they brought their view of the eldership with them. In 1720, the Synod of Philadelphia approved the Adopting Act, which called for substantial subscription to the Westminster Standards by Presbyterian elders.[30] In 1789, the Presbyterian Church in the United States of America held its first General Assembly in Philadelphia. The new denomination adopted a Form of Agreement that had been drafted the previous year. The Form of Agreement included a Constitution and a lightly revised version of the Westminster Confession of Faith. According to the chapter in the Constitution titled "Of Ruling Elders,"

> Ruling elders are properly the representatives of the people, and chosen by them for the purpose of exercising government and discipline in conjunction with pastors or ministers. This office has been understood by a great part of the Protestant Reformed Churches, to be designated in the Holy Scriptures by the title of governments, and of those who rule well, but do not labour in the word and doctrine.[31]

---

29. "The Westminster Assembly Directory for Church Government," Of the Officers of the Church, cited in *Paradigms in Polity*, 262.
30. James E. McGoldrick, *Presbyterian and Reformed Churches: A Global History* (Grand Rapids: Reformation Heritage, 2012), 200. Exceptions were made for articles 20 and 23, which addressed the role of civil magistrates and their relationship to the church.
31. The chapter is cited in numerous guides to presbyterian polity, including Hodge, *The Church and Its Polity*, 263, and Joan S. Gray and Joyce C. Tucker, *Presbyterian Polity for Church Officers*, 2nd ed. (Louisville: Westminster-John Knox, 1990), 37.

Contemporary Presbyterian affirmations of a twofold eldership are in continuity with the earliest Presbyterian denomination in the United States. The same is true of Reformed denominations with historic ties to the Continental Reformed traditions. Groups such as the CRC and RCA have adopted the Three Forms of Unity, including the distinction between ruling elders and teaching elders.

A Presbytery of Elders

In addition to the belief in two types of elders, presbyterian polity is characterized by the way the elders exercise authority within the church. Presbyterians argue that Christ is Lord of the church and that he has entrusted his authority to the whole church. The congregation chooses elders to represent them in the church's governance, so Christ's authority entrusted to the church is specifically delegated to the elders. In turn, the elders govern a local congregation by exercising Christ's authority on behalf of the congregation that they serve. As Sean Lucas notes, "All church power is granted to officers through the call of Jesus Christ, which comes by the consent of the church."[32]

Elder authority also extends beyond any given local church. Presbyterians advocate connectionalism through a system of graded church courts "reflecting mutual accountability, dependency, and submission among them."[33] These courts, which may be called by a variety of names, are bodies of elders that exercise governance over groups of churches. The idea of a court is important to presbyterians, even if it sounds unusual to others. As Lucas argues, "The word [court] reminds us that when elders gather together to do the work of the church, they are King Jesus' governing body, and their meetings are formal meetings presided over by King Jesus."[34] Presbyterian denominations as ecclesiastical bodies are defined by these courts, creating a single Presbyterian (or Reformed) Church that is embodied in affiliated local congregations. Lucas summarizes this understanding of connectional polity: "*In Presbyterianism, the parts are in the whole and the whole is in the parts.*"[35]

---

32. Lucas, *What Is Church Government?*, 19.
33. Reymond, "The Presbytery-Led Church," 95.
34. Lucas, *What Is Church Government?*, 23.
35. Ibid., 25 (emphasis original).

The Biblical Evidence

Presbyterians use several lines of biblical argumentation to make the case that churches are ruled by groups of elders. They point out that the New Testament churches included both apostles and pluralities of elders (Acts 11:30; 20:17; 21:18; Phil. 1:1). In fact, assuming that Titus and Timothy were evangelists or some other apostolic representative, the New Testament never provides an example of a single elder ruling over a congregation. Per the previous section, New Testament elders were divided into those who merely helped to govern the church and those who also taught (1 Tim. 5:17), though all elders performed at least some ministerial functions such as anointing and praying for the sick (James 5:14). They further note that the apostles or their representatives appointed and ordained the elders who labored alongside them in the New Testament churches (Acts 14:23; Titus 1:5).

More to the point, presbyterians argue that elders shared in the governance of these churches with the apostles. Apostles, of course, were directly appointed by Christ and held authority over the entire church, but presbyterians argue the apostles shared their authority with elders. Together, apostles and elders reached authoritative decisions on behalf of the churches they represented (Acts 15:1–29). When the office of apostle ceased around the turn of the second century, elders remained and continued to rule the churches with apostolic authority. John Murray summarizes this understanding of the eldership:

> Rule by elders is the apostolic institution for the government of the local congregation, and this involves the principles of plurality and parity. The inference is inescapable that this is a permanent provision for the government of the churches. Since the apostolate is not permanent, and since there is in the New Testament no other provision for the government of the local congregation, we must conclude that the council of elders is the only abiding institution for the government of the church of Christ according to the New Testament.[36]

---

36. Murray, "The Government of the Church," 342–43.

Presbyterians also believe the New Testament teaches that elders rule groups of churches through trans-congregational church courts. The key passages for this argument are Acts 15:1–29 and Acts 16:4, which recount the so-called Jerusalem Council and its aftermath. To summarize, some men, presumably Judaizers, were teaching that one must be circumcised in order to be saved. Paul and Barnabas argued with these men to no avail before being sent by the church at Antioch to consult with the apostles and elders in Jerusalem. At the resulting meeting, the believers with Pharisaical backgrounds sided with the Judaizers, while Peter argued that gentiles could come into the new covenant without going through Judaism. The other apostles and elders sided with Peter and wrote a circular letter outlining the details of the decision. Silas and Judas Barsabbas were appointed to return to Antioch with Paul and Silas and carry the letter to the Antioch Church. In the following days, Paul and Barnabas separated during their subsequent missionary journey. Paul was joined by Timothy, and "As they went on their way through the cities, they delivered to them for observance the decisions that had been reached by the apostles and elders who were in Jerusalem" (Acts 16:4).

For presbyterians, the Jerusalem meeting is the first example of a church court where groups of elders (and apostles) made a decision that was binding on all the churches.[37] As Michael Horton argues, "the main outlines of a presbyterian polity can be seen in the Jerusalem Council of Acts 15, where a local church dispute was taken to the broader assembly of the church."[38] John Murray agrees, noting that Acts 15 provides, "for us a pattern of consultation and adjudication that cannot be neglected in the permanent government of the church."[39] Charles Hodge affirms the presbyterian interpretation, though he suggests that in smaller churches the members can act for themselves without the representation of the

---

37. Interestingly, Benjamin B. Warfield rejected the majority presbyterian view, arguing that the Jerusalem Council was a unique event, that it is not a paradigm for presbyterianism, and that its decision was not binding on other churches. See the discussion in Fred G. Zaspel, *The Theology of B. B. Warfield: A Systematic Summary* (Wheaton, IL: Crossway, 2010), 528–29.

38. Michael Horton, *The Christian Faith: A Systematic Theology for Pilgrims on the Way* (Grand Rapids: Zondervan, 2011), 858.

39. Murray, "The Government of the Church," 344.

eldership.[40] Robert Reymond summarizes the importance that Acts 15 holds for presbyterian traditions: "Presbyterians believe that the New Testament teaches in a schematic way ecclesiastical 'connectionalism' between local churches, presbyteries, and a general assembly because they see it being lived out by the church in Acts 15!"[41]

Reymond makes four arguments to support the presbyterian interpretation. First, the elders of the Antioch Church, which Reymond calls the "Antioch presbytery," did not believe it could make a decision about the debated matters for itself, so it appealed for a larger meeting of elders in Jerusalem. Reymond suggests its possible elders from other cities also attended. Second, the Antiochene elders appointed Paul and Barnabas as their delegates to meet "with the Jerusalem presbytery in a general assembly." Third, the resulting letter was circulated "with the presumption on the part of the Jerusalem assembly that its instructions were to be heeded and to be viewed by all the churches as church law." Fourth, Judas Barsabbas and Silas were sent to Antioch alongside Paul and Barnabas as "unbiased witnesses" to confirm the Jerusalem assembly's authoritative decision for the Antiochene elders.[42]

Historical Development

As with the twofold eldership, presbyterian connectionalism arose during the Reformation era. Like later presbyterians, reformational presbyterians argued that their polity closely followed the apostolic pattern. They claimed that innovations entered into church government during the Patristic era, particularly the gradual separation of bishops from elders. As the understanding of the bishopric developed into a proto-episcopal structure, bishops began to exercise authority over all the churches in a region, while elders (increasingly called *priests*) were tasked with ministering to particular congregations. Presbyterians did not look on episcopacy as a favorable development, particularly because of the way this polity was frequently abused by the medieval Catholic Church in the West. For example, after surveying the transition from presbyterianism to episcopacy during the Patristic era, John

---

40. Hodge, *Discussions in Church Polity*, 124–25.
41. Reymond, "The Presbytery-Led Church," 109.
42. Ibid., 108–9.

Calvin argues that apostolic polity reached the height of its corruption in the medieval papacy.[43] Calvin and other Reformed leaders rejected episcopacy and introduced presbyterian polity into their churches, arguing the latter recovers the biblical form of church government.

By the 1540s, presbyterian polity was emerging in Reformed cities all over Europe. For example, in Geneva, Calvin outlined the roles of the Company of Pastors and the Consistory in his *Ecclesiastical Ordinances* (1541).[44] The Company of Pastors was a church court comprised of clergy that governed the affairs of all the pastors in the city. The Consistory was a church court comprised of both pastors and lay elders, which governed the affairs of the laity in Geneva. These two groups of elders oversaw the doctrine and discipline of the churches in Geneva, often working in close tandem with the secular magistrates in the city.[45] For Calvin, these church courts apparently functioned in the place of church councils. Though Calvin esteemed the first four ecumenical councils of Nicaea, Constantinople, Ephesus I, and Chalcedon, he did not believe that ecumenical councils were authoritative and argued that all councils should be subjected to biblical scrutiny.[46]

Variations on this proto-presbyterian approach was duplicated in other Continental Reformed Churches.[47] In 1559, the French Huguenots set up a Consistory that was modeled after the Genevan polity. The French pattern was even closer to modern presbyterianism. It called for a series of church courts, called General Councils, that moved from the Consistory, which was city-wide, to a Colloquy, which covered a wider area. A Provincial Synod included multiple Colloquies, while a National Synod included all the Provincial Synods. Each of these courts was made up of both pastors and ruling elders, though sometimes deacons

---

43. See Calvin, *Institutes of the Christian Religion*, 4:5.
44. Some presbyterian groups capitalize the names of their church courts, while others do not do so. In this chapter, I have followed whatever convention is used in the particular source I am referencing.
45. Gordon, *Calvin*, 127, 133–35. David Hall points out that the freedom of the Consistory to act apart from interference from the secular authorities in Geneva was the greatest obstacle of the Geneva Reformed Church during Calvin's lifetime (see Hall, "John Calvin's View of Church Government," 399).
46. Calvin, *Institutes of the Christian Religion*, 4:9:8; 4:9:12–14.
47. Philip Benedict provides a helpful table that demonstrates the various forms of presbyterian polity adopted by Reformed Churches during the sixteenth century (see Benedict, *Christ's Churches Purely Reformed*, 284).

could take the place of ruling elders.[48] The Church Order of Dort, adopted at the Synod of Dort in 1619, called for a series of similar courts divided into the Consistory, Classical Meetings (Classis), the Particular Synod, and the General or National Assembly. Each court exercised authority over the lower levels of courts.[49]

Reformational presbyterians in the British Isles advocated a similar approach to church courts. In the Scottish Kirk, Andrew Melville and other presbyterians drafted *The Second Book of Discipline* (1578), which refined the earlier polity manual written by John Knox in 1560. This second document called for four different types of church courts, all of which were assemblies of elders. The first level of assembly represented particular churches or groups of churches in a given locale. The next assembly represented all the churches in a province. Subsequent assemblies represented the entire nation and even groups of nations that adhered to the Reformed faith.[50] A form of this polity prevailed in the Scottish Kirk after it became permanently Presbyterian in 1707. The Westminster Assembly Directory for Church Government affirmed a similar presbyterian polity that moved from assemblies of elders in local churches to assemblies representing multiple nations. The nature and jurisdiction of each assembly was discussed. The document also calls the most local assembly of elders a presbytery.[51]

These documents provide the blueprint for the polity practiced by Presbyterian denominations in the English-speaking world. For example, in America, the Act of Adoption (1720) and Form of Agreement (1789) guaranteed that American Presbyterians adopted a fully presbyterian polity, including connectionalism. A connectional approach continues to prevail among American Presbyterians. For example, in the PCA, the church courts are Sessions, Presbyteries, and the General Assembly. Sessions govern local churches, Presbyteries govern all the churches in a region, and the General Assembly governs the en-

---

48. See the editors' introduction and the text of the "Ecclesiastical Discipline, 1559," in *Paradigms in Polity*, 134–39.
49. "The Church Order of Dort. 1619/Christian Reformed Church Order, 1914," Articles 29 and 36, in *Paradigms in Polity*, 179–180.
50. "The Second Book of Discipline, 1578," Chapter VII: Of Elderships and Assemblies of Discipline, Article 2, in *Paradigms in Polity*, 240.
51. "The Westminster Assembly Directory for Church Government," in *Paradigms in Polity*, 263–68.

tire denomination.[52] In the Associate Reformed Presbyterian Church, the corresponding levels of church courts are called the Sessions, the Presbyteries, and the General Synod.[53] In the PC-USA, the four church courts are the Session, Presbytery, Synod, and General Assembly.[54]

Among denominations with ties to the Dutch Reformed tradition, the terminology varies from Presbyterian denominations, but the basic polity remains intact. In the RCA, the local church court is the consistory and the area court is the classis. Regional synods and the General Synod constitute the higher courts.[55] The CRC divides its courts into councils (local church), classis (regional), and a synod (America and Canada).[56] In the United Reformed Church of North America, the courts include the Consistory (local church), classis (regional), and synod (national).[57]

CRITIQUING PRESBYTERIANISM

Presbyterian polity is certainly appealing. The twofold eldership offers a vision of shared leadership that reflects a more biblical approach than polity structures that revolve around a single pastor or give too much authority to biblical officers like deacons or extra-biblical committees. Presbyterian connectionalism attempts a balanced middle between a hierarchical episcopalianism and a more democratic congregationalism. The former has too often been characterized by corruption or theological declension while the latter is too often prone to schism and often simplistically equates the priesthood of all believers with having a vote in church meetings. Nevertheless, while appealing, I believe the presbyterian vision of church polity is a less faithful adaptation of New Testament polity

---

52. See *The Book of Church Order of the Presbyterian Church in America*, Chapters 10–14.
53. *The Standards of the Associate Reformed Presbyterian Church* (n. p.: General Synod of the Associate Reformed Presbyterian Church, 2008), 220–38, available online at http://www.arpsynod.org/downloads/Standards.pdf (accessed December 21, 2012).
54. Gray and Tucker, *Presbyterian Polity for Church Officers*, 57–69, 103–18.
55. See https://www.rca.org/organized (accessed December 21, 2012).
56. See http://www.crcna.org/welcome/christian-reformed-church-governance (accessed December 21, 2012).
57. "Church Order of the United Reformed Churches in North America," 5th ed. (2010), Chapter 2: Ecclesiastical Assemblies, Articles 16–36, available online at https://www.urcna.org/urcna/officialDocuments/5ChurchOrderoftheURCNA-FifthEdition.pdf (accessed December 21, 2012).

than a plural-elder-led congregationalism. In this section, I will offer a friendly critique of presbyterianism from the latter perspective.

All Elders Teach and Rule

Historically, ecclesiastical polities have developed around the priority given to one of the three terms translated in English Bibles as "elder," "pastor," "bishop," and "overseer." This includes presbyterianism, which derives its name from its emphasis on the rule of elders. Nevertheless, as Mark Dever argues, "the New Testament refers interchangeably to elders, shepherds or pastors, and bishops or overseers in context of the officers in the local church."[58] *Presbyteros* (elder) occurs seventeen times and is the most common term for this office (e.g., Acts 11:30; 15:2; 20:17; 1 Tim. 5:17; Titus 1:5; 1 Peter 5:1). *Episkopos* (bishop, overseer) occurs four times when referring to the leadership office in the church (Acts 20:28; Phil. 1:1; 1 Tim. 3:2; Titus 1:7). *Poimēn* (pastor, shepherd) is only used once to refer the leadership office (Eph. 4:11), though it is used frequently in reference to Jesus (John 10:11; Heb. 13:20; 1 Peter 2:25; 5:4).

These three terms are used interchangeably in several key New Testament passages about church leadership. Peter uses the verbal forms of *episkopos* and *poimēn* to describe the role and responsibility of elders in 1 Peter 5:1–2:

> So I exhort the elders [*presbyterous*] among you, as a fellow elder and a witness of the sufferings of Christ, as well as a partaker in the glory that is going to be revealed: shepherd [*poimanate*] the flock of God that is among you, exercising oversight [*episkopountes*], not under compulsion, but willingly, as God would have you; not for shameful gain, but eagerly.

In these verses, Peter understands elders to be those who pastor and oversee the congregation whom they serve.

---

58. Mark Dever, *The Church: The Gospel Made Visible* (Nashville: B&H Academic, 2012), 55. For a monograph that develops this thesis in detail, see Benjamin L. Merkle, *The Elder and Overseer: One Office in the Early Church* (New York: Peter Lang, 2003). Merkle condenses his argument into chapter one in *40 Questions About Elders and Deacons*, 76–83 (see also his *Why Elders?*, 17–27).

Similar language is used by Luke in Acts 20. In Acts 20:17, Paul sends for the elders of the church at Ephesus: "Now from Miletus he sent to Ephesus and called the elders [*presbyterous*] of the church to come to him." Once they arrive, Paul tells them that the Holy Spirit has made them overseers of the church and he charges them to pastor or shepherd God's flock: "Be on guard for yourselves and for all the flock, among which the Holy Spirit has made you overseers [*episkopous*], to shepherd [*poimainein*] the church of God which He purchased with His own blood" (Acts 20:28 NASB). According to Paul, elders are bishops who pastor God's people.

Paul also uses these terms interchangeably in his letter to Titus:

> This is why I left you in Crete, so that you might put what remained into order, and appoint elders [*presbyterous*] in every town as I directed you—if anyone is above reproach, the husband of one wife, and his children are believers and not open to the charge of debauchery or insubordination. For an overseer [*episkopon*], as God's steward, must be above reproach. (Titus 1:5–7a)

In this passage, Paul instructs Titus to appoint elders in every town in verse 5. He then provides Titus with a list of qualifications for elders in verses 6–9, but in verse 7, her refers to these elders as overseers. As with his recorded sermon to the Ephesian elders in Acts 20, in his letter to Titus, Paul understands an elder and an overseer or bishop to be two ways to refer to the same office. Ben Merkle argues Titus 1:5–7a is the most convincing passage that demonstrates that the term "elder" and "overseer" are interchangeable terms.[59] John Hammett aptly summarizes the New Testament's usage of these words: "Clearly, the term to be used for the leaders of the church does not seem to have been a major concern of the writers of Scripture."[60]

Presbyterians agree with baptistic congregationalists that bishops and pastors or teaching elders are one and the same; the difference lies in the distinction between teaching elders or pastors and ruling elders,

---

59. Merkle, *Why Elders?*, 20.
60. Hammett, *Biblical Foundations for Baptist Churches*, 163.

the latter of whom are not pastors. As mentioned in the previous section, presbyterians base this distinction on their interpretation of 1 Timothy 5:17: "Let the elders who rule well be considered worthy of double honor, especially those who labor in preaching and teaching." Presbyterians contend that this verse indicates that all elders rule, but not all labor in preaching and teaching. The former includes both ruling and teaching elders, while the latter is limited to teaching elders or pastors.

Historically, Baptists have rejected the presbyterian understanding of 1 Timothy 5:17 and the twofold eldership that presbyterians claim the verse affirms.[61] Other passages indicate more clearly that all elders are called not only to the ministry of leading or ruling, but also to the ministry of teaching. In his letter to Timothy, Paul writes, "Therefore an overseer must be above reproach, the husband of one wife, sober-minded, self-controlled, respectable, hospitable, *able to teach*" (1 Tim. 3:2, emphasis added). Paul argues that all elders/pastors/bishops must be able to teach. There is no mention of elders who do not teach. In his letter to Titus, Paul writes, "He must hold firm to the trustworthy word as taught, so that he may be able to give instruction in sound doctrine and also to rebuke those who contradict it" (Titus 1:9). The "he" in question here is the elder (v. 5) or overseer (v. 7) whom Titus is vetting as he appoints leaders for the churches in every town. All of these elders/overseers should be able to provide positive teaching about sound doctrine and refute false doctrine. Again, no allowance is made for elders who do not teach.

Because of these passages, Baptists interpret 1 Timothy 5:17 to be about the respect (particularly in the form of financial compensation) due to especially gifted elders rather than some distinction between ruling and teaching elders. 1 Timothy 3:2 has already indicated that all elders must be able to teach. Now, two chapters later, Paul is arguing

---

61. Interestingly, some eighteenth-century Baptists in America affirmed a twofold eldership, but without embracing the idea of authoritative ruling elders. For these Baptists, many of whom were affiliated with the Philadelphia Baptist Association, ruling elders were congregational role models who assisted the pastor in leading the church, albeit the final authority rested with the congregation rather than the pastor and elders. According to Greg Wills, this practice was out of vogue by about 1820. See Greg Wills, "The Church: Baptists and Their Churches in the Eighteenth and Nineteenth Centuries," in *Polity: Biblical Arguments on How to Conduct Church Life*, ed. Mark E. Dever (Washington DC: Center for Church Reform, 2001), 33–34.

that the church should provide generous remuneration for those elders who are exemplary in their leadership, especially those who are gifted teachers of the Word. For this reason, in many Baptist churches with a plurality of elders one or more of those pastors who are especially gifted teachers are set apart and compensated. For example, in our church, all of our elders are competent Bible teachers, but our senior pastor, Andy Davis, is widely considered to be an exceptional Bible teacher.[62] For that reason, we pay him to be the primary (though not sole) elder who preaches in our Sunday morning corporate worship gatherings and to provide full-time, intentional oversight to our church's preaching and teaching ministry.

For Baptists, while 1 Timothy 5:17 makes a distinction among elders, it is a distinction of personal giftedness rather than a formal distinction between two classes of elders.[63] All elders rule and teach, though different elders may emphasize one task more than the other, depending upon an elder's degree of giftedness in each responsibility and the particular needs of the congregation the elder serves. This is especially evident among staff elders. Many churches employ one or more pastors who focus upon the ministry of preaching or teaching, but also employ other pastors who focus upon administration. Leadership teams that include unpaid elders may also divide these pastoral responsibilities in similar ways. As long as all the pastors meet the biblical qualifications of an elder, such arrangements are matters of prudence that are contextual to each congregation. Phil Newton does a fine job of summarizing the historic Baptist view of elders: "It can be argued that some [elders] excel in teaching while others excel in governing, but to make a distinction seems artificial."[64]

Elder Leadership and Congregational Cooperation

Presbyterians not only argue for a twofold eldership, but they also argue for groups of elders who exercise authority over groups of churches. They exercise this authority through a series of interconnected church

---

62. Andy Davis is also a contributor to this volume. See chapter 11.
63. See William Williams, "Apostolical Church Polity," in *Polity*, 533; Merkle, *40 Questions About Elders and Deacons*, 84–88.
64. Newton, *Elders in Congregational Life*, 51.

courts that make key decisions for churches at the local, regional, and national levels. For presbyterians, this binding, connectional authority is what it means for elders to rule the church. They argue that the so-called Jerusalem Council of Acts 15 provides the prototype for a church court making an authoritative decision on behalf of all the churches that are represented by that court. Presbyterians believe that the New Testament pattern of leadership is ruling through connectionalism. This connectionalism results in ecclesial bodies that transcend local congregations. Simply put, Presbyterian or Reformed churches are local expressions of larger bodies such as the Presbyterian Church in the USA or the Reformed Church in America.

Congregationalists, including most Baptists, reject a presbyterian reading of Acts 15. Baptists counter the presbyterian view on at least two fronts. First, beginning at the level of local churches, Baptists typically have a different understanding of what it means for elders to "rule" a congregation. For Baptists, ruling does not mean exercising final authority, but rather providing spiritual leadership through godly example and sound biblical teaching. As D. A. Carson notes,

> [W]e have too often envisaged church authority flowing in straight lines, whether up or down, instead of recognizing the somewhat more fluid reality of the NT. The normal responsibility for and authority of leadership in the NT rests with the bishops-elders-pastors; but if they are interested in pursuing biblical patterns of leadership, they will be concerned to demonstrate observable growth not only in their grasp of truth but also in their lived discipline (1 Tim. 4:14–16). They will comprehend that spiritual leadership, far from lording it over others (Matt. 20:25–28), is a balanced combination of oversight (1 Tim. 4:11–13; 6:17–19; Titus 3:9–11) and example (1 Tim. 4:12; 6:6–11, 17–18; 1 Peter 5:1–4), which, far from being antithetical, are mutually reinforcing. By the same token such leaders prefer not to dictate terms but to lead the church into spiritually minded consensus.[65]

---

65. D. A. Carson, "Church, Authority in the," in Walter A. Elwell, ed., *Evangelical Dictionary of Theology*, 2nd ed. (Grand Rapids: Baker Academic, 1999), 250–51.

John Hammett notes that Baptists normally understand ruling to mean directing, which is consistent with their congregational polity.[66] This is why most Baptist churches with a plurality of elders (including my church) refer to themselves as "elder-led" rather than "elder-ruled"; we are making a distinction between our polity and that of our presbyterian friends.

For Baptists, the final earthly spiritual authority is the congregation itself, which comes to a consensus under the lordship of Christ through their corporate searching of the Scriptures. The "flow chart" for this sort of christocentric congregationalism looks different than presbyterian polity. For Baptists, the church is ruled by Christ, governed by its membership, led by elders, and served by deacons. Elders are the spiritual leaders of the church and they ought normally to be followed (Heb. 13:17), but elders are ultimately accountable to the congregation that has called them. When elders embrace heresy, engage in unrepentant sin, or exercise abusive leadership, they answer to the final authority of the congregation, not vice versa. Elders are first and foremost members of the body and subject to the same discipline as the rest of the congregation.

Second, Baptists and other congregationalists normally challenge the presbyterian understanding of Acts 15 and its meaning for church polity.[67] Presbyterians make a number of assumptions about the "Jerusalem Council" that simply cannot be proven.[68] First, they assume the presence of multiple congregations in Jerusalem and Antioch. Second, they assume that all the congregations in each city was governed by presbyteries. Third, they assume that the presbytery in Antioch sent Paul and Barnabas as their official representatives to a general assembly of elders and apostles in Jerusalem. Finally, they assume that the decision made by the general assembly is a binding church law rather than a contextual decision for a particular season in redemptive history. While the presbyterian reading is certainly plausible, it seems more likely that presbyterians read their convictions into the text rather than

---

66. Hammett, *Biblical Foundations for Baptist Churches*, 142.
67. Interestingly, some nineteenth-century Baptists adopted a more or less presbyterian view of Acts 15, but argued it was a unique, non-repeatable event with special authority because of the participation of the apostles (see W. B. Johnson, "The Gospel Developed through the Government and Order of the Churches of Jesus Christ," in *Polity*, 173–75, and J. L. Reynolds, "Church Polity of the Kingdom of Christ," in *Polity*, 343).
68. For example, see Reymond, "The Presbytery-Led Church," 95–109.

finding their views articulated by the text. As Hammett notes, "All of these [presbyterian] assumptions are simply that: assumptions that are not mentioned, much less proven in Scripture."[69]

Baptists and most other congregationalists opt for voluntary congregational cooperation over the binding denominational connectionalism of presbyterianism. Baptists base their "associational principle" of voluntary interchurch cooperation in large part off of the very same passage that presbyterians use to argue for their connectionalism: Acts 15.[70] This was the case with the earliest Baptist associations in America. James Sullivan contends that for the Baptists who formed the Philadelphia Association in 1707, "The scriptural bases for the district association had been found in such passages as Acts 15 and Galatians 2."[71] In a 1805 treatise on church discipline and polity written for the churches of the Philadelphia Association, Samuel Jones made the same argument.[72] In their influential 1774 essay on church discipline, the Charleston Association argued that Acts 15 provides the biblical precedent for associations.[73]

Like their forebears, contemporary Baptists frequently look to Acts 15 for justification for voluntary cooperation. For example, Danny Akin finds six ways that Acts 15 affirms voluntary congregational cooperation rather than presbyterian connectionalism. First, the local church at Antioch sent Paul and Barnabas to Jerusalem and the local church in the latter city received these men (Acts 15:2–4). Second, the Antioch church's decision to send Paul and Barnabas arose from that church's voluntary initiative to address a particular problem; the process was bottom-up rather than top-down. Third, once the meeting convened, the entire congregation listened to the discussion among the apostles and elders (Acts 15:12). Fourth, not just the apostles and elders, but the "whole church" chose men to accompany Paul and Barnabas with

---

69. Hammett, *Biblical Foundations for Baptist Churches*, 142. See also Merkle, *40 Questions About Elders and Deacons*, 31–37.
70. Walter B. Shurden, "The *Associational Principle*, 1707–1814: Its Rationale," *Foundations* 21, no. 3 (July–September 1978): 211–24, and Winthop Hudson, "*The Associational Principle among Baptists*," in *Baptists: The Bible, Church, Church Order, and the Churches. Essays from Foundations: A Baptist Journal of History and Theology*, ed. Edwin Gaustad (New York: Arno Press, 1980), 10–23.
71. James L. Sullivan, *Baptist Polity As I See It* (Nashville: Broadman, 1983), 96.
72. Samuel Jones, "A Treatise of Church Discipline, and a Directory," in *Polity*, 157.
73. "A Summary of Church Discipline Shewing the Qualifications and Duties of the Officers and Members of a Gospel Church," in *Polity*, 132.

the decision reached by the meeting (Acts 15:22). Fifth, the letter was sent by the apostles, elders, and whole church at Jerusalem, and it was directed to the whole church at Antioch (Acts 15:23). Finally, the whole church at Antioch received the letter (Acts 15:30) and rejoiced over its content (Acts 15:31). As Akin notes, Acts 15 shows that "congregational involvement and action are present at every turn."[74]

Baptists argue that the polity of the New Testament is a combination of apostolic authority and congregational authority—what I call "apostolic congregationalism." Clearly, the apostles and their representatives exercised authority over the churches, at least those they directly planted. Nevertheless, the congregations themselves made certain key decisions related to membership and leadership. According to Matthew 18:15–20 and 1 Corinthians 5, the entire congregation is normally to be involved in membership matters, particularly the exercise of church discipline.[75] According to Acts 6, the entire congregation is involved in the selection of deacons. The Pastoral Epistles lay out qualifications for elders and deacons, implying that congregations were expected to vet and choose their leaders. (Though Titus appointed the first elders in the churches he planted—see Titus 1:5.) Since Baptists (like presbyterians) argue that the apostolic office ceased around the end of the first century, we maintain that the best adaptation of New Testament polity to contemporary churches is congregationalism.

I would argue the healthiest form of congregationalism is one that is led by a plurality of elders in a church that takes seriously the doctrines regenerate church membership and the priesthood of all believers.[76] Congregationalism does not entail a pure democracy wherein the

---

74. Daniel L. Akin, "The Single-Elder-led Church," in *Perspectives on Church Government*, 30–31. See also J. C. Bradley, *A Baptist Association: Churches on Mission Together* (Nashville: Convention Press, 1984), 16; James W. [Jim] Richards, "Cooperation among Southern Baptist Churches as Set Forth in Article 14 of the Baptist Faith and Message," in *The Mission of Today's Church: Baptist Leaders Look at Modern Faith Issues*, ed. R. Stanton Norman (Nashville: B&H Academic, 2007), 149.

75. For a helpful introduction to church discipline written from a Baptist perspective, see Jonathan Leeman, *Church Discipline: How the Church Protects the Name of Jesus* (Wheaton, IL: Crossway, 2012).

76. For helpful introductions to these doctrines and other important Baptist ecclesiological distinctives, see the essays in John S. Hammett and Benjamin L. Merkle, eds., *Those Who Must Give an Account: A Study of Church Membership and Church Discipline* (Nashville: B&H Academic, 2012).

membership makes nearly every decision. Indeed, in the New Testament elders were clearly responsible for the overall teaching and shepherding ministry in the churches. Following the New Testament precedent, congregationalism requires that the whole church must arrive at a consensus about key matters such as the selection of elders and deacons and the maintenance of the church's membership. Though not biblically mandated, as a matter of prudence it also seems appropriate for the entire congregation to also vote on matters such as the church's budget, major expenditures, and the purchasing and selling of church property.

CONCLUSION

This chapter has attempted to summarize presbyterian polity and offer a friendly critique from a Baptist perspective. Presbyterian polity is characterized by two distinctives. First, presbyterians affirm a twofold eldership that distinguishes between ruling elders and teaching elders. Second, presbyterians argue for a connectional polity wherein groups of elders exercise authority over groups of churches by means of church courts. To varying degrees, this leadership structure is embraced by Presbyterian and Reformed denominations, as well as many evangelical churches that do not self-identify with historic Reformed traditions.

While presbyterians rightly emphasize a plurality of elders, they make a false distinction between ruling and teaching elders. All elders should be able to teach the Scriptures and lead the congregation by example and intentional shepherding. While presbyterians rightly emphasize the interconnectedness of local churches, they assume too much in arguing for connectional courts of elders. Churches can and should voluntarily cooperate together for the sake of the gospel under the lordship of the Head of the Church, Jesus Christ, but there is no New Testament warrant for connectionalism. I am immensely thankful for my presbyterian friends, who have taught me much about the Christian life. But at the end of the day, a plural-elder-led congregationalism seems to be the best way to apply New Testament polity and leadership to contemporary Christian churches.

CHAPTER 8

A Cousin of Catholicism:
The Anglican Understanding of Church Leadership

Jason G. Duesing[1]

A glance at one scene of the title page of Henry VIII's *Great Bible* (1540) reveals the essence of an Anglican understanding of church leadership. Seated on a throne raised to the heavens, the king, as both monarch and head of the church, dispenses his translation of the Bible to parishes through the Archbishop and to citizens through the head of state. The people receive the word of God with varying degrees of interest but the majority respond with the cry "VIVAT REX," or "Long live the King."[2] There is no longer a Pope that stands between God and King and yet the King acts very much like a Pope. Such is the complex nature of leadership in the Church of England. A cousin once removed from Roman Catholicism, the Church of England still bears a family resemblance.

The purpose of this chapter is to analyze and critique the Anglican view of church leadership. Recognizing that I am writing about Anglicanism to a largely non-Anglican audience,[3] I will present an overview

---

1. Jason G. Duesing (PhD, Southwestern Baptist Theological Seminary) is Provost at Midwestern Baptist Theological Seminary in Kansas City, Missouri.

2. Diarmaid MacCulloch observes, "the message was one of unity: two estates, clerical and lay, harmoniously and gratefully receiving the word of God from the hands of a benevolent monarch, and drawing from it his preferred message of discipline and obedience" (*Thomas Cranmer: A Life* [New Haven, CT: Yale University Press, 1996], 238).

3. While I will use the terms "Anglicanism" and "Church of England" interchangeably for this chapter, the term "Anglicanism" should properly find use in reference to the period of church development in England after the mid-seventeenth century as the term did not come into regular use until the nineteenth century to describe this time. The use of "Church of England" should be employed for any time after the English Reformation.

of the historical and theological development of church leadership in the Church of England throughout the Early Church, Middle Ages, Reformation, and Modern eras. I will conclude the chapter with a few brief statements regarding my own perspective as a Baptist evangelical.

HISTORICAL AND THEOLOGICAL DEVELOPMENT

Eamon Duffy observes that just like in the novel and film *Jurassic Park*, the Roman Catholic liturgy, buildings, and ministerial orders are the mosquitos trapped in amber, "vestiges of that past which were to prove astonishingly potent in reshaping the Church of England's future."[4] While there is basic agreement that the break with Rome in the sixteenth century marked the beginning of the Church of England, great debate surfaced throughout the ensuing years over the extent to which the Church of England truly separated. Since the Church maintained much of its Roman garb and ecclesiastical structure, some have argued that there exists more continuity and closeness with Rome and especially the Early Church. These "Anglo-Catholics" maintain their Anglican identity but walk closely to the Tiber River.[5] However, the more reformation-minded Anglicans assert that a sharp discontinuity with Rome took place when the Church of England formed, though they uphold an affinity with the Early Church as well.[6] The result is a continuum of historical perspec-

---

See "Anglicanism," in F. L. Cross and E. A. Livingstone, eds., *The Oxford Dictionary of the Christian Church* (Oxford: University Press, 1997), 65–66; Paul Avis, "Great Britain," in Alister McGrath, ed., *The SPCK Handbook of Anglican Theologians* (London: SPCK, 1998), 3–4; Diarmaid MacCulloch, *The Later Reformation in England, 1547–1603* (New York: Palgrave, 2001), 85; J. Robert Wright, "Anglicanism, *Ecclesia Anglicana*, and Anglican: An Essay on Terminology," in Stephen Sykes and John Booty, eds., *The Study of Anglicanism* (London: SPCK, 1988), 424–29. My thanks to Zachary Bowden for his keen comments to assist the completion of this chapter.

4. Eamon Duffy, "The Shock of Change: Continuity and Discontinuity in the Elizabethan Church of England," in *Anglicanism and the Western Christian Tradition*, ed. Stephen Platten (Norwich: Canterbury Press, 2003), 63–64.

5. To enter the city of Rome from the North or to enter Vatican City from Rome one must cross the Tiber River. The phrase "crossing the Tiber" has been used to describe those who have converted to Roman Catholicism from other traditions. See Stephen K. Ray, *Crossing the Tiber: Evangelical Protestants Discover the Historical Church* (San Francisco: Ignatius Press, 1997).

6. MacCulloch comments, "Let us not be under any illusion: there was an English Reformation, and within a century of Henry VIII's break with Rome in 1533, it had made England a strongly Protestant country" (Diarmaid MacCulloch, "The Church of England 1533–1603," in *Anglicanism and the Western Christian Tradition*, ed. Stephen Platten, 18).

tives that range from continuity on the one hand to discontinuity on the other, each having direct implications for the understanding of Anglican Church leadership.[7] However, setting aside the debate over the extent to which Roman Catholic ecclesiology influenced the Church of England, this chapter will show that though independent from Rome, the Anglican perspective on church leadership retains the genetic Catholic blueprint first established in the third century.[8]

Early Church[9]

"Christianity came late to the province."[10] By this Malcolm Lambert means that Christianity likely arrived in Britain from European missionaries during the third century though it did not emerge as an established tradition until the late fourth century while still under the rule of the Roman Empire. Surviving Germanic attack in the fifth century, Christians in Britain contributed to the broader theological development with the controversialists, Pelagius and Faustus,[11] as well as the expansion of their faith to neighboring Ireland. There was some ecclesiastical structure present as Patrick (the would-be saint), kidnapped and taken as a slave to Ireland when a teen, was the son of a deacon. After enduring for a time, he escaped only to sense the call of God to return to "come to the Irish people to preach the Gospel . . . so that I might give up my free birthright for the advantage of others."[12] In this quadrant of the history of Christianity, a three-tiered model of hierarchical church oversight had developed consisting of bishops, elders, and deacons. Further, many church leaders began to identify these offices with

---

7. Duffy, "The Shock of Change," 42–64.
8. Carl Trueman notes that the retention of Roman Catholic DNA is more than likely simply due to the fact that "while church leadership at the top changed when Protestantism arrived, most parishes would have continued to have the same pastors and priests as before" (*The Creedal Imperative* [Wheaton, IL: Crossway, 2012], 112).
9. See Michael A. G. Haykin's chapter in this volume for an extensive treatment of this era outside and including England.
10. Malcolm Lambert, *Christians and Pagans: The Conversion of Britain from Alban to Bede* (New Haven, CT: Yale University Press, 2010), 4.
11. Michael A. G. Haykin, *Rediscovering the Church Fathers: Who They Were and How They Shaped the Church* (Wheaton, IL: Crossway, 2011), 136–37.
12. *Confession of St. Patrick*, 37, http://www.ccel.org/ccel/patrick/confession.viii.html (accessed April 21, 2013).

the Old Testament priesthood as seen in the *Constitutions of the Holy Apostles*, "For [the bishops] are your high priests, as the presbyters are your priests, and your present deacons instead of your Levites."[13] These developments only served to elevate the office of bishop and, though distant from Rome, England increasingly came under such oversight.

By the late sixth century, the churches throughout the Mediterranean region followed the increasing consensus that the bishop of Rome held greater authority over all other bishops. The bishop of Rome served in succession to the Apostle Peter and due to the predominant interpretation of Matthew 16, Peter was given apostolic authority above the other Apostles.[14] The bishop of Rome, as father of all churches, became known as the Pope. Thus, when Pope Gregory called the monk Augustine (not the fifth-century bishop of Hippo), to advance Christianity within the kingdom of Kent, Augustine went. Christianity had some presence in the area as the queen of the region, Bertha, claimed Christ. However, for King Aethelberht, there was resistance but only for a time as he welcomed Augustine and his party of forty men to the capital in Canterbury. After the conversion of many, including the king, Augustine received ordination as bishop and established a monastery.[15] The story of Augustine's arrival is central to the eighth-century historian and monk, Bede, who composed a history of Christianity in England, the *Historia Ecclesiastica*. Bede confirms that once the king "believed and was baptized . . . greater numbers began daily to flock together to hear the Word."[16] Further, he reviews at length the questions that Augustine presented to Pope Gregory regarding the role of a bishop in England.[17] Thus, the presence of Rome shaped episcopal organization during the earliest days of the English Church.[18] As the church grew and solidified, the advocacy of the monarchy for this structure as

---

13. *Constitutions of the Holy Apostles*, 2.4.25, in *ANF*, 7.410. For broader explanation of these and related developments see Gregg R. Allison, *Historical Theology* (Grand Rapids: Zondervan, 2011), 593–95.

14. Allison, *Historical Theology*, 596–98. See also the chapters by Michael Haykin and Gregg Allison in this volume.

15. Lambert, *Christians and Pagans*, 164–200.

16. Bede, *Ecclesiastical History of England*, 1.26.

17. Ibid., 1.27.

18. Allison, *Historical Theology*, 590, explains that well into the third century the terms for elders and bishops were used interchangeably, even though Ignatius and Cyprian had developed a three tiered model of bishops, elders, and deacons that increasingly became standard.

well as Bede's influential history only served to perpetuate the Roman model in England.[19]

Middle Ages[20]

Christians in England saw the Church in Rome continue to grow in power and territory during the centuries that comprise the Middle Ages, but not without consequence. "The Catholic world of the pre-Reformation West," MacCulloch explains, "had two pillars to support it: first, a devotional pattern centered on the power of the mass and the power of the clergy who performed it, and second, the unity provided by the Pope."[21] In addition to unity, the Pope also had power but not unchecked power devoid of dissenting opinions. Anselm, born in Italy, served as Archbishop of Canterbury from 1093–1109 and though known more for his theological works, he spent a significant amount of his time as archbishop in conflict over the dynamics of church leadership in England. At issue was his relationship to William II and the king's refusal to recognize the authority of the pope. Further, Anselm believed that "former popes had assigned the whole area of the British Isles to the jurisdiction of the Archbishop of Canterbury" and he "saw his relationship with both popes and kings as essentially pastoral."[22] But, when the king refused to allow Anselm to convene an ecclesiastical council, the archbishop sought papal aid in Rome. Eventually, the king and Anselm would come to terms, and Anselm returned to convening councils and nominating bishops, thus establishing further the unique identity of Canterbury.[23]

Another archbishop that serves as an example of the development of church leadership in England is Thomas Becket. Once the friend and

---

19. Richard Turnbull notes, "The Church of England (and Anglicanism more widely) especially, but not only, in its more Catholic understanding, reflects the triumph of the Roman model in its ecclesiological and leadership patterns very deeply indeed" (*Anglican and Evangelical?* [London: Bloomsbury, 2007], 7).
20. See Gregg R. Allison's chapter in this volume for an extensive treatment of to the role of the papacy up to the twentieth century.
21. MacCulloch, *Later Reformation*, 4.
22. R. W. Southern, "Anselm [St Anselm] (c.1033–1109)," *Oxford Dictionary of National Biography* (Oxford: Oxford University Press, 2004), http://www.oxforddnb.com/view/article/572 (accessed April 26, 2013).
23. Ibid.

chancellor to Henry II, upon his installation in Canterbury Becket's loyalties transferred to the church. As Becket asserted his understanding
of the role of the archbishop, the king responded with the *Constitutions
of Clarendon,* clarifying what he saw as "acknowledged customs," which
included the clear hierarchy of archdeacon to bishop to archbishop to
"the lord the king."[24] Like Anselm, Becket appealed to Rome and left
England. After several years of attempting reconciliation, Becket returned even though much was still unresolved. He zealously took up
his responsibilities as archbishop according to how he saw fit. Tragically, Henry II had him murdered in Canterbury Cathedral.[25]

In the thirteenth century, Pope Boniface VIII attempted to insert his
authority into the affairs of the kings of England and France only to have
them refuse his edict, a precursor of the future defiance of another English king, Henry VIII. The result was a standoff that ended when Boniface VIII died and led to the curtailment of papal influence for the next
seventy years.[26] The authority of the Pope would be reestablished, though
not without controversy, as the fourteenth century saw great disagreement and schism over the rightful claim to the Holy See. This conflict led
to the rejection of papal authority in favor of rule by councils in the early
fifteenth century. Eventually, Pius II reclaimed the papacy with considerable authority and power.[27] During this time of turbulence, the English churches continued steadily under the threefold structure of church
leadership. However, the highest office of church leadership was increasingly known for corruption, immorality, and extravagance.

One dissenting voice came from England in the person of John
Wycliffe. During the fourteenth century, Wycliffe rose to a position of
theological prominence as an academic at Oxford when the university
was merely two centuries young. From this post Wycliffe spoke against
the abuses of the church and called for many reforms. In his work *On
Simony* Wycliffe railed against the Roman Catholic practice of selling
spiritual things over which they had no dominion and also questioned

---

24. "The Constitutions of Clarendon (1164)," in Gee, Henry, and William John Hardy, ed.,
    Documents Illustrative of English Church History (New York: Macmillan, 1896), 68–73.
25. Frank Barlow, "Becket, Thomas (1120?–1170)," *ODNB*, http://www.oxforddnb.com/view/
    article/27201 (accessed December 28, 2012).
26. Allison, *Historical Theology*, 599.
27. Ibid., 601.

the authority of the Pope to appoint bishops. "[A]t one time there was a law that either God would make the determination or the community to be governed would choose for itself a priest or bishop. But now an election by ordinary people is excluded."[28] Wycliffe had a deep concern for the character of those in church leadership and the priority they gave to shepherding the people rather than to political power.[29] In other writings, Wycliffe questioned the extent of the Pope's authority and, as a result, received a Papal Bull of excommunication.[30]

Though Wycliffe's attempts at reform did not gain any lasting traction, aside from his English translation of the Bible, he and his followers did give the laity a picture of what church leadership could look like and an awareness of the need for a genuine corrective. Of MacCulloch's two pillars supporting Roman Catholicism, in the years following the 1530s, "Papal overlordship was decisively repudiated, but the old devotional world was treated in a much more ambiguous fashion."[31]

Reformation

William Tyndale, trained at Oxford, surfaced as another who raised ecclesiological questions. Failing to obtain support from the church hierarchy, he traveled to Antwerp and eventually published a New Testament in English. Tyndale had an intense interest in church leadership, as he found the structures and claims of the Roman Catholic Church untenable.[32] His *Obedience of a Christian Man* (1528) advocated the rejection of any form of allegiance to the established church while it encouraged obedience to the magistrate. However, his *Practice of the Prelates* (1530) opposed Henry VIII's plans to divorce his wife as unscriptural and Tyndale became a wanted man.[33] Inspired by the humanist Erasmus, Tyndale's English New Testament, published in the face of royal opposition, would serve as a foundation for future Bibles

---

28. John Wycliffe, *On Simony*, trans. Terrence A. McVeigh (New York: Fordham University Press, 1992), 84.

29. Ibid., 90; Allison, *Historical Theology*, 601.

30. G. R. Evans, *John Wyclif: Myth and Reality* (Downers Grove, IL: InterVarsity Press, 2005), 172

31. MacCulloch, *Later Reformation*, 5.

32. David Daniell, *William Tyndale: A Biography* (New Haven, CT: Yale University Press, 2001), 79.

33. Ibid., 201.

in English, even those authorized by the monarchy. In 1528, the soon to be Lord Chancellor, Thomas More, published his *A Dialogue Concerning Heresies*, a tract pointed at Tyndale. During the 1520s, More engaged Martin Luther in debate, defending Henry VIII and showing his Roman Catholic loyalties. In his *Dialogue*, More called into question Tyndale's translation specifically as it concerned Tyndale's preference for translating *ecclesia* as "congregation" rather than "church."[34] Tyndale followed Erasmus in his translation, notes Richard Marius, as "Both men were striving to get away from the sense of the church as a hierarchical institution; both wanted to emphasize the spontaneous gathering together of like-minded Christians."[35] Tyndale responded to More in his *An Answer* (1531), defending his translation of *ecclesia* as congregation to show that an *ecclesia* is "a multitude or company of gathered people in one, of all degrees of people" and not merely the stratified clergy, which is what most people considered at that time to be the church.[36] This led to further excoriation of Tyndale by More and by 1536 Tyndale was apprehended and executed for heresy.[37]

Henry VIII's handling of Tyndale reveals the complexities and compromise that surrounded the birth of the Church of England. [38] Obsessed with a desire to secure a male heir to the throne, the king desired a new wife in place of Catherine of Aragon for, as A. G. Dickens writes, "No

---

34. Thomas More, *A Dialogue Concerning Heresies*, Parts I & II, ed. Thomas M. C. Lawler, Germain Marc'hadour, and Richard C. Marius (New Haven, CT: Yale, 1981).
35. Richard Marius, *Thomas More: A Biography* (New York: Alfred A. Knopf, 1984), 321–22. See also Patrick Willis, "*Ekklesia* and the English Translation Debate of the Sixteenth Century" (unpublished PhD seminar paper, Southwestern Baptist Theological Seminary, Fort Worth, TX, 2012).
36. William Tyndale, *An Answer to Sir Thomas More's Dialogue*, Henry Walter, ed. (Cambridge: University Press, 1850), 12. In addition, Tyndale also defended his translation of *presbyterous* as seniors or elders rather than priests.
37. Daniell, *William Tyndale*, 382.
38. Historians of the English Reformation have debated how exactly the events transpired that brought about the sixteenth century transformation of English culture. Essentially, there are two perspectives: The traditional view championed by A. G. Dickens sees the Reformation as a rapid anti-clerical movement at the popular level. The revisionist view articulated by Christopher Haigh understands the Reformation as an independent pro-clerical Reformation which came together over time. See A. G. Dickens, "The Early Expansion of Protestantism in England 1520–1558," in *Archiv für Reformationsgeschichte* 78 (1987): 187–221; Christopher Haigh, "The Recent Historiography of the English Reformation," in *Historical Journal* 25 (1982): 995–1007.

English King had lost so many children."[39] His request for a divorce, denied by the Pope, sent Henry VIII reeling and, in addition to the eventual arrival of a son, a new trajectory for Christianity in England was born.[40] Thomas Cromwell served as Henry VIII's primary legal minister and architect of the move to sweep "away the papal connection and monasteries, while legally subordinating the national Church to the control of the Crown in Parliament."[41] In 1534, the Parliament renounced Papal authority and affirmed that "the Bishop of Rome has not, in Scripture, any greater jurisdiction in the kingdom of England than any other foreign bishop."[42] Further, they passed *The Supremacy Act* and installed the king as the "supreme head of the Church of England."[43] Henry VIII's second marriage to Anne Boleyn saw no male heir but a daughter, Elizabeth. His third wife, Jane Seymour, however, gave birth to a son, Edward. By the time of Henry VIII's death, the formation of church leadership in the Church of England continued to develop through the reforming leadership of Archbishop Thomas Cranmer.

Under the nine-year-old boy king Edward VI, the architects of the Church of England strived to maintain many of the preexistent physical, organizational, and ceremonial Roman Catholic structures while rewriting the founding theological documents to ensure separation greater than land and sea. The attempted balance they sought to strike can best be seen in the doctrinal documents they produced. As Gerald Bray explains, Cranmer designed these to cover doctrine, devotion, and discipline where the "Articles provided its doctrinal framework,

---

39. A. G. Dickens, *The English Reformation*, 2nd ed. (University Park: Pennsylvania State University Press, 1989), 126. Due to the fact that Catherine was first the widow of Henry's brother, many in England, including Henry, came to believe that the lack of a male heir was due to the judgment of God following Leviticus 20:21, "If a man takes his brother's wife, it is impurity. He has uncovered his brother's nakedness; they shall be childless."
40. Ibid., 127–29. While the divorce of Henry VIII remains at the center of the English Reformation, the degree to which it served as a catalyst is a matter of complex debate. As Dickens notes, Henry VIII likely would have preferred unity with Rome should they have granted his divorce. However, there were many problems already extant with Catholicism in England that, regardless of the King's acceleration of the separation, would have inaugurated such in the subsequent years.
41. Ibid., 206.
42. "Abjuration of Papal Supremacy by the Clergy (1534)," in *Documents*, ed. Henry Gee and William John Hardy, 251–52.
43. "The Supremacy Act (1534)," in *Documents*, ed. Henry Gee and William John Hardy, 243–44. See also Allison, *Historical Theology*, 604–5.

the Prayer Book settled the pattern of its devotional life and the Ordinal outlined what was expected of the clergy, whose role was the key to the church's discipline."[44] What is now known as *The Thirty Nine Articles* began in 1536 with just ten and then expanded under the influence of Cranmer to forty-two. Under Elizabeth I, the *Articles* were reviewed and in 1571 they were adopted in final form at thirty-nine total. Bray classifies the large middle section, Articles 9–34, as the Protestant doctrines, signaling England's allegiance with the churches of the Reformation at large., Bray identifies Articles 35–37 as the Anglican doctrines as they "deal with matters specific to the Church of England."[45] Article 32 affirms that bishops, priests, and deacons can seek marriage. Article 36 speaks to the consecration of the bishops and ordering of priests and deacons according to the pattern established by Edward VI. Article 37 asserts the Church of England's independence from the Bishop of Rome and recognizes the King's role in governing estates but not the ministry of God's Word or Sacraments.

In 1549, Cranmer published the *Book of Common Prayer* [BCP], a significant liturgical first for the English language[46] that was carefully designed so that "the old vestments and much of the old ceremonial could be used with it, despite the radical shift in its underlying theology."[47] As the government gave Cranmer and his theologians more freedom to advance reforms, they continued to revise the BCP. In terms of how that affected church leadership, the 1552 BCP revision diminished the language of priests offering sacrifices in favor of their functioning as pastors and teachers.[48] The BCP would shape England's political, social, and religious history, even influencing Shakespeare to the degree that the BCP is what one scholar calls Shakespeare's "great forgotten source."[49] *The Ordinal* first appeared in 1550 during the time

---

44. Gerald Bray, *The Faith We Confess: An Exposition of the Thirty-Nine Articles* (London: Latimer Trust, 2009), 1.
45. Bray, *The Faith We Confess*, 15.
46. Trueman, *Creedal Imperative*, 111.
47. MacCulloch, *Later Reformation*, 14.
48. Ibid., 15–16. MacCulloch notes, "The 1552 Book was the ultimate expression of Cranmer's theological outlook."
49. "Shakespeare's Book of Common Prayer" http://bostonglobe.com/ideas/2012/11/25/shakespeare-book-common-prayer/oooN896q4eGDtNfWoe5NJK/story.html (accessed November 26, 2012).

Cranmer was making significant changes. Designed to give direction for the ordination of what will be known as the "threefold ministry" of bishops, priests, and deacons, this manual provides clarity with regard to the function of Anglican Church leadership. No one was to serve in one of these offices unless "he be called, tried, examined and admitted thereunto, according to the Form hereafter following."[50]

Upon Henry VIII's death, his first daughter, Mary, assumed the throne. Mary I had not abandoned Roman Catholicism and thus desired to halt the reforms and redirect the Church of England back toward Rome. Soon, Parliament repealed the ecclesiastical legislation of Edward VI, but as Dickens relates they "would accept a return to the last years of Henry VIII but not a return to the Middle Ages."[51] Mary I did eventually succeed in reuniting the Church of England with Rome and then proceeded to execute the likes of Thomas Cranmer and others for heresy. Many Protestants fled the country, including a large number that gathered in Frankfurt under the leadership of John Knox. A native of Scotland, Knox served in the counsel of Edward VI and also agitated against Mary I. The gathering of exiles first in Germany and then in Geneva picked up the reformation trajectory of Cranmer, and they began developing their own translation of the Bible in English.[52] Mary I succumbed to cancer in 1558 and with her death came the end of her reactionary movement.

Enter the regal Elizabeth I. As Alister McGrath describes, under her dynasty the Church of England emerged "as a harassed monarch looked for ways to achieve a workable middle way that would find acceptance among both traditional Catholics and those who had been deeply influenced by the ideas of Luther and Calvin."[53] Elizabeth I's 1559 *Supremacy Act* required every ecclesiastical person to vocalize an oath stating that they "do utterly testify and declare in my conscience, that the queen's highness is the only supreme governor of this realm, and of all other her highness's dominions and countries, as well in all

---

50. Brian Cummings, ed., *The Book of Common Prayer: The Texts of 1549, 1559, 1662* (Oxford: Oxford University Press, 2011), 622.
51. Dickens, *English Reformation*, 288.
52. Ibid., 343–44.
53. Alister E. McGrath, *The Renewal of Anglicanism* (Harrisburg, PA: Morehouse, 1993), 11.

spiritual or ecclesiastical things or causes."[54] The subsequent *Uniformity Act* repealed many of the actions of Mary I and reinstated use of the BCP as well as requiring that those "inhabiting within this realm, or any other the queen's majesty's dominions, shall diligently and faithfully, having no lawful or reasonable excuse to be absent, endeavour themselves to resort to their parish church or chapel" or face the correction or punishment of Church censure.[55] Elizabeth I oversaw a revision of the BCP in 1559 that made only slight revisions to the 1552 BCP but also brought back some of the ceremonial forms of the 1549 BCP.[56] For matters related to church leadership, the offices of bishop, priest, and deacon remained unchanged from even the pre-reformation days.[57]

During the days of Cranmer, John Jewel joined the reformation movement while a student at Oxford. While Mary I reigned he lived in exile but as soon as Elizabeth I claimed the throne, Jewel returned to England as one of the early supporters of Elizabeth I's reforms. Appointed Bishop of Salisbury in 1560, Jewel advocated for the rightful place of the Church of England to separate from Rome. In response to Pope Pius IV's criticisms, Jewel wrote a brief treatise in Latin defending the Church of England.[58] By 1564, Jewel's *Apology* appeared in English and many read of his conclusion regarding Rome, "We truly have renounced that Church, wherein we could neither have the Word of God sincerely taught, nor the sacraments rightly administered, nor the Name of God duly called upon."[59] Regarding church leadership, Jewel supported his conclusions both with Scripture and testimony from the early church to show that no basis existed for a single bishop or Pope to have supreme jurisdiction over other churches.[60] His appeal to tradition did not supersede Scrip-

---

54. "The Supremacy Act (1559)," in *Documents*, ed. Henry Gee and William John Hardy, 442–58.
55. "The Supremacy Act (1559)," in *Documents*, ed. Henry Gee and William John Hardy, 458–67.
56. MacCulloch, *Later Reformation*, 25. There is a sense in which while the names of the offices remained unchanged their function altered over the centuries. See chapter 6 of Malcolm B. Yarnell, III's *Royal Priesthood in the English Reformation* (New York: Oxford University Press, 2014).
57. Ibid., 29.
58. John Craig, "Jewel, John (1522–1571)," *ODNB*, http://www.oxforddnb.com/view/article/14810 (accessed July 20, 2005).
59. John Jewel, *The Apology of the Church in England* (London, 1564), 136, http://www.gutenberg.org/files/17678/17678-h/17678-h.htm#startoftext (accessed April 28, 2013).
60. Ibid., 34.

ture but rather showed that the Church of England more authentically connected to the first six centuries.[61] Jewel published *A Defense of the Apology* in 1567 in response to Thomas Harding's volume, *An Answer to Master Jewel's Challenge*. This confrontation brought the debate to a large audience and by 1577 many bishops were requiring all parishes to purchase copies of Jewel's *Apology*, the *Defense*, or both.[62]

By the 1570s, many of the reformation advocates dating back to the Edward VI era faded from the scene and a new generation of Puritans began to advocate for more reforms. Centered around the university in Cambridge, these "keen-minded young enthusiasts" did not see Elizabeth I's actions as permanent and were "convinced that a further alteration of the ecclesiastical system was necessary."[63] Dubbed "the marching wing of the Church of England" these zealous Puritans first followed Thomas Cartwright in a movement against the episcopal form of church leadership.[64] As Lady Margaret Professor, Cartwright used his Spring lectures on the Book of Acts to critique the Church of England. "That the names and functions of archbishops and archdeacons ought to be abolished. . . . That the government of the church ought not to be intrusted to bishops' chancellors or the officials of archdeacons, but every church ought to be governed by its own ministers and presbyters."[65] These actions led to the removal of Cartwright from the professorship and he departed for Geneva.[66] In 1572, John Field and Thomas Wilcox helped draft the Puritans' *Admonition to the Parliament*. Patrick Collinson confirms, "The *Admonition* was more outspoken than anything that had yet been published by protestants against protestants."[67] Regarding church leadership in the Church of England, the *Admonition* addressed, in part, the Ordinal's direction for

---

61. As early as 1559, Jewel sent for the challenge in a sermon that "if any learned man of our adversaries be able to bring any one sufficient sentence out of any old doctor or father, or out of any general council, or out of the holy Scripture, or any one example out of the primitive church for the space of six hundred years after church" in support of Roman teachings then, "I would give over and subscribe to him" (Craig, "Jewel, John," *ODNB*). See also Turnbull, *Anglican and Evangelical?*, 25.

62. Craig, "Jewel, John," *ODNB*.

63. M. M. Knappen, *Tudor Puritanism* (Chicago: Chicago University Press, 1939), 219.

64. Michael J. McClymond and Gerald R. McDermott, *The Theology of Jonathan Edwards* (New York: Oxford University Press, 2012), 43–44.

65. B. Brook, *Memoir of the Life and Writings of Thomas Cartwright* (London: John Snow, 1845), 69–70.

66. Knappen, *Tudor Puritanism*, 225.

67. Patrick Collinson, *The Elizabethan Puritan Movement* (Oxford: Clarendon Press, 1967), 119.

consecrating bishops as "a thing word for word drawn out of the Pope's pontifical."[68] Field and Wilcox would spend a year in jail.

Not all Cambridge graduates of this era seeking change were content to labor within the existing hierarchical structure. Robert Browne represents the first to publish the views of several that had rejected episcopal authority and met in private gatherings appealing to Scripture for their own "prayer, preaching, and sacraments."[69] Browne's congregation had met during the early 1580s but due to increased scrutiny by ecclesiastical officials, they fled to the Netherlands. In 1583, Browne published *A Treatise of Reformation without Tarrying for Anie,* a volume of wide-reaching significance that B. R. White terms, "the first sustained attempt by an English Separatist to produce a consistent doctrine of the Church."[70] Browne confirmed the right of the Queen to have jurisdiction in all civil matters, but called upon church leaders to remove themselves from monarchial oversight of matters spiritual. "My kingdom, says Christ, is not of this world, and they would shift in both Bishops and Magistrates into his spiritual throne to make it over this world."[71] In the following years Browne returned to England and upon his arrest for his publications he recanted and submitted to the authority of the Archbishop.[72] Subsequent Separatists who did not submit were imprisoned and executed.

When John Whitgift became Archbishop in 1583 he gained new ground toward the subjection of Puritans and Papists within the Church of England as well as the Separatists outside the Elizabethan Church.[73] In a series of articles he published for distribution to all dioceses, Whitgift announced that anyone exercising an ecclesial function in a church must subscribe that "the Book of Common Prayer, and of ordering bishops, priests, and deacons, containeth nothing in it con-

---

68. W. H. Frere and C. E. Douglas, eds., *Puritan Manifestoes* (London: SPCK, 1907), 30.
69. B. R. White, *The English Separatist Tradition* (Oxford: Oxford University Press, 1971), 24.
70. Ibid., 66.
71. Robert Browne, *A Treatise of Reformation without Tarrying for Anie,* in *The Writings of Robert Harrison and Robert Browne,* ed. Leland H. Carlson and Albert Peel (London: George Allen and Unwin, 1953; reprint 2003), 155. Spelling modernized.
72. Michael E. Moody, "Browne, Robert (1550?–1633)," *ODNB,* http://www.oxforddnb.com/view/article/3695 (accessed July 25, 2005).
73. MacCulloch, *Later Reformation,* 41.

trary to the word of God."[74] Not long thereafter the Puritan attempt to transform the leadership structure of the Church of England diminished and to avoid the consequences that befell many Separatists, the Puritans retreated to give "priority to the cultivation of the individual soul."[75] The return of the Puritans to Cambridge came at the time of Richard Hooker's *Of the Laws of Ecclesiastical Polity*, a work considered "a charter document for Anglicanism."[76] Whereas Jewel defended the Church of England against the Roman Catholic critique, Hooker defended it against the Puritan and Presbyterian onslaught.[77] With regard to church leadership he emphasized the roles of tradition and reason functioning in support of Scripture and argued that the Puritans were wrong to downplay church practices based on tradition in areas where Scripture did not speak.[78] He affirmed the priority of the episcopate: "let us not fear to be herein bold and peremptory, that if anything in the Church's government, surely the first institution of bishops was from heaven, was even of God, the Holy Ghost was the author of it."[79] With this established balance in place, Hooker and Whitgift strengthened the centrist Church of England that the queen desired. Many may have doubted whether Elizabeth I could have taken the reins of this melodramatic monarchy, but quickly she showed that in matters of church, just as in matters of state, that though "I have the body, but of a weak and feeble woman, but I have the heart and stomach of a King, and of a King of England too."[80]

While examination of the ensuing eras follows, it is important to note the overarching significance of the sixteenth century for the de-

---

74. "Articles Touching Preachers and Other Orders for the Church," in *Documents,* ed. Henry Gee and William John Hardy, 482.
75. MacCulloch, *Later Reformation,* 51.
76. Avis, "Great Britain," 9. McGrade comments, "In the course of its eight books, the *Laws* deals with issues between conformists and nonconformists, episcopalians and presbyterians, and Rome and the Church of England in greater depth than any previous treatment" (A. S. McGrade, "Hooker, Richard [1554–1600]," *ODNB,* http://oxforddnb.com/view/article/13696 [accessed July 20, 2005]).
77. John Booty, "Standard Divines," in *The Study of Anglicanism,* ed. Sykes and Booty, 164.
78. Turnbull, *Anglican and Evangelical?,* 26.
79. John Keble, *The Works of That Learned and Judicious Divine, Mr. Richard Hooker: with an Account of His Life and Death* (Oxford: Clarendon Press, 1876), 168, http://anglicanhistory.org/hooker/7/7.160–169.pdf (accessed April 29, 2013).
80. Janet M. Green, "'I My Self': Queen Elizabeth I's Oration at Tilbury Camp," *The Sixteenth Century Journal* 28, no. 2 (Summer 1997): 421–45. Spelling modernized.

velopment of the Church of England, especially with regard to church leadership. Oliver O'Donovan writes, "The Tudor church has exercised the most profoundly formative role in determining what Anglicanism ever since, in all its varieties, has been and now is. Each century has left its stamp on us; but the sixteenth has determined the shape of the whole."[81]

Post-Reformation

Paul Zahl believes that "Elizabeth's 'Anglicanism' was and is a wax nose. It can be shaped in a Protestant direction, and it can be shaped in a Catholic or non-Roman but 'high-church' direction. It can even be shaped in a 'liberal' or 'broad-church' direction."[82] Like Janus, the centuries following the reformation of the Church of England have seen multiple shaped noses. The ascension of James I to the throne in 1603 breathed new hope into the lives of the Puritans though soon the King would clarify that he would make few changes. When a thousand Puritan ministers petitioned the King for relief regarding several church practices, James I heard their plea but only provided small concessions.[83] James I's renewed focus on the BCP allowed for a greater tolerance toward Rome than had existed during Elizabeth's reign. One of the principle figures for this development both in the seventeenth century and for future eras was Lancelot Andrewes. The Bishop of Winchester, Andrewes participated in the translation of the Authorized Version of the Bible and in his writings affirmed the strong connection the Church of England had with the early church.[84] After his death in 1626, Archbishop William Laud, supported by the new King Charles I, began to spread Andrewes' views through the publication of his works to assist in their "reorientation of national worship from sermons to sacrament and prayer."[85] Those who supported the renewed emphasis on royal supremacy and the elevation of the epis-

---

81. Oliver O'Donovan, *On the Thirty-Nine Articles: Conversations with Tudor Christianity* (London: SCM Press, 2011), 5.

82. Paul F. M. Zahl, "The Bishop-Led Church," in *Perspectives on Church Government*, ed. Chad Owen Brand and R. Stanton Norman (Nashville: B&H, 2004), 222.

83. "The Millenary Petition," in *Documents*, Henry Gee and William John Hardy, 508.

84. Roger Steer, *Guarding the Holy Fire* (Grand Rapids: Baker, 1999), 59–60.

85. P. E. McCullough, "Andrewes, Lancelot (1555–1626)," *ODNB*, http://www.oxforddnb.com/view/article/520 (accessed April 29, 2013).

copate became known as the Caroline Divines and would serve as fore-runners for the later High Church views of Anglo-Catholics. By reacting against the Puritans, the followers of Laud peculiarly saw themselves as charting an even more accurate course than Elizabeth I's via media between Canterbury and Rome.[86]

A dissenting voice appeared during the early seventeenth century in Thomas Helwys. Having traveled from Puritanism to Separatism, Helwys was a member of the first congregation on English soil to observe baptism only for believers.[87] Motivated by the sole authority of Scripture, Helwys published *A Short Declaration of the Mystery of Iniquity* (1612). A tract that called for universal religious freedom, Helwys' *A Short Declaration* also identified the Church of England as the Second beast of Revelation 13. The First beast is Rome and the Second remains connected to the first through the hierarchical structure of church leadership. "This hierarchy of archbishops and lord bishops are the image of the beast, let all behold the names of blasphemy which it bears."[88] Helwys took issue with the attribution of the spiritual titles held by those connected to temporal offices. He further critiqued the Puritans for their presbyterian structure of church leadership as a "hierarchy, a decreeing synod, which would have been no more pleasing to God than a hierarchy of archbishops" as such would rule over consciences.[89] Helwys, in turn, advocated for a congregational authority of church leadership.[90] The appearance of this work led to Helwys's apprehension where he likely died in prison.

During the 1640s, England's preoccupation with its Civil War led to a radical transformation of the understanding of church leadership.[91]

---

86. Turnbull, *Evangelical and Anglican?*, 27–28.
87. Stephen Wright, "Helwys, Thomas (c.1575–c.1614)," *ODNB*, http://www.oxforddnb.com/view/article/12880 (accessed July 24, 2007).
88. Thomas Helwys, *A Short Declaration of the Mystery of Iniquity*, in Joe Early, Jr. *The Life and Writings of Thomas Helwys* (Macon, GA: Mercer University Press, 2009), 176.
89. Ibid., 230.
90. Ibid., 223. Helwys also condemned the Separatists stating that even though they are no longer organizationally connected to the Church of England and thereby to Rome, they, in fact still have a tie due to their recognition of the baptism from the Church of England.
91. While traditionally called the Civil War, Carl Trueman notes that while the conflict was an internal one consisting of a war between Parliament and Crown, "it also involved both Scots and Irish and more than one phase of military conflict. Thus, it is now known in some quarters as the Wars of the Three Kingdoms" (*Creedal Imperative*, 125). See also John Morrill, *The Nature of the English Revolution* (London: Longman, 1993).

Following the execution of Archbishop Laud and Charles I, congregations were permitted to "determine their forms of Christian teaching
and worship" so long as they did not insist upon Roman Catholic or
Anglican practices.[92] One example of an Anglican serving during this
period is the curate in Kidderminister, Richard Baxter and his work,
The Reformed Pastor. Baxter's understanding of church leadership focused on the pastoral oversight of a congregation in addition to the
oversight of oneself.[93] As N. H. Keeble notes, Baxter distinguished
himself from the Caroline Divines as he advocated the plain preaching
of the Puritans and "had no patience with such preaching as that of
Lancelot Andrewes, which 'did but play with holy things.'"[94] In contrast
to Baxter, the poet John Milton engaged Andrewes during the Civil
War and advocated for a congregational form of church leadership.[95]
In his *The Reason of Church Government*, Milton specifically attacks
the notion that episcopacy is grounded in the Old Testament priesthood. "If therefore the superiority of Bishopship be grounded on the
Priesthood as part of the moral law, it cannot be said to be an imitation;
for it were ridiculous that morality should imitate morality, which ever
was the same thing. This very word of patterning or imitating excludes
Episcopacy from the solid and grave Ethical law, and betrays it to be
a mere childe of ceremony."[96] In July 1643 an assembly of theologians
met to discuss "the settlement of the Government and Liturgy of the
Church of England."[97] The Westminster Assembly, infused with Scottish Presbyterians, began to overhaul the entire Anglican experiment.
The BCP was replaced and the *Westminster Confession* adopted.[98] How-

---

92. William P. Haugaard, "From the Reformation to the Eighteenth Century," in *The Study of Anglicanism*, ed. Sykes and Booty, 20.
93. Richard Baxter, *The Reformed Pastor* (London, 1656).
94. N. H. Keeble, "Baxter, Richard (1615–1691)," *ODNB*, http://www.oxforddnb.com/view/article/1734 (accessed April 30, 2013).
95. David Loewenstein, ed., *John Milton Prose* (West Sussex: Wiley-Blackwell, 2013), 61–62. Gordon Campbell, "Milton, John (1608–1674)," *ODNB*, http://www.oxfordodnb.com/view/article/18800 (accessed April 30, 2013).
96. John Milton, *The Reasons of Church Government Urg'd against Prelaty* (1642), 1.3, http://www.dartmouth.edu/~milton/reading_room/reason/book_1/index.shtml (accessed April 30, 2013).
97. *The Westminster Confession of Faith* (Atlanta: Committee for Christian Education & Publications, 1990), xiv.
98. B. B. Warfield, *The Westminster Assembly and Its Work* (Oxford: Oxford University Press, 1932; reprint, Grand Rapids: Baker, 2003).

ever, such advancements toward a presbyterian structure of church leadership soon ended.[99]

Charles II reclaimed the throne in 1660 and with him came a return to the elevation of the episcopacy that developed during the reign of Charles I. By 1662 Charles II revised the BCP, the Ordinal, and passed an *Act of Uniformity* as well as a *Corporation Act* that required repudiation of the Solemn League and Covenant established during the interregnum.[100] The stalwart Puritan ministers, some one thousand, who felt they could not subscribe to these new parameters were ejected from their churches in 1662.[101] As Paul Avis concludes, "From this point onwards there was a strengthening of the divine right of bishops rather than of kings."[102] Following Charles II's death, his brother James II became king and advocated for more toleration toward Roman Catholics within the Church of England. In the Glorious Revolution, William of Orange laid claim to the throne in 1688, sending James II into exile. While soon establishing religious toleration outside of the Church of England, except for Roman Catholicism, many bishops refused to pledge supremacy to the new monarch as they felt allegiance to Charles II and James II. These "non-jurors" were permitted to continue ministering and their presence continued to advance the high-church views of the Caroline Divines.[103]

While the eighteenth century saw the expansion of the Church of England and the growth of evangelical movements led by John Wesley

---

99. Trueman, *Creedal Imperative*, 126.
100. "The Corporation Act," in *Documents*, ed. Henry Gee and William John Hardy, 594. In 1643, Parliament saw the need to align with Scotland for military reinforcement against the Royalists. In exchange for aid, Parliament agreed to the Solemn League and Covenant, which assured Scotland of her Presbyterian system of government and churches and intimated that England would move to adopt the same. See G. M. Trevelyan, *England Under the Stuarts* (London: Methuen & Co., 1904; reprint, London: Routledge, 2002), 244–45.
101. Haugaard comments, "Episcopal polity was rapidly reasserted at the Restoration, and, in spite of presbyterian expectations and royal promises, there was no compromise on the requirement of episcopal ordination. With the departure of Protestant dissenters, protests against episcopal government within the Church ceased. However, in spite of confident assertions of the importance of 'apostolic succession' in the episcopal office, nearly all seventeenth-century Anglicans qualified their claims for episcopacy, as Hooker had done, by a recognition that circumstantial necessity might dictate another course" ("From the Reformation to the Eighteenth Century," 26).
102. Avis, "Great Britain," 15–16.
103. Steer, *Guarding the Holy Fire*, 77–79.

and George Whitefield, there was a general consensus that doctrinally "the Church of England was both Catholic and Reformed" with its church leadership still intact even though in practice the church waned.[104] Though loyal to the historic doctrines and documents of the Church of England, Whitefield increasingly received criticism from the bishops for his open air preaching.[105] Whitefield, in turn, expressed his displeasure with the poor character of many of the Anglican clergy and began to move away from their oversight. He writes, "The whole world is now my parish. 'Tis equal to me whether I preach in a field or in a church."[106] Wesley, too, came to a place as seeing the world as his home for ministry though he saw his Methodist movement as an "evangelist order" within the Church of England to combat what he saw as a climate of apathy.[107]

Modern Era

From the nineteenth century to the present the Church of England has seen three distinct groups emerge within the Anglican Communion; or as Zahl explains, "It is actually three churches within one organization."[108] For the Liberal Protestants, the Anglo-Catholics, and the Evangelicals there exists a diversity of views with regard to church leadership.[109] With the advent of the Enlightenment, many in the Church of England

104. Avis, "Great Britain," 17.
105. Boyd Stanley Schelenther, "Whitefield, George (1714–1770)," *ODNB*, http://www.oxforddnb.com/view/article/29281 (accessed May 2, 2013).
106. Ibid. See also Graham C. G. Thomas, ed., "George Whitefield and Friends: The Correspondence of Some Early Methodists," in *National Library of Wales Journal* 27.1 (1991), 91.
107. Albert C. Outler, ed., *John Wesley* (Oxford: Oxford University Press, 1964), 20–22. The attacks by Anglicans for his use of lay preachers and other "irregularities" led eventually to an increasing separation and disagreement over church structure and order. Eventually Methodism would establish itself as its own denomination. See Henry D. Rack, "Wesley, John (1703–1791)," *ODNB*, http://www.oxforddnb.com/view/article/29069 (accessed May 2, 2013).
108. Zahl, "The Bishop-Led Church," 224.
109. There have been various attempts at unification of the diverse theological and geographical bodies that comprise the Anglican Communion in the modern era. One effort originated in the mid-nineteenth century and has occurred in subsequent intervals is the Lambeth Conferences. A synod of bishops, the Conference convenes at the bequest of the Archbishop of Canterbury. In 1888, the Conference adopted the Quadrilateral statement on Anglicanism in an attempt to establish a core consensus for unity. The fourth statement signals that the churches should agree that the role of the "Historic Episcopate" is a part of the foundation necessary for unity. See Perry Butler, "From the Early Eighteenth Century to the Present Day," in *The Study of Anglicanism*, ed. Sykes and Booty, 40.

joined the practice of focusing on the role of reason in addition to tradition and Scripture for shaping the life of the church.[110] Identified first as the Latitudinarian movement for its tendency to grant wide discrepancy for all matters of theological difference, the Liberal wing of Anglicanism emphasized the *adiaphora* or large area of things indifferent with regard to liturgy, doctrine, and church leadership.[111] With a growing acceptance of the rise of biblical criticism and other movements of the theological left, the Liberal Protestants[112] continued to expand their influence into the twentieth century while drifting further from their theological roots of the sixteenth century.[113] Here is where the employment of the hierarchical structure of church leadership exercised significant sway over the churches. For example, in recent decades the Church of England has acted upon and approved practices contrary to the historic teaching and understanding of Scripture with regard to the ordination of homosexual priests.[114] As it pertains to the evangelical American congregation, The Falls Church, the result has been the diocese reclaiming the church's property in response to the congregation departing to join a more conservative communion.[115]

The Anglo-Catholic perspective grew in the first half of the nineteenth century in response to a sermon by curate John Keble and then the work of Edward Pusey and John Henry Newman. Known as the Oxford Movement, these Anglicans responded both to parliamentary influence and Protestant liberalism in the church and identified with the high-church emphases of the seventeenth century. Elevating

---

110. Trueman states that the drift toward liberalism over the history of Anglicanism "is, by and large, a history of failure to apply the *Thirty-Nine Articles* and to carry forward the theology they contain" (*Creedal Imperative*, 115).

111. Perry Butler, "From the Early Eighteenth Century to the Present Day," 35–36.

112. See Benjamin Jowett, "On the Interpretation of Scripture," in *Essays and Reviews*, ed. John W. Parker (London, 1860), 330–433, and the works of F. D. Maurice and Robert Gore for examples.

113. Bray, *The Faith We Confess*, 2, observes that "The Articles of Religion have not been revised or supplemented, but if anything they have suffered an even more drastic fate—they have been sidelined and ignored instead!"

114. William L. Sachs, *Homosexuality and the Crisis of Anglicanism* (Cambridge: Cambridge University Press, 2009).

115. Greg MacDonald, "Va. Supreme Court rules on ownership of The Falls Church," *Fairfax Times*, http://www.fairfaxtimes.com/article/20130426/NEWS/130429290/1117/va-supreme-court-rules-on-ownership-of-the-falls-church&template=fairfaxTimes (accessed April 26, 2013).

the role of tradition alongside Scripture, the Anglo-Catholics sought a higher standard of worship and even a revival of monastic orders. As MacCulloch notes, "The Elizabethan Church Settlement had created a cuckoo in a nest, a Protestant theological system and Protestant programme for national salvation sheltering within a largely pre-Reformation Catholic church structure; now the structure began to reassert its fascination, and aroused theological interest in the Catholicism which had created it."[116] The cuckoo in the nest, the Oxford Movement, though opposed by many, would have "a decisive effect on the pattern of Church life in Britain and beyond."[117] One issue related to church leadership is the advocacy of apostolic succession. In Newman's *Tracts for the Times* he urges clergy to "Exalt our Holy Fathers, the Bishops, as the Representatives of the Apostles, and the Angels of the Churches; and magnify your office, as being ordained by them to take part in their Ministry."[118] Keble maintains that the Bishops have, through succession, received the commission of Jesus and thus Christians should not desire to separate from the Episcopal communion for this succession is "the best external security I can have."[119] Newman especially built a bridge to Rome and argued that the *Thirty Nine Articles* "may be subscribed by those who aim at being catholic in heart and doctrine."[120] The Anglo-Catholic position remains attractive for many who find the role of tradition equal or superior to Scripture. For them, this unique perspective on church leadership within the Church of England is the ultimate expression of authentic Anglicanism.[121]

The Evangelical Anglicans of the modern era are the descendants of the Whitefield and Wesley movements during the eighteenth century. And, much like the Puritans of the sixteenth and seventeenth centuries, many of the evangelicals could be found at Oxford or Cambridge. In

116. MacCulloch, *Later Reformation*, 78.

117. "Oxford Movement," in *The Oxford Dictionary of the Christian Church*, 1206.

118. Tract 1, "Thoughts on the Ministerial Commission," http://anglicanhistory.org/tracts/tract1.html (accessed May 3, 2013).

119. Tract 4, "Adherence to the Apostolic Succession Is the Safest Course," http://anglicanhistory.org/tracts/tract4.html (accessed May 3, 2013).

120. Tract 90, "Introduction," http://anglicanhistory.org/tracts/tract90/introduction.html (accessed May 3, 2013).

121. Todd D. Hunter, *The Accidental Anglican: The Surprising Appeal of the Liturgical Church* (Nottingham: InterVarsity Press, 2011).

part this was due to the long tenured churchman and preacher, Charles Simeon.[122] Another significant evangelical figure was J. C. Ryle, bishop of Liverpool. Ryle regularly defended evangelical claims against the Anglo-Catholic and Liberal Anglicans. Seeking first for fairness, he wrote, "In a fallen world like ours, and in a free country it is vain to expect all men to see all things alike: but so long as a brother walks loyally within the limits of the Articles and Prayer Book, let us respect him."[123] Ryle affirmed the threefold ministry of church leadership that "from the beginning there have been bishops, priests, and deacons" but he refused that "bigoted cry, 'No Bishop, no Church.'"[124] Further, he said, "We give to our Bishops as much honour and respect. . . . We thoroughly believe the Episcopal government, rightly administered, is the best form of Church government that can be had in this evil world. But we steadily refuse to believe that Bishops are infallible."[125]

In the twentieth and twenty-first centuries, evangelicals in the Church of England have followed John Stott and J. I. Packer, two churchmen who through their preaching and writing have shaped the broader evangelical movement.[126] While remaining loyal to the Church of England, they have spoken against theological liberalism as well as attempted where possible to work with Catholics. In the 1960s, they were challenged to leave the Church of England on the basis of putting doctrine first. Rather, they chose to stay and, like the Puritans, attempted change from within.[127] Contemporary Anglican evangelicals like Richard Turnbull describe the evangelical perspective on church leadership as one of priority, stating "Anglican Evangelicals draw their basic understanding of the Church firstly from the pages of the New

---

122. Perry Butler, "From the Early Eighteenth Century to the Present Day," 33. See also, Leonard W. Cowie, "Simeon, Charles (1759–1836)," in *ODNB*, http://www.oxforddnb.com/view/article/25559 (accessed May 3, 2013).
123. G. R. Balleine, *A History of the Evangelical Party in the Church of England* (London: Longmans, Green, and Co., 1908), 279.
124. J. C. Ryle, *Knots Untied* (London: Wm. Hunt and Co., 1898), 15.
125. Ibid., 14. See also Steer, *Guarding the Holy Fire*, 196–202.
126. See the evangelical movement in Australia in Michael P. Jensen, *Sydney Anglicanism: An Apology* (Eugene, OR: Wipf & Stock, 2012).
127. Steer, *Guarding the Holy Fire*, 210–35. For more on the call to leave the Church of England, see Carl Trueman, "J. I. Packer: An English Nonconformist Perspective," in *J. I. Packer and the Evangelical Future*, ed. Timothy George (Grand Rapids: Baker, 2009), 115–30.

Testament and secondly from the Thirty-Nine Articles." Then he appeals to *adiaphora*, "Key to Anglican Evangelical ecclesiology is the
recognition that a detailed blueprint is not laid down."[128] Paul Zahl likewise speaks of *adiaphora* and priority: "Church questions are penultimate ones in the Bible. They are penultimate in the Bible because the
evidence in Scripture is multiple, not necessary, and therefore univer-
salizable. Anyone who argues in favor of the universality of a particular
New Testament polity will always have to devalue or deemphasize one
or another conflicting text."[129] For Peter Toon, "apostolic succession"
is not an unbroken line of individual bishops but rather a statement of
connectivity the office of the bishop as whole has with all other bishops
in time past and future.[130] Toon sees the greater potential for unity to
come from this form of church leadership due to its connectivity with
the authority of Christ. Finally, John Webster believes that the episcopate is an "ordered, institutional implication of the gospel."[131] Rather
than focus on an argument from historical succession, Webster argues
that the bishop, through his role of gathering the congregation around
the gospel, exercises the designed oversight necessary to achieve unity.[132] Anglican Evangelicals emphasize, wherever they feel possible, the
priority of Scripture over tradition and reason. With regard to church
leadership this places them in the closest position historically to the
rest of the Reformation tradition.

"I have told a complicated story, and that is necessary, because
Henry VIII made his Reformation a complicated matter."[133] Following
MacCulloch's disclaimer, I affirm that the review of the historical and
theological development of church leadership in Anglicanism is intri-
cate. However, despite the dramatic convulsions that took place, one
can see that Eamon Duffy, too, has a point. Embedded in the genetic
makeup of the Church of England, like mosquitos trapped in the amber
of *Jurassic Park*, resides a nascent Roman Catholic ecclesial hierarchy.

---

128. Turnbull, *Anglican and Evangelical?*, 112.
129. Zahl, "The Bishop-Led Church," 212.
130. Peter Toon, "Episcopalianism," in *Who Runs the Church? 4 Views on Church Government*,
     ed. Steve B. Cowan (Grand Rapids: Zondervan, 2004), 38.
131. John Webster, "The Self-Organizing Power of the Gospel of Christ: Episcopacy and Com-
     munity Formation," in *International Journal of Systematic Theology* 3, no. 1 (March 2001): 70.
132. Ibid., 77.
133. MacCulloch, "The Church of England 1533–1603," 23.

As many have sought to advance or diminish this aspect of Anglicanism, the core three-tiered church structure never changed from the early church to the present.

CONCLUSION

"One of the first steps toward the theological renewal of Anglicanism must be the re-examination of our cherished claims to distinctiveness, to ensure that we are not simply perpetuating unjustifiable misjudgments concerning our past heritage."[134] Alister McGrath rightly notes the propensity of Anglicanism to drift toward cherished traditions. After examining the historical development of Anglicanism with regard to views on church leadership, I conclude with three brief statements of evaluation. First, as MacCulloch states, "Yet the story of Anglicanism, and the story of the discomfiture of Elizabeth's first bishops, is the result of the fact that this tension between Catholic structure and Protestant theology was never resolved."[135] Even though officially separate from Rome politically and otherwise, there remains an inherent connection through their polity and specifically through their continued use of the hierarchical system of church leadership. Without this connection there would not be the reoccurring talks of the Church of England returning to the "Mother Church."[136] Second, in this history of the Church of England there are very few who attempt to make a biblical case for their offices of church leadership. Even if one appeals to the secondary nature of these doctrines, the New Testament is not silent about the matter and the biblical evidence leans strongly in favor of the argument that the terms for bishop and elder are used interchangeably.[137] Third, while an appeal to Scripture is lacking, the overwhelming reli-

---

134. McGrath, *The Renewal of Anglicanism*, 66.
135. MacCulloch, *Later Reformation*, 29.
136. Rachel Donadio, "Tensions Linger Between Pope and Anglicans" http://www.nytimes.com/2010/09/22/world/europe/22pope.html?_r=1&&gwh=1BEF4D0C87D36CDADC FC942B45404870 (accessed April 20, 2013); Rachel Donadio and Laurie Goodstein, "Vatican Plan to Ease Conversion of Anglicans," http://www.nytimes.com/2009/10/21/world/europe/21pope.html?gwh=69512009D74367A41C4A42504811A3EA (accessed April 20, 2013).
137. See Gregg R. Allison, *Sojourners and Strangers: The Doctrine of the Church* (Wheaton, IL: Crossway, 2012), 260; Benjamin L. Merkle, *The Elder and Overseer: One Office in the Early Church* (New York: Peter Lang, 2003).

ance upon tradition is the very thing that causes the complexity and confusion within the Anglican Communion when seeking to understand church leadership. The use of tradition is a helpful tool but in the end, remains a record of the activities and constructions of failed men and women. For these reasons, I cannot agree with my fellow Baptist, E. Glenn Hinson's assessment that "the Church of England is our mother church by way of the Puritans. A Baptist joining an Anglican or Episcopal Church is going home."[138] For example, I do not think Thomas Helwys, from his prison cell, and other persecuted seventeenth-century London Baptists would agree with that sentiment. However, though the Church of England is the cousin of Catholicism, Baptists and other free churches share the Scriptures as our common source of authority. Because many Anglicans treasure Scripture, there lies the beginning of a basis for discussion about church leadership.

At the conclusion of Diarmaid MacCulloch's award-winning biography of Thomas Cranmer, he answers the hypothetical question of what would have occurred if Mary I failed to become queen and the Edwardian reformation continued. Seeing a dramatic yet more stable series of events unfold, MacCulloch concludes that "England would have become the most powerful political player in the Reformed camp, with Cranmer a cordial if geographically distant partner with John Calvin."[139] While the force and facts of history do seem to affirm this potential trajectory, one equally wonders if the Puritan penchant for the study and preaching of Scripture would have led the Church of England beyond an embrace of presbyterian church leadership to a congregationalism comprised of free churches, separate from the state, and no longer the cousin of Catholicism.

---

138. E. Glenn Hinson, *A Miracle of Grace: An Autobiography* (Macon, GA: Mercer University Press, 2012), 355.
139. MacCulloch, *Thomas Cranmer*, 619.

CHAPTER 9

Baptists and a Plurality of Elders

Shawn D. Wright[1]

For all of their emphasis on Scripture's role in regulating how local churches should be ordered, Baptists have been surprisingly quiet about the necessity of having a plurality of elders in their churches. Their *raison d'être*, the very idea that called them into existence, was their insistence that the Bible alone should determine how their churches would be organized.[2] Yet, they have largely remained silent about the New Testament pattern of having multiple elders in each church. Hence emerges the paradox of Baptists and plurality of elders. Claiming to be the consistent followers of Scripture, Baptists have allowed other concerns to trump the clear pattern of plural elders found in the New Testament.

Baptists are too large and diverse a group to adequately cover in this chapter. An introductory caveat is therefore important. This study is not a chronological look at Baptist thought on plurality to show development over time. That would be a wonderful approach, but it is not realistic given the paucity of sources that address the issue. I have instead asked the question, What did Baptists coming out of the Particular, or Calvinistic, stream think about having a plurality of elders in their churches? That question has focused this study to Particular Baptists in England beginning in the 1600s and follows that stream in their American descendants, especially in the South.

---

1. Shawn D. Wright (PhD, The Southern Baptist Theological Seminary) is Associate Professor of Church History at The Southern Baptist Theological Seminary in Louisville, Kentucky.
2. One prominent historian of the Baptists rightly comments, "The most fundamental contribution which Baptists made to Christian theology was a new vision for the visible Church" (William Brackney, *The Baptists* [Westport, CT: Greenwood Press, 1988], 37).

The sources are overwhelmingly quiet on the issue. There were those, especially English Baptists in the seventeenth century, who advocated plurality. Additionally, there were Scottish and Welsh Baptists who had a Presbyterian-like system of one teaching elder and multiple ruling elders. This, though, was one of the factors which distinguished them from the majority of English Baptists who had just one pastor in their churches and a plurality of deacons.[3] A few voices advocated plural eldership in America. For example, W. B. Johnson in 1846 urged the recovery of plural elders in Southern Baptist churches.[4] E. C. Dargan did the same thing about sixty years later.[5] Recently there has been an outpouring of support of plural elders among American Baptists.[6] These few instances, however, are just that: few. The overwhelming view of Baptists has been to speak of the leader of the church in the singular; he is "the local preacher."[7] The question before us is, Why?

The course of this chapter will be simple. After briefly noting the pattern of plurality in the New Testament and the ecclesiastical setting out of which Baptists emerged, we will see that some early Particular Baptists did indeed have plural elders. That practice, however, quickly dissipated, more out of neglect than outright disagreement it seems. The bulk of the chapter will consist of suggested reasons that plural elders continued to be neglected in the Baptist tradition until a recent resurgence of this ecclesiology.

---

3. Brian Richard Talbot, "The Origins of the Baptist Union of Scotland, 1800–1870" (PhD thesis, University of Sterling, 1999), 1–3, 34, 129–30; James M. Renihan, *Edification and Beauty: The Practical Ecclesiology of the English Particular Baptists, 1675–1705* (Waynesboro, GA: Paternoster, 2008), 100–1.

4. W. B. Johnson, *The Gospel Developed through the Government and Order of the Churches of Jesus Christ*, in Mark E. Dever, ed., *Polity: Biblical Arguments on How to Conduct Church Life* (1846; reprint, Washington, DC: Center for Church Reform, 2001), 190–94.

5. Edwin Charles Dargan, *Ecclesiology: A Study of the Churches*, 2nd rev. ed. (Louisville: Charles T. Dearing, 1905), 89–90, 171, 179–81.

6. See, for example, Mark Dever, *Nine Marks of a Healthy Church* (Wheaton, IL: Crossway, 2000), 215–18; idem, *By Whose Authority? Elders in Baptist Life* (Washington, DC: 9Marks, 2006); idem, *The Church: The Gospel Made Visible* (Nashville: B&H, 2012), 56–61; John S. Hammett, *Biblical Foundations for Baptist Churches: A Contemporary Ecclesiology* (Grand Rapids: Kregel, 2005), 177–89; Phil A. Newton, *Elders in Congregational Life: Rediscovering the Biblical Model for Church Leadership* (Grand Rapids: Kregel, 2005); Benjamin L. Merkle, *40 Questions about Elders and Deacons* (Grand Rapids: Kregel, 2008), 161–96; idem, *Why Elders? A Biblical and Practical Guide for Church Members* (Grand Rapids: Kregel, 2009).

7. J. M. Stifler, "The Gospel Ministry," in *Baptist Doctrines*, ed. Charles A. Jenkens (St. Louis: C. R. Barns, 1890), 299.

BIBLICAL DATA AND THE ECCLESIASTICAL SETTING

The clear pattern in the New Testament is of a plurality of elders, all of whom are able to teach and rule, in each local church. Almost everywhere where elders are spoken of, they are mentioned in the plural. It will be useful to have the most pertinent texts before us.

- And when they had appointed elders for them in every church, with prayer and fasting they committed them to the Lord in whom they had believed. (Acts 14:23)

- Now from Miletus he sent to Ephesus and called the elders of the church to come to him. (Acts 20:17)

- To all the saints in Christ Jesus who are at Philippi, with the overseers and deacons (Phil. 1:1)

- Do not neglect the gift you have, which was given you by prophecy when the council of elders laid their hands on you. (1 Tim. 4:14)

- Let the elders who rule well be considered worthy of double honor, especially those who labor in preaching and teaching. (1 Tim. 5:17)

- This is why I left you in Crete, so that you might put what remained into order, and appoint elders in every town as I directed you. (Titus 1:5)

- Is anyone among you sick? Let him call for the elders of the church, and let them pray over him, anointing him with oil in the name of the Lord. (James 5:14)

- So I exhort the elders among you, as a fellow elder and a witness of the sufferings of Christ, as well as a partaker in the glory that is going to be revealed. (1 Peter 5:1)

In addition to these instances, plural elders are often mentioned in regards to the church in Jerusalem (Acts 11:30; 15:2, 3, 6, 22–23; 16:4; 21:18). The pattern is clear: more than one elder per a local congregation.

It is important at the outset that we understand the New Testament's teaching on this topic. John Hammett summarizes the biblical material well:

> When one looks at the verses containing the words *elder, overseer,* and *pastor*, a consistent pattern of plurality emerges. The church in Jerusalem is spoken of eight times in the books of Acts as having elders; the church in Ephesus had elders (Acts 20:17); the churches to which James wrote had elders (James 5:14), as did the churches to which Peter wrote (1 Peter 5:1). Perhaps the strongest support is found in Acts 14:23: 'Paul and Barnabas appointed elders for them in each church.' *Elder* is used in the singular only three times; once in a generic sense (1 Tim. 5:19) and twice for an individual (2 John 1; 3 John 1). There is no verse describing anyone as *the* elder of a church. *Overseer* is only used as a term for a church office four times. Three times it is used in a generic sense (1 Tim. 3:1–2; Titus 1:7). The one place where it refers to the officers of a specific church it is used in the plural, for the overseers of the church in Philippi (Phil. 1:1). The one place where *pastor* is used for a church office it is in the plural, though not referring to a specific church (Eph. 4:11).[8]

In addition to this, Hammett notes, "when church leaders are referred to in other ways, the pattern is the same," in 1 Thessalonians 5:12 and Hebrews 13:7, 17, 24.[9] The New Testament model is that each congregation is led by a plurality of elders/overseers/pastors.

---

8. Hammett, *Biblical Foundations*, 178.
9. Ibid. Merkle similarly argues that, "In every case that the term 'elders' is used in the New Testament it is found in the plural (except in 1 Tim. 5:19). This strongly suggests that the New Testament church was governed by a group of qualified leaders and not by one individual" (Benjamin L. Merkle, "Hierarchy in the Church? Instruction from the Pastoral Epistles concerning Elders and Overseers," *SBJT* 7, no. 3 [2003]: 39).

As they emerged out of the Puritan tradition, seventeenth-century Particular Baptists in England saw dissenting churches all around them with ecclesiastical structures having a plurality of elders. The Presbyterians had a teaching elder-ruling elders scheme in place. They inherited the ecclesiastical model set in place by Calvin in Geneva.[10] This Presbyterian system received classical expression in 1645 when the divines of the Westminster assembly penned *The Form of Presbyterial Church Government*. Even closer to the Baptists were the Puritan Congregationalists. The most influential English Congregational theologians of the seventeenth century, Thomas Goodwin and John Owen, both advocated a presbyterian-like teaching elder-ruling elders system.[11] This system was also represented in the New England Congregational *Cambridge Platform* (1649).[12]

Given this historical background, it is no surprise that some prominent early Baptist congregations had a plurality of pastors. When John Bunyan (d. 1688) assumed the pastorate of his church, the two previous pastors "resigned the pastoral office to him, and were considered afterwards as elders or ministers."[13] The influential pastor, William Kiffin (d. 1701), was also open to the notion of multiple elders. His church's records tell us that in 1690 Richard Adams was ordained as an elder "in conjunction with brother William Kiffin." Sixteen years later the church called a brother to serve as co-elder with Adams, who was instructed to recite at the ordination that "my brother Mark Key is by this church appointed or ordained a joint elder, pastor or overseer with myself over her."[14] Similarly, the church records at London's prominent Petty France church state that

---

10. See, e.g., Elsie Anne McKee, "Calvin's Teaching on the Elder Illuminated by Exegetical History," in *John Calvin and the Church: A Prism of Reform*, ed., Timothy George (Louisville: Westminster/John Knox, 1990), 147–55.

11. See Thomas Goodwin, "The Government of the Churches of Christ" in *The Works of Thomas Goodwin*, (1861–1866; reprint, Eureka, CA: Tanski, 1996), 11:132–79, 285–359; John Owen, "The True Nature of a Gospel Church and Its Government" in *The Works of John Owen* (1850–53; reprint, Edinburgh: Banner of Truth, 1968), 16:1–208.

12. For more on Baptists' ecclesiastical setting, see Samuel E. Waldron, "Plural Elder Congregationalism," in *Who Runs the Church? Four Views on Church Government*, ed. Paul E. Engle and Steven B. Cowan (Grand Rapids: Zondervan, 2004), 199–202.

13. Joseph Ivimey, *A History of the English Baptists* (London: n.p., 1811–1830), 2:35. I have standardized spelling, capitalization, and abbreviations in older quotations to conform to modern usage.

14. Renihan, *Edification and Beauty*, 99.

"On the 21st of the 7th month, brother Collins and brother Coxe were solemnly ordained pastors or elders in this church."[15]

Several other examples confirm that some early Baptist churches had multiple elders. When the Broadmead Baptist Church of Bristol's pastor (whom they called their "teaching elder") was imprisoned because of persecution against Baptists, they had ruling elders who were able to step up and fulfill many of the tasks—except to administer the Lord's supper—that the teaching elder had previously done. Their records include this entry: "Joseph Clarke and James Lewis were, at a day of prayer, admitted members of this congregation, (although we had no pastor), by our two ruling elders laying before them, in the presence of the church, their duties to God, the church, and the world."[16] In Kent, in 1657, it was recorded "that some [men] as helps of government may very much help the elders [in] their work so that they may not leave their callings but contrariwise work with their hands at all seasonable time."[17] In addition, James Renihan notes of the churches which sent representatives to the 1689 assembly that released the Second London Confession of Faith that the majority "were committed to a plurality and parity of elders in their churches." He goes on, to note, however, that "This is not to say that all of the churches had such a plurality, in fact many did not."[18] Plural eldership was common, if not the norm, in the late seventeenth century.[19]

---

15. Ibid.
16. Roger Hayden, ed., *The Records of a Church of Christ in Bristol, 1640–1687* (N.p.: Bristol Record Society, 1974), 205.
17. "Two Association Meetings in Kent, 1657," *Transactions of the Baptist Historical Society* 3 (1912–1913): 249.
18. Renihan, *Edification and Beauty*, 101.
19. Some queries of Baptist congregations to their local associations about the validity of having plural elders also show that in the seventeenth century English Baptists were asking questions about plural eldership. The Abingdon Association in 1654, for example, made a statement, suggesting that they were reacting against the teaching-ruling elder distinction: "That the office of pastors, elders and overseers or bishops is but one and the same and that it is the duty of every elder as well to teach as to rule in the church whereof he is an elder" (B. R. White, ed., *Association Records of the Particular Baptists of England, Wales and Ireland to 1660. Part 3. The Abingdon Association* [London: Baptist Historical Society, 1974], 134). The following year the association contradicted a brother who promoted a teaching elder-ruling elder distinction (see White, *Association Records. Part 3*, 138).

The Decline of Plurality

At least five factors influenced Baptists not to maintain the practice of plural elders over time. The first one is that Baptists were congregationalists; they had reasons to doubt that a plural elder system could be reconciled with real congregational authority. Second, Baptists developed a complex hermeneutic for interpreting the plurality passages in the New Testament. This allowed them to favor the Scripture's teaching on congregational authority over the Scripture's teaching on plurality. Third, Baptist confessions did not mandate that churches should have a plurality of elders. They were intentionally ambiguous, which led to the demise of plurality over time. Fourth, the practice of prominent Baptist leaders—some of whom explicitly opposed plural elders—downplayed the importance of having multiple elders in a church. Fifth, Baptists lacked enough qualified men who could serve as elders in a congregation. These factors combined to make plural elders, which was perhaps the slight majority view of Baptists in the mid-1600s, a rare practice among English and American Baptists in the following generations.

The Congregation's Fear of Unbiblical Domination

A primary reason that Baptists by and large shied away from having a plurality of elders was their fear that such an arrangement would bring about elder domination over the local congregation. Such fear of domination overturned the biblical pattern that gave the final authority not to individuals or pastors within the church, but rather to the congregation as a whole. As a nineteenth-century American asserted, "Every Baptist church is a republic in miniature. 'The government is in the body' is a sentiment dear to every member of the denomination. . . . 'The church is the highest ecclesiastical authority on earth.'"[20] Based on Christ's words in Matthew 18:17 ("if he will not hear the church"), Benjamin Keach (d. 1704) asserted that "the power of the keys is in the church. . . . It is not said, if he will not hear the

---

20. Adiel Sherwood, "Extracts from Sherwood's History of Georgia Baptists, no. 2: Religious Liberty," *The Christian Index* (June 2, 1843): 341.

elder, or elders."[21] Their fear of unbiblical elder domination stemmed from their equating plural elders with the typical Presbyterian teaching elder-ruling elders system. Proof for this comes more from Baptists' penchant to attack presbyterianism with its ruling elders than it does from their positive program for single eldership. This helps to explain the paradoxes of their ecclesiology given their historical setting and their desire to be biblical. Their developed hermeneutic was that the authority-of-the-congregation passages provided the key to interpreting the plural elder passages.

In the first place, we must notice that Baptists were not so obsessed with potential abuse of power by plural elders that they were freewheeling libertarians. To the contrary, they recognized that pastors were a blessing from God given by him for the good of the congregation. Churches did not elect officers begrudgingly, but they did so thankfully because they knew that it was unto the church that "Jesus had given such gifts [the officers] as the fruit of his ascension for the gathering and edifying of his church."[22] The Abingdon Association reiterated this view in 1654: "the offi[ces of e]lders and deacons are ordained of the Lord for the [good] of his church and, therefore, it is the duty of every church very diligently to endeavour, and very earnestly to seek unto the Lord, that they may enjoy the benefit of these his gracious appointments, remembering God's promise to give his people pastors according to his own heart (Jer. 3.15)."[23] Pastors were a gift from God, to be honored and received with joy by the Lord's people.

Baptists were careful, though, to limit the authority which was given to the pastors. The pastor was the under-shepherd of Jesus Christ, the Chief Shepherd. As such the pastor's authority derived from his faithfulness to Christ, especially as shown in his careful exposition of

21. Benjamin Keach, *The Glory of a True Church, and Its Discipline Display'd*, in Mark E. Dever, ed., *Polity: Biblical Arguments on How to Conduct Church Life* (1697; reprint, Washington, DC: Center for Church Reform, 2001), 71.

22. White, *Association Records. Part 3*, 171.

23. Ibid., 134. Compare the assertion of Knollys to this effect: "Gospel-government is ordained and appointed of God for the well-being of his church: The church of God cannot have a well-being without Christ's instituted gospel-government" (Hanserd Knollys, *The World That Now Is; and the World That Is to Come; Or the First and Second Coming of Jesus Christ* [London: Tho. Snowden, 1681], 53).

Christ's word.[24] Thus, Nehemiah Coxe (d. 1688) was careful to define the areas in which obedience to the pastor was required:

> It is not a blind obedience that the apostle requires, nor such as shall suppose a legislative power in church-officers, but an orderly subjection to them acting in their office according to the law and testament of Jesus Christ; even a ready obedience to the word of God dispensed by them, and humble submission to their just reproofs and ministerial correction. . . . But when the law of Christ is observed, and a conformity, with that urged, by the evidence and demonstration of, truth from the holy Scriptures, herein the obedience of the people is justly expected.[25]

The pastor was to be obeyed not because of his office, but as he acted in his role "according to the law and testament of Jesus Christ," that is, according to the guidelines which Jesus set down for the pastor's duties in Scripture. This would result, then, not in servile acquiescence to a pastor but in "ready obedience to the word of God." The church was to submit to Christ's words, not to the pastor. Thus, Coxe concluded that when the Scriptures have been faithfully expounded "herein the obedience of the people is justly expected."[26]

---

24. A telling example of the manner in which a congregation believed they, not their pastor, were the final authority in the church comes from the ministry of Benjamin Keach. For almost twenty years, Keach tried to convince his congregation to allow the singing of hymns in their Sunday worship services, but the members did not think this practice was biblical. So Keach continued to try to persuade them, until finally they saw the wisdom of what he was advocating. But they did not simply submit to their pastor until they became convinced that his views were biblical. For almost two decades the pastor was unable to get his way. On the "hymn-singing controversy," see J. Barry Vaughn, "Benjamin Keach," in *Baptist Theologians,* eds. Timothy George and David S. Dockery (Nashville: Broadman, 1990), 53–55; Michael A. G. Haykin, *Kiffin, Knollys and Keach: Rediscovering Our English Baptist Heritage* (Leeds: Reformation Today, 1996), 91–96; Bill Leonard, *Baptist Ways: A History* (Valley Forge, PA: Judson, 2003), 58–60.
25. Nehemiah Coxe, *A Sermon Preached at the Ordination of an Elder and Deacons in a Baptized Congregation in London* (London: Tho. Fabian, 1681), 33–34.
26. It was probably because of the elders' authority in teaching the Scriptures that most Particular Baptists made, in the words of the Charleston Church Discipline, a distinction between elders who were "the highest office in the church," and deacons who were "employed in the inferior services of the church" (James Leo Garrett, *Baptist Church Discipline* [Nashville: Broadman, 1962], 31, 34).

This was the common view among Baptists seen, for example, in Hanserd Knollys in the seventeenth century and two hundred years later in W. B. Johnson.[27] In the nineteenth century, J. L. Reynolds noted that churches needed to "ascertain that a pastor is to execute only the laws of Christ; that [when] his power is restricted within these wholesome and well-defined limits, all just grounds of jealousy are removed; he and his people are equally under obligation to the Redeemer."[28] Christ ruled his church through the Scriptures and pastors had a derivative authority as they faithfully expounded that word and led the church to obey it.[29]

It was this biblical-theological understanding of the elder's role in teaching and applying Scripture which led most Baptists to oppose the notion of a plurality of elders in each congregation. Many felt that a plurality of elders equaled having one teaching elder and multiple ruling elders. But ruling elders were anathema to most Baptists, for they adamantly opposed having persons in the congregation who had authority but whose authority was not derived from Christ's authority in Scripture. Thus, Coxe in 1681 stated that "it is evident the Holy Ghost intends no distinction, or preeminence of office among" elders.[30] It was the duty of each elder to teach as well as to rule. The Abingdon Association declared in 1654 that "it is the duty of every elder as well to teach as to rule in the church whereof he is an elder."[31] The West Country Association followed suit the next year: "it is the office of an elder both to

---

27. Knollys specifically limited the pastor's authority to that which they were charged to do by Christ "according to the laws, constitutions and ordinances of the gospel" which I think means the pattern and exposition of Scripture (Knollys, *World That Now Is*, 56–57). Johnson likewise emphasized the pastor's derivative authority from the Scriptures: "Governing, not as lords, but as examples; feeding, which implies speaking the word of the Lord, from the experience of his power; watching for souls, warning and admonishing them; laboring in word and doctrine, by preaching the word, being instant in season, out of season; taking heed unto themselves and to all the flock. These seem to be the prominent duties of the bishopric" (*The Gospel Developed*, 82).

28. J. L. Reynolds, *Church Polity, or The Kingdom of Christ, in Its Internal and External Developments*, in Mark E. Dever, ed., *Polity: Biblical Arguments on How to Conduct Church Life* (1849; reprint, Washington, DC: Center for Church Reform, 2001), 356.

29. This view of the derivative authority of the pastor and the priority of the congregation was codified in Baptist confessions. See, for example, Renihan, *Edification and Beauty*, 103–4.

30. Coxe, *Sermon*, 18.

31. White, *Association Records, Part 3*, 134.

teach and rule."[32] An elder's duty was to teach the Scriptures; only such a man could also rule.

Baptists felt that ruling elders seized privileges and duties from the congregation that had rightly been delegated only to the church. Thus, a nineteenth-century correspondent in Kentucky's Baptist state paper, *The Western Recorder*, responded to a letter-writer who had promoted ruling elders by saying:

> To make this passage [1 Tim. 5.17] authorize an office, whose incumbents possess the governing power in the church, is to bring the passage in direct conflict with God's plan of church government. For ruling in the church must include the admission and dismission of members, and the choice of officers, as well as the discipline of those who are disorderly; but these are all plainly shown in the word of God to be the prerogatives of the church, and not of its officers.[33]

Similarly, writing in 1885 J. H. Spencer regarded ruling elders as one of the "early customs in our Baptist churches that do not prevail at the present time." According to Spencer, ruling elders came to Kentucky through the Separate Baptists who had learned this practice from New England Congregationalists. He argued, however, that ruling elders never fit comfortably in Baptist church polity because "every member of a Baptist church is under obligation to discharge all the duties here assigned to ruling elders."[34] The office of ruling elder was disallowed because such officers usurped the rightful authority of the congregation.

First Timothy 5:17, "Let the elders who rule well be considered worthy of double honor, especially those who labor in the preaching and teaching," was the key text for Baptists as they sought to discov-

---

32. B. R. White, ed., *Association Records of the Particular Baptists of England, Wales and Ireland to 1660. Part 2. The West Country and Ireland* (London: Baptist Historical Society, 1973), 60.
33. J. C. M., "Eldership," *Western Recorder*, 15 February 1868, 1.
34. J. H. Spencer, *A History of Kentucky Baptists from 1769 to 1885* (Cincinnati: J. R. Baumes, 1885), 1:485. The records from Kentucky dealing with elders are sparse. The Elkhorn Baptist Association was founded in 1785 and in 1787 voted to correspond with the Philadelphia Association because they were both Calvinistic in doctrine. Through 1850 Elkhorn's minutes reveal only one question about the sanction of plural elders in a congregation (ibid.).

er God's mind on the issue of ruling elders. Although they differed slightly from each other in their interpretations, they were united in opposing the usual Presbyterian exegesis of this verse. Presbyterians used this as proof for having two types of elders—teaching and ruling. Not so most Baptists.

Responding to a brother's expressed unease about the notion that every elder should teach as well as rule, the Abingdon Association in 1655 averred that "the saying of the apostle in 1 Tim. 5.17 must not be conceived to imply that there were elders ruling well who yet were not at all exercised in the word and doctrine, but rather to signify that the elder's pains in the word and doctrine was a special thing for which he was to be honoured."[35] All elders were to rule God's household well and therefore were to be highly honored in the church. Likewise all elders were to labor at preaching and teaching. The congregation was to esteem highly those elders who preached and taught faithfully and who also governed the church well.

John Gill (d. 1771) also denied that 1 Timothy 5:17 prescribed ruling elders who were distinct from teaching elders. There was only one office of elder given to the church. Those occupying this office were both to rule and to teach the Scriptures: "There are no other that rule in churches, but such who also speak to them the word of God."[36] Further, Gill maintained, as did the Abingdon Association in the previous century, that elders were of two different sorts: one type "do not take so much pains in the ministry of the word; whilst others of them both rule well and labour in the word." It is only the latter category "who are to be reckoned deserving of the honour hereafter mentioned."[37]

In America 1 Timothy 5:17 was discussed intermittently in the state and regional Baptist papers during the nineteenth century. This was probably because of Baptists' on-going desire to controvert Presbyterian ecclesiology. For example, in 1867 the editor of *The Western Recorder* responded to a letter which advocated having a plurality of elders, including ruling elders, in each congregation. He saw no indication from 1 Timothy 5:17 that Paul here taught the necessity of ruling

35. White, *Association Records. Part 3*, 138.
36. John Gill, *An Exposition of the New Testament in Which the Sense of the Sacred Text Is Taken* (1852; reprint, Atlanta: Turner Lassetter, 1954), 2:614.
37. Ibid.

elders, explaining that Paul distinguished between some elders who worked especially hard at their pastoral labors and others who did not labor so vigorously:

> We do not understand that the apostle distinguishes between the rank or office of the eldership, and conditions of honor, and the especial honor, upon their rank or office; but he distinguishes between the degree of efficiency in the persons of the same rank and office, and he makes the honor, or, the especial honor, depend upon the degree of their efficiency. "Let the elders who rule well be accounted worthy of of [*sic*] *double* honor, especially they who *labor* in word and doctrine." This is unquestionably the true emphasis of the passage.[38]

At the end of the nineteenth century, William Williams repeated the standard explanation that Baptists had developed in response to presbyterianism. Taking notice of the key word "especially," he averred that it "introduces a specification of particular persons belonging to the same general class."[39] In other words 1 Timothy 5:17 expresses "a *personal* distinction among those of the same official class and with

---

38. E. M. Dudley, "New Testament Eldership," *Western Recorder*, 27 April 1867, 2. The following year a writer in the *Western Recorder* caustically commented on the Presbyterian use of "especially" in 1 Timothy 5:17: "allow me to ask if it is not a just ground of suspicion against any system, that its sole foundation is one adverb in the New Testament?" (J. C. M., "Eldership," 1). Baptists judged the Presbyterian exegesis of this verse to be opposed by the sum of the New Testament's teaching. This explanation seems to have been common among Baptists. In 1842 a writer in Georgia's *Christian Index* repeated the substance of Gill's argument. He commented that the explanation of the apparent distinction between teaching and ruling elders is "that in the days of the apostles, as in our day, some ministers were more exclusively devoted than others to the great work of preaching the gospel." Therefore what Paul taught here was "that the elders, or pastors, who rule well, that is, who preserve a due discipline in the churches, are to be accounted worthy of double honor, but more especially those who are careful not only to maintain a proper discipline, but are indefatigable and persevering in their endeavors to instruct people in the doctrines of the gospel" (Chattahoochee, "The Identify of Bishops and Presbyters or Elders," *The Christian Index*, 26 August 1842, 541).

39. William Williams, *Apostolical Church Polity*, in Mark E. Dever, ed., *Polity: Biblical Arguments on How to Conduct Church Life* (1874; reprint, Washington, DC: Center for Church Reform, 2001), 534. The Authorized Version translation is, "Let the elders that rule well be counted worthy of double honour, especially they who labour in the word and doctrine."

respect to the discharge of duties which all might equally perform."[40] Their exegesis of 1 Timothy 5:17, comparing it to the sum teaching of the New Testament, convinced Baptists that the office of ruling elder deprived the congregation of its rightful authority.

Their handling of Hebrews 13:17 similarly shows that Baptists placed the issue of multiple elders squarely in their larger biblical-theological understanding of the way that Christ ruled the church. This verse exhorts believers to "Obey your leaders and submit to them, for they are keeping watch over your souls, as those who will have to give an account." How could Baptists salvage congregational authority from this? In their effort to submit to the word of God, Particular Baptists in fact often dealt with this verse.

Placing the emphasis on "obey," "leaders," and "submit," those holding a more Presbyterian-like understanding of the relationship between elders and the congregation gravitated towards this text. For instance, the Welsh Baptists—whom we have seen followed the teaching elder-ruling elders scheme—explained the duty of church members to their pastors in these words: "Submit to and obey them (Heb. 13.17)."[41] They included no discussion of the extent to which the congregation was obliged to obey. It appeared to be a blanket statement.

In contrast, most Baptists qualified this assertion based on their understanding of Christ's means of ruling the local church. We previously noted Coxe's, Johnson's, and Reynolds' views that the elder's authority derived only from his faithful dispensing of the word of God. Importantly, Coxe tied this explication of the church's duty to its elders to Hebrews 13, for he began his discussion by stating, "You owe submission and obedience to them in the discharge of their office, and in the exercise of that rule and oversight which Christ has committed to them for your edification; obey them that have the rule over you, and submit yourselves (Heb. 13.17)."[42] Other Baptists likewise limited the scope of this verse. Commenting on the meaning of Hebrews 13:17, in 1655 the Abingdon Association stated, "In v.17 they are called upon

---

40. Ibid., 533.
41. B. R. White, ed., *Association Records of the Particular Baptists of England, Wales and Ireland to 1660. Part 1. South Wales and the Midlands* (London: Baptist Historical Society, 1971), 12.
42. Coxe, *Sermon*, 33–34.

to yield due submission to their pastors who then lived and watched for their souls who, feeding them with knowledge and understanding, were undoubtedly careful to speak unto them the word of God."[43] The allusion to Hebrews 13:7 ("Remember your leaders, those who spoke to you the word of God. Consider the outcome of their way of life, and imitate their faith") was common in the arguments of Particular Baptists. Those who were to be obeyed (v. 17) were those who taught the word of God (v. 7). The church was to obey its elders as they faithfully taught the Scriptures.

We must note, however, that ruling elders were never the norm among Baptists. They were not represented at the assembly that released the 1689 Confession.[44] For the most part, ruling elders in Baptist churches were limited to a few geographical areas. They were a distinguishing feature of "Scotch Baptist" churches as opposed to the "English Baptist" churches in Scotland that had only a single pastor.[45] They were also a feature of some Welsh Baptist congregations, as the South Welsh Baptist Association records from the mid-seventeenth century reveal. In 1653 the association agreed to send a letter to one of its member churches "to advise them if they have any fit members to choose more elders to rule or teach that church, and to advise them to submit in the Lord to such as are or shall be chosen elders among them."[46] The next year, 1654, the association included the office of ruling elder as one of the three biblical types of elder; the other two were pastor and teacher. They said "the ruling elders, or helping office [role] is, to oversee the lives and manners of men: to whom also double honor is due (1 Tim. 5.17; Rom. 12.8). He must also take care of God's house (Heb. 13.17; 1 Tim. 3.5)."[47] In America two groups of Baptists had ruling elders, at least for a while.[48] The Separate Baptists inherited the practice of ruling eldership from the Con-

---

43. White, *Association Records. Part 3*, 138.
44. See Renihan, *Edification and Beauty*, 101.
45. Talbot, "Origins of the Baptist Union," 1–2, 129–30; Robert G. Torbet, *A History of the Baptists*, 3rd ed. (Valley Forge, PA: Judson, 1963), 92–94; H. Leon McBeth, *The Baptist Heritage: Four Centuries of Baptist Witness* (Nashville: Broadman, 1987), 309.
46. White, *Association Records. Part 1*, 7.
47. Ibid., 11.
48. Writing in 1859, David Benedict recounted that ruling elders entered some Baptist churches through "the New Light stir" leading to the Separate Baptists. But "at present I know of no church of our persuasion where this office is maintained" (David Benedict, *Fifty Years among the Baptists* [New York: Sheldon, 1860], 167).

gregationalists they emerged from in the 1750s. They did not, however, maintain that ecclesiology for long when they came to the South.[49] The Philadelphia Association Baptists also practiced ruling eldership.

The course of ruling elders in the prominent Philadelphia Association in America illustrates Baptists' tendency and concern to protect their churches from ruling elders. The association's genesis in 1707 is of great interest for it "originated with churches planted by members from Wales."[50] As we have seen, the Welsh were out of the mainstream of English Particular Baptist church government in their advocacy of a teaching elder-ruling elder system. The Welsh brought this ecclesiology with them to Philadelphia, as the first entry in the association's minutes demonstrates:

> In the year 1710, several able men, ministers and elders, and in the following year also, came over from south Wales and the west of England—as the Rev. Mr. Nathaniel Jenkins, Mr. John Burrows, Mr. Abel Morgan, and some that had been ruling elders in the churches they came from—all of them men long concerned in the affairs of the churches and associations in their own countries.[51]

In addition, the records of the Welsh Neck church, one of the four founding churches of the association, indicate that early in its existence it had men identified as "elder," "minister," and "ruling elder" who served the church.[52] Some churches, at least, in the Philadelphia

49. "In its early history, this association [Sandy Creek Separate Baptists] held many sentiments of a peculiar nature which do not now prevail. . . . They also retained the office of ruling elders, eldresses, and deaconesses, and to weekly communion" (Geo. W. Purefoy, *A History of the Sandy Creek Baptist Association, from Its Organization in A.D. 1758, to A.D. 1858* [New York: Sheldon & Co., 1859], 6–67). We also know of Shubal Stearns, one of the leading Separate Baptists, that "In 1759 he was ordained a ruling elder" (Robert Baylor Semple, *History of the Rise and Progress of Baptists in Virginia* [Richmond: John O'Lynch, 1810], 18).

50. A. D. Gillette, ed., *Minutes of the Philadelphia Baptist Association, 1707–1807: Being the First One Hundred Years of Its Existence* (1851; reprint, Springfield, MO: Particular Baptist Press, 2002), 3.

51. Ibid., 25.

52. *Records of the Welsh Tract Baptist Meeting, Pencader Hundred, New Castle County, Delaware, 1701 to 1828*, vol. 1, Papers of the Historical Society of Delaware, XLII (Wilmington: The Historical Society of Delaware, 1904), 39.

Association seemed to take for granted the ecclesiology which they had inherited from Wales.[53]

An examination of the two association-sponsored documents on ecclesiology reveals, however, that the association was fighting a losing battle to maintain ruling elders in its churches. In 1743 the association adopted *A Short Treatise of Church-Discipline* composed by Benjamin Griffith. After discussing the church and its ministers, Griffith addressed the office of ruling elder. The propriety of the office was assumed:

> Ruling elders are such persons as are endued with gifts, to assist the pastor or teacher in the government of the church. ... The works of teaching and ruling belong both to the pastor; but in case he be unable, or the work of ruling too great for him, God has provided such for his assistance, and they are called ruling elders (1 Tim. 5.17), helps (1 Cor. 12.28), governments, or he that rules (Rom. 12.8). .... experience teaches us the use and benefit of such rulers in the church, in easing the pastor or teacher, and keeping up the honour of the ministry.... Their office only relates to rule and order, in the church of God, and does not include teaching.[54]

Fifty-five years later the association approved a new document which provided guidelines for local church practice. *A Treatise of Church Discipline* of 1798, written by Samuel Jones, is remarkable for the light it sheds on the reception of ruling elders in the association at the close of the eighteenth century. Jones wrote,

> Concerning the divine right of the office of ruling elders, there has been considerable doubt and much disputation. We, therefore, had a thought of passing it over in silence;

---

53. In the first hundred years of the association's minutes, four queries about elders were addressed to the association. Each of them—from 1728, 1738, 1746, and 1767—assumed the validity of the office of ruling elder (see Gillette, *Minutes*, 29, 39, 52, 102).

54. Benjamin Griffith, *A Short Treatise Concerning a True and Orderly Gospel Church,* in Mark E. Dever, ed., *Polity: Biblical Arguments on How to Conduct Church Life* (1743; reprint, Washington, D.C.: Center for Church Reform, 2001), 98.

but, on farther consideration, concluded to state briefly the arguments on both sides, then subjoin a few general observations, and so let the churches judge for themselves, and practice as they shall see fit.[55]

Between 1743 and 1798 churches debated the validity of this office. Whereas the propriety of having ruling elders was taken for granted in 1743, by 1798 "much disputation" had taken place about these officers.

Unfortunately, the association records are silent about the nature and extent of these debates. The following points, though, seem warranted. First of all, just as the Welsh were out of the mainstream of English Particular Baptist church order, so their heirs in the colonies must have felt themselves to be out of touch with the bulk of Calvinistic Baptists. In the second place, Benjamin Keach and John Gill were influential in this association, and both of these pastor-theologians, as we shall see, downplayed the necessity of plural elders and attacked the notion of ruling elders. Their prestige and persuasiveness must have induced at least some churches to abandon their Welsh heritage. Finally, the association's confession, adopted in 1742, was identical to the Second London Confession on the matter of church officers. Its ambiguity, which we shall note below, would not have encouraged the propagation of a plural elder system.

The demise of plural elders is also seen in the Charleston Association. The Philadelphia Association helped found this southern association in 1751, an association that was to play a dominant role in the life of Baptists in the South. Surprisingly, plural eldership seems never to have been an issue in this association. One would have expected that since Charleston had close ties to Philadelphia it would at least have had some discussion about the validity of plural elders. Yet, the association's minutes through 1858 do not even mention one query from a church about elders. Nor was there any indication that elders were ever an issue of debate or discussion among its churches.[56]

---

55. Samuel Jones, *A Treatise of Church Discipline, and a Directory,* in Mark E. Dever, ed., *Polity: Biblical Arguments on How to Conduct Church Life* (1805; reprint, Washington, D.C.: Center for Church Reform, 2001), 145. See Francis W. Sacks, *The Philadelphia Baptist Tradition of Church and Church Authority, 1707–1814: An Ecumenical Analysis and Theological Interpretation* (Lewiston, NY: Edwin Mellen, 1989), 715.

56. For example, Charleston's *Summary of Church-Discipline* mentions only the pastor and deacon as church officers. No hint is made of a plurality of elders (*A Summary of Church-*

So Baptists on both sides of the Atlantic were adamant that Christ alone should rule his church and that he did this as pastors faithfully taught Christ's word to the church. Churches then were to exercise their spiritual privilege of submitting to Christ, but never to a person who did not come in Christ's name. This dual passion—for the sole authority of Christ in the church and for the church's freedom from tyrannous leaders—caused Baptists to be very wary of a plurality of elders in their churches, especially as they cast a wary glance at those practicing the teaching elder-ruling elder model.

Baptist Hermeneutic

Baptists have been a people devoted to the Bible. For them, it is essential to follow the clear teachings of Scripture, not only for one's personal salvation, but also for the organization of our churches. B. R. White, one of the deans of Baptist studies in the twentieth-century, noted that early English Baptists "assumed that the Bible . . . provided the final and authoritative teaching for all necessary matters concerned with the true nature and constitution of the Church." Therefore, they also presupposed "that in the apostolic age the Church was organised and constituted according to one pattern and that the New Testament provided enough evidence of that pattern to enable those who came after to reconstruct it."[57]

The record is full of Baptists advocating something like the "regulative principle," the view that Christ in his word regulates both how the church should worship and how it should be organized. The Second London Confession (1689) argued that "The whole counsel of God

---

Discipline, Shewing the Qualifications and Duties of the Officers and Members of a Gospel-Church, in Mark E. Dever, ed., *Polity: Biblical Arguments on How to Conduct Church Life* [1774; reprint, Washington, DC: Center for Church Reform, 2001], 119–22). Richard Furman (d. 1825) was one of the most influential pastors in this association until his death in 1825. Therefore his *Sermon, on the Constitution and Order of the Christian Church* of 1791 is probably important regarding his, and the association's, views about elders. In this sermon Furman set forth a fine exposition of the duties of pastors, yet not even one time did he allude to a plurality of elders. It was assumed throughout that the "pastor" was the sole elder of the congregation (see Richard Furman, *Sermon, on the Constitution and Order of the Christian Church* [Charleston, SC: Markland and McIver, 1791]).

57. B. R. White, *The English Baptists of the Seventeenth Century*, A History of the English Baptists, vol. 1 (London: Baptist Historical Society, 1983), 10.

concerning all things necessary for His own glory, man's salvation, faith and life, is either expressly set down or necessarily contained in the Holy Scripture; unto which nothing at any time is to be added, whether by new revelation of the Spirit or traditions of men."[58] J. L. Reynolds clearly advocated this same approach in 1849. Everything necessary to know about the church, and what churches are obligated to follow, is laid down in the Bible:

> As the kingdom of Christ is a subject of pure revelation, it may justly be expected that every thing pertaining to its nature, and to the external organizations by which its principles are to be diffused among men, will be found in the inspired volume, in which that revelation is deposited. . . . The Scriptures are a sufficient rule of faith and practice. The principles of ecclesiastical polity are prescribed in them with all necessary comprehensiveness and clearness.[59]

Baptists believed that both apostolic commands and examples are authoritative in churches. These examples need not be extensive either. A classic instance is the way in which the pattern of receiving the word, then being baptized, then devoting oneself to the apostles' teaching and to the fellowship of the church, and then being admitted to the breaking of bread in Acts 2:41–42 was used as an argument for the practice of close communion.[60] Christ inspired the examples in Scripture as much as the precepts. Both were authoritative.

---

58. *Second London Confession* 1.6. Coxe sounded a similar note a few years earlier: "The edification and beauty of the church is much concerned in her order, not such an order as superstition will dictate, or litigious nicety contend for, but such as we have already described; which sets her in a conformity with Christ's will; and particularly the filling up of the offices which he has appointed, with persons duly qualified for the administration of them, and the regular acting both of officers and members in their respective places" (*Sermon*, 10).

59. Reynolds, *Church Polity*, 305. This same sentiment was repeated later in one of the most significant ecclesiologies to be written by Southern Baptists in the nineteenth century. See J. L. Dagg, *Manual of Theology. Second Part: A Treatise on Church Order* (1858; reprint, Harrisonburg, VA: Gano, 1990), 84–86.

60. See, e.g., William Kiffin, *A Sober Discourse of Right to Church-Communion* (London: George Larkin, 1681); Andrew Fuller, "The Admission of Unbaptized Persons to the Lord's Supper Inconsistent with the New Testament," in *Complete Works of Andrew Fuller* (Harrisonburg, VA: Sprinkle Publications, 1988), 3:508–15.

This insistence on authoritative precept and practice was jettisoned, however, when it came to plural elders. When they addressed this issue, most Baptists argued that the clear pattern of plurality in the New Testament churches need not be followed. There were circumstances in the first century that called for a plurality of elders. But since modern churches did not find themselves in the same circumstances, they were not required to follow the pattern of plurality. This has been a consistent hermeneutical argument of Baptists over the centuries. Three examples will demonstrate this interpretive paradigm.

John Gill argued that the New Testament example of a plurality of elders was illustrative, but not prescriptive. Commenting on Philippians 1:1, he acknowledged that "bishop" and "elder" referred to the same office.[61] Then he argued that there had been more than one elder in the church at Philippi and so there may be more than one now in a church if this is necessary. In other words, the practice at Philippi was not prescriptive:

> [T]here were, and so may be, where there is necessity for it, more pastors or bishops than one in a church; unless it can be thought that there were more churches than one in each of these cities; or that the pastors of adjacent churches are here included; neither of which seem to be a clear case, but the contrary: but then these pastors or bishops were all upon an equal foot: one had not any authority or power over another, or more authority than another; they were not metropolitan or diocesan bishops, but pastors of a particular church; and were neither lords over one another, nor of God's heritage.[62]

Gill apparently feared Presbyterianism, for he argued that if there were more than one elder per congregation, none should have authority over any other, nor should any be in a position to lord it over the church. In a similar manner, he neutered Titus 1:5 of any prescriptive force. "Elders"

---

61. When commenting on Acts 20:17, James 5:14, and 1 Peter 5:1, however, he did not even mention the number of elders addressed in those texts (see Gill, *Exposition of the New Testament*, 1:959; 2:802, 844).
62. Ibid., 2:461.

here, he said, meant more than one elder, but he advanced the opinion that there were probably numerous churches on Crete, so there was no reason to assume from this text that a congregation must have more than one elder.[63]

William Williams manifests a second instance of this hermeneutic, from the late nineteenth century. Williams said that, "temporary reasons growing out of the peculiar exigencies of the time, would seem to demand a plurality of elders in the primitive churches, and the Saviour adjusted the supply to the demand in accordance with the temporary exigency."[64] He acknowledged that "In most, if not all the apostolic churches, there was a plurality of elders." That arrangement, however, was not obligatory on churches today. There were circumstances in the early church which rendered a plurality of elders "very advantageous, if not absolutely necessary." For instance, since the apostolic churches tended to be large, "As a matter of prudence, the whole church could not ordinarily meet together." Therefore they needed "a plurality of elders to instruct these several sections of the church." In addition, Williams argued, "If Christianity, in its incipiency, is to make any headway against this overwhelming tide of superstition and corruption, there would seem to be a demand for a greater number of preachers than one elder to every church." Finally, according to Williams's reading of the setting of the early church, "persecution would be most likely to fall upon the leaders, the elders" so churches needed more than one elder to maintain a constant teaching and leadership ministry in the church even in the face of a forced exile of one of the elders.[65]

Recently, Daniel Akin has also advocated this interpretive paradigm. He notes that the New Testament pattern is always of a plurality of elders in a congregation.[66] Yet, he argues that "it is important

---

63. Ibid., 2:650.
64. Williams, *Apostolical Church Polity*, 532.
65. Ibid.
66. "The argument for a plurality of elders, pastors, overseers, leaders is easier to make [than the single elder position] based upon the biblical evidence. For example, every time *elder* (*presbuteros*) appears in the context of church leaders, it is always in the plural (e.g., Acts 14:23; 16:4; 20:17; 21:18; 1 Tim. 5:17; Titus 1:5; James 5:14; 1 Pet 5:1)" (Daniel L. Akin, "The Single-Elder-Led Church: The Bible's Witness to a Congregational/Single-Elder-Led Polity," in *Perspectives on Church Government: Five Views of Church Polity*, eds. Chad Owen Brand and R. Stanton Norman [Nashville: B&H, 2004], 64).

to take into consideration the reality of the house church in the early history of Christianity" as churches ask if they must follow this pattern today. Although the apostolic churches initially met in a single home, as they "grew and multiplied it was necessary to move into additional houses. This, of course, required multiplication of leadership as well."[67] He concludes that the New Testament "does not provide a precise manual on how the structure of church government should be organized" and "allows flexibility on this point. Both a single elder and a plurality of elders within a congregational structure fit the pattern of church government and polity that emerges from a study of the New Testament."[68]

Although they have maintained that the apostolic churches had a plural eldership and that apostolic practice was binding, Baptists have suggested reasons that made that pattern necessary in the first century. But those reasons no longer exist. Plural eldership made sense in the past, but it is not necessary any longer.

Ambiguity of Baptist Confessions

Particular Baptists historically subscribed to confessions and creeds and required brethren who wished to associate with them to do the same.[69] Their confessions were important in maintaining their belief and practice. Significantly, the most influential Baptist confessional documents were decidedly ambiguous concerning the number of elders each church should have. Following are the pertinent sections on church leadership from the most significant Baptist confessions. The ambiguity is apparent. Churches holding to plural elders could subscribe to each confession. But since the plural title for pastor was used generically of all the churches subscribing to the confession, churches holding to a single pastor could also subscribe.

---

67. Ibid., 64–65.
68. Ibid., 25–26.
69. See Silas M. Noel, "Circular Letter on Campbellism's Objection to Confessions (1826)," in H. Leon McBeth, ed., *A Sourcebook for Baptist Heritage* (Nashville: Broadman, 1990), 241–43; Reynolds, *Church Polity*, 334–41; Thomas J. Nettles, *The Baptists: Key People Involved in Forming a Baptist Identity. Vol. 1: Beginnings in Britain* (Fearn, Scotland: Christian Focus, 2005), 46–48.

- *First London Confession (1644)*: "every Church has power given them from Christ for their better well-being, to choose to themselves meet persons into the office of pastors, teachers, elders, deacons"[70]

- *First London Confession (1646)*: "every church has power given them from Christ, for their wellbeing, to choose among themselves meet persons for elders and deacons"[71]

- *Second London Confession (1689)*: A particular church "consists of officers, and members; and the officers appointed by Christ to be chosen and set apart by the church (so called and gathered) for the peculiar administration of ordinances, and execution of power, or duty, which he entrusts them with, or calls them to, to be continued to the end of the world, are bishops or elders and deacons."[72]

- *New Hampshire Confession (1833/1853)*: A church's "only proper officers are bishops or pastors, and deacons, whose qualifications, claims, and duties are defined in the epistles to Timothy and Titus."[73]

- *The Abstract of Principles (1858)*: "The regular officers of a church are bishops or elders, and deacons."[74]

- *The Baptist Faith and Message (1925)*: A church's "Scriptural officers are bishops, or elders, and deacons."[75]

- *The Baptist Faith and Message (1963)*: A church's "Scriptural officers are pastors and deacons."[76]

---

70. William L. Lumpkin, *Baptist Confessions of Faith*, rev. ed. (Valley Forge, PA: Judson, 1969), 166.
71. *The First London Confession of Faith, 1646 Edition* (Rochester, NY: Backus, 1981), 13.
72. Lumpkin, *Baptist Confessions*, 287. Samuel Waldron thus seems mistaken to suggest that this confession "suggests that each church should have a plurality of elders" (Waldron, "Plural Elder Congregationalism," 201). See Renihan, *Edification and Beauty*, 101.
73. Lumpkin, *Baptist Confessions*, 365–66.
74. http://www.sbts.edu/about/truth/abstract/.
75. http://www.sbc.net/bfm/bfmcomparison.asp.
76. Lumpkin, *Baptist Confessions*, 396; http://www.sbc.net/bfm/bfmcomparison.asp.

- *The Baptist Faith and Message (2000)*: A congregation's "scriptural officers are pastors and deacons."[77]

We are left to surmise why there is decided ambiguity in the confessional tradition. At the simplest level, this ambiguity was essential to account for the views of prominent early Baptists. For example, Keach would not have subscribed to the 1689 Confession if it mandated a plurality of elders, but Coxe and Collins would not have subscribed to it if the confession contained a prohibition against the practice. So the confessions were probably intentionally ambiguous to reflect the differing opinions among the churches.

Although some interpreters have argued that the demise of plurality was indicated confessionally in the Baptist Faith and Message's dropping "elders" between the 1925 and 1963 editions, this does not seem accurate.[78] They suggest that the practice was common until the early twentieth century. As we have already observed, this does not fit the historical record. Rather, Baptists were following the pattern of synonymous titles for pastors in the New Testament. In the New Testament there is one office, or position of leadership, having three different titles associated with it: "pastor," "elder," and "overseer." This is clearly seen in Paul's last interaction with the leadership of the church in Ephesus. In Acts 20:17 Paul calls for "the elders" (*presbuterous*). Then in v. 28 he reminds these same people that God has made them "overseers" (*episkopous*) and urges them to "care for" or "shepherd" the flock, which is the verbal form of the word we usually translate "pastor." So for Paul, "elder" = "pastor" = "overseer/bishop."[79] In Titus the apostle similarly refers to the same leaders as "elders" and "overseers" (Titus 1:5, 7).[80] Baptists noted this interchangeability of terms. When they called a pastor, "elder," it does not signal that they held to plurality. More often than not they were using the terms synonymously.[81]

---

77. http://www.sbc.net/bfm/bfmcomparison.asp.
78. For example, see Newton, *Elders in Congregational Life*, 27.
79. See Merkle, "Hierarchy," 32–33.
80. Ibid., 35.
81. "The term 'elder,' as a proper distinction for our ministers of all grades, old or young, in my early day, was, and indeed from time immemorial it has been, the usual title for them. Office instead of age has always been intended by it. . . . I have often been amused in our region of the country, where the Baptists were the first settlers, and where they always have

This ambiguity in the confessional statements was significant. On the one hand, it signaled to Particular Baptist churches that although ecclesiology was important the number of elders a congregation had was not of the utmost importance. Certain things about the church in the 1689 Confession, for instance, were givens: the church was local and universal, the initiatory rite into the church was baptism after one came to faith in Christ, the final authority in the church resided in the congregation, and elder/overseer/pastor and deacon were the two offices of the church. But by its absence from the confessions, the number of elders was deposed to the status of secondary importance. The number of elders a church had could be decided by other factors.

Non-plurality Position of Prominent Pastor-Theologians

Baptists were also influenced away from a plural elder position by the practice and writings of prominent Baptist pastor-theologians. Significantly, the three arguably most influential pastors of the seventeenth and eighteenth centuries wrote works which specifically argued against the necessity of multiple elders per congregation. Their influence was monumental, and their views undoubtedly persuaded countless pastors and fellowships that plural elders were not necessary in each church.

No pastor from the seventeenth century was as influential among Particular Baptists as Benjamin Keach. Yet, in all his years as a pastor, Keach never had other elders serving with him in his church. He spelled out his views on the plurality of elders very clearly in his work *The Glory and Ornament of a True Gospel-Constituted Church* (1697). Here Keach posed a question, "Are there no ruling elders besides the pastor?," the answer to which proves he did not consider co-elders to be a necessity: "There might be such in the primitive apostolical church, but we see no ground to believe it an abiding office to continue in the church, but was only temporary."[82] Keach was, of course, here directly countering the (typically Presbyterian) practice of having ruling elders, but his use of the singular "the pastor" suggests that in his understanding there was only

---

been numerous, to hear our old-fashioned people, especially among the sisterhood, apply the term 'elder' to ministers of other denominations as freely as they do to their own order" (Benedict, *Fifty Years*, 166–67).

82. Keach, *Glory of a True Church*, 68–69.

one pastor per congregation. Throughout the rest of this work Keach seemed purposefully not to take a strong position on the issue by constantly referring to those in the congregation's pastoral ministry as "elder or elders." Those influenced by Keach would not be drawn to plurality.

Before looking at the views of the two prominent pastors from the eighteenth century we should look more closely at some of Keach's contemporaries. For example, Renihan is certainly right to point to Kiffin as one who had a co-pastor. Yet, he fails to mention that this inauguration of a co-pastorate happened late in Kiffin's ministry. For the bulk of his pastorate Kiffin functioned as the lone elder and did not advocate plural eldership. One is left with the impression that there were circumstances at work in Kiffin's or the congregation's life which made a co-pastorate expedient, though not requisite. Similarly, though Ivimey claimed that at the inception of his ministry Bunyan had a plurality of elders, Bunyan seems never to have written on this topic. Hercules Collins (d. 1702) will serve as a final example. He had ample opportunity to address the issue of a plurality of elders in his *Some Reasons for Separation from the Communion of the Church of England*, which was written to clarify the reasons behind the Baptists' separation from the established church. Yet, he did not. In fact, a debate he had with his congregation while he was imprisoned makes it clear that his church had no elders beside him.[83] William Collins's and Nehemiah Coxe's congregation is one of the only prominent seventeenth-century Baptist churches that had a plurality of elders. Most of the well-known churches had only a single pastor, or they were silent about their practice to the contrary.

John Gill had a far-reaching influence on Baptists in the eighteenth and nineteenth centuries through his prominent London ministry and his plentiful writings. As we have seen, Gill argued against the necessity of a plurality of elders in a local congregation. In his massive *Body of Divinity* (1769), Gill wrote approximately forty-five pages on the nature of the church. Of these, about fifteen were devoted to pastoral leadership within the congregation. Yet, he never even raised the issue of the number of pastors a congregation should have. It appears that he did not consider the position important enough even to offer a refutation

---

83. Ernest F. Kevan, *London's Oldest Baptist Church: Wapping 1633–Walthamstow 1933* (London: The Kingsgate Press, 1933), 66–67.

of it. Throughout his discussion of pastoral ministry he simply referred to the "pastor" in the singular as a given entity.[84]

An insight into Gill's opinion about plural elders was conveyed by his biographer, John Rippon. When Gill was advanced in years, his church suggested getting a co-pastor to help him with his ministry. He wrote the church a letter in response saying,

> That Christ gives *pastors* to churches is certain, but that he gives *co-pastors* is not so certain. A co-pastor is an officer the Scripture is entirely silent about—and which is much the same thing as if a woman should marry another man, whilst she is under the law, dominion, and power of her former husband.[85]

In private Gill lamented to his family about the prospect of having a co-elder, complaining that "I should not like a co-pastor to hang about my neck, nor an assistant to be dangling at my heels."[86] Therefore, either by silence (as in his theology and most of his biblical expositions) or by arguing for a single pastor, Gill communicated that the norm was to be one elder per church.[87]

Andrew Fuller (d. 1815) also exercised great influence among Baptists in the eighteenth and nineteenth centuries. Like Keach and Gill, he did not think a plural elder system was obligatory on all congregations. The key principle for organizing a church, Fuller wrote, is that all things be done in the way that is most "fitting," that is, in the way which seems right to the church, as long as their practice does not contradict

---

84. John Gill, *A Complete Body of Doctrinal and Practical Divinity: Or a System of Evangelical Truths, Deduced from the Sacred Scriptures* (1809; reprint, Paris, AR: Baptist Standard Bearer, 1995), 862–76.

85. John Rippon, *A Brief Memoir of the Life and Writings of the Late Rev. John Gill, D. D.* (Harrisonburg, VA: Gano Books, 1992), 130.

86. Rippon, *Brief Memoir*, 131.

87. The Philadelphia Association, the most influential Particular Baptist body in America, wanted Gill's works to be in the hands of all the pastors in its churches (Gillette, *Minutes*, 229, 439). Gill's influence spread much broader than just the Philadelphia area. According to Wills, his works "had wide influence among Baptists," and in Georgia Jesse Mercer promoted the sale of Gill's commentaries to Baptist pastors (Gregory A. Wills, *Democratic Religion: Freedom, Authority, and Church Discipline in the Baptist South, 1785–1900* [New York: Oxford University Press, 1997], 85–86).

the clear biblical witness.[88] He argued that the New Testament did not require more than one elder per church:

> A large church or congregation, where much service was to be done, required seven deacons; and where they abounded not only in numbers, but also in spiritual gifts, they commonly, if not always, seem to have had a plurality of bishops or elders.—With respect to us, where the reason of the thing exists—that is, where there are churches whose numbers require it, and whose gifts admit of it—it is well to follow this part of their example; but for a small church to have more pastors than one appears to be as unnecessary as to have "seven" deacons. Such a rule would favour idleness, and prevent useful ministers from extending their labours. To appoint two or three to a station which might be filled by one must have a tendency to leave many other places unoccupied, and so contract instead of enlarging the kingdom of Christ.[89]

In England, it was not until the ministry of C. H. Spurgeon (d. 1892) in the late nineteenth century that a prominent pastor practiced a plurality of elders in his church. However, Spurgeon did not promote his views forcefully. For instance, during the many years of his editorship of *The Sword and the Trowel*, Spurgeon only included one article which mentioned the plural elder practice of his church. Yet, even this account was descriptive, not prescriptive.[90] American Baptists were even quieter, as we have already observed, apart from a few advocates like W. B. Johnson. For most of Baptist history, no prominent Baptist pastor-theologians advocated plural eldership in their churches.

---

88. Andrew Fuller, "Thoughts on the Principles on which the Apostles Proceeded, in Forming and Organizing Christian Churches, and Regulating Various Religious Duties," *Works*, 3:453. According to Fuller, the New Testament did not contain a blueprint for church government; rather, it contained a broad pattern which should be emulated by churches: "to attempt to draw up a formula of church government, worship, and discipline, which shall include any thing more than general outlines, and to establish it expressly on New Testament authority, is to attempt what is utterly impracticable" (ibid., 3:452).

89. Fuller, *Works*, 3:454.

90. J. A. Spurgeon, "Discipline of the Church at the Metropolitan Tabernacle," *The Sword and the Trowel* (February 1869): 198–206; http://sites.silaspartners.com/cc/article/0,,PTID314526_CHID598016_CIID1552894,00.html.

Lack of Qualified Elders

Demographics also contributed to the lack of plural elders among Baptists. There was a dearth of qualified men to fill the office.[91] Since Baptists were reticent to have ruling elders, they could have adopted the position of co-teaching elders. Such elders had to be capable teachers and preachers. That is where the problem lay with many Baptist congregations, for their fidelity and submission to the Bible would not allow them to lower the standards for their pastors. If they did not have qualified men to serve as elders in a congregation, they would strive just to have one qualified pastor. Thus, the lack of qualified plural elders contributed to the practice of single eldership in most Baptist churches.

Perhaps, then, due to the larger pool available from which to draw, larger metropolitan churches would be the most likely congregations to have more than one qualified man to be their pastor. That, at least, seems to have been the case at the Petty France church with its pastors Coxe and Collins. As T. E. Dowley recounts,

> On 21 September 1675 William Collins and Nehemiah Coxe were ordained elders of Petty France. Collins had received an unusually long and thorough education by contemporary Baptist standards, and undertook a continental tour to France and Italy to broaden his experience. He graduated B.D., but despite efforts to attract him into the Anglican ministry, accepted a call to minister at Petty France in 1675. Coxe was a qualified physician.[92]

It seems unlikely such gifted men would have been tempted to serve a small rural congregation.

---

91. Dealing with the 1650s, White mentioned "the problem of the lack of men with leadership qualities from which so many Calvinistic Baptist churches suffered at this period" (B. R. White, "John Miles and the Structures of the Calvinistic Baptist Mission to South Wales 1649–1660," in *Welsh Baptist Studies* [n.p.: South Wales Baptist College, 1976], 55). My reading of association records suggests that the problem was endemic to the Particular Baptists of England in the seventeenth century.

92. T. E. Dowley, "A London Congregation during the Great Persecution," *Baptist Quarterly* 27 (1978): 234.

The famine of qualified leadership was clear in the association records on both sides of the Atlantic. The Charleston Association's experience was typical. In 1851, the association wrote, "we have to mourn over the great destitution of ministers within our bounds; truly, 'the harvest is great, but the laborers are few.'"[93] Many congregations could not find one qualified pastor, let alone a plurality of them.[94]

Certainly other factors influenced Baptists not to practice a plurality of elders in their churches. The rapid growth of Baptists in America in the nineteenth century combined with the rising independent ethos in American churches may have confirmed Baptists in their practice of non plurality. Baptists also would have naturally wanted to avoid guilt by association with those holding plural elders, not only Presbyterians but, even more troubling, Sandemanians and Campbellites.[95] We need to remember, though, that these factors did not cause the decline of plural eldership. They rather encouraged a long-standing practice of single eldership in Baptist churches.

CONCLUSION

I began this chapter with a caveat. A second one is in order by way of conclusion. Historical investigation is not the same as advocacy. It is instructive for us to consider what Baptists thought about a plural eldership and to see why they have overwhelmingly advocated a single

---

93. *Minutes of the Charleston Baptist Association, at Its One Hundredth Anniversary: Held with the First Baptist Church, Charleston, S. C. November 1–4, 1851, Together with the Centennial Sermon* (Charleston, SC: A. J. Burke, 1851), 9.

94. Related to this dearth of qualified pastors was some churches' dispatching of their "qualified brethren"—men who had the congregation's approval to preach and who were thus often in training to become pastors—to sister fellowships seeking pastors of their own. For instance, in 1655 the English Midlands Association's churches agreed that one of their responsibilities to other congregations within the association consisted "in sending their gifted brethren to use their gifts for the edification of the churches that need the same: as they shall see it seasonable, as the church at Jerusalem sent Barnabas to Antioch (Acts 11.22)" (White, *Association Records. Part 1*, 21). Lending gifted brothers to needy churches is never mentioned as a deterrent to plural elders, but it follows that this practice would take qualified men away from a congregation leaving the church with a smaller pool from which to select a plurality of elders.

95. Newton, *Elders in Congregational Life*, 96; Hammett, *Biblical Foundations*, 179–80; Talbot, "Origins of the Baptist Union," 35–36, 58; on Baptists' controversies with Campbellism, see McBeth, *Baptist Heritage*, 375–80, and Torbet, *History of the Baptists*, 269–75.

pastor model of leadership. Although the seventeenth century saw several plural elder Baptists, they were the minority even then, and the fact that many of them advocated a teaching-ruling elder distinction made them suspect to congregationally-minded Baptists. Combined with the other factors we noted, plural eldership never gained much traction in Baptist churches.

At least it did not until quite recently. As noted earlier, there has been a recent resurgence of advocacy of plural elders among Baptists. This is as it should be, given Baptists' long-standing commitment to the authority of Scripture and to the regulative principle. The New Testament pattern is clear: plural elders in one church. Baptists need to wrestle with the implications of this pattern for their local churches.

Taking Baptists' historical concerns about plural eldership into account, here are several suggestions for churches wishing to implement plural elders. First of all, agreeing with the ambiguity of Baptist confessions, we need to remember that a church may be a legitimate church apart from having a plural eldership. Several things—such as the preaching of the gospel, the implications of the gospel for the practice of believer's baptism, and ultimate congregational authority—should be givens in Baptist churches. These are parts of the *esse* ("being") of the church. Plural elders are not; rather, they are expressions of the *bene esse* ("well-being") of the church.[96] A church can exist apart from plural elders. It cannot exist apart from the gospel.

In the second place, Baptist churches that opt for a plural eldership must be certain to have an elder-led, not an elder-ruled, church. Baptists were right historically to oppose any system of elders that usurped the rightful authority of the congregation. As the New Testament teaches and our confessions have historically affirmed, the final authority in the church is the congregation. The elder is to lead, and he leads as he faithfully teaches and persuades according to the word of God. Hebrews 13:7, 17 is very instructive here. The congregation is to obey its leaders and submit to them. But those they are called to obey are the ones who faithfully teach the word of God to them. In other words, the pastor's authority is derivative. Christ is the head of the church, and he rules the church through his word as his Spirit ap-

---

96. On *esse* and *bene esse*, see Renihan, *Edification and Beauty*, 90.

plies the word to the church. So the elder leads the church to listen to its Lord. Christ, not the elder, is the Lord.[97]

Additionally, if a congregation chooses to have a plurality of elders it must make sure that there is parity among the eldership. That is to say, the elders must be equal in authority. Baptists have been correct in noting that 1 Timothy 5:17 does not teach the separate office of "ruling elder." All elders are to have oversight of the congregation; and all elders must be able to teach. Not only will this allow the congregation to be benefit from more than one gifted man serving as Christ's under-shepherd over them, but it will also protect them from having one pastor ruling them with little or no accountability.[98]

In conclusion, the question of plural eldership is a fascinating example of the limitations of the study of history for determining what we should do in our churches. As Christians we must approach the historical data humbly, seeking to learn from those who have preceded us. This is one of the great benefits of historical inquiry. And it is incumbent upon us to face the historical material honestly, even when the material is limited. Such is the case in the circumstance of Baptists and a plurality of elders. Even when we find that there is not much historical data on Baptists and a plurality of elders, we can learn a great deal from them when we see the reasons why they did not want to have plural elders. But having seen the limitations of the historical material, we are forced as Christians to fall back on God's word as the only source of authority in our churches. For us, the ultimate question is not, What did Baptists practice historically? The important question for us is, What does the Bible say? Baptists have not said much about elders over the course of their history. But the Bible does. What are we to do with that data in our churches?

---

97. This might allay the fears of some commentators who assume that having a plural eldership necessarily means that the congregation loses its ultimate authority. See, e.g., Wring's misunderstanding of the plural elder position, especially of Capitol Hill Baptist Church's view of plural eldership (Robert A. Wring, "An Examination of the Practice of Elder Rule in Selected Southern Baptist Churches in the Light of New Testament Teaching" [PhD diss., Mid-America Baptist Theological Seminary, 2002], 143, 152, 168, 185, 214–15). For an example of one church's attempt to balance elder leadership with ultimate congregational authority, see the constitution of Clifton Baptist Church, Louisville, Kentucky. http://cliftonbaptist.org/wp-content/uploads/2011/10/Constitution-of-Clifton-Baptist-Church.pdf.

98. This may also be a reason to question the appropriateness of referring to one of the church's elders as "senior pastor." See my article: http://www.9marks.org/journal/case-against-senior-pastor.

CHAPTER 10

Putting It All Together: A Theology of Church Leadership

Bruce A. Ware[1]

The importance of church leadership can so easily be either over-stated, or understated. Overstatements are often in the form of asserting that only "professional," formally trained, and ordained men should rightly be understood as ministers in the church. While the provision of trained, recognized leaders surely is a gift to any church (more below), it simply is not the case that these, and these alone, are the ministers of the church. Paul makes clear in Ephesians 4:11–13 that, as important as these formal leaders are, their primary function is to train the members of a local church to carry out the work of service to grow one another up in Christ. So, who truly are the "ministers" of the church? These are the members, trained and equipped by formal leaders, to be sure, but members who themselves are gifted and called to serve one another in the body of Christ until all are built up to the measure of the stature that belongs to the fullness of Christ (Eph. 4:13).[2]

But understatements of the importance of church leadership also abound. Often these come in the form of minimizing the usefulness of

---

1. Bruce A. Ware (PhD, Fuller Theological Seminary) is Professor of Christian Theology at The Southern Baptist Theological Seminary in Louisville, Kentucky.
2. I once served on part-time staff at a church where the church worship folder listed the names and positions of each of the staff members, as well as the names of the elders and deacons. But at the top of this list of names of staff, elders, and deacons, was this first heading: "Ministers." And following "Ministers," it read, "The Members of Our Church." The symbolism of this spoke volumes to members, regular attenders, and visitors alike. Those who are called and equipped for ministry are, not merely the pastor, or his associate, or the elders, or deacons, but more comprehensively, all of the membership of the church. They are the ministers of the church.

formal training, of a studied approach to understanding the content of the Bible and the Christian faith, and of a preparedness in communicating well that faith once for all delivered to the saints (Jude 3). Evidently the apostle Paul was deeply concerned about the need for capable and competent church leaders, as is evidenced by his appeal to Timothy to train others in what he had been taught so that they will then be able to carry on this training to yet another generation (2 Tim. 2:2), and from his instruction to Titus to proceed to appoint elders in every city (i.e., the churches in those cities) as he had previously directed him to do (Titus 1:5). Churches lacking strong leaders are left, in most cases, to flounder, whereas churches with strong and competent leaders have resources for knowing and carrying out God's purposes that all benefit from.

If the importance of church leadership can be wrongly overestimated or underestimated, it is incumbent upon us to consider what the New Testament teaching of leadership is for the church. The purpose of this chapter, then, is to endeavor to synthesize some of the most important aspects of New Testament teaching on the nature and expression of the leadership God has designed for the church. Since this chapter proposes to develop a relatively brief theology of leadership from the New Testament, there is much that will, of necessity, only be touched upon which, in a more specialized treatment, might be developed much more extensively.[3] But perhaps a broad overview of a theology of leadership for the church may prove helpful in keeping in place what is essential while allowing differences among us to exist on secondary and tertiary matters. Just what value does the New Testament give to church lead-

---

3. Many very fine book-length treatments of church leadership, and more narrowly of church elders and deacons, are available. Among those I would recommend highly are these: Thabiti M. Anyabwile, *Finding Faithful Elders and Deacons* (Wheaton, IL: Crossway, 2012); Mark Dever, *A Display of God's Glory: Basics of Church Structure—Deacons, Elders, Congregationalism, and Membership*, 2nd ed. (Washington DC, IX Marks, 2001); Benjamin L. Merkle, *40 Questions about Elders and Deacons* (Grand Rapids, MI: Kregel, 2008); R. Albert Mohler, Jr., *The Conviction to Lead: 25 Principles for Leadership that Matters* (Bloomington, MN: Bethany House, 2012); Alexander Strauch, *Biblical Eldership: An Urgent Call to Restore Biblical Church Leadership* (Colorado Springs, CO: Lewis & Roth, 1995); Timothy Z. Witmer, *The Shepherd Leader: Achieving Effective Shepherding in Your Church* (Phillipsburg, NJ: P&R, 2010); and Timothy S. Laniak, *Shepherds after My Own Heart: Traditions and Leadership in the Bible*, NSBT 20 (Downers Grove, IL: InterVarsity Press, 2006).

ership, and how should this leadership function so that Christ and his purposes for the church are advanced? To these questions we now turn.

CHRIST, THE CHIEF SHEPHERD AND LORD OF THE CHURCH

A theology of leadership for the church must (yes, must!) begin with a recognition that the church of which we speak is the church *of Jesus Christ* and of no one else. Surely we all recognize that we speak with dangerously imprecise and potentially misleading language when we speak of this as "Charles Spurgeon's church," or that as "Adrian Rogers's church," since every church that truly is a church, is a church under the sole Lordship and ultimate Leadership of the One Head of the Church, the Lord Jesus Christ. So, the first thing about church leadership to be clear on is this: only Jesus Christ has rights of absolute leadership and authority over any and every local church, as he is head and lord over all of the church.[4] Consider some of the ways that the New Testament highlights the highest position and absolute primacy of Christ over all of the church, as Supreme Leader of all other leaders within the church.

Christ, the Chief Shepherd of the Church (1 Peter 5:1–4)

Peter's reference in 1 Peter 5 of Christ as the "chief Shepherd" (5:4) is highly instructive. While elders are called by Peter to "shepherd the flock of God" (5:2), the reference to Christ as the Chief Shepherd immediately puts their role in its proper perspective and orientation. While their responsibility is sobering and must be carried out with integrity, selflessness, and with rightful and upbuilding authority (5:2–3), these elder shepherds must always bear in mind that they are under the

---

4. It should be noted that the NT term for church, *ekklesia*, is used both of the church universal (i.e., all of those, in all of history, who have trusted Christ alone for the forgiveness of their sin and their only hope for eternal life) and for local churches (i.e., local assemblies or congregations of believers who covenant together and meet regularly for the preaching of God's word, the administration of the ordinances, and for the encouragement, admonition, and accountability of the followers of Christ). Some examples where *ekklesia* is used of the universal church are: Matthew 16:18; Acts 9:31; 1 Corinthians 15:9; Ephesians 1:22–23. And some examples where *ekklesia* is used of local congregations are: Matthew 18:17; 2 Corinthians 8:1; Colossians 4:15; Revelation 2:1.

authority of One who stands always over and above them. They do not have the final word, nor is their work their own to decide. They are, in short, under-shepherds.

As under-shepherds, then, they stand in a relation to Christ in a manner even greater than that in which their own people stand to them. They must acknowledge that their role and all it involves is simply and solely to carry out the will of another, to advance the work of one greater. And this cannot be a matter merely of formal acknowledgement; it must rather be a matter of daily and prayerful submission. These elders, though they have authority and are called to lead their sheep along paths of life and renewal, are under authority themselves— every moment, in every decision, with every conflict, and in every relationship. There must be a deeply self-conscious awareness that they must be and do, only rightly and properly, what Christ wants of them to be and do. Glad and willing submission, then, is the first hallmark of those in positions of New Testament leadership.

"I Will Build My Church" (Matt. 16:18)

Another confirmation of the supreme leadership position possessed by Christ alone comes with Christ's declaration that he will build *his* church. Even though Christ delegates a significant role to Peter as the possessor of the keys to the kingdom (Matt. 16:19), nonetheless all that Peter does, and all that others who join the work of building the church will do, must be seen as under the sole authority of Christ who sovereignly rules in the building of his own church.

It truly is a marvel that Christ has designed that part of the way in which he will build his church is through the active participation of others. Church members are all gifted, and leaders are provided, all for the carrying out of this work of building the church of Jesus Christ. But the temptation is ever-present to think that, since we have such important work to do, and we labor at times with such passion and endurance, that it really is "our" kingdom that we are building. But if this labor and toil truly does contribute to the building of the church, then two things are true. First, the very power or energy by which we exert such labor was itself given to us by Christ for the accomplishment of the work he kindly, in his mercy, gave us to do (1 Cor. 15:10;

Col. 1:28–29). And second, all work done to the glory of God and the advancement of Christ's kingdom is fully and, in reality, the work of Christ himself. When Christ says, "I will build my church," there is no percentage of that work that is left to others to fulfill. All of a leader's work, then, when done such that the church truly is advanced, is the work ultimately of Christ and not his own.

The Lordship of Christ over All, for the Church (Eph. 1:20–23)

A third passage highlights the supreme authority that Christ has been given, an authority which he wields for the sake of the advance of the very church over which he stands as its head. In Paul's prayer in Ephesians 1:15–23, he revels in the work that the Father accomplished in raising Christ from the dead and seating him at his right hand far above every authority, and power, and name both now and in the age to come (1:20–21). And while this supremacy of position over all powers has enormous implications for the affairs of nations and the unfolding of the history of world governments, to be sure, the primary stress Paul makes is not there. Yes, Christ is given authority over all nations, peoples, powers, and dominions, but the primary and ultimate purpose for this absolute authority possessed by Christ alone is this: as absolute authority over all, he is given as head over all these things to the church, which is his own body, the fullness of him who fills all in all (1:22–23).

This is an astonishing reality! The One who has been granted unparalleled and uncontested authority over everything in heaven and earth is the very One who is placed as ultimate authority over and leader of the church. Analogies of this reality at the human level pale. What would you say if the one who stepped forward to pay off your debts was the billionaire just announced in the *Wall Street Journal* to be the wealthiest man in the world? Or what if the person put in charge of handling the computer redesign for your business had just won an award for being the most ingenious and knowledgeable computer designer in the industry? These, and any other, analogies are simply feeble in comparison. Jesus Christ, the risen Victor over Satan and sin, is now granted, by virtue of the efficacy of his atoning work and triumphant resurrection, to be given authority over absolutely everything in existence—an authority which once established will never, ever end. And it is this Jesus who is given this authority over all, not primarily to rule all else, but primarily and most centrally to rule and build his own church. How amazing and unrivaled is his absolute authority, under which all church leaders serve.

The Primacy of Christ in All of the Metaphors for the Church

Finally, that church leaders, as well as all church members, are under the sole authority of Christ can also be seen by observing the metaphors that the New Testament uses of Christ and his church. Regardless of the metaphor, the centrality, primacy, and ultimacy of Christ is evident, while all others—including all church leaders—are dependent upon and in subjection to this Lord. Recall, for example, the metaphor of Christ as the vine and his people as branches (John 15:1–5), showing their need to receive from him the supply of life-giving nourishment that only he can provide. Or consider Christ as the bridegroom and the church as his bride (2 Cor. 11:2; Eph. 5:25–27; Rev. 19:7–9) where Christ's authority and loving care for the church ensures her future purity and holiness by the work he will bring to pass. Or recall Christ as the head of the body (Eph. 1:22–23; Col. 1:18) and Shepherd of his sheep (Luke 15:3–7; John 10:1–18) and Cornerstone of the building (Eph. 2:19–22; 1 Peter 2:4–8), all of which place Christ as the central figure and show the church as dependent upon and under the ultimate leadership of the Lord Christ.

The first truth of church leadership that the New Testament announces, then, is this: all such leadership, regardless of titles, or training, or longevity, or position, or reputation, or prestige, is under the one and absolute authority of Christ. Leaders, then, lead as they are led by Christ; they teach as they are taught of Christ; they build in the manner by which they have been instructed by Christ; and they labor for the glory, not of themselves, but for the glory of the One to whom belongs all glory and honor and praise—the Lord Jesus Christ. As supreme leader, teacher, and builder, Christ alone has unchallenged authority over every leader and every church. Jesus' words, "I will build my church," must remain on the minds and in the hearts of every church leader who truly seeks to lead within the church of Jesus Christ.

ELDERS/OVERSEERS/PASTORS:
THE UNDER-SHEPHERDS FOR THE CHURCH

Having established the sole and absolute authority of Christ over his church, we turn now to New Testament teaching on those who are called, equipped, and qualified to lead within local churches. Two offices are referred to and described in the New Testament, which provide for the church her two main bodies of leaders. Elders (or overseers, or pastors) are given primary spiritual leadership in local churches, and deacons are responsible for the every-day and practical needs of local communities of believers. When the members of each leadership group understand and carry out their respective roles, local churches experience health and strength. We will consider each leadership group briefly to see in what respects they are to lead within the church.

Three Greek Terms, Six English Terms, One Office

It appears from various contexts in the New Testament that the three Greek terms, *presbyteros*, *episkopos*, and *poimēn*, all refer to the same office, an office we will refer to (for convenience as well as current custom in some congregations) as the office of "elder." To make matters even more confusing for English readers, each of these three Greek terms can be rendered with at least two common English terms. So, *presbyteros* is commonly translated as "elder" or "presbyter," *episkopos* is rendered "overseer" or "bishop," and *poimēn* refers either to "shepherd" or "pastor." What evidence is there that these terms refer to the same office?[5] Consider the following.

In Acts 20, when Paul calls the leaders of the church at Ephesus to meet with him, he requests that "the elders" (20:17) come. Yet, as he addresses them, he warns them to be on the guard for themselves and for all the flock, among which the Holy Spirit has made them "overseers," to "shepherd" the church of God (20:28). It is evident, then, that Paul's calling of the "elders" and the coming of the "overseers" refer to the same group of leaders, leaders who are respon-

---

5. In support of this reading, see esp. Benjamin L. Merkle, *The Elder and Overseer: One Office in the Early Church* (New York: Peter Lang, 2003).

sible to "pastor" or "shepherd" the flock of believers in the church at Ephesus. All three designations, then, are given to this one group of church leaders.

Another text where all three designations are used is in 1 Peter 5:1–2. Here Peter exhorts the "elders" among the scattered believers to whom he writes to "shepherd" the flock of God, among whom they are given "oversight." Although both "shepherd" and "oversight" are expressed in verbal forms rather than as nouns, it is clear again that elders shepherd and oversee the congregation.

Not only do all three terms apply to this spiritual leadership office in the church, each of these terms presents some of what is involved in the work of those who carry out this office. Elders, as "elders," are to be "seasoned" in the faith. As Paul says in 1 Timothy 3, overseers are to be able to teach (3:2), implying they have learned already the fundamentals of biblical teaching and the Christian faith, and they are not to be new converts (3:6), implying that there is both some life experience and some gained humility and strength of character that has come in their walk with the Lord. Although elders do not have to be truly old men, they should be mature and seasoned Christian men, neither too young in age nor young in the faith. The term "overseer" adds the dimension that these spiritual leaders must be men who take and exercise responsibility for the well-being of those under their charge. They are to train their children at home indicating their ability to provide training, instruction, and discipline within the church. And they are to exercise their authority in ways that bring benefit and strength to the church (see 1 Peter 5:3). Also, the term "shepherd" or "pastor" (as is more commonly used) adds the dimension of tender care, provision, and protection of the flock. One calls to mind the good shepherd of Psalm 23 and John 10 who seeks good pasture and clear water for his flock, all the while watching carefully to defend against the attempt of any predator to harm any of his sheep. The terms elders, overseers, pastors refer to one and the same office held by those with a richness and integrity of spiritual life and experience, oversight responsibility for the spiritual well-being of the church, and a watchful care for others that Christ has ordained as one of the greatest means for the growth and maturity of his people.

Elder Qualifications and Responsibilities

Paul took the qualifications and responsibilities of elders seriously. Both in his first letter to Timothy (1 Tim. 3:1–7) and in his letter to Titus (Titus 1:5–9), he specifies the characteristics that must be true of an elder if he is to fulfill with integrity this noble calling within a local church. As for qualifications, the emphasis in both passages rests on the character of the man of God who aspires to the office of elder. These requisite character qualities relate both to his public demeanor (e.g., above reproach, respectable, not combative, having a good reputation with outsiders, hospitable) and to his personal, even private, life (e.g., temperate, prudent, gentle, peaceable, not addicted to wine, free from the love of money, self-controlled). What both sets of characteristics display is a man who has grown much in his relationship with the Lord, who lives humbly before God and others, and who wants to reflect the character of Christ and the fruit of the Spirit. Maturity, godliness, integrity, honesty, humility, kindness, faithfulness—these are the kinds of characteristics that must mark the life of a man who aspires to become an elder.

But beyond these character qualifications, some other characteristics required of an elder need also to be noted, ones which relate directly to some of the responsibilities that must be carried out by elders. For example, an elder is to manage the children of his own household, giving evidence that he is able to manage and care for those in the church as well (1 Tim. 3:4–5; Titus 1:6). An elder, then, cannot be haphazard, thoughtless, or negligent about the manner in which he oversees the culture and activities of his own home. He must have a vision for his own family, leading them to grow in the knowledge of God and of the gospel that shows an intentionality and discipline that is needed if he is to be an effective spiritual leader in the church. I do not think that this qualification is given to rule out mature single men or husbands who have no children from becoming elders (recall that both Jesus and the apostle Paul were both single, yet I dare say no one would dispute their qualifications to be elders!). Rather, how a father raises his children, with the thought, care, foresight, and planning necessary to lead them to a growing understanding and faith, is a clear and common indicator of the kind of man the members of a church should consider for the position of elder. So, the point is not that one *has* to be a father, but rather that one has to have the discipline and intentionality necessary to be effective in spiritual leadership of the church—which discipline and intentionality are often displayed by how a father conducts himself with his children.

Here, then, is a qualification that leads to a responsibility. Elders need to display an approach to life that is serious about pursuing spiritual growth, with a plan and discipline that marks their own lives and their leadership in their homes (if married with children). This qualification is stressed precisely because one of the most important responsibilities of those in the office of elder is to give careful, intentional, and purposeful, planning and forethought to those kinds of things that will best facilitate the spiritual growth of those under their charge. When elders get preoccupied with so many details (even good and important ones) and neglect the burning question of what can best assist the growth of the flock in their embrace of the gospel and the knowledge of God and his word, one central and crucial elder responsibility remains unfulfilled.

Another qualification that extends naturally into a central responsibility of elders comes in the very brief statement in 1 Timothy 3:2, that an elder must be "able to teach." One may easily infer that if an elder must be able to teach, he must first have been taught. In other words, this qualification requires not only that the elder can communicate (i.e., he has the capacity to teach something to others), but it requires that he know the truth of the Christian faith sufficient to be a reliable and faithful teacher of that truth.

Support for this understanding of "able to teach" comes from the longer statement of this qualification in Titus 1:9. Here Paul says that an elder must "hold firm to the trustworthy word as taught, so that he may be able give instruction in sound doctrine and also to rebuke those who contradict it." Here is a fuller and more textured statement of the simpler "able to teach" requirement of 1 Timothy 3:2. Clearly elders must have an accurate understanding of and faithful adherence to the "trustworthy word as taught" to them, in order for them to be able to pass on this message faithfully to others. Notice that elders are to "give instruction" with sound teaching, indicating that this message is itself life-giving and growth-producing. What elders have primarily to give to their people is the truth of the message they themselves have first received.

There is, however, another side of this teaching responsibility as Paul's instruction to Titus makes clear. Not only must elders be able to teach the trustworthy message they have received but they also must be ready and able to refute those false teachings that would contradict the faith and bring harm and destruction to those who would embrace those teachings. Elders, in a word, must exercise both an offensive and defensive strategy in their teaching of their people. They cannot devote time exclusively to constructive teaching of the truth when false teaching is in the air and threatens to undermine the faith of the flock. They must make it their business to know what false views are circulating, especially ones that have gained inroads into the minds of their own people. They must know those false teachings, represent them accurately, and then refute them in ways that pull their people back, as it were, from the edge of a jagged and life-threatening cliff. But a constant diet of defensive teaching, which excessively warns about error and false teaching, likewise fails to provide the hope and truth needed for people to embrace fully the glory of Christ and his gospel. Positive and consistent teaching of the truth is what will bring people hope and life. The truth, Jesus said plainly, is what sets us free (John 8:32). Both defensive warnings and refutations, along with offensive admonitions and instruction are needed to fulfill the responsibility of the elders of a local church, and discernment is called for in how best to bring both kinds of teaching to one's flock.

One added feature of the teaching role of elders can be seen from some other places where Paul expresses his attitude concerning that which elders ought to be devoting themselves. In 1 Timothy 5:17 he commends elders who rule well as worthy of double honor, and then adds, "especially those who labor in preaching and teaching." In his closing comments to Timothy, Paul writes, "I charge you in the presence of God and of Christ Jesus, who is to judge the living and the dead, and by his appearing and his kingdom: preach the word; be ready in season and out of season; reprove, rebuke, and exhort, with complete patience and teaching" (2 Tim. 4:1–2). Both passages demonstrate the special importance Paul ascribes to the teaching and preaching ministry of elders.[6] I

---

6. We are not asserting that Timothy held the office of elder because Timothy's position is best described as an apostolic delegate (which has more authority than an elder). However, Timothy's role does overlap with that of the elders in several places.

think it is fair to say that there is nothing more central to an elder's calling, or of greater potential benefit for the people of God, or closer to the heart of God and his desire for his people, than that elders take up their teaching and preaching responsibilities with earnestness, sobriety, faithfulness, diligence, and joy. Although elders are more than this, they simply cannot be less or other than those committed with heart and soul to bring the word of God to the people of God. Here, then, lies the chief responsibility of the office of elder.

Plurality of Elders

Both New Testament descriptive and prescriptive accounts unite to indicate that the eldership of New Testament churches was plural, not singular. Descriptively, consider some of the statements made in the Book of Acts and elsewhere regarding elders of local churches. Acts 11:30 records Barnabas and Saul as bringing contributions to the "elders" of the brethren living in Judea. Even clearer, Acts 14:23 indicates that Paul and Barnabas appointed "elders" in every church, after prayer and fasting. Also, in Acts 20:17 Paul sends for the "elders" of the church at Ephesus to come to him, and when he addresses them, he does so in the plural, referring to them as "overseers" of the church (Acts 20:28). Then, Acts 21:17–18 gives us a reference to James and all of the "elders" of the church in Jerusalem. Add to these the reference in James 5:14, instructing one who is sick to call for the "elders" (plural) of the church (singular) to come and pray. So, it is clear from these descriptive statements that each church had a plurality of elders.

One prescriptive account confirms what we have just seen, when Paul commands Titus to set in order the things that remain in the establishing of churches, which involves appointing "elders in every town" as he had instructed him previously (Titus 1:5). In case one wonders if this passage requires an understanding of a plurality of elders for each local church, it should be kept in mind that Paul's goal was to see a church established in each town or city. It is most probable, then, that appointing elders (plural) in every town amounted to appointing elders (plural) in every church (singular), i.e., the church that was planted in each particular town.

What are some of the implications of a plurality of elders for understanding leadership in the church? Consider these three observations.

First, that God designed a plurality of elders for each local church implies that no one person has the sufficient gifting, or energy, or insight, or perspective, to fulfill all that is needed in the governing and teaching of a local church. Not only do many hands often make light work, many hands often make better and more complete work. The vertical dependency that every elder should feel (and feel deeply) toward God is expressed, in part, by a horizontal dependency on one's fellow elders. No one is adequate in himself, but together a plurality of elders can provide collectively what is lacking from any one person individually. Second, a plurality of elders also implies a division of labor. Although there are common goals and responsibilities for all of the elders together (see discussion above), there are also certain needs that can be attended by one or another elder, leaving others free to attend to different needs and responsibilities. For example, although all the elders must be "able to teach," not all of them will necessarily be responsible to preach on a given Sunday. So, those not "tasked" with preparing to preach might devote time to small group discipleship, or counseling, or greater hospitality. The avenues for spiritual growth of God's people are many, and with a plurality of elders, there can be different men travelling different avenues. Third, the encouragement and stimulation that members of an elder board can provide to one another is incalculable. Times of sharing, praying, admonishing, discussing, caring among a group of elders are potentially precious times that can do much for the spiritual encouragement and strengthening of those elders. To know that you are not in this alone, but that you have other like-minded, spiritually-minded, men who will pray fervently with you, think carefully with you through issues, and decide with you how best to proceed is invaluable. This is a great benefit to those elders and to the churches they are called to shepherd.

Male Elders

Finally, the office of elder in the New Testament is restricted to qualified men. When Paul gave his instructions on the qualifications of elders in both 1 Timothy 3 and Titus 1, he included in both passages that an elder should be the "husband of one wife." Whether he had in mind here that concurrent polygamy (having multiple wives at one time), or serial polygamy (having multiple wives through divorce and remarriage), or both, were forbidden, one thing is clear—the elder in view was male. Only qualified males may be considered to be elders of local churches.

Another indication that Paul had in mind only qualified men for elders is his prohibition in 1 Timothy 2:12, that women are not permitted "to teach" or have authority over men. But then in the next chapter, Paul indicates that elders must be "able to teach" (1 Tim. 3:2), which surely would include the teaching of both men and women. The logic, then, is clear. If elders must be qualified to teach, and their audiences would include both men and women, but if women are not permitted to teach men, then it follows that women cannot be elders.

This clearly does not mean that any man, simply because he is male, may become an elder. Many other qualifications and factors must also be considered. But it does mean this, that among those factors which one considers, the gender of the person is relevant in determining what he/she is qualified to do. Furthermore, while it might have been natural for Paul to say in 1 Timothy 2:12 that he forbids a woman from being an elder (with a focus on the office), he does not say this. Instead, Paul focuses on the functions that are particular to elders—teaching and exercising authority—and says that a woman may not carry out these functions with men. Obviously this means that a woman may not be an elder, since she may not do what elders are called principally to do, that is, teach and rule (cf. 1 Tim. 5:17). But this also means that women may not teach men the content or truths of the Christian faith, or provide spiritual leadership of men, whether or not the office of elder is in view. That the function, not the office, is what Paul prohibits, means that there are contexts other than just those carried out formally by elders in local churches in which women should not participate.

If, for example, a woman teaches a mixed (male and female) adult Sunday School class in the church, one might think this permissible since one does not have to be an elder to teach an adult Sunday School class. But the question now is this: as she teaches this adult Sunday School class, if men are present, is the woman teacher violating what is stated in 1 Timothy 2:12 that a woman is not to teach men? The answer, without question, is "yes." Therefore, faithfulness to this text would mean that women should not teach a mixed adult Sunday School class since to do so violates Scripture. Much the same could be said of any number of para-church ministry gatherings. Since 1 Timothy 2:12 does not specifically prohibit women from being elders, per se (which is tied to local churches), but prohibits women from carrying out the functions of teaching spiritual truth and providing spiritual leadership to men, then this biblical teaching applies as much to any Christian para-church gathering as it does to one taking place during the gathering of a local congregation. The teaching leadership of the church, and of Christians more broadly, is to be done by qualified men. Elders specifically, then, can only be such qualified men, among the many other requirements that must be true of them to hold this sobering and honorable office.

DEACONS: THE SERVANTS OF PRACTICAL NEEDS FOR THE CHURCH

Meaning of Deacons

The English word, deacon, is a transliteration, not a translation, of the word *diakonos*, used in the Greek New Testament. The translation of *diakonos* is, simply, servant. Consequently, we get our first insight into the office of deacon—deacons are servants of the members of a local church, whose goal it is to help them with practical needs that they face in their every-day lives. Deacons, then, are leaders along with elders, but their style of leadership and the roles that they carry out differ remarkably from those of elders. Whereas elders have overall leadership of all the flock, with particular responsibility for the spiritual growth and well-being of those under their charge, deacons rather lead in organizing and assisting "services" to the church body so that the many practical needs those church members have might be cared for.

Where did the office of deacon originate? Many believe that it came into existence fluidly, as it were, because of the needs of the moment in the early church. Acts 6 records for us the resentment that occurred when the Greek-speaking, Jewish Christian widows were overlooked in the serving of food, which indicated a favoritism—intended or not—of the Aramaic-speaking, Jewish Christian widows. This problem was brought to the apostles, who instructed the congregation to select seven men who were of high reputation among the believers and who were directed by the Spirit and his wisdom, to be brought together to administer the distribution of the food in a fair and rightful manner. Although these seven men are not called "deacons," they are called "to serve" (*diakonein*)—the verbal form of the noun, deacon. Instructive here also is the fact that the apostles deliberately chose not to solve this problem themselves by serving the food daily to these needy widows, since to do so would take them away from the responsibilities they were deeply concerned to fulfill—their own devotion to prayer and to the study and ministry of the word of God to the congregation (Acts 6:2, 4). So, while these early "deacons" led in the administration and organization of meeting this practical need within the church, they thereby permitted the apostles (who will soon be functionally replaced, as it were, by elders; cf. 2 Tim. 2:2) to continue their spiritual leadership of the church. Deacons, then, are specially called by God to serve the physical, social, and practical needs of the followers of Christ in local churches. Elders, on the other hand, have larger oversight of the whole church with special focus on the spiritual well-being and development of the body. When elders focus on their primary calling and when deacons focus on their primary calling, this allows the church to function smoothly and properly. Put simply, when elders and deacons carry out what God has designed each office to do, needs of both soul and body, deep spiritual and internal needs and practical everyday needs, are met.

Deacon Qualifications and Responsibilities

One might think that qualifications for deacons will be significantly less than for elders, since elders must care for the doctrine of the church, combat false teaching, and inculcate truth in the lives of their people, whereas deacons care "merely" for the "physical" side of people's needs. Amazingly, this way of thinking is not reflected in the teaching of the New Testament. Even back in Acts 6, with the occasion that (in all likelihood) brought about the first "deacons" of the early church, notice what the Twelve said the congregation should consider as they selected these seven men to serve tables: "pick out from among you seven men of good repute, full of the Spirit and of wisdom, whom we will appoint to this duty" (Acts 6:3). And of Stephen (the first of the seven then mentioned), we read, "and they chose Stephen, a man full of faith and of the Holy Spirit" (Acts 6:5), and then the other six names are listed. As a result, the bar for character qualifications to serve as deacons is set as high as it is for elders, as it relates to the spiritual devotion, dependence, and wisdom of those who qualify.

The parallel nature of the requisite qualifications of elders and deacons is confirmed, then, when Paul articulates his list in 1 Timothy 3:8–13. As one reads through the items listed, it is clear that Paul has in mind that both the requisite "public" and "personal" characteristics of the elder/overseer must also be true for one who would aspire to the office of deacon. One who qualifies as a deacon must have character qualities that relate both to his public demeanor (e.g., worthy of respect, not excessive in drinking wine, husband of one wife, and manager of his own home, tested and shown to be blameless before others) and to his personal, even private, life (e.g., holding the mystery of faith with conviction, not hypocritical, not greedy, possessing genuine and growing faith). What both sets of characteristics display is a man who has grown much in his relationship with the Lord, who lives humbly before God and others, and who wants in what he does to reflect the character of Christ and the fruit of the Spirit. Maturity, godliness, integrity, honesty, humility, kindness, faithfulness—these are the kinds of characteristics that must mark the life of a man who aspires to become, and is affirmed by others as, a deacon. Why are essentially the same public and personal character qualities required of deacons as for elders? It is because deacons, too, minister the grace of God to others, and they do so formally and officially in the name of the local church, and more importantly, as representatives of Christ. Because they represent Christ and the church in their service, they must be godly people, and they must minister in ways that adorn the gospel.

A notable difference in the two lists of characteristics relates centrally to fundamental role differences that exist between elders and deacons. Whereas elders must be "able to teach" (1 Tim. 3:2) and to exhort in sound doctrine and refute error (Titus 1:9), deacons, in contrast, must hold "the mystery of the faith with a clear conscience" (1 Tim. 3:9). In short, though deacons must know the faith once for all given to the saints and embrace this as their own conviction, with a clear conscience, they are not called, necessarily, to be able to teach the faith to others in the church. Of course, nothing states that they cannot teach others, if they are qualified on other grounds for doing so. But "able to teach" is not their calling or responsibility as deacons. It is also worth noting that when Paul ends his discussion on deacon qualifications, his final word of encouragement to them is not, "if you do a good job as a deacon, you will be preparing yourself one day to be an elder!" No, Paul does not see the deacon role as inferior or lesser, so that becoming a deacon should be seen as the stepping stone to the greater elder role. Rather, he seems to think of deacons as being confirmed and affirmed as deacons, such that as they serve well as deacons, they will "gain a good standing for themselves and also great confidence in the faith that is in Christ Jesus" (1 Tim. 3:13). In other words, deacons who serve well as deacons will be approved by God and blessed for the faithfulness in which they execute their servant roles.

Absent from this list of deacon qualifications (1 Tim. 3:8–13), though, is any mention specifically of what they are to do. Nor does one find elsewhere in the New Testament specific role responsibilities of deacons stated. This indicates, then, a common understanding of diaconal roles that was simple enough and widely affirmed so that no specific instruction was needed. Consequently, this gives us even more reason to look back at Acts 6 as the "prototype" of deacon roles and responsibilities. What are deacons? They are servants of the members of a local church whose primary calling and responsibility is to identify, administrate, and care for the practical everyday needs of the body. In Acts 6, the specific need related to the daily serving of food. But surely, this is just one specific type of ministry deacons may have. While the principle of what deacons are to do is indicated in Acts 6, the specific task of serving tables should not be seen as the only way in which this principle is applied. The occasional nature of how the office of deacon developed in Acts 6 suggests otherwise.

This means, then, that we should think of the responsibilities of those who hold the office of deacon in "occasional" or fluid ways. Just as the specific need for waiting tables occasioned the selection of "servants" to help fill this needed deficiency in Acts 6, so too the specific physical and practical needs in our churches should be the occasion for conceiving how qualified deacons could be called out to assist in meeting those needs. Church bodies differ in the kinds of needs they have, and so too deacon groupings should be formed that best serve the needs of that particular church, at that particular time. It might also be the case that needs that were present at one time diminish, while others become more prominent over time. If so, the structure and responsibility of deacons should adjust to the needs, so that just as the seven were called out in Acts 6 to meet the present need, so newly conceived deacon responsibilities can be realized that will meet the church's current needs. We should not get in a rut with our deacon structure so that outdated needs are "served" while present and real felt needs go unmet. Flexibility, creativity, and continuous re-evaluation, then, are needed in order for deacons truly to fulfill their calling to help meet the present physical and social needs of fellow believers.

Male and Female Deacons

Whereas elders may only be qualified men, there is evidence that the office of deacon is filled by both qualified men and women. At one level, this should not be surprising, since there is nothing in the office or role of deacons that violates the specific roles and responsibilities reserved for elders. Elders are responsible to teach the Scriptures and the content of the faith of the church to the whole of the church body, and they are to exercise oversight over the whole of the church and direct the spiritual growth and development of the church's members. Neither of these roles— teaching and ruling—is given to deacons, so in principle, no violation of elder responsibilities occurs as women serve as deacons in the church.

But beyond this observation that elder roles are not compromised if women serve as deacons, are the indicators in Scripture for women deacons. Part of the evidence for female deacons is Paul's reference in Romans 16:1 to Phoebe, "a servant of the church at Cenchreae." The word "servant" here is the word *diakonon*, from *diakonos*, normally translated elsewhere in the New Testament as "deacon." Beyond this, perhaps the strongest indication for women who serve as deacons comes from Paul's deliberate address to "women" as he discusses the qualifications for deacons. First Timothy 3:11 reads, "[Women] likewise must be dignified, not slanderers, but sober-minded, faithful in all things." The opening word of this verse, *gunaikas*, literally refers to "women." And when one inquires which "women" Paul is likely referring to, it would seem there are only two viable possibilities. One would be that Paul has in mind the women who are wives of deacons, and this understanding is reflected in some English translations that open the verse with, "Wives" (so ESV, HCSB, NIV[84], NKJV). Support for this rendering contextually comes significantly from the following verse (3:12) where Paul instructs that deacons must be husbands of one wife. Thus, if deacons (as a whole) must be husbands of one wife, they (as a whole) must be male. Therefore, the reference to "women" in 3:11 must be to their wives.

But one other possibility must be considered; that is, that Paul speaks in 3:11 of "women deacons." The main reason for thinking that Paul had in mind women who serve as deacons, and not wives of deacons is this: if Paul was so concerned with the qualifications of the wives of deacons that he would devote a special listing of character qualities that must be true for them, lest a given married man not be able to serve as a deacon were his wife not also qualified, then why does he not also propose this same requirement when it comes to elders? If wives of deacons must be women of upstanding character for their husbands to serve as deacons, how much more, or so it would seem, would Paul care about the character of the wives of those who would serve as elders? This seems especially so when we consider how significant the wives of elders often are in our churches. Therefore, it would seem altogether appropriate for Paul to address the wives of elders as part of the qualifications of the men who would be selected as elders. But interestingly, he does not. However, when it comes to deacons, he does devote special attention to these "women."

But what of the reference in 3:12 to "husband of one wife"? It may be that Paul "inserts" his discussion about female deacons when he does, right after the listing of character qualities that deacons must have (ending at 3:10), and then considers character qualities of women deacons (3:11). Following this, he then returns to male deacons in 3:12 to stress the importance of them serving as heads of their homes, leading their families as is only appropriate for a Christian husband and father to do. And since such leadership of the home is not an appropriate qualification for the woman of the home, he specifies only men in this last verse (3:12) of deacon qualifications. Read this way, the logic or flow of thought of our passage might be as follows: the character qualifications of deacons (3:8–10), given first, are more specifically directed to men, but appropriate also for women who are considered for the office of deacon. This is followed, then, by some specific qualifications that Paul relates directly to women being considered as deacons (3:11), after which he then concludes with the qualification of being a responsible leader in the home, which applies specifically to male, but not female, deacons.

The women of 3:11, then, are most likely women deacons, whose calling and role is—along with qualified men who serve as deacons—to give prayerful, intentional thought and energy to how best to meet specific daily, and physical, practical needs of those in the local body of believers. To give an example, the church where I am a member has many young families who are at the stage in life where they are growing their families. One of the most regular and pressing needs among our church family is for care to young mothers. What a marvelous contribution women deacons make here, where much of the need these mothers have can best be met by other women. Meals, help with childcare, etc., involve largely (not exclusively) the help of godly and Spirit-filled women. So in our church, an "occasional" need (that has become somewhat permanent!) is the need for women to care for young mothers. A cadre of qualified women to "serve" in this way, then, is a blessing to all. Of course, a church like ours may have this need met without having women deacons. But how much more meaningful is their service when it is recognized by the church as a whole, where women are identified for their Christ-like character and called out formally to serve as deaconesses, officially representing Christ and this local church as they carry out their service. Just as the apostles saw the formal calling of the Seven in Acts 6 as an important part of meeting the need to serve tables, so today the formal identification and calling of "servants," both men and women, provides a dignity and sobriety to the office while also accomplishing the meeting of needs.

ELDER LEADERSHIP, CONGREGATIONAL RULE

How should leaders in the church, particularly elders who have responsibility for the overall direction and spiritual well-being of the church, relate to the congregation in terms of decision making and authority? Does the New Testament teach a full "elder-rule" model where elders decide all things related to the church while the congregation is responsible only to submit to any and all elder decisions? Or does the congregation have absolute authority (at the human level) over all things so that elders are only advisory, at best? It seems clear from an examination of all of the teaching of the New Testament that the answer is this: elders are given authority in the church to lead the church forward in its overall direction and in regard to the spiritual edification of the people, yet congregations are also given authority as the final court of appeal, an ultimate (at the human level) kind of authority that all in the church, including its leaders, should acknowledge and embrace. We might describe this blend of authority structures with this phrase: churches are to be elder led, and congregationally ruled. This blend best accounts for the teaching of the New Testament both on the proper authority of elders and the ultimate authority of the congregation in the decision making of the church.

Responsible Elder Leadership within the Church

The New Testament teaching of the responsibility of elders to lead their churches forward spiritually is abundant and clear. As we have already seen elders have primary responsibility for the doctrinal fidelity of the church and for the care of the souls of the church's members. And precisely because they (not the church as a whole) have this responsibility, it stands to reason that they also have authority to carry out plans designed to move the church forward spiritually. Their spiritual authority flows from the spiritual responsibilities they have been given.

One of the strongest and most sobering expressions of this elder authority that is due to elder responsibility comes from the writer to the Hebrews, who admonishes, "Obey your leaders and submit to them, for they are keeping watch over your souls, as those who will have to give an account. Let them do this with joy and not with groaning, for that would be of no advantage to you" (Heb. 13:17). Notice the authority they have ("obey your leaders and submit to them") flows out of the sobering and weighty responsibility that they are given ("for they are keeping watch over your souls, as those who will have to give an account"). Because elders have the burden of the souls of the flock on their shoulders, their authority in spiritual matters should be acknowledged and followed. Their biblical and doctrinal teaching should be embraced, their directives for spiritual growth should be followed, and their counsel for spiritual well-being should be welcomed.

Ultimate Congregational Authority within the Church

But this is not the whole picture. Elder authority in the New Testament is not exclusive authority, nor is it absolute authority, nor is it ultimate authority. Of course, in the fullest sense of each of these qualifiers, only Christ has exclusive, absolute, and ultimate authority. But at the human level, the final and ultimate authority within a local church does not rest with the elders but with the congregation. Perhaps a few examples will help us see this.

Jesus spoke to his disciples about what to do when a brother sins. He instructs them to follow a procedure that begins with personally confronting the wayward brother. If that proves ineffectual, one is to take one or two witnesses also in confronting the brother's sin. And if that likewise fails to elicit the brother's repentance, the final step is this: "tell it to the church" (Matt. 18:17). Notice that the final appeal is not, "tell it to the elders." This is highly significant since the disciples of Jesus are those who will soon become the apostles of the early church who might think that they, or the elders who follow after them, would be this highest authority at the human level. But no, this is not what Jesus said. It is not the designated leaders of the church who have highest authority in this matter but the congregation as a whole.

Or consider again the very interesting account of the selection of the first "servants" or deacons of the church in Acts 6. We noted before that the apostles told the congregation to select seven men who were full of the Spirit and wisdom who could serve tables as was needed. Here is a wonderful example, then, of "elder led, congregational ruled." Although these are apostles, not elders, they represent the official teaching leaders of the church (recall again their commitment to the ministry of the word in 6:2 and 4). As those responsible for the overall well-being of the church, they decide that there needed to be officially-acknowledged "deacons" who will formally be called out to meet the pressing need of the moment. But when it comes to just who those deacons will be, the apostles tell the congregation (literally, "the full number of the disciples," in 6:2) to make the selection. So, the apostles lead in providing the structure for meeting the need, but the congregation bears the final and ultimate authority in selecting who those deacons will be.

Other indicators of the ultimate authority that resides only in the congregation as a whole can be seen in Acts 13:1–3 where the church as a whole is confronted by the Holy Spirit for the sending out of Barnabas and Saul as missionaries. Similarly in Acts 15:22 the church as a whole, along with the apostles and elders, chose men to accompany Paul and Barnabas in taking a letter to other churches expressing the decision of the Jerusalem Council.

So, while elders have enormous responsibility for the spiritual nurture, cultivation, protection, and development of members of the church, the church as a whole has ultimate responsibility in those decisions that affect the ministries and personnel of the church. A kind of shared authority, then, is in view in the New Testament, and it seems that this is both biblical and eminently wise. If exclusive authority resided in the elders alone, or in congregations alone, one can imagine far greater abuses that might occur. But with a balance of primary spiritual authority residing in elders, and ultimate ministry authority given to the congregation as a whole, we see a wisdom of accountability and dependence that surely does provide for a healthier outworking of the authority structure of the church.

CONCLUSION: LAYERS OF LEADERSHIP, ALL UNDER CHRIST

The theology of church leadership found in the New Testament, then, involves various layers or levels of authority and responsibility. The Lord Jesus Christ has the only truly and finally ultimate authority over all, and he has been given authority over all of creation in order to execute his plans and purposes for building his church. Any local church that truly is a church is under his highest authority for all that it is and should do.

Under Christ, then, he has designed that there be trained leaders who bear the responsibility for the spiritual growth and development of the church, guarding the church from error, and graciously leading the church along paths of truth, hope, and joy. But along with these spiritual leaders, Christ has also designed that there be leaders who assist in the practical needs that members of the church will face. Here, godly and Christ-like character is just as important as with those who are spiritual leaders, for both (elders and deacons) represent Christ as they minister, whether they minister the word of Christ (elders), or food and water in the name of Christ (deacons), to others.

And then, along with elders and deacons, the membership of the church itself has a place in leadership, in that they, not merely those chosen to lead spiritually and practically, bear responsibility before God for discerning the will of Christ in regard to the ministries and mission of the church. Leadership in the church of Jesus Christ, then, is layered. It involves all at some levels, while it recognizes some especially suited and qualified at other levels. But all recognize that they serve and lead and carry out their responsibilities only and always under Christ, the highest and only truly ultimate authority for any local church, as he is for the universal church. Leading in the church of Jesus Christ, under Christ, for the glory of God in Christ, is one of the greatest privileges and responsibilities given to mortal men. May we all assume the roles and stations given us, by God's grace, and see them fulfilled in such a manner that it is evident that here, in these ministries and through these callings, Christ is at work building *his* church.

CHAPTER 11

Leading the Church in Today's World: What It Means Practically to Shepherd God's Flock

Andrew M. Davis[1]

Scripture gives an amazingly wide range of descriptions of the human race. On the one hand, God created humanity in his image to glorify him in ways no other part of his creation can. But on the other hand, the people of God are again and again called sheep: "He is our God, and we are the people of his pasture, and the sheep of his hand" (Ps. 95:7). God testifies to the incredible capabilities of our race under leadership saying, "If as one people speaking the same language they have begun to do this, then nothing they plan to do will be impossible for them" (Gen. 11:6). As human beings are strongly led, organized, and all moving in one direction, God himself says there is no limit to what we can do. But as people are like sheep: weak, defenseless, short-sighted, slow, delicious, and stupid—they are the perfect prey in a world full of predators. Therefore, they are totally dependent on shepherds to feed, lead, and protect them.

As Jesus was looking over a crowd of people, he had compassion on them because they were "harassed and helpless, like sheep without a shepherd" (Matt. 9:36). Albert Mohler, in a recent commencement address delivered at the Southern Baptist Theological Seminary, put the neediness of the sheep very poignantly: "Specialists in the science of animal husbandry point out that sheep cannot survive without a shepherd. Take away all the shepherds, and the sheep will surely perish.

---

1. Andrew M. Davis (PhD, The Southern Baptist Theological Seminary) is Senior Pastor of First Baptist Church in Durham, North Carolina.

They will be lost, starved, and torn apart by predators. The [sheep], as we know it, is a species that survives only by human intervention. And Christ's Church is described, not coincidentally, as sheep who need a shepherd."[2] Charles Jefferson, nineteenth-century pastor and author of *The Minister as Shepherd*, spoke specifically of the need sheep have to be led:

> Sheep are not independent travelers. They must have a human conductor. They cannot go to predetermined places by themselves. They cannot start out in the morning in search of pasture and then come home at evening time. They have, apparently, no sense of direction. The greenest pasture may be only a few miles away, but the sheep left to themselves cannot find it. What animal is more incapable than a sheep? He realizes his impotence, for no animal is more docile. Where the shepherd leads, the sheep will go. He knows that the shepherd is a guide and that it is safe to follow him.[3]

For this reason, Scripture repeatedly testifies concerning the need for God's people to have godly shepherds. This is the most common and powerful image of the ministry given us in the Bible. In John 21, the resurrected Christ reinstated Peter to his role as a leader in the church after he had denied Jesus three times. So, three times, Jesus asked Peter, "Do you love me?" Three times, Peter affirmed his love for Jesus. Three times, Jesus commanded Peter to shepherd his beloved people: "Feed my lambs" (v.15); "Tend my sheep" (v.16); "Feed my sheep" (v.17).

It is the middle of these three commands that attracts our special attention in this book. The first and third commands of John 21:15–17 both have to do with "feeding" the sheep of God, which means the ministry of the word of God. The middle command, "tend my sheep,"

---

2. R. Albert Mohler, "Feed My Lambs—The Tender Courage of the Christian Ministry," http://www.albertmohler.com/2012/12/07/feed-my-lambs-the-tender-courage-of-the-christian-ministry/ (accessed 27 December, 2012).

3. Charles Edward Jefferson, *The Minister as Shepherd* (1912; repr. Fincastle: Scripture Truth, n.d.), 47. Cited by Alexander Strauch, *Biblical Eldership: An Urgent Call to Restore Biblical Church Leadership*, rev. and exp. ed. (Colorado Springs: Lewis and Roth, 1995), 25–26.

employs the Greek verb ποιμαίνω, which communicates a strong sense of leadership, authority, and rule. John uses the word four times in the book of Revelation, and in every case it refers to Christ's leadership and authority to rule, sometimes with a "rod of iron" (Rev. 2:27; 7:17; 12:5; 19:15). Peter was called to be an under-shepherd, and as such, he commanded other under-shepherds not to "lord it over" the flock (1 Peter 5:3). But there is no doubt that Jesus wanted Peter (and all other apostles and elders) to lead his flock.

Throughout this volume, we have analyzed the topic of church leadership from biblical, historical, and theological perspectives. Now, we desire to address the topic of shepherding God's flock practically, in the context we find ourselves in today. The issue of leadership is one of the most vital facing the church of Christ today. John MacArthur says a "crisis of leadership faces both the world and the church."[4] Mohler says that hotel conference rooms overflow with people eager to learn from various speakers on the topic of leadership, and observes that colleges and universities now offer degree programs on leadership studies. And yet, he says, "something is missing."[5] What the church needs in every generation are blood-bought, Spirit-anointed, biblically driven leaders who are not mere managers, but who are compelled to apply the timeless truth of Scripture to a constantly changing world in constant rebellion against God. Mohler speaks poignantly of this kind of leader—one driven by deep convictions that lead irresistibly to actions: "Convictions are not merely beliefs we hold; they are those beliefs that hold us in their grip."[6]

DEFINITION OF CHRISTIAN LEADERSHIP

How shall we define leadership, and most especially, leadership done by the elders of a church? John MacArthur states, "To put it simply, leadership is influence. The ideal leader is someone whose life and character motivate people to follow. . . . By contrast, much of the world's 'leader-

---

4. John MacArthur, Jr., *The Book on Leadership: The Power of a Godly Influence* (Nashville: Nelson, 2004), 3.
5. Albert Mohler, *The Conviction to Lead: Twenty-five Principles for Leadership That Matters* (Minneapolis: Bethany House, 2012), 15.
6. Ibid., 21.

ship' is nothing but manipulation of people by threats and rewards."[7]
Another writer notes, "Leadership is the process of motivating people."[8]
Andy Stanley gives something of a definition of leadership in his epilogue: "By God's divine and mysterious appointment you have been
blessed with *the ability to command the attention and influence the direction of others*. You are a leader."[9] Harris Lee focuses on the attainment
of goals: "Leadership is that which moves persons and organizations
toward the fulfillment of their goals."[10] Kenneth Gangel's definition hits
the mark well: "[Leadership is] the exercise of one's spiritual gifts under
the call of God to serve a certain group of people in achieving the goals
God has given them toward the end of glorifying Christ."[11] Mohler focuses on the convictions that drive a leader, asking if they are the right
ones. He says that many may study leadership and the techniques of
influencing people, and they may be experts on getting people moving,
climbing a steep ladder of sacrifice rung by rung, but is the ladder lean-
ing against the right wall? Mohler writes, "I believe that leadership is all
about putting the right beliefs into action, and knowing, on the basis
of convictions, what those right beliefs and actions are."[12] He adds very
powerfully later in his book, "When you enter the room, trust and confidence had better enter with you. If not, leadership is not happening.
How could it? Leadership is about a sense of direction and purpose,
and a competence that puts the room at ease."[13]

Having read all of these insights, this is my definition: *Christian
leadership is the God-given ability through the Holy Spirit to influence
people by word and example to achieve God's purposes as revealed in the
Scriptures.* A Christian leader is a change-agent, a fork in the road, a
force for change, smelling salts in the nostrils of the semi-conscious,
a sharpened scalpel in the hands of the Great Physician. I sometimes
compare the church to one of those old sawmills constructed by the
side of a river, which can cut tons of lumber a day (representing good

7. MacArthur, vi–vii.
8. Harold Myra, ed., *Leaders* (Waco, TX: Word, 1987), 158.
9. Andy Stanley, *Next Generation Leader: Five Essentials for Those Who Will Shape the Future* (Sisters, OR: Multnomah, 2003), 161 (emphasis mine).
10. Harris W. Lee, *Effective Church Leadership* (Minneapolis: Augsburg Fortress, 1989), 27.
11. Kenneth O. Gangel, *Feeding and Leading* (Wheaton, IL: Victor, 1989), 31.
12. Mohler, 26.
13. Ibid., 84.

works done for God) when the river is running well, but which comes to a standstill when little or no water flows by it. Extending the image, I have imagined that upstream are blocks of ice containing ample water supply to cut all the lumber in the county. God uses a leader's fiery words, fervent example, and warm embrace like the sun, to melt the frozen resources of the people of God and cause them to flow freely, turning the wheels of the church's industry.

Twelve Practical Elements of Christian Leadership

What, then, are some practical guidelines for the leadership of Christ's church? How can the timeless principles of God's perfect word be lived out in our twenty-first century for the shepherding of Christ's blood-bought people? I would like here to lay out twelve practical elements of Christian leadership for your prayerful consideration.

1. Trust the Sufficiency of Scripture for a Vision of Christian Leadership

One of the issues dividing Christian writers on leadership is the value of seeking leadership models from the non-Christian world. There is no doubt that secular history is full of inspiring examples of leadership. I am captivated by the fearlessness of Alexander the Great, who, in 325 BC, was besieging the Multanese Citadel in what is modern-day Pakistan. His soldiers, weary of the long campaigns, were dragging their feet in ascending the walls to conquer the citadel. Alexander became incensed, grabbed a ladder himself, ascended it ahead of his troops, and actually jumped down within the enemy fortress to fight completely alone! His troops, shocked by the boldness of their king, immediately followed him and fought savagely to rescue him from trouble. Never was there a more courageous example of leading from the front. Or again, consider the strategic boldness of George Washington's midnight crossing of the ice-choked Delaware River on Christmas night, 1776, to surprise the Hessian forces celebrating in Trenton. His previously demoralized army was immediately infused with hope after the twin victories at Trenton and Princeton, and the Continental cause was revitalized. Or reflect on the wisdom shown by Abraham Lincoln in assembling a "team of rivals" to serve as his cabinet, political opponents who were anything but "yes-men," but who were the most gifted leaders of his party.[14] Or marvel at the ability with mere words to inspire a whole nation to fight with dogged determination shown by Winston Churchill in the days England faced Nazi Germany alone in World War II. Secular history is filled with dynamic leaders who are tempting role models for prospective church leaders to emulate.

In our times, however, it is not so much military or political figures to which church leaders are drawn. More and more, it is the example of successful business leaders that seem difficult for Christians to resist. MacArthur writes, "I recently read a Christian book that analyzes the entrepreneurial and administrative techniques used at Google, Amazon, Starbucks, Ben and Jerry's, Dell Computers, General Foods, and several other prestigious secular corporations. The authors of that book occasionally try to insert a biblical proof-text or two to buttress some of the principles they teach, but for the most part, they uncritically accept whatever seems to produce 'success' as a good model for church leaders to imitate."[15]

While I do not repudiate valid insights on leadership these writers and seminar speakers can present to the church, I am zealous here to argue for the sufficiency of Scripture for the leadership of a local church. It stands to reason that, if godly leadership is vital to the health and fruitfulness of every generation of churches throughout redemptive history, then everything we need for that leadership must be available to us in the Bible. I doubt that John Maxwell or Andy Stanley would contend that the church cannot be well-led without insights from modern business leaders.

Even more to the point, Jesus Christ himself drew a strong contrast between the patterns of worldly leaders and those he is commanding for the church: "You know that the rulers of the Gentiles lord it over them, and their high officials exercise authority over them. Not so with you. Instead, whoever wants to become great among you must be your

---

14. Doris Kearns-Goodwin, *Team of Rivals: The Political Genius of Abraham Lincoln* (New York: Simon and Schuster, 2005).

15. MacArthur, vii.

servant, and whoever wants to be first must be your slave—just as the Son of Man did not come to be served, but to serve, and to give his life as a ransom for many" (Matt. 20:25–28). Clearly, the "rulers of the Gentiles" carried themselves in a way that would have been completely unacceptable for the leaders of the church. Their arrogance, selfishness, vainglory, corruption, cruelty, love of money, love of pleasure, and yearning for human praise was diametrically opposed to the patterns of leadership Jesus himself displayed in true servanthood: washing the disciples' feet (John 13:1–17) and going to the cross for the sins of his people (Matt. 13:28). The essence of biblical leadership is self-denial and servanthood to God and to God's people.

Fundamentally and practically, leadership in the twenty-first century must be derived from precepts and examples in the Bible, just as it has been for the first twenty centuries of church history. The Bible has been sufficient for godly leadership in every generation (2 Peter 1:3). Go to the Scriptures for the qualifications of elders (1 Tim. 3:1–7, Titus 1:5–9), for commands to elders for the conduct of ministry (Acts 20:17–35, 1 Peter 5:1–4, 1 and 2 Timothy, Titus), and for rich examples of both successful and failed leaders (cf. Joshua, Judges, 1 & 2 Samuel, 1 & 2 Kings, 1 & 2 Chronicles, Nehemiah, Acts). Everything needed for leadership in this century will be there. Now, I truly believe secular thinkers can highlight themes and bring up valid insights on leadership, but at best, they serve to draw our attention to what was already available in Scripture. If they serve as a "common grace" display of some helpful leadership principles, then they are useful. But the Scriptures are sufficient.

2. Embrace Plurality of Elders in a Congregational Context

Ever since the Reformation, there have been vigorous debates about the most biblical form of church government, and the whole purpose of this volume is to trace out biblical, historical, and theological insights on this very topic. While I cannot hope to write the final word on that topic here, I believe it is worthwhile to speak of the practical benefits of understanding the plurality of elders in a congregational setting. It is my conviction that this is the most biblically accurate structure for church leadership and shepherding, and as such, is the one most likely to result in maximum fruitfulness for the people of God.

The concept of a plurality of elders is taught many places in Scripture and defended in this volume as well. For me personally, the most powerful New Testament passages teaching this structure are Titus 1:5 (in which Paul says he left Titus in Crete to appoint elders in every town), Acts 14:23 (in which Paul and Barnabas appointed elders in each church), Acts 20:17 (in which the elders of the Ephesian church come to Miletus to meet with Paul), and James 5:14 (in which the elders of the church are summoned to pray for the sick). Also of interest is the clear sense of shared leadership in the Jerusalem council on circumcision in Acts 15 in which no one man seems to have final authority, but rather James seems to sum up the insights presented by Paul, Barnabas, Peter and others.

The concept of congregationalism is most clearly seen in the Lord's instructions concerning church discipline (Matt. 18:15–17) in which the final "court of appeal" is the church. It is also on display in the church's selection of the "Seven" (commonly called Deacons) who cared for the Greek-speaking widows in Acts 6, as well as the apostle Paul's passion in holding the church of Galatia accountable for the false teaching they were putting up with (cf. Gal. 1:6–9). In congregationally governed churches, only the congregation can elect elders, and only the congregation can remove them by discipline if needed.

The dynamic of the plurality of elders in the context of congregational polity is complex. Once the church has identified godly men to serve in this role by the criteria of 1 Timothy 3:1–7 and Titus 1:5–9, and has established them in their office, it must now follow the leadership of those godly men, as Hebrews 13:17 clearly commands: "Obey your leaders and submit to their authority. They keep watch over you as men who must give an account. Obey them so that their work will be a joy, not a burden, for that would be of no advantage to you." Yet, the church should continue to evaluate the doctrine and lifestyle of the leaders to be sure they conform to the biblical "patterns" (Gk. τύπος; see 2 Timothy 1:13 for the pattern of doctrine, and Phil. 3:17 for the pattern of lifestyle). The congregation is to be like the Bereans who listen eagerly to the teaching of the elders, and then search the Scriptures daily to confirm that what they heard was biblical. In the same way, they are to observe the lives of the elders for obedience in keeping with the teachings, for Jesus warned that false teachers, wolves in sheep's clothing, can be discerned by their fruit (Matt. 7:16).

The church's scrutiny of the elders is no different than how the elders should be scrutinizing themselves, for Paul commanded Timothy, "Watch your life and your doctrine closely" (1 Tim. 4:16). Yet, the church should scrutinize in a respectful way, more passively than actively, not with suspicion or assumption of wrongdoing. I have likened it to the difference between the active and passive sonar of a submarine. A submarine can know the objects in the water around it either by sending out a strong ping of active sonar (which will betray its position to any other ships), or by the finely honed precision of passive sonar, listening carefully and analyzing every sound in the water. So, in the absence of problems, a grateful and submissive congregation should assume the clear right teaching and the apparent godliness of their elders is what it appears to be, just as the elders, "in the judgment of charity" assume that the Christian profession of the flock is what it appears to be.

We can see the wisdom of God in this marvelous pattern of church government. Plurality of elders (1) protects elders from too much praise and too much blame; (2) affords built-in accountability for the elders in their personal holiness and walks with Christ; (3) helps eliminate blind spots both in doctrine and in ministry; (4) enables elders to feed on each other's passion and courage; and (5) enables the various leadership gifts and styles of different men to be fully used for the health of the body. In my experience serving with a body of elders, I have observed some elders with strong gifts of administration serve ably as chairman of the elders, tasked with the responsibility of organizing and facilitating the elders' meetings, thus ensuring maximum efficiency and productivity during those times. I have also observed some with a special sensitivity to counseling, or to evangelism, or to financial wisdom, or to prayer, or to compassion for the needy, come to the fore at various times and decisively influence the direction of the elders. Here we see in a microcosm the beautiful imagery of the Body of Christ in which different men have different gifts and lead in different ways. Yet, we also are continually seeing the hand of God in bringing us to unity in the Spirit, one in heart and mind on an amazingly wide variety of issues in the life of the church.

3. Understand God's Ultimate End: His Glory in the "Two Infinite Journeys"

It is impossible for anyone to lead without knowing the final destination. Jesus likened the false teachers of his day to "the blind leading the blind," and said that both will fall into the pit (Matt. 15:14). So, elders must have a firm sense of the final destination to which the church should be heading, or their leadership will be just as faulty. The blindness of the Pharisees came from their unbelief, for faith is the eyesight of the soul by which we may know the invisible spiritual world and the will of God. So by faith, the elders must discern that the "end for which God created the world"[16] is his own glory. In the same way, the end for which God redeemed his people through Christ is the same—his own glory (Isa. 43:7). So, whether we eat or drink or whatever we do, including every aspect of church ministry, our ultimate motive must be to glorify God (1 Cor. 10:31).

But what does it mean for an individual or church to "glorify God?" What has God left us in the world to do? I believe the Bible teaches that we are here to make progress in two infinite journeys: the internal journey of sanctification, and the external journey of disciple-making through missions. These two journeys are alluded to in Philippians 1 by Paul's twin use of the Greek word προκοπή (progress). In Philippians 1:12, Paul speaks of the progress of the gospel as a result of his imprisonment, since the brothers in the Lord are now even more courageous in preaching the gospel. This is the external journey of evangelism/ missions. In Philippians 1:25, Paul speaks hopefully of his release from prison so that he can continue with the Philippian Christians for their "progress and joy in the faith." Progress in the faith for existing Christians is sanctification, gradual growth into personal holiness in full conformity to Christ. As in John Bunyan's classic, *Pilgrim's Progress*, the word "progress" indicates long and arduous journeys, journeys which I call "infinite," not because we will never finish them, but because each will continue to lay out before us as long as we live, and because only by

---

16. This striking phrase comes from Jonathan Edwards, "Dissertation on the End for Which God Created the World," in *The Works of Jonathan Edwards* (Peabody, MA: Hendrickson, 2000), 1:94–121.

the infinite power of Almighty God can we make a single step forward in either journey.

And no local church can prefer one journey to the other; both must be held together in perfect harmony. No healthy church can be only a "soul-winning" church that neglects discipleship, or a "deeply doctrinal" church that neglects evangelism and missions. Every good church tends to drift toward one or the other, while false churches deny both. The elders must discern their own tendencies, so they can avoid this drift. If a church should willingly embrace one infinite journey to the detriment of the other, they will eventually lose both. For if a church decides to go wholly after soul-winning and to be shallow on discipleship, the sins in the lives of the people will overwhelm the church and the leaders so that no one is doing any evangelism a generation later. And if the church retreats from the unregenerate world to study the "meat of the word" and become ivory-tower experts in theology, their growth will falter and become corrupt within a short time. So the elders of a church must understand the central call to shepherd their flock—each individual sheep—toward Christ-like maturity, and to keep boldly advancing the gospel in their region (evangelism) and to the ends of the earth (missions). The glory of God through the daily progress of the flock in each of these symbiotic journeys is the ultimate end of the church. Toward this end all elders must lead.

4. Seek Directly from God the Particular Mission for Your Church

The two infinite journeys are universal calls to every local church all over the world. But God has specific works for each local assembly to do that are unique to that church and to that era of history. Ephesians 2:10 says, "We are his workmanship, created in Christ Jesus to do good works which God prepared in advance for us to do." Just as those good works are tailor-made for each individual Christian, so they are also for each local church. Christ's "Letters to the Churches" in Revelation 2–3 give a strong sense of this diversity. For example, Jesus says to the church in Pergamum, "I know where you live—where Satan has his throne" (Rev. 2:13). To live "where Satan has his throne" was a specific challenge not given to each of the seven churches, just to the one at Pergamum. In the same way, Christ gives specific messages beginning with "I know" to each of the seven churches, speaking words tailor-made to each unique set of circumstances.

God has set before each local church an array of both challenges and opportunities, and the combination of those is unique to each church. It is for the elders of the church to discern both the challenges and the opportunities, and to craft a ministry strategy as the Lord leads by his Spirit. And the elders should specifically seek that direction from the Lord in prayer and in his Word. One of the significant qualities of David as a leader after God's own heart was his regular habit of inquiring of the Lord concerning what to do next. A prime example of this occurs in 1 Samuel 23:1–13 concerning the town of Keilah. David was told that the Philistines were attacking and looting Keilah. David inquired of the Lord three times concerning Keilah, gaining different insights each time. David's habit of seeking specific strategies from the Lord is in direct contrast with Saul, whose tragic epitaph in 1 Chronicles 10:13–14 underscores how much this pattern of inquiring of the Lord means to God: "Saul died because he was unfaithful to the Lord; he did not keep the word of the Lord and even consulted a medium for guidance, and did not inquire of the Lord. So the Lord put him to death and turned the kingdom over to David son of Jesse."

The same pattern of seeking guidance is found in Acts 16:6–10 in which the Spirit blocks Paul and Silas from preaching in the province of Asia and in Bithynia. Rendered motionless, they waited on the Lord and God gave Paul a vision of a man of Macedonia saying, "Come over and help us" (v. 9). This was the guidance they needed and a new mission strategy emerged, focusing westward on Greece and Europe rather than eastward toward Asia. In the same way, the elders of a local church should ask, "Lord, give us wisdom to know what ministries and missions you are giving us to do." James 1:5–8 says that if we lack wisdom, we should ask God in faith, trusting that he will guide us. Elders who make their own decisions apart from seeking God's will in prayer are little different in spirit than King Saul.

Each local church should have a clear sense of calling from God in the external journey of evangelism and missions. They should understand their own church's gifts and interests, and match those up with effective strategies for winning the lost in the community around them. For example, the church at which I serve has a large number of medical professionals as church members, and we are in an urban setting. God has led us to match those up with a regular "health fair" event at our church in which our doctors, dentists, nurses, and nutritionists can serve the people of the community while our evangelists share the gospel of Jesus Christ with those who come.

Concerning missions "to the ends of the earth," I think American churches should realize how richly blessed we are with resources that enable us to be involved in strategizing and planting churches among unreached people groups around the world. The gospel of the Kingdom must preached in the whole world as a testimony to all peoples before the end can come (Matt. 24:14). As a Southern Baptist church, we give financially to the mission efforts of the denomination, which sends out over five thousand missionaries all over the world. But we have also adopted an unreached people group in East Asia, and some of our church members are there now as church planters. We also keep in active contact with seven other family units who are church members and who are working in various places in the world. We seek to "hold the ropes"[17] for them in a variety of ways: short-term teams to visit them and assist them, care packages, Skype and emails, prayer meetings for specific needs they have, financial resources for projects they want to do, etc.

In addition, it is important for the elders of a church to discern the specific ways that Satan is attacking the truths of God's word in our particular age, for as Paul says, "We are not unaware of his schemes" (2 Cor. 2:11). Satan's schemes for the American church in the twenty-first century include an array of potent threats: pluralism, sexual immorality, abortion, the homosexual agenda, secularization, materialism, post-modernism. Godly leaders must discern the "signs of the times" (Matt. 16:3) and ask what God what he wants us to do to respond to these Satanic schemes.

---

17. William Carey's famous phrase to the Baptist Missionary Society in England, urging them to continue supporting him in prayer and financially as he set out for India: "I will descend into the dark hole of heathenism, but you must continue to hold the ropes for me."

5. Inspire the Flock by Unleashing the Word

In 1948, twenty-two-year-old J. I. Packer heard Dr. D. Martyn Lloyd-Jones preach for the first time. He never forgot that experience: "I had never heard such preaching...[delivered] with the force of electric shock, bringing to at least one of his listeners more of a sense of God than any other man."[18] The word of God, preached with clarity, skill, and deep conviction, has the power to transform hearts and rearrange lives—power that can feel like an "electric shock." All leaders have the power to inspire people to sacrifice, to shock people out of complacency and disengagement to full commitment. A Christian leader must inspire based on the truth of God's word. The hearers should be having an encounter with the living God; the eyes of their hearts should be opened weekly to the future glory of a multitude greater than any could number from every tribe, language, people, and nation standing before the throne dressed in white, calling out "Salvation belongs to our God, and to the Lamb" (Rev. 7:10). This vision can only come by the word of God, and it is by preaching with the anointing of the Spirit that a man of God can best lead the flock.

A godly Christian leader must stand in front of the people of God week after week endued by the Holy Spirit to unleash the truths of Scripture line after line. He must speak as one speaking "the oracles of God" (1 Peter 4:11). The word must work on his own heart first, then he can unleash the same power on the people that has already changed his own heart. As John Bunyan put it, "I preached what I smartingly did feel."[19] For myself, I lead others best to conviction and repentance when I have first been convicted and have repented.

Recently, as I was preaching through the Book of Hebrews, I came to the description of the word of God in Hebrews 4:12: "For the word of God is living and active. Sharper than any double-edged sword, it penetrates even to dividing soul and spirit, joints and marrow; it judges the thoughts and attitudes of the heart." I pondered this sharp, double-edged sword for a while, comparing it to 2 Timothy 2:15: "Do your best to present yourself to God as one approved, a workman who does

18. Christopher Catherwood, *Five Evangelical Leaders* (Wheaton: Harold Shaw, 1985), 170.
19. John Bunyan, *Grace Abounding to the Chief of Sinners*, in *The Works of John Bunyan* (Carlisle, PA: Banner of Truth Trust, 1991), 1:42.

not need to be ashamed and who rightly divides (ὀρθοτομέω; *ortho* = right or straight, *tomeo* = to cut) the word of truth." A skilled preacher "cuts open" the word so it can "cut open" the people. The best illustration I could come up with was of a large, fresh orange cut open by a sharp knife, releasing into the air the distinctive fragrance of citrus. As the knife releases the full effect of the orange, so an expository sermon releases the full effect of the text on the people.

By means of this passionate unleashing of the word of God, a Christian leader must lead. We desire people to make sacrifices for Jesus because they understand his will, delight in his glory, and consider their lives worth nothing to them if only they may finish the race and complete the task the Lord Jesus has given to them (cf. Acts 20:24). The word of God alone has the power to transform their hearts (Rom. 12:2) so they follow Christ in the healthiest way possible along the twin paths of the two infinite journeys.

6. Be Patient but also Bold in Leading the Flock Toward Change

Paul commanded his young pastoral protégé, Timothy, to lead his flock with "great patience and careful instruction" (2 Tim. 4:2). People do not naturally welcome the changes that are the essence of the two infinite journeys. Churches have the tendency toward static security and the creeping rigor mortis of traditionalism precisely because change is scary and unsettling. As the leader continues to point the way forward, he will continually be facing resistance and resentment from some members of the flock who would rather settle down and be comfortable. This is why the ministry calls for "great patience." Jacob spoke to his brother Esau about the limitations of his family: "My lord knows that the children are tender and that I must care for the ewes and cows that are nursing their young. If they are driven hard just one day, all the animals will die" (Gen. 33:13). So also a leader should understand the pace of his flock, and be humble, realizing that the Lord has been amazingly patient with him as he has developed; so he must give others time to grow used to new ideas and embrace them.

On the other hand, a Christian leader must be bold when the time comes to move, and not hold back fearfully. It is so easy for a leader to be intimidated by the obstacles that oppose a certain course of action, especially the reluctance of the people themselves. But there is a time for decisive action, and no one can lead without courage. The source of a Christian leader's courage must be his own vibrant walk with Jesus Christ, fed daily in his quiet time. As he takes in God's word, his mind is renewed and his vision clears. People become small and God becomes infinitely great again. "Fear of man will prove to be a snare, but whoever trusts in the Lord is kept safe" (Prov. 29:25). The "trust" in that verse is another word for faith, the eyesight of the soul. When you read Scripture, you see passages like this one: "He sits enthroned above the circle of the earth, and its people are like grasshoppers. He stretches out the heavens like a canopy, and spreads them out like a tent to live in. He brings princes to naught and reduces the rulers of this world to nothing" (Isa. 40:22–23). The faithless ten spies who spread a cowardly report about the Promised Land and led Israel to doubt God in Numbers 13 had the "grasshopper" analogy backwards: "All the people we saw there are of great size. . . . We seemed like grasshoppers in our own eyes, and we looked the same to them" (Num. 13:32–33). Isaiah says that all the nations are like grasshoppers to God, like a drop from a bucket and like dust on the scales. A leader needs to marinate his mind in such passages so that he can lead forth into whatever "Promised Land" God has in store for the people he's leading.

7. Recruit, Train, and Unleash Gifted Laborers

Two different passages liken the church of Jesus Christ to a body, with various parts, all of them prepared in different ways to serve Christ. Romans 12:4–6 uses this image: "Just as each of us has one body with many members, and these members do not all have the same function, so in Christ we who are many form one body, and each member belongs to all the others. We have different gifts, according to the grace given us." First Corinthians 12:12–31 develops this concept much further. Spiritual gifts are vital to the healthy functioning of the church, and one of the main functions of the pastor-teachers is to "prepare God's people for works of service so the body of Christ may be built up until we all reach unity in the faith." (Eph. 4:12–13). It is important to read this passage carefully—the "works of service" build up the body of

Christ to full maturity, and these are done by God's people, not by the leaders alone. The leaders, especially by the ministry of the word (note that the "apostles, prophets, evangelists, pastors and teachers" of verse 11 all focus on the word of God), prepare God's people to do the good works that build the body. The leaders cannot do all those works by themselves, nor should they. It is by the Spirit-empowered use of spiritual gifts that each member of Christ's church can offer a life of service to the Savior, and no one can do another's good works for him or her.

As the leader understands the "big picture" mentioned above—the glory of God in the two infinite journeys—and has sought, together with his fellow elders, the specific mission of that local church from God himself, the time comes to recruit gifted co-laborers to achieve that mission. Some may have the gift of organization (administration) to help with the nuts and bolts of planning. Some may have the gift of faith, to pray and spread a buoyant confidence that God will bless this effort. Some may have the gift of giving, to fund the extra needs that the work will require. Some may have the gift of service, to do all the hidden tasks that make it possible. Some may have the gift of evangelism, to make the work eternally fruitful through the winning of souls to Jesus. Some may have the gift of teaching, to build up those brought to faith in Christ. Some may have latent gifts of leadership, and are themselves being prepared by this project to be future leaders of the people of God. The Body of Christ must be challenged and employed to use the gifts God has given, so that none of the talents may be hidden in the ground.

When it comes to identifying those gifts, two parallel verses have been indispensable for my understanding—Romans 12:3 and Hebrews 10:24. Romans 12:3 says, "For by the grace given me I say to every one of you: Do not think of yourself more highly than you ought, but rather think of yourself with sober judgment, in accordance with the measure of faith God has given you." Since Paul goes on to speak of the varieties of gifts/roles for people in the Body of Christ (vv. 4–8), in verse 3 he wants each person, in order to find his/her place of service in the Body of Christ, to *think* about himself or herself. What an interesting command! In context, if you want to know where you fit in, then (1) present your body as a living sacrifice (v. 1); (2) be transformed in your mind (v. 2); and (3) think about yourself with sober judgment by faith (v. 3). The elders would do well to make sure each member of the flock follows this three-step process so that not one of Christ's laborers will be idle.

The other side of this process is laid out in Hebrews 10:24. Many translations render it similarly to the NIV's "Let us consider how we may spur one another on to love and good deeds." The goal of the consideration is "love and good deeds," but in these translations, the topic of the consideration is a method: "Let us consider *how*. . . ." But this is inaccurate grammatically. The direct object of the verb "consider" is "one another," so the focus of the thinking is *people*, not method: "Let us consider *one another*. . . . The Body of Christ should be thinking about other members of the Body of Christ as *people*, in order to stimulate (provoke) each one to love and good deeds. This, then, is both sides of the equation. Romans 12:3 says that each member should think of himself/herself with sober judgment, to find out where he/she fits in service to Christ. Hebrews 10:24 says we should also be thinking of each other in the exact same way, to make sure that each member is doing the ministry God has prepared. Elders should lead the way in the "considering" commanded by Hebrews 10:24, making specific prayers to God for each member by name, asking "Lord, how have you gifted _____ to serve you in this Body?"

Having enabled the Body to identify gifts, the next step for the elders is to train up those gifts to a high level of skill: "Fan into flame the gift of God which is in you through the laying on of my hands"(2 Tim. 1:6) Each gift must be developed, and the members must be told, "give yourself fully to these things, so that everyone may see your progress" (1 Tim. 4:15). Note that the word "progress" here is the same Greek word that we studied earlier in Philippians 1:12 and 1:25. We make progress in the internal and external journeys when we also make progress in our spiritual gifts! The training of the members of the Body for skillful service to Jesus is a high priority for the leaders of a local church.

Finally, after recruiting and training the members, it is now time for the leaders to unleash the church to do the ministry God has prepared for them. It is important for leaders to delegate ministry tasks to others, and then stay out of the way and not micromanage how they do these tasks. As the apostles said concerning the "seven" who would look after the food distribution to the Greek-speaking widows, "We will turn this responsibility over to them, and give our attention to prayer and the ministry of the word" (Acts 6:3–4). The Greek word translated "turn this responsibility over" is καθίστημι which carries a strong meaning of putting someone in charge of something. The elders of the church must oversee generally the direction of the church, but ministries must be entrusted to gifted co-laborers who take full responsibility for the daily outworking of these ministries.

8. Lead by Example

It is obvious that the centerpiece of Christ's incarnation is his atonement for our sins by his physical body and blood (Col. 1:22, Heb. 2:14). Yet it is also right for us to meditate upon the purpose of Christ's incarnation in giving us a perfect example to follow. Christ lived out a life "born of a woman, born under the law" (Gal. 4:4) not only to redeem us from the law (v. 5), but also teach us how to live in such a way that the righteous requirements of the law might be fully met in us, who do not live by the flesh but by the Spirit (Rom. 8:4).

The night before he died, Jesus washes his disciples feet as a clear display of loving servanthood and godly leadership: "Now that I, your Lord and Teacher, have washed your feet, you also should wash one another's feet. I have set you an example that you should do as I have done for you" (John 13:14–15). In the same way, Peter says that Jesus has given us an example of submissive suffering under ungodly oppressors: "if you suffer for doing good and you endure it, this is commendable before God. To this you were called, because Christ suffered for you, leaving you an example, that you should follow in his steps" (1 Peter 2:20–21).

The apostle Paul certainly understood this, and willingly and courageously set himself forward as a leader by example: "Be imitators of me as I am of Christ" (1 Cor. 11:1). Again he writes, "For you yourselves know how *you ought to follow our example.* We were not idle when we were with you, nor did we eat anyone's food without paying for it. On the contrary, we worked night and day, laboring and toiling so that we would not be a burden to any of you. We did this, not because we do not have the right to such help, but in order *to make ourselves a model* for you to follow" (2 Thess. 3:7–9, emphasis added).

He commanded Timothy to do the same for his flock: "Don't let anyone look down on you because you are young, but *set an example* for the believers in speech, in life, in love, in faith and in purity" (1 Tim. 4:12, emphasis added). In fact, the earlier verse cited on the daily life "pattern" in Philippians 3:17 shows how Paul understood a central part of discipleship to be the imitation of a lifestyle learned by example: "Join with others in *following my example*, brothers, and take note of those who live according to the pattern we gave you" (emphasis added).

This "pattern" of practical holiness and Christlikeness is therefore essential to the work of the church in discipleship. It extends to all areas of daily life. Leaders should teach their flock by the clear example of how to pray, evangelize, study the Bible, love and lead a wife, train children, deal with adversity, face persecution, make difficult decisions, and put temptations to death by the Spirit. This kind of "life on life" role modeling is very difficult to achieve in the busy, twenty-first century setting in which we find ourselves. It is far easier to have a scheduled Bible study on Thursday afternoon in the pastor's office than to observe him making a household budget or disciplining a child. One of the biggest sacrifices for a busy leader is to open his life and his home to a young disciple so he can lead by example. This is precisely why elders are required to be "hospitable" (1 Tim. 3:2, Titus 1:8), in order that they may make their daily lives an example to the flock.

It is especially important that the flock see a conspicuous pattern of personal holiness in the lives of their elders. In his classic on pastoral ministry *The Reformed Pastor*, Richard Baxter led his fellow pastors to consider in great depth Paul's admonition to the Ephesian elders, "Take heed therefore unto yourselves, and to all the flock, over the which the Holy Ghost hath made you overseers." (Acts 20:28 KJV). Half of his work focused on the first part, "Take heed unto yourselves," and he poured out his words in a fiery passion for the holiness of other pastors:

> Take heed to yourselves, lest you live in those sins which you preach against in others, and lest you be guilty of that which daily you condemn. Will you make it your work to magnify God, and, when you have done, dishonor him as much as others? Will you proclaim Christ's governing power, and yet contemn (sic) it, and rebel yourselves? Will

you preach his laws, and willfully break them? If sin be evil, why do you live in it? If it be not, why do you dissuade men from it? If it be dangerous, how dare you venture on it? If it be not, why do you tell men so? If God's threatenings be true, why do you not fear them? If they be false, why do you needlessly trouble men, with them, and put them into such frights without a cause.[20]

In addition to personal holiness, I think it is just as vital for the church to see elders leading in the hardest areas of ministry—evangelism, missions, and facing persecution. In the regions of the world where the church is illegal (e.g., Muslim and Communist countries), local church pastors are often singled out for special abuse: "Strike the shepherd, and the sheep of the flock will be scattered" (Matt. 26:31). By their courage and cheerful willingness to suffer and die for Christ, they enable others to speak the word of God more courageously and fearlessly (cf. Phil. 1:14). In our context, the culture is one of religious freedom, but with an increasing hostility to evangelical ("missional") Christianity. Leaders cannot merely verbally exhort their congregations to be bold in evangelism; they must lead by example, by a regular pattern of stepping out in faith to share the gospel, graciously accepting the social coldness, rejection, low-grade hostility, and sometimes verbal abuse that may come. In the same way, leaders cannot merely verbally exhort members to go on short-term mission trips to Haiti or Bangladesh; they must lead by example, showing a willingness to step out of the comfort of our affluence to be deprived for Jesus. The sheep will gladly follow such bold shepherds.

9. Protect the Flock from Satan's Attacks as You Make Progress

As the mission of the church unfolds, and the Lord begins to bless these journeys with fruit, it is inevitable that Satan will unleash powerful attacks to hinder the progress. The elders are called to protect the flock from these attacks. By far, the most common attack on fruitful minis-

---

20. Richard Baxter, *The Reformed Pastor* (Portland, OR: Multnomah, 1982), 28.

tries is discouragement. Satan knows that our offensive weaponry is irresistible, mighty for the pulling down of spiritual strongholds (2 Cor. 10:3–5). He also knows that our defensive armor is impenetrable, able to extinguish all the flaming arrows he hurls at the Christian soldier (Eph. 6:10–19). Therefore, his best bet is to keep the Christian warrior from ever taking the field against him. He will lie to the Christian, saying in effect, "You have labored to no purpose; you have spent your strength in vain and for nothing" (Isa. 49:4). He will cause us to look out over the harvest of our efforts and find nothing but crop failure. Or, he will tempt us toward sin in order to accuse us of our sins and get us depressed. Or, he will greatly heighten the discouragement attending normal, earthly trials, like illness or financial struggles, and cause the Christian laborer to cease striving for the glory of God.

It is amazing to study how many choice laborers in the Lord have been overwhelmed with discouragement at some time in their lives. Martin Luther was so discouraged by the slow progress of the Reformation in Wittenburg that he gave up preaching for over a full year, 1529–1530. Adoniram Judson, the astonishingly fruitful missionary to Burma, was so discouraged after his wife's death that he dug his own grave and sat by it for hours, staring into it. Charles Spurgeon spoke of the "minister's fainting fits," battles every faithful servant of God has with discouragement. In order for a leader to battle the dark satanic attack of discouragement in others, he must first face it himself and defeat it.

So also, Satan will seek to derail a flourishing ministry with other attacks as well: disunity (as people argue over both significant and petty issues), vainglory (as some servants seek honor and praise above others), distraction (as Satan tries to draw a church off from the powerfully effective ministry it's doing to some cul-de-sac of lesser activities), and of course, sin (perhaps sexual, perhaps financial, perhaps marital, etc.). These all have a terribly deadening effect on the progress of the church. The most potent satanic attacks in church history have been doctrinal, as Satan raises up even members from within a church body to attack the doctrinal integrity of a church, as Paul warned: "Even from your own number men will arise and distort the truth in order to draw away disciples after them" (Acts 20:30). Doctrinal attacks are the worst because they have the power to alter the gospel message itself, and Paul warned plainly: "But even if we or an angel from heaven should preach a gospel other than the one we preached to you, let him be eternally condemned" (Gal. 1:8).

So, a faithful shepherd of the sheep must recognize this diverse satanic arsenal of attacks against a fruitful church, and craft "precious remedies for Satan's devices."[21]

10. Continually Evaluate Fruitfulness

In John 15, Jesus likens the relationship between himself and his disciples to that of a vine and branches: "I am the vine and you are the branches" (John 15:5). He says that if we remain in intimate spiritual connection with him, we will bear eternal fruit. In that teaching, he says his Father is the "vinedresser," who is constantly tending the vine for maximum fruitfulness: "He cuts off every branch in me that bears no fruit, while every branch that does bear fruit he prunes so that it will be even more fruitful" (John 15:2). The home base of this analogy is that ongoing purification of every Christian in sanctification, for the verse literally says the Father "cleans" (*kathairei*) every branch so that it will be maximally fruitful. It is so wonderful that, in verse 3 Jesus assures all true Christians, "You are already clean because of the word I have spoken to you." So the Father "cleans" those in sanctification who are already "clean" though justification.

But this image also relates to the need for fruitful Christians and churches to be constantly discerning about the most fruitful works in which they can be involved, and pruning those that are not so fruitful. Discerning between good, better, and best is a challenging aspect of leadership. Churches can get cluttered up with dozens of seemingly productive ministries that are actually having a net diluting effect on the church's eternal fruitfulness. Therefore, there are always aspects of seemingly fruitful activity that have to be trimmed off in order that the individual or church may be even more fruitful. And that takes Spirit-led wisdom, great tact, and significant courage. The leader must constantly assess the ministries of the church with a clear eye, and ask,

---

21. Thomas Brooks's phrase in his *Precious Remedies to Satan's Devices* (Carlisle, PA: Banner of Truth Trust, 2008).

"Lord, how can we be even more fruitful for your glory? Are there some seemingly fruitful things we are doing that we should stop doing?" And then, he should listen and act.

Over this past year, the elders our church have benefitted from reading and meditating on Colin Marshall and Tony Payne's excellent book, *The Trellis and the Vine*.[22] The book says that church leaders must make a careful and wise distinction between the living vine (the people of God as they grow in Christ through evangelism and discipleship) and the trellis (support structures the church ministries do that are not directly involved in the growth of the vine, but which aid it). They note that churches have the tendency to develop ever more elaborate trellises to the neglect of the vine work they should be doing. I recommend this book for developing a very helpfully critical eye at every aspect of church life, asking constantly, "Is this ministry actually helping to grow the vine, or are we just expanding the trellis?"

11. Pray and Wait upon the Lord for the Harvest

It is fascinating to me how many agricultural parables and illustrations there are in the New Testament, likening the growth of the Kingdom of God to a seeds that fall on good soil yielding a harvest, a mustard seed, growing wheat, spreading yeast, a vine, a fig tree, a vineyard, etc. These agricultural parables teach us the incredible patience a Christian leader must have as God does his sovereign work on the human heart. James 5:7–8 teaches this clearly: "Be patient, then, brothers, until the Lord's coming. See how the farmer waits for the land to yield its valuable crop and how patient he is for the autumn and spring rains. You too, be patient and stand firm, because the Lord's coming is near." Just as a farmer can't go out two days after planting the seed and pull the stalk up out of the seed and make it become ready for harvest, so an elder cannot force the growth in the hearts of his people that he would like to see.

God wants leaders to learn to wait on him for the harvest, to learn to look to him for everything. This development of God-centered endurance for the final outcome is especially expressed in prayer. The leader

---

22. Colin Marshall and Tony Payne, *The Trellis and the Vine* (Kingsford: Matthias Media, 2009).

should renew his faith daily in the certainty of God's ultimate glory in the complete salvation of his elect, and give voice to that faith in prayer for the Lord Jesus Christ to do what he has sworn that he will do. Four times in John 6, Jesus said he would most certainly raise up on the last day (in resurrection bodies) all of those that the Father had given him:

- And this is the will of him who sent me, that I shall lose none of all that he has given me, but *raise them up at the last day*. For my Father's will is that everyone who looks to the Son and believes in him shall have eternal life, and *I will raise him up at the last day*. (John 6:39–40, emphasis added)

- No one can come to me unless the Father who sent me draws him, and *I will raise him up at the last day*. (John 6:44, emphasis added)

- Whoever eats my flesh and drinks my blood has eternal life, and *I will raise him up at the last day*. (John 6:54, emphasis added)

By meditation and fervent prayer, the leader will take his changeful heart with its wavering faith and faltering hopes, and immerse it in the ocean of God's sovereignty. He will emerge from that bath renewed and refreshed and able to lead again.

12. Continually Give All Glory to God, Both Inwardly and Publicly

Every gifted and effective leader in church history has been tempted to think too highly of himself and forget that in God alone he lives and moves and has his being. Pride is the deadly enemy of God's glory, and it is especially endemic among gifted leaders. God's flock needs their leaders to believe with all their hearts that, apart from Christ, they could have done nothing, and to say often with their mouths, "To God alone be the glory."

Paul humbled himself completely before the Corinthian church with these words: "I planted the seed, Apollos watered it, but God made it grow. So neither he who plants nor he who waters is anything, but only God, who makes things grow" (1 Cor. 3:6–7). In one sense, according to Paul, the human laborers are *nothing*, and God alone is everything. Do you believe this? Really? Ironically, the more God blesses your ministry, the harder it is to believe. But God requires it, for he opposes the proud, but gives grace to the humble (James 4:6).

So also God humbled Moses at the burning bush by the way he answered his question, "Who am I, that I should go to Pharaoh and bring the Israelites out of Egypt?" (Ex. 3:11). God said, "I will be with you" (v. 12). This may seem to be a total disconnect, as though God didn't hear Moses' question. But God definitely did hear Moses question, "Who am I, that I should go?" (v. 11). Moses was looking inwardly at his own resources and finding them inadequate. And so they were . . . infinitely inadequate. The answer is perfect—"I will be with you" (v. 12). In other words, your question is irrelevant. It doesn't matter who you are ultimately; it only matters who I am.

God has entrusted a weighty responsibility on his under-shepherds, but his sovereign power is sufficient for them to be faithful and fruitful in that responsibility. The shepherding of Christ's sheep requires skill and passion, insight and dedication. The word of God and the indwelling Spirit of God are powerful and effective for training and equipping servants to shepherd the sheep that Christ bought with his blood. The twelve insights in this chapter are drawn from the Scriptures in the hope that each reader of this book will learn more and more to rely on the all-sufficient word of God to complete the task Christ has assigned to each one.

SCRIPTURE INDEX

Mark

Acts

Romans

1 Corinthians

2 Timothy

Titus

Philemon

Hebrews

James

1 Peter

ANCIENT SOURCES INDEX